RESEARCH DESIGN EXPLAINED

RESEARCH DESIGN EXPLAINED

Mark Mitchell

Beaver College

Janina Jolley

Clarion University

Holt, Rinehart and Winston, Inc.

New York • Chicago • San Francisco • Philadelphia
Montreal • Toronto • London • Sydney • Tokyo

This book is dedicated to our parents

Acquisitions Editor	**Susan Meyers**
Development Editor	**Kirsten Olson**
Senior Project Manager	**Sondra Greenfield**
Production Manager	**Annette Mayeski**
Design Supervisor	**Gloria Gentile**
Cover Photograph	**Pete Turner/Image Bank**

Library of Congress Cataloging-in-Publication Data

Mitchell, Mark L.
    Research design explained.

    Bibliography: p.
    Includes index.
    1. Research—Methodology. 2. Research—Moral
and ethical aspects. 3. Experimental design.
I. Jolley, Janina M. II. Title.
Q180.55.M4M57 1988   001.4   87-25990

ISBN 0-03-004024-8

Request for permission to make copies of any part of the work should be
mailed to:
Permissions
Holt, Rinehart and Winston, Inc.
111 Fifth Avenue
New York, NY 10003
PRINTED IN THE UNITED STATES OF AMERICA
Published simultaneously in Canada

8 9 0 1   090   9 8 7 6 5 4 3 2 1

Holt, Rinehart and Winston, Inc.
The Dryden Press
Saunders College Publishing

PREFACE

When we first began teaching research design, we were excited about introducing students to a new way of looking at the world. We wanted to show them that by looking through the eyes of a psychological researcher, they could discover facts that no one has ever known before; they could evaluate the validity of claims made by other researchers; they could understand why psychology was a science; and they could appreciate why many psychologists are thrilled that psychology is a science.

Unfortunately, while we were trying to show students that research design is a logical and valuable way of looking at the world, the textbook they were reading was sending them the opposite message. This was true no matter what text we used. Some texts sent the message: "Research design is easy—It's just a bunch of terms, sayings, bits and pieces that you need to memorize, just like any other course." Others sent the message: "Research design is something that scientists do—It's too complicated for you to understand."

Because of our frustration with existing texts, we consulted several publishers. Although most were interested, we found that Holt, Rinehart and Winston best understood what we wanted to do: Write a book that was intelligible, but meaty; a book that would engage students to *think* about research design, to *understand* design, and to be able to evaluate the pros and cons of the many decisions a researcher must make. A book that took advantage of the fact that the goal of research design courses is not just to know several terms, but to learn a new way of thinking about the world. In short, a book that followed the way the best design courses are taught.

Holt is publishing this book because they understood our vision and were willing to give us enough time to refine the text until we were happy with it. They waited while our first four drafts were scrutinized by Robert Tremblay, a professional writer, to whom we owe more than we can repay. They waited until we let students review our manuscript. When Holt finally got the manuscript and sent it out to reviewers, they had to wait an additional six months while we responded to reviewer comments. Then, when they got the comments back from a second set of reviewers, they waited another year and a half as we revised the manuscript again. The result is not only that we spent our youth writing this book (we were both 25 years old when we started this book, we're now over 30), but also that we are very pleased with it.

Why are we pleased with the book? Primarily, because of the following features:

1. **Ethical considerations.** Our strong emphasis on ethics is a rarity in research design texts. Whereas most texts spend only a few pages listing

the American Psychological Association's Ethical Principles, ethical considerations are infused throughout our text. Rather than give them an encyclopedic version of ethics, we show students how ethical considerations are present during each step of the research process.

2. **Integration.**   Our text is organized around the student research project. This unifying focus gives our book a coherence that other texts ("expanded glossaries") lack. Students readily appreciate how each step in the research process builds on previous steps. They come to appreciate research as a meaningful and *logical process*, rather than a collection of unrelated concepts and actions.

3. **Writing style.**   Our personal, easy-to-read style will encourage students to actually read the book. Consequently, students will be less intimidated by the course and professors will be freed from the task of translating an inaccessible text.

4. **Depth.**   Don't let our engaging writing style fool you. Our text has greater depth than most undergraduate texts and many graduate texts. We prove that a textbook can be both meaty and palatable.

5. **Balanced coverage of experimental and nonexperimental designs.**   Professors can use our book regardless of whether they emphasize experimental or nonexperimental designs.

6. **Practical advice.**   Novice researchers need all the advice they can get. Our book is loaded with practical tips for every step of the research process. From how to come up with a research idea to how to greet subjects to conducting a literature search—our text won't leave your students in the dark.

7. **A logical and flexible plan of the book.**   Although we ordered the chapters in a way that made sense to us and our students, we realized that there are many other orders that make just as much sense. Therefore, as much as possible, we made each chapter (or set of chapters, in the case of the experimental design chapters) independent. You'll find that you can easily omit chapters or cover them in a variety of orders. In short, this text can easily adapt to virtually all of the different ways of teaching the research design course.

PLAN OF THIS BOOK

You've seen that research psychologists are aware of the responsibilities and challenges of studying behavior. What you haven't seen is the wide range of methods psychologists use to meet these challenges and responsibilities. Shrewd investigators may use a single subject or thousands of subjects; human subjects or animal subjects; laboratory studies or field studies; experiments or surveys, depending on ethical considerations and their research goals.

This book will help you become a shrewd investigator by showing you how to generate research ideas; how to manipulate and measure the variables you're interested in; how to collect data objectively; how to maximize internal, external, and construct validity; how to choose the right design for your particular research question; how to test subjects ethically; how to interpret your results; and how to communicate your findings.

Thus, in Chapter 1 you'll learn why psychologists conduct research and why you might join them in the quest for knowledge. In Chapter 2, you'll learn how to use your creative potential to develop exciting research ideas. In Chapter 3, you'll take the first step toward testing those ideas: learning how to devise or select measures and manipulations that have construct validity. In Chapter 4, you'll encounter the obstacles to establishing internal validity. In Chapter 5, you'll read about the easiest way to achieve internal validity: the simple experiment. In Chapters 6 and 7, you'll learn about methods that build on the simple experiment's strengths, but have better construct and external validity. In Chapter 8, we describe two designs that you can use to increase the external validity of research: experiments done in the field and within-subjects experiments. In Chapter 9, you'll have a chance to exercise both your critical and creative thinking skills by first criticizing published research and then coming up with clever ways to improve that research. In Chapter 10, you'll deal with threats to internal validity without relying on statistics. Specifically, you'll learn two methods that often have remarkable external validity: single-subject designs and quasi-experimental designs. In Chapter 11, you'll discover research methods you can use if your primary goal is to describe behavior. In Chapter 12, you'll learn how to use the three most popular descriptive methods: surveys, questionnaires, and interviews. Finally, in Chapter 13, we'll show you how to integrate what you know to plan and execute an ethical research study.

Appendixes: Last, but Not Least

The appendixes are in the back of the book, but they aren't meant to be read last. Appendix A, "Ethical Guidelines for Research," should certainly be read before planning a study. In addition, you'll probably want to read Appendix B, "Library Resources," and Appendix C, "Using the Computer in Research," prior to running your study. Finally, if you are not planning to go to graduate school, you'll want to read Appendix D, "Marketing Your Research Skills," and Appendix E, "Statistics and Random Numbers Tables."

ABOUT THE AUTHORS

After graduating summa cum laude from Washington and Lee University, Mark L. Mitchell received his M.A. and Ph.D. degrees in psychology from The Ohio State University. He is currently a member of the faculty of Beaver College.

Janina M. Jolley graduated with great distinction from California State University at Dominguez Hills and earned her M.A. and Ph.D. in psychology from The Ohio State University. She is currently a consulting editor of *The Journal of*

Genetic Psychology and *Genetic Psychology Monographs.* Her previous book is the acclaimed, *How to write psychology papers: A Student's survival guide for psychology and related fields,* which she wrote with J. D. Murray and Pete Keller. She is currently an Associate Professor of Psychology at Clarion University.

Drs. Mitchell & Jolley are married to research, teaching, and each other—not necessarily in that order.

ACKNOWLEDGMENTS

Writing *Research Design Explained* was a monumental task that required commitment, love, effort, and a high tolerance for frustration. If it had not been for the support of our friends, reviewers, family, publisher, and students, we could never have met this challenge.

Robert Tremblay has our undying gratitude for the many hours he spent critiquing the first draft of our book. We appreciate the insightful opinions of our colleagues who have reviewed our book: Rick J. Scheidt, Kansas State University; Kenneth L. Leicht, Illinois State University; Lynn Howerton, Arkansas State University; Neil J. Salkind, Kansas State University; Sandra L. Stein, Rider College; Ross A. Thompson, University of Nebraska; George L. Hampton III, University of Houston—Downtown; Kenneth B. Melvin, University of Alabama; Steven P. Mewaldt, Marshall University; John P. Brockway, Davidson College; John C. Jahnke, Miami University; and Helen J. Crawford, University of Wyoming. We are also indebted to many people at Holt, Rinehart and Winston, from Susan Meyers, the Acquisitions Editor, who shared our vision of what the ideal design text should be, to Kirsten Olson, our insightful Development Editor, and Sondra Greenfield, our meticulous Project Manager, who helped us come as close to our vision of the ideal text as we could.

Yet, all of this expert help might have gone to waste, had it not been for the daily encouragement and advice we received from out students. We owe them a great deal, especially Rob Alling, Shari Custer, Jane Clever, Kathi Foley, Barbara Olszanski, Lynda Paulding, Melody Sample, Linda Taylor, and Kelly Thompson.

Finally, we offer our gratitude to Agatha and Zelda for allowing us the time to complete this project.

CONTENTS

RESEARCH DESIGN EXPLAINED

1

THE HUMANE ART OF SCIENTIFIC RESEARCH

Mommy, where do facts come from?

RESEARCH AND KNOWLEDGE

Why Are Psychologists Interested in Research?

Since the first cave-dweller, humans have been asking themselves: "Why are people the way they are?" Everyone seems to have an opinion about what causes someone to break the law, be a hero, flunk a class, or run for president.

As a result of humanity's speculations, we have many "theories" of human nature. Most of these theories sound reasonable, yet they often contradict each other. For every opinion someone offers us, another person can offer an opposing opinion. Although all of these theories may be equally logical, they can't all be correct (see Box 1-1).

As psychologists, our task is to find out which theories are correct. We are put in much the same situation as a detective in a good murder mystery. The detective has three or more theories of how the victim was killed and each theory proposes a different murderer. The detective can only find the true murderer by collecting evidence that will refute some of the theories and lend support to others. Similarly, psychologists—detectives of the mind—systematically collect information to enable them to distinguish between idle speculation and fact.

Our search for information has been remarkably successful. In the last 100 years psychology has made significant progress in understanding human behavior. To see the effect of research on the teaching and practice of psychology, compare introductory psychology textbooks published in 1910, 1930, and 1950 with one another and with a current text. Even a cursory examination will dramatize two facts. First, research has radically changed knowledge in every field of psychology. Second, the rate of research discovery rather than slowing down is accelerating—especially in the fields of counselling, developmental, personality, cognitive, physiological, social, and applied psychology.

Because research has contributed to every area of psychology, even former opponents of research now praise research. For example, Abraham Maslow (1970), the founder of the "Third Force," an approach that rebelled against scientific psychology, wrote: "Clearly, the next step for this psychology and philosophy is research, research, research. . . ." (p. 1).

Why Should You Be Knowledge-able about Research?

Reading and Evaluating Research

Clearly, research is a rich source of information. Understanding research will enable you to learn about the latest discoveries in your area of interest. To illustrate, suppose you're particularly interested in the psychology of dating behavior or in treatments for depression. What would you do to find out more about these topics?

Since you're unfamiliar with research, you may not read original research articles. Instead, you might read about research in a textbook. Although reading about

---

BOX 1-1   The Inconsistency of Common Sense

Absence makes the heart fonder,
    BUT
Absence makes the heart wander (Out of sight, out of mind).

Like attracts like,
    BUT
Opposites attract.

Haste makes waste,
    BUT
A stitch in time saves nine.

Too many cooks spoil the broth,
    BUT
Two heads are better than one.

To know you is to love you,
    BUT
Familiarity breeds contempt.

---

research in a textbook is helpful, it may not give you the information you need. The discoveries you're interested in may be so new that they won't appear in any textbook for several years. Furthermore, only a fraction of research finds its way into textbooks. Even if a textbook reports the results you are interested in, a summary of those findings may be incomplete. Thus, if you rely primarily on textbooks, you may be left with sketchy summaries of the few out-of-date studies selected by the textbook's authors.

However, once you become more familiar with the process of research, you can read the original sources themselves. You will have direct access to the latest research discoveries. Instead of textbook authors deciding what you should (and should not) know, you can decide for yourelf what information is of value.

Evaluating Research "Facts"

If you understand research, you will not only be able to get recent, first-hand information, but you will also be in a position to critically evaluate that information. Because research is the source of information and because you'll know the strengths and weaknesses of different sources (research methods), you'll be able to judge how much weight you should place on a particular research finding—a very useful skill, especially when you encounter two conflicting research findings.

No matter what you do in the future, you'll need to read and evaluate the merit of specific research findings. If you become a counselling psychologist, you'll want to use the best, most up-to-date treatments for your patients. If you become a manager, you'll want to know the most effective management techniques. If you become a parent, you'll want to evaluate the relative effectiveness of different child-rearing strategies. To get accurate answers to any of these questions, you will need to understand research. Unless you understand the process of research, you'll be limited by insufficient, out-of-date, and inaccurate information.

Conducting Research

Another reason you should understand research is so you can do research yourself. Few things are as exciting as doing research. As Carl Rogers (1985) said, "We need to sharpen our vision of what is possible . . . to that most fascinating of all enterprises: the unearthing, the discovery, the pursuit of significant new knowledge" (p. 1).

In this book, we hope to encourage you to join researchers in trying to get good information that will help people. We'll begin by taking you inside the mind of a research psychologist so you can see the obstacles to getting good information. Then, we'll outline our strategy for teaching you how to overcome these obstacles.

THE RESEARCHER'S PERSPECTIVE

Psychological researchers are at once optimistic and skeptical. Although they hope to harness the power of science to make as much progress in understanding human behavior as chemists have made in understanding molecules, research psychologists realize that their subjects (rats, pigeons, apes, humans, etc.) can't be studied the same way that objects are studied.

To appreciate how sensitive research psychologists are to the unique challenges and responsibilities involved in studying the behavior of living things, let's see how a research psychologist would react if someone ignored these challenges and responsibilities. For example, suppose that a novice investigator tries to model his psychological research after the following chemistry experiment:

> A chemist has two test tubes. Both test tubes contain a hydrogen and oxygen mixture. She leaves the first test tube alone. She heats the second test tube over a flame. She observes that water forms only in the second test tube. Since there was only one difference between the two test tubes (the heat), she concludes that the heat caused the difference in the behavior of the two groups of molecules. That is, she concludes that the heat caused the hydrogen and oxygen to combine.

Instead of filling two test tubes with hydrogen and oxygen, the chemistry major fills two rooms with both men and women. He treats both groups identically, except that he makes the second group's room 30 degrees warmer than the first group's. Then, he compares the behavior of the two groups and observes more aggression in the second room. The chemistry major then concludes that warmer temperatures make people more aggressive.

Because of the vast differences between humans and molecules, the experienced research psychologist would have four sets of very serious questions about the chemistry major's study. The first three deal with the validity of our novice investigator's conclusions. The last, and most serious, deal with whether it was ethical to perform the study.

The research psychologist realizes that measuring and manipulating human behavior, thoughts, and feelings is much more difficult than measuring and manipulating the behavior of molecules. Therefore, her first question would be: Is there sufficient **construct validity**? i.e., Did the investigator really measure and manipulate the **constructs** (aggression and temperature) he thought he was measuring and manipulating? Because humans are so unlike molecules, the research psychologist would have four major reasons for doubting that the novice's temperature-aggression study had adequate construct validity.

> **What Is Being Studied?: Construct Validity**

First, unlike molecules, human subjects may not passively accept manipulation. If you heat molecules in a test tube, they get warmer. But if you put people in a warm room, they may compensate by taking off their sweaters, coats, and ties, by opening windows, or by fanning themselves.

Second, unlike the purely physical reactions of molecules, human subjects bring a wide variety of psychological reactions to a situation. They may very well interpret the researcher's treatment differently from what he intended. Thus, even if the novice investigator did make the subjects warmer, this treatment may have had other, unintended side effects. The group in the warm room may be frustrated about not being able to cool off the room or they may be angry at the investigator for his lack of consideration in putting them in an uncomfortable room. Thus, this group's aggressiveness may not be a reaction to the temperature per se, but the result of frustration at not being able to open the windows, anger at the investigator, or some other side effect of the treatment.

Third, unlike molecules, people know they're in a study and may act accordingly. In our novice's study, subjects will probably realize that they're being observed and have been deliberately placed in an abnormally warm room. Thus, they may conclude that they're supposed to act differently because of the heat. They may even guess that the heat is supposed to make them more irritable and aggressive. If they like the investigator, they may try to give him the results they think he wants. They may therefore act aggressively just for the investigator's benefit. Although the subjects are just playing along, the investigator may think he's assessing their real reactions.

Fourth, unlike weighing the amount of water produced by a chemical reaction, it's hard to measure something as abstract and intangible as aggression. The chemistry major may have misinterpreted "kidding around" as aggression or considered only acts of physical violence as evidence of aggression. When a researcher has to infer a subject's state of mind, he may make a mistake.

In short, since people think and feel and since, as social scientists, we often want to measure these thoughts and feelings, studying human beings is much more difficult than studying molecules. Therefore, this aggression research, like any research, can be flawed if the subjects guess what the study is about, if investigators misinterpret their subjects' behavior, or if they misinterpret how their subjects will perceive a given treatment or situation.

The knowledgeable researcher's second question would concern **internal validity**: "Did the treatment cause the effect?" If the study clearly establishes that the treatment caused the warm-room group to behave differently from the normal-room group, the study has internal validity. If something other than the treatment may have caused

> **What Caused the Effect?: Internal Validity**

the groups to behave differently, the study doesn't have internal validity. In this study, the experienced researcher realizes that many things, other than the treatment, might account for the difference in behavior.

She might start by questioning whether the groups were identical before the study began. Specifically, she might ask: "Could it be that the warm-room group was naturally more aggressive than the normal-room group?".

Next, she might wonder if the groups were treated identically in every respect except for the treatment (the room temperature). She would ask questions such as: "Were the groups tested in the same room? At the same time of day? By the same experimenters?". If she found any nontreatment differences between the two groups, she would entertain the possibility that these differences, rather than the treatment, caused the groups to differ from one another.

In short, the experienced researcher realizes that establishing internal validity for a psychological study is more difficult than for the chemistry experiment. Unlike molecules, all humans aren't identical. As a result, it's hard to start off with two identical groups of people. Also, unlike molecules, which can be tested in a vacuum or a test tube, people can't be isolated from nontreatment factors. Therefore, it's hard to treat two groups of subjects identically in every respect.

Can You Generalize the Results?: External Validity

Even if the results in this particular study were due to the treatment, the researcher would question the study's **external validity**, i.e., whether the treatment would have the same effect outside this study. The research psychologist would have several reasons to question the aggression study's external validity.

First, since people differ, a result that occurs with one group of people might not occur with a different group of people. The novice investigator might have obtained different results if he'd studied all female groups instead of mixed-sex groups or if he'd studied Russian sixth-graders instead of American college students.

Second, since people change over time, a result obtained today may not hold in the future. Perhaps research in aggression will virtually eliminate aggression, so that 500 years from now, a researcher repeating this study would find no instances of aggression in either group!

Third, since people's behavior may change depending on the situation, the results might not hold in another setting. For example, suppose the investigator used a very sterile, artificial laboratory situation to eliminate the effects of nontreatment factors. By isolating the treatment factor, the investigator may have succeeded in establishing internal validity. However, results obtained under such controlled situations may not generalize to more complex situations where other factors might come into play. For instance, these results might not apply to aggression in the workplace, at home, or outdoors.

In short, even if temperature increased aggression in this particular lab with this particular group of subjects at this particular time, the researcher wouldn't automatically assume that temperature would have the same effect in future studies conducted in different settings with different subjects.

Is the Study Ethical?

Although there are many differences between molecules and humans, the researcher realizes that the two most important differences are: 1) Molecules don't have rights, but people do, and; 2) Chemists have no responsibility for the welfare of molecules involved in their studies, but psychologists have a responsibility for the welfare of their subjects. Therefore, in the researcher's mind, the most important question about the study is whether it should have been done.

In deciding whether the subjects' rights were protected and whether the novice investigator lived up to his responsibilities, the researcher would consult the "Ethical principles in the conduct of research with human participants" published by the American Psychological Association (APA, 1981a). These principles are listed in Appendix A.

Human Subjects' Rights

As the APA's ethical research principles point out, human subjects have the right to know what will happen in the study, the right to refuse to be in the study, and the right to anonymity. According to these principles, the chemistry major should have told his subjects that the study would involve sitting in a warm room with a group of people; knowing this, the subjects should have freely volunteered to be in the study and been allowed to quit the study at any point. Furthermore, the chemistry major should have taken extensive precautions to ensure that no one other than the investigator found out how each subject behaved during the study.

Investigators' Responsibilities

The "principles" discuss not only subject rights but investigator responsibilities as well. According to the APA's ethical principles, the investigator is responsible for behaving in an ethical manner and, under some circumstances, may be responsible for ensuring that others also behave ethically. For example, if the novice had others working on the aggression study, those people would be responsible for their own behavior, but the investigator would also be responsible for their conduct. In other words, if the people working with or for the investigator behaved unethically, the investigator couldn't avoid responsibility by saying that he didn't misbehave or that he didn't know what the others were doing.

Furthermore, the investigator should try to anticipate all possible risks to his subjects and protect them from these risks. In this study, he should have taken steps to prevent his subjects from suffering because of the heat (heart attack, heat stroke) or aggression (hurt nose, hurt feelings, hurt relationships).

Yet, taking preventative measures is not enough. The investigator should also try to find out if anyone has been harmed. The investigator can't merely assume that no one has been harmed. Instead, he must actively look for evidence of harm. He should probe the subjects to find out if anything unpleasant happened to them. Of course, if he detects harm, he should try to undo that harm.

Finally, the investigator should inform each subject about the study's purpose. Informing the subjects about the study is the least the investigator can do to compensate them for their participation. Furthermore, informing them about the study may help assure subjects that their reactions are not unusual. For example, some of the subjects might think themselves anti-social or highly aggressive if they aren't told that the study was designed to make them act and feel that way.

Beyond Rights and Responsibilities

Unfortunately, the researcher can't determine that the study was ethical simply by observing that the investigator followed a few simple rules. Instead, as the first sentence of the APA's Principles states, "The decision to undertake research rests upon a **considered judgment** by the individual psychologist about **how to best contribute to psychological science and human welfare**." (emphasis added).

This sentence has two important implications. First, it means that even if none of the principles were compromised, the study would still be unethical if it was unlikely to contribute to psychological science and human welfare. Second, it means that the investigator might compromise some of these principles and still be ethical if the expected benefits of the study would compensate for those compromises. Consequently, an important step in determining whether the study was ethical is determining the likelihood that the study would lead to human betterment.

The experienced researcher would determine whether the chemistry major's study might lead to human betterment by evaluating the importance of the research question and how well the study could answer that question: the internal, external, and construct validity of the study. Unfortunately, determining the value of the research question is highly subjective. One person may find the idea very interesting, another may find it extremely dull. In the aggression study, the novice may believe that determining the relationship between temperature and aggression is extremely valuable and might lead to ways of preventing riots. Others, however, may disagree. A novice investigator should always consult and defer to a higher authority's opinion. **Never conduct a study without the approval of your professor**!

The problem of assessing the potential value of a piece of research is further complicated because no one knows what the researcher will discover. A study that looks promising may reveal nothing. On the other hand, many scientific studies designed to answer one question have ended up answering a very important, but unrelated question (Coile and Miller, 1984). Because it's so hard to judge the value of a research question, the experienced researcher would probably acknowledge that the chem major's research question has some merit.

The only reason to consider the research question totally worthless would be if it had already been answered. For example, suppose there was an abundance of research on aggression and temperature, including several studies very similar to our novice's. Suppose further that the chem major wouldn't have done his study if he'd known about this published research. In other words, the only reason he performed the study was that he was too lazy to do a proper review of the literature. Under these circumstances, the experienced researcher would consider the study unethical. No investigator has the right to put subjects at any risk, no matter how small, if the study has no chance of contributing to human betterment.

But unless the chem major made the serious mistake of not doing a literature review, evaluating the importance of a research question is very subjective. Therefore, to estimate the potential value of the research, the experienced research psychologist would rely more heavily on the less subjective judgment of how well the study would answer the research question. That is, she would ask whether the study would provide valid data. Of course, she wouldn't consider the study worthless if it failed to have high levels of all forms of validity. (Few studies even attempt to have high levels of all three validities.) However, she would demand a reasonable level of at least one kind of validity.

After carefully considering the potential value of the study, the research psychologist would again consider the potential risks to the subjects. If the benefits greatly outweighed the risks (the ends justify the means), she would believe that conducting the study was ethical.

Ethics: Concluding Remarks

In short, the psychological researcher's most important concerns about this aggression study are ethical concerns. Indeed, since ethical concerns include concerns about validity and since the goal of research is human betterment, you could argue that ethical concerns are the researcher's only concerns.

But what if the study had used animals instead of human subjects? In that case, you might think the psychologist wouldn't be concerned about ethics. Nothing could be further from the truth. Psychologists have always been concerned about the ethics of animal research, and, in recent years, animal rights have received more attention from the APA than human rights. If the aggression study had used animals as subjects, the researcher would have consulted the APA's (1981b) "Ethical principles for the care and use of animals" listed in Appendix A. If the study were done unethically, the investigator would be severely punished. Not only does the APA refuse to publish an unethical investigator's research, it may also rescind the offending investigator's membership in the association.

PLAN OF THE BOOK

You have seen that research psychologists are aware of the responsibilities and challenges of studying human and animal behavior. What you haven't seen is the wide range of methods psychologists use to meet these challenges and responsibilities. Shrewd investigators may use a single subject or thousands of subjects; human subjects or animal subjects; laboratory studies or field studies; experiments or surveys, depending on ethical considerations and their research goals.

This book will help you become a shrewd investigator by showing you how to generate research ideas, manipulate and measure the variables you're interested in, collect data objectively, ensure validity, choose the right design for your particular research question, treat subjects ethically, interpret your results, and communicate your findings. We hope you'll use this knowledge to join the most fascinating quest of our time—exploring the human mind.

THE CASE OF THE MURDERED TWIN

"Mother Murders Son for Inheritance. Twin Brother Mourns," blared the headlines. According to the article, Scotland Yard had found overwhelming evidence of the mother's guilt. In fact, they had arrested the distracted woman even before they received an eyewitness account of the murder from the twin's brother.

"Watson, can you pack a bag? I'd like to look into this matter," said Holmes.

"Certainly, Holmes. But it's an open and shut case," I replied.

"Perhaps, Watson, perhaps. But even if the case is closed, we should take advantage of this occasion to meet the twin. You see, he's a research psychologist."

When we arrived at the house where the atrocities had transpired, Holmes greeted the twin with unreserved enthusiasm. "Hello, I'm Sherlock Holmes. I've heard a great deal about you. You are quite a psychologist!"

The twin reciprocated. "And I've heard quite a bit about you, Mr. Holmes."

"Well, that's to be expected. We're both in the same business—trying to get inside people's heads. We both try to find out what happened and why it happened," said Holmes.

"Yes, but you look for motives in the real world. Your work is truly exciting. I just do experiments in my dreary little lab," the twin replied, modestly.

Holmes persisted. "Not at all, my dear fellow. We both dig for facts and uncover new evidence. We both question common sense and look for possibilities and explanations for events that others have overlooked."

"Well, perhaps, but your techniques are so creative," said the twin.

"You are too modest. Please tell me about your research," insisted Holmes.

The twin pushed the request aside, saying "Oh, it's dull. I simply manipulate statistics, really."

Suddenly, Holmes pounced. "You fiend! You are not Dr. Ardlich, but Mr. Ardlich. You killed your twin brother, the esteemed Dr. Ardlich, framed your mother, and then assumed your brother's identity.

"Last night during dinner, you drugged both your mother and brother. After murdering your brother, you arranged things in the kitchen and in your brother's room to incriminate your own mother. What sort of vile creature premeditates such a crime? What misguided brilliance! You willed your money to your mother to attract suspicion to her, but actually, you planned to inherit her money after she was sent to the gallows."

We took a sullen Ardlich to Scotland Yard. On our way back to Baker Street, Holmes revealed how he knew that the twin was Mr. Ardlich rather than Dr. Ardlich. "Surely it's obvious, my dear Watson. His lack of enthusiasm for his work tipped me off. He didn't display any of the enthusiasm and excitement that we investigators get when the game is afoot. The thrill of the chase and the joy of the search were absent in him. But there was much more. He believed that research is highly statistical. Any investigator knows that statistics are just a tool, a means to an end, not an end in themselves. He showed similar ignorance with regard to laboratories. He felt that research only involved laboratory experiments. This is false. Not only did the late Dr. Ardlich do many experiments outside of the lab, but he also used a variety of non-experimental research methods."

MAIN POINTS

1. Research is a logical, proven, and ethical way of obtaining important information about human behavior.
2. The researcher's primary concern is to do ethical research. Of course, part of being ethical is ensuring that your study has some degree of internal, external, and/or construct validity.
3. If a study has internal validity, it establishes that a particular cause results in a certain effect.
4. The study's external validity is the degree to which its findings can be generalized to other people, places, and times.
5. Researchers do studies in a variety of settings on a wide range of subjects to maximize external validity.
6. When investigators are studying the factors they claim to be studying, their research has construct validity.

KEY TERMS

construct validity
internal validity
external validity

EXERCISES

1. A police officer puts a drunk in a blue room. The prisoner acts in a way that the officer describes as "violent." Then, the officer moves the prisoner to a pink room. This prisoner then acts in a way that the officer describes as "less violent."
   a. A scientist doubts that the pink room changed the prisoner's behavior. Instead, she thinks the change in the prisoner's behavior in the pink room might just be a coincidence. The prisoner may have changed his behavior for reasons that have nothing to do with the pink room (the prisoner has calmed down by the time he enters the pink room). Since the scientist doubts that the pink room caused the effect, she questions the study's _____ validity.
   b. A second scientist believes that even if the pink room changed this particular prisoner's behavior (That is, the study had _____ validity), there would be serious doubts about whether the pink room would change the behavior of sober prisoners. The second scientist questions the degree to which the results would generalize; i.e., he questions the study's _____ validity.

c. A third scientist believes that even if the pink room did cause a change in the prisoner's behavior, the change probably wasn't due to the prisoner being calmed down by the pink colors in the room. Instead, the scientist thought the prisoner was less violent in the pink room because the officer was nicer to him in the pink room. The officer was nicer to him in the pink room because the officer expected the prisoner to be less violent in that room. Thus, the pink room works because the officer expects it to work and changes his behavior accordingly, not because pink soothes the prisoner. In this case, since the scientist is questioning whether the treatment is working for the reason the officer claims, the scientist is questioning the study's _____ validity.

2. What concerns would you have about the validity of the study described above? Why?

3. Can you have external validity without internal validity?

4. A researcher does a study using only male subjects. Another researcher finds that the results do not hold for female subjects. The fact that the original study's results do not generalize to female subjects reflects a problem with the original study's _____ validity.

5. Is it ethical to treat a patient with a method that hasn't been scientifically tested? Why or why not?

6. How are the APA's ethical guidelines similar to the ''golden rule''? How do they differ?

7. Do you think individual researchers are capable of making responsible judgments about whether their research is ethical? Or, should committees make these decisions? If so, who should serve on these committees?

8. The APA's ethical principles are general guidelines for researchers. Do you support the idea of general guidelines or do you think there should be hard and fast rules that all researchers must obey? If you support the idea of establishing some absolute laws for researchers, what would your laws be? If you don't think absolute rules should be enacted, why not?

9. Two of the most ethically questionable studies in the history of psychology are Milgram's (1974) obedience study (where subjects were told to deliver dangerous shocks to an accomplice of the experimenter) and Zimbardo's (1974) prison study (where well-adjusted students pretended to be either prisoners or guards). In both of these studies, there would have been no ethical problems at all if subjects had behaved the way common sense told us they would. No one would have obeyed the order to administer the shocks and no one would have mistreated the ''prisoners.'' Argue that the inability to know how subjects will react to a research project means that research should not be done. Then, argue the opposite side of the coin: Because we can't yet predict human behavior, certain kinds of research should be performed to find out the answers to these important questions.

10. A study is done of whether drivers stop to help a woman who is having car trouble. On Sunday, the subjects see a man helping a woman a half-mile before they see the ''woman in distress.'' On Monday, subjects don't see a model. More people stop to help on Sunday than on Monday. The researchers argue that their research shows that exposure to a helpful model makes people more helpful.

    a. Alice says that the effect may not be due to the model at all. Instead, people may be more likely to help on Sunday because they don't have to get to work or because they have just returned from church. Alice is questioning the study's _____ validity.

    b. Joe notes that the study was done in the suburbs. He doesn't feel that the results would hold in the country or in the city. He also feels that the results would not hold in Europe, because he thinks people are more helpful there. Joe is questioning the study's _____ validity.

c. Sue wonders whether the model really increased helping or whether the model made men feel less inhibited about trying to "pick up" a woman. She suspects that many of the men who stopped were not stopping just to be helpful. Furthermore, she wonders whether the reason more people stopped after seeing the model was that they slowed down to see why the car was off the road. Since they had already slowed down, they were able to stop more easily when they saw someone who needed help. Sue obviously has doubts about the study's _____ validity.

2

GENERATING THE RESEARCH HYPOTHESIS: TAPPING INTUITION AND THEORY

OUTLINE

Behind every great research project, there is a great research hypothesis.

If you do not ask specific questions, I can not be responsible for your misinterpretation of the answer.

—SOLITAIRE *Live and Let Die*

OVERVIEW

We do research to get answers to questions. Therefore, to do research, we must start with a research question that can be answered. This question is usually stated as a **hypothesis**—an idea, a prediction, capable of being disproven.

Unfortunately, many people, in their eagerness to get an idea that can be tested, generate boring research hypotheses. This is a shame because dull, uninspired hypotheses lead to dull, uninspired research projects.

To do exciting research, you must begin with a question that's worth answering. Once you have an interesting question, then you can start figuring out how you'll convert this question into a testable, research hypothesis.

But how do you get an interesting question? There are three major sources of research questions: intuition, theory, and existing research. In this chapter, you'll learn how to tap two of these sources: intuition and theory. In Chapter 9, once you have a better understanding of the terms used in journal articles, you'll learn how to get research ideas by reading research.

After you've learned to extract fascinating ideas from intuition and theory, you'll learn how to convert these ideas into testable research hypotheses. Thus, by the end of this chapter, you should be well on your way to conducting creative, exciting, and fruitful research.

USING INTUITION TO GENERATE RESEARCH IDEAS

Shared Intuition: Common Sense

Two Kinds of Intuition: Shared and Personal

Intuition isn't a magical quality that only a gifted few possess. On the contrary, all members of a society share the same intuition in the form of common sense. Common sense, like an informal theory, gives us general rules from which we can deduce specific hypotheses. These hypotheses help us understand the world and predict what will happen next. For instance, suppose we know that Jim and Joan are two very different people. What would happen if we put them together? Our common sense tells us that opposites attract. Therefore, we conclude that Jim and Joan will be attracted to each other. Our conclusion is an example of **deduction**—applying a general rule to a specific situation. (A problem with common sense, however, is that it also tells us that "like attracts like." Therefore, we could also predict that Jim and Joan will not like each other.)

Personal Intuition: Uncommon Sense

In addition to being given common sense rules, we create our own unique "uncommon sense" rules by finding patterns in our personal experiences. These uncommon sense rules are often formed by **induction**, i.e., creating a general rule by seeing similarities among several specific situations. For example, after seeing people fight repeatedly in bars, you may induce that alcohol leads to aggression.

Capitalizing on Your Intuition

You will find that your intuition is a valuable source of potential research ideas—if you concentrate exclusively on generating ideas about real-life behavior. When you begin thinking of ideas, don't worry about whether your idea is a testable one. Just generate as many ideas as you can. Once you have completed this first step, you can move on to the second step—deciding which ideas are testable.

Unfortunately, the natural way to begin thinking of research ideas is to take a more direct approach. Rather than generating ideas about real-life behavior (step 1) and then narrowing down these ideas (step 2), the natural tendency is to combine these two steps—thinking about what can be done in a lab. Although this shortcut is tempting, using it will prevent you from fully capitalizing on your intuition. If you constantly remind yourself of the following four facts, you'll be able to resist this temptation.

First, you're probably more interested in real-life behavior rather than "what could be done in the lab" and are therefore more likely to think longer about real-life behavior than laboratory behavior. Since creative ideas are largely the result of persevering (Pronko, 1969), you're more likely to produce creative ideas about real-life behavior than laboratory behavior.

Second, research suggests that the more broadly defined the problem, the more creative the solutions (Adams, 1974). Trying to come up with an idea about behavior is less restrictive than coming up with an idea that can be tested in a laboratory. Thinking of ideas that can be tested in a laboratory is extremely restrictive, especially since research doesn't have to be done in a lab.

Third, although you don't have a lifetime of experience in a lab, you do have a lifetime of experience in real-life. As Wolfgang Kohler showed in 1925, you're much more likely to be creative in an area in which you have some background than one in which you don't.

Fourth, in trying to generate an idea that can be tested in a laboratory, you tend to do two things simultaneously: produce the idea and evaluate how testable it is. Many psychologists believe that the key to creativity is keeping the production and the criticism of ideas separate. Indeed, the number one rule on brainstorming is that no idea is to be criticized and eliminated until the idea-generation stage is completed. And it works (Meadow, Parves, and Reese, 1959.) We have found that students prefer to use the two-step (generate ideas, then narrow down) model, than to try to go directly to an idea that can be tested. They find that the two-step approach makes it relatively easy to come up with ideas and that their final hypotheses are really interesting.

Although the process of producing ideas can be relatively easy, it's usually difficult to generate the first one. Perhaps this is because students are afraid of not having a perfect idea. Excessive self-criticism is a common barrier to creative thinking (Adams, 1974). Remember, the first idea doesn't have to lead to the Nobel Prize. Try to think of it as just a step to the next idea, and to the next. In the early stages of generating ideas, you should emphasize quantity over quality. Once you have a large pool of ideas, you can then start judging their relative merits as hypotheses.

To help you get the first idea and to get in the habit of generating ideas without judging them, we've developed the following techniques. We think you'll find these "ice-breakers" both fun and useful.

1. **THINK OF SOME "OLD SAYINGS."** Although old sayings are stated as fact, they're really assumptions—assumptions that can often be tested. For example, Stanley Schachter (1959) tested the saying that "Misery loves company." More recently, Latane, Williams, and Harkins (1979) tested the hypothesis that "Many hands make light the work" (they discovered that the hypothesis was false). Although some old sayings have been tested, others remain untried. Perhaps you could test hypotheses generated from common sense such as "The more, the merrier," or "Familiarity breeds contempt."

Rather than testing old sayings, you might try to refine them. For example, you might ask yourself, "Under what circumstances is the old saying accurate?" Or, you might try to reconcile the inconsistencies of common sense. For example, when does "like attract like" and when "do opposites attract?" Under what circumstances are "two heads better than one" and when is it better to do it yourself (after all, "too many cooks spoil the broth" and "nothing is worse than a committee")?

2. **ANALYZE SONGS.** Many songs suggest ideas about why people do the things they do. Some psychologists have already taken advantage of some of the hypotheses provided by songs. For instance, Pennebaker, et al. (1979) investigated the hypothesis proposed by the country song "The girls get prettier at closing time" (They discovered that women appeared more attractive to men as closing time approached). Perhaps you can convert some of your favorite songs into research ideas. Some songs only offer questions "Why do fools fall in love?", whereas others make predictions. For instance, Survivor's "Eye of the Tiger" proposes that success can decrease motivation. So, listen to records as a means of getting research ideas.

3. **LITERATURE OFTEN GIVES THE READER EXPLANATIONS** for why people act in certain ways or stimulates the reader to generate explanations. For example, many of Shakespeare's works suggest unconscious influences on behavior, e.g., Lady Macbeth washing her hands in an attempt to remove her guilt in the king's death from her conscience. Less lofty literature may suggest ideas, if only because the author is restating common sense.

Even the lowest forms of literature can provide you with research ideas. For instance, tabloid newspapers such as the *National Enquirer* present intriguing ideas stated as documented fact. Some of these ideas can be tested and may occasionally

Eleven Ways to Tap Your Intuition

prove correct. For example, in one issue, a tabloid asserted that deliberately smiling would improve your mood. This idea appears to be correct (Zuckerman, et al., 1981). If nothing else, reading tabloids should stimulate you to hypothesize about why people read them!

4. **FIND A PERSON WHO DISAGREES WITH YOU** about almost everything and then argue with him or her about the effects of various activities. Many of these arguments can be converted into research projects. For example, suppose your acquaintance feels that jogging increases creativity and you don't. Or suppose you feel that fast-talkers are more persuasive, but your acquaintance vehemently disagrees. If neither of you can use logic to win these arguments, you have an ideal situation (for generating hypotheses, not for friendship). If you can't prove your acquaintance wrong, then it's time to get evidence to show that you're right: It's research time. So, seek out those quarrelsome friends and argumentative acquaintances, or play the role of "devil's advocate" if you really need a research hypothesis.

5. **LOOK THROUGH A DICTIONARY OR A THESAURUS.** Start at any page and begin looking for a personality trait (e.g., aggressive, creative, persistent). Once you find a trait, look for its noun form. Aggressive would become aggression, creative would become creativity, persistent would become persistence, and so on. The first of these trait nouns you find can be what you try to measure. Then, think about factors that might influence this trait. If you can't think of anything, go back to the dictionary again. Flip through the pages, looking at a couple of words on each page. Ask yourself if these words could have anything to do with your first trait noun. If the answer is yes, you may have a research idea.

An example will give you a clearer picture of how this method works. You pick up a dictionary, open it near the middle, and start looking for traits. You find the word "nervous." Your dictionary informs you that nervous is an adjective, but that "nervousness" is a noun. You now know what you want to measure. Next, you need to find a factor that would affect nervousness. On a lark, you start looking for words that start with "ba." You dismiss babble, baby, and bachelor. However, baboon, baccarat (a gambling game), backbiting, the backfiring of a car, bacteria, badge, bad-mouthing, bagpipes (especially off-key), balloons (popping), bang (as from a gun), barbarity, barometer (Say, do changes in air pressure make people nervous?), barracuda, basil (Does the smell of the herb make people less nervous?), bat, battle, bawl, and bazooka, all have some appeal.

You'll probably eliminate some of these variables (e.g., barracuda, battle, and bazooka) because you wouldn't want to expose your subjects to danger. However, you still have many factors you could study. Some of these variables are easy to manipulate, such as the scent of basil, the presentation of loud noises, and so on. The other variables can also be manipulated if you use a little imagination. For example, although you may not be able to actually release a bat into the room, you could suggest its presence by saying, "Don't mind the bat."

6. **TELEVISION COMMERCIALS** are another source of ideas. Ask yourself what makes a certain commercial effective—or ineffective. For example, suppose you think the television commercial for "Scrumptious Candy" is ineffective because it's too serious, but you think the ad for "Jerby's Candy" is effective because it's funny. You now have a hypothesis: Humor increases the effectiveness of a persuasive message.

7. **ATTACK A PRACTICAL PROBLEM.** Practical problems are often good sources of hypotheses because they are easy to visualize and because different people have different "solutions" to almost any given problem. For example, consider the problem of spouse abusers. Some people think that spouse abusers should be arrested. Others believe that abusers should be separated from their families. Still others feel that spouse abusers should be left alone. As a matter of fact, in Minneapolis, a study was conducted (Sherman & Berk, 1984) to choose among these "solutions." On the basis of random assignment, police either removed the abusive spouse from the home, arrested him, or left him alone. Several months later, social workers went back to the home to check on the family. Results of this experiment showed that one night in jail decreases spouse violence.

Of course, just because the hypothesis comes from a practical situation doesn't mean that the research needs to be conducted in the field. For example, laboratory studies on violence, productivity, jury decision making, eyewitness testimony, perceptual factors that cause accidents, were all inspired by practical problems.

Suppose you're concerned about the effect of television violence on aggression. Specifically, you're concerned about television shows that include scenes in which hundreds of shots are fired without a serious injury occurring. You feel that this kind of violence could lead to more viewer aggression than equally violent shows where people get hurt. You don't have to take over a major television network to test this hypothesis. Instead, you could make several videotapes: one that had no violence, one that had violence with people getting killed, and one that had the same violence but with few consequences. Next, you could randomly assign subjects to watch one of the three films (no-violence film, violence-without-consequences film, or violence-with-consequences film) and then measure aggression. You could conduct the entire study without leaving the comfort of the lab.

8. **LOOK AT SURVEYS AND STATISTICS THAT NEWSPAPERS, MAGAZINES, AND TELEVISION COMMENTATORS PRESENT.** Each day, you're bombarded with statistics that no one bothers to explain. For example, you might read that 61% of the people believe television news is more objective than newspaper news. Or, you may hear that the home-court advantage is very important in basketball. If you can come up with a possible explanation for a given fact, then you may be able to do a research project to test this explanation.

9. **CREATE A NEW SITUATION.** Rather than trying to model the real-world, you might try to create conditions that have never occurred outside the lab. Just as a chemist can create new molecules, you can create new, never-before-experienced environments. You could then expose people to conditions they would never experience in real life. In short, you can ask "I wonder what would happen if . . . ?" questions. There are numerous, new experiences to which you could expose people (or animals)— from novel scents, to special diets, to films of self-actualized models.

10. **TAKE ADVANTAGE OF NEW MEASURING INSTRUMENTS.** A new measuring instrument may open up a new psychological frontier, thereby allowing you to be a pioneer. Many psychologists have greatly benefited from using such newer and better mousetraps as the Skinner box, the memory drum, the electroencephalogram (EEG), the prisoner's dilemma game, The Bem Androgeny Scale, the Minnesota Multiphasic Personality Inventory (MMPI), and the Buss Aggression Machine.

New instruments allow you to manipulate variables that have been manipulated thousands of times before, but with a new perspective. For instance, medical research institutes spend thousands of dollars to gain access to the newest measurement device so they can be the first to see how the measure is affected by such well-known variables as caffeine, alcohol, and exercise. Fortunately, new psychological measuring tools are usually less expensive and more easily accessible than medical instruments. In fact, many of our newest tools are paper-and-pencil devices (e.g., psychological tests, interview forms, attitude scales). These paper and pencil tools can often be copied from recent journal articles.

Not all psychological devices are so easily obtained however. Unfortunately, some of these measuring instruments may be beyond your (or even your department's) budget. To avoid the expense problem (and become famous to boot), invent a way of measuring a heretofore uninvestigated variable. Hints on developing measurement tools will be discussed in the next chapter.

11. If you're still stuck for an idea, **ASK YOURSELF WHAT FACTORS ARE DECREASING YOUR CREATIVITY.** You could then do research to investigate these factors.

The Art of Creating Intuitive Hypotheses: A Summary

You can generate research ideas if you're persistent and concentrate on trying to discover why people or animals act the way they do. To focus on this task, you can use two basic approaches.

First, you can take advantage of existing common sense. You can find common sense ideas by reading literature, listening to songs, or thinking about old sayings. Second, you could stimulate your intuition by thinking about how to solve a practical problem, creating what you'd consider the ideal situation for a certain event to occur, explaining a statistic, figuring out the motive behind a character in a novel, thinking about how a new measuring device would be affected by certain factors, talking to people whose intuitions differ from yours, reconciling apparent contradictions, glancing through a dictionary, analyzing ads, or even reflecting on why you're having problems coming up with an idea.

BOX 2-1   Eleven Ways to Tap Your Intuition

1. Test or refine a proverb.
2. Analyze songs.
3. Test assumptions about human nature that are stated in classic or popular literature.
4. Transform the opposing views of an argument into a research idea.
5. Look through a dictionary for interesting research variables.
6. Analyze television commercials.
7. Attack a practical problem.
8. Try to explain survey and research findings reported in the media.
9. Create a new situation.
10. Use a new measuring instrument.
11. Investigate factors that decrease your creativity.

GETTING IDEAS FROM THEORY

Thus far, we have concentrated on generating ideas from our own informal observations and from common sense. Yet, following hunches isn't the only or even the
most preferable method of generating ideas. Many psychologists prefer ideas drawn
from theory.

Theory and Research

A **theory** is a set of propositions from which a large number of *new* observations can
be deduced. Not surprisingly, theories are proven sources of hypotheses. For example,
"germ theory" led to the discovery of bacteria responsible for certain diseases, "gene
theory" led to the discovery of DNA, Newton's theory of gravity led to the discovery
of Neptune, Einstein's theory of relativity led to the development of nuclear weapons,
and social learning theory has led to thousands of studies. Thus, theory, like intuition,
is a good source of research ideas. But why do many psychologists prefer theory to
intuition?

What Is a Theory?

First, theories tend to be more internally consistent than common sense or intuition.
That is, a theory usually doesn't contradict itself. Common sense, on the other hand,
often contradicts itself ("absence makes the heart grow fonder," "absence makes the
heart wander").

The Advantages of Using Theory to Generate Ideas

Second, theories tend to be more consistent with existing facts than common
sense or intuition. Inductive theories are constructed by systematically collecting data
and carefully analyzing the data for patterns. Deductive theories are molded by facts:
if a deduction is incorrect, the theory is changed or abandoned. Thus, unlike common
sense and intuition, theories don't ignore facts.

Third, theories aren't restricted to making common sense predictions. They
can make predictions that are counterintuitive. For example, social learning theory,
contrary to popular wisdom, predicts that punishment will not be an effective way of
changing behavior. By definition, intuition can only lead to intuitive hypotheses.

Fourth, theories summarize and organize a great deal of information. Thus,
rather than producing scattered, isolated bits of trivia like some intuitive research
does, theory-based research can relate to and build on existing work.

Despite their similarities, all theories aren't equally useful for helping you to generate
testable ideas. Therefore, when choosing a theory, make sure that it's testable. Testable theories make specific, observable predictions about what will happen in the
future.

The Qualities of a Helpful Theory: In Search of Testability

Prediction Rather than Postdiction

To make testable predictions, the theory must tell you what will happen in the future.
Not all theories make such predictions. Instead, some only explain what happened
after the fact. For example, McDougall's (1908) instinct theory explains that things
happen by instinct but doesn't tell us when to expect instincts to be aroused or how
to tell whether someone has a high level of instinct. The adage "Hindsight is always
better than Foresight" tells us that it's easier to look back on experiences and think
we see a trend, than to predict future events.

Prediction Rather than Predictions

To be testable, a theory must be capable of making one and only one prediction about what would happen in a certain situation. To illustrate the problem of making more than one prediction, consider Freudian theory. According to Freudian theory, receiving a severe beating from one's father would result in either:

1. no effect (we forget it: repression)
2. no apparent effect (we try not to think about it: suppression)
3. deep anger and resentment at people similar to our father (displacement)
4. great love for our father (reaction formation)
5. hate for ourself (internalization)

Precision in Prediction

Some theories purport to make predictions about the future, but the predictions are so vague as to be untestable. An extremely vague prediction reminds us of the fortune cookies that read "You will make a decision soon."

Precision is the reason we often value math in theories. We don't like math for math's sake, but math tends to be specific. For instance, the statement "People taking the drug will remember twice as much as those not taking the drug" is more precise (and mathematical) than the statement "People taking the drug will remember more than those not taking the drug."

Operationalism

Even if a theory makes specific, unambiguous predictions about the future, these predictions must be publicly observable for the theory to be testable. For example, even though the statement: "If you've lived a good life, you'll go to heaven" is a specific prediction about future events, it can't be scientifically tested. Such a prediction is not scientifically testable because we can't find any publicly observable, physical evidence to help us determine whether or not a person has gone to heaven. In other words, we can't provide an **operational definition**—a publicly observable way to measure or manipulate—of "gone to heaven." Such metaphysical (beyond the physical world) statements as "gone to heaven" are beyond the reach of science and therefore are best left to theologians. Analogously, a few scientists have argued that science and psychoanalysis are mutually exclusive because psychoanalysis is based upon an acceptance of the unconscious—an intangible that can't be observed. Such is the fate of theories whose variables cannot be operationalized.

We should caution, however, that not all variables in a theory must be directly observable. Many theories discuss **hypothetical constructs**: entities that we can't, with our present technology, observe directly. Love, learning, and memory are all hypothetical constructs because they're invisible. However, although hypothetical constructs can't be seen, we can measure them if we can see their traces. The responsible theory leads us to observable traces, or imprints, of the hypothetical construct. With enough indirect, physical evidence, scientists can make a very convincing case for the existence of an invisible entity (a hypothetical construct). Thus, although no one has ever seen an electron, physicists have proved that electrons exist.

BOX 2-2   Qualities of a Testable Theory

Predicts the future

Predicts one outcome per situation

Makes precise predictions

Is operational—the variables you are studying are publicly observable

---

In psychology, the challenge has not been to see inside the atom, but to see inside the mind. Like electrons, mental states can't be directly observed. For example, we can't observe learning directly. However, we can see its effect on performance, i.e., we can operationally define learning as an increase in performance. Thus, if we see people improve their performance after practicing a task, we conclude that learning has occurred. Similarly, we can provide operational definitions for such intangible, hypothetical constructs as hunger, thirst, mood, love, etc.

Finding a Theory

You now know how to judge whether a theory can help you generate research ideas. But where do you find theories?

Preparing to Take Advantage of a Helpful Theory

From our earlier discussion, you might expect to find theories in the form of a list of hypotheses, as shown in Box 2-3. Unfortunately, psychological theories, especially ones that are broad in scope, are rarely presented so elegantly. Instead, psychological theories may ramble on for hundreds, even thousands of pages. For example, Gall's theory of phrenology (the study of the shape and contours of the head) occupied seven volumes. Even with more accepted theories, hypotheses and core assumptions are often hidden among tons of verbiage.

Faced with the problem of a clumsily stated theory, what's a theory-oriented researcher to do? The theory-oriented researcher has two basic options. One option is to read summaries of the theory. Reading a textbook summary should at least acquaint you with some of the theory's propositions. The problem with this approach is that a textbook summary may oversimplify the theory. The researcher who relies exclusively on textbook summaries may be accused of ignoring key propositions of the theory or of using a **"straw" theory**—an exaggerated, oversimplified caricature of the theory. Therefore, in addition to reading textbook summaries, you should discover how other researchers have summarized the theory. To find these summaries, consult journal articles that describe studies based on the theory (e.g., "Elation and depression: A test of opponent process theory"). Usually, the beginning of these articles includes a brief description of the theory the study tests.

The second option is to read the theory and generate a complete list of its propositions yourself. Authors of recently developed theories often describe their theories in the *American Psychologist*. If you are interested in a more established theory, you should be able to find a textbook that includes a reference to the original statement of the theory. In addition, the *Psychological Abstracts* (see Appendix B) or your

---

BOX 2-3 Theory of Social Comparison Processes
Leon Festinger (1954)

Hypothesis 1—There exists, in the human organism, a drive to evaluate his opinions and his abilities.

Hypothesis 2—To the extent that objective, nonsocial means are not available, people evaluate their opinions and abilities by comparison respectively with the opinions and abilities of others.

Hypothesis 3—The tendency to compare oneself with some other specific person decreases as the differences between his opinion or ability and one's own increases.

Hypothesis 4—There is a unidirectional drive upward in the case of abilities, which is largely absent in opinions.

Hypothesis 5—There are nonsocial restraints that make it difficult or even impossible to change one's ability. These nonsocial restraints are largely absent from opinions.

Hypothesis 6—The cessation of comparison with others is accompanied by hostility or derogation to the extent that continued comparison with those persons implies unpleasant consequences.

Hypothesis 7—Any factors that increase the importance of some particular group as a comparison group for some particular opinion or ability will increase the pressure toward uniformity concerning that ability or opinion within that group.

Hypothesis 8—If persons who are very divergent from one's own opinion or ability are perceived as different from oneself on *attributes consistent with the divergence*, the tendency to narrow the range of comparability becomes stronger.

Hypothesis 9—When there is a range of opinion or ability in a group, the relative strength of the three manifestations of pressures toward uniformity will be different for those who are close to the mode of the group than those who are distant from the mode. Specifically, those close to the mode of the group will have stronger tendencies to narrow the range of comparison and much weaker tendencies to change their own positions compared to those who are distant from the mode of the group.

---

professor may be able to lead you to books or review articles devoted to the theory. These articles will help keep you up-to-date about the changes in the theory.

Which of these options should you use? Perhaps the most prudent strategy is to select a theory based on textbook descriptions of the theory. Then, if the original theory is extremely lengthy, rely on review articles or textbooks to obtain its main principles. If the original statement of the theory is brief (e.g., Kelley's attribution theory, Festinger's social comparison theory, equity theory, Latane's social impact theory, Seligman's learned helplessness theory, Solomon's opponent processes theory, Aaronson's gain-loss theory of attraction) or if the theory explicitly states its propositions, as do many learning theories (e.g., Guthrie's contiguity theory, Hull's drive reduction theory, Anderson's associative network theory), read the original source.

Deducing Hypotheses from Theory

Once you understand the theory, your task is to apply your powers of deduction. You have these powers or you wouldn't have been able to pass high-school geometry or write an essay. In fact, much of your everyday thinking involves deductive logic. For example, you may say, "The important thing about a college education is learning how to think. This assignment doesn't help me learn how to think. Therefore, this assignment is not important to my college education." This statement is an example of deductive logic. The premises may not be sound, but the logic is.

In deducing hypotheses from theory, you will use the same deductive logic illustrated above. That is, you'll apply a general rule to a specific instance. The only difference is that the general rule comes from a theory instead of from the top of your head. To reassure yourself that you can apply deductive reasoning to propositions that were made up by someone else, try this deductive reasoning test:

1. All people treated like b turn out c.
2. Person A is being treated like b.
3. Person A will turn out _____ .

1. All behavior can be changed by controlling its consequences.
2. Bob's behavior is bad.
3. Bob's bad behavior can be changed by _____ .

As you can see, if set up correctly, deductive logic is as simple as a-b-c. Often, you will be able to generate hypotheses by applying the theory's abstract hypotheses to concrete situations. You'll soon discover that (to paraphrase Kurt Lewin), "there is nothing as useful as a good theory for generating hypotheses." The problem is often the same one we have when presented with a large dessert tray—knowing where to start!

Four Ways to Use a Theory

1. **BROADEN THE THEORY'S HORIZON.** One place to start is by trying to broaden the theory. The breadth of a theory may be increased by testing whether it will hold in different situations. For example, you might ask whether a theory developed on rats applies to humans (or vice versa). Or you might try to apply deductions from the theory to a practical problem, or situation that interests you. Basically, you're just

asking the question, "where could this theory be applied?" For instance, dissonance theory defines dissonance as an unpleasant state that occurs whenever a person has two thoughts that she thinks are inconsistent. You could simply ask yourself, "where does dissonance occur?" Does it occur on the job? In a hospital? In psychological therapy?

The "where does the theory apply" question is often asked of theories. For example, much of the research in nursing, medicine, marketing, politics, religion, crime, personnel relations, advertising, and consumer behavior involves applying basic psychological theories to different situations. When you stretch a theory by expanding its scope, you're improving the theory. If the theory passes your test, it has more power. If the theory flunks your test, you have defined its boundaries.

2. TAKE IT TO THE LIMIT. In addition to determining to what phenomena the theory applies, you can determine to what degree it applies. In other words, you can see whether it holds in the extremes. For example, if a theory predicts that increasing rewards will lead to greater liking of the task, you might see whether extremely large rewards lead to even greater liking (comparing first-graders who either receive a nickel or a dollar for five minute's work). Again, if the theory passes your test, you have extended the theory's scope; if it fails, you have documented its limits.

3. IMPROVE ITS ACCURACY. Instead of extending the theory, you may choose to increase its precision. For instance, you may want to more accurately map the relationship between reward and effort. Is the relationship a straight line (what slope?), a curve, a parabola? This mapping will require accurate measurement of both variables (reward and effort) and may seem rather dull. However, the more precise a rule, the more useful it is. Wouldn't you prefer specific directions such as, "Go straight for a mile and a half, then turn right" to general directions such as, "Turn to the right up the road a piece"?

Historically, psychologists have become famous by carefully mapping functional relationships between variables. For example, Fechner's psychophysics mapped the relationship between physical stimulation and sensation, providing the impetus for the development of psychology as a science. Fechner's general finding—that the more intense the stimulus, the more intensely we feel it—was not that exciting. The exciting thing was that he was able to so precisely specify the relationship between stimulation and sensation.

More recently, Latane's Nida's, & Wilson's (1981) theory of social influence has been acclaimed, although by itself it is not unique. It says that the more people in the group, the more influence the group can have. It is unique, however, in describing with more accuracy than any previous theory, how much more influence the group will gain by adding members. Thus, the precision of a theory is of enormous value. Being specific is often the only thing that distinguishes the scientist's prediction from common sense predictions. Therefore, if you can improve a theory's precision, you have made quite a contribution.

4. GO FOR THE JUGULAR. Another tactic is to try to design an experiment that tests whether the core assumptions of the theory are valid. This involves attacking the heart of the theory. For instance, cognitive dissonance theory assumes that dissonance (having two beliefs that you think are contradictory) is an unpleasant, tense state. You might try to induce and maintain dissonance in subjects and determine if they find dissonance an unpleasant, tension-arousing state. If subjects feel decreased tension, it seems that you have disproved a core assumption of the theory. If you succeed in disproving a core assumption of a theory, you have accomplished a lot.

However, whether you disprove a prediction from a theory or one of the theory's core assumptions, the theory will probably not simply disappear. Rather than "throwing the baby out with the bath water", an established theory is usually modified and patched up after a damaging attack. Thus, Darwin's theory of evolution, Adam Smith's theory of capitalism, and Festinger's theory of cognitive dissonance survive today but not in their original forms.

Why Established Theories Persist

Modifying an existing theory to fit the facts is part of the scientific ideal. Theories are, after all, tentative explanations of behavior and are meant to be tested and refined. However, for whatever reason, some theories (Freud's theory of person-ality, Kohlberg's theory of moral development, Erikson's theory of psychosocial de-velopment) become so accepted that they survive intact even when the evidence contradicts some of their basic tenets.

Theories Make Sense of Our World

One possible explanation for the persistence of these theories is that accuracy may not be the most vital quality of a theory. Theories organize our world for us, keeping us from chaos. If some scientists dread chaos much more than inaccuracy, they may not abandon a theory unless they find another that can take its place. Their situation may be like that of someone flying above the clouds in a balloon. If they find that the balloon is drifting off course and there are a few holes in it, they do not, however, jump out—even though they know that it is full of hot air. They might, however, allow themselves to be rescued by another balloon.

"Crucial" Studies Are Rarely Crucial

Because scientists tend to jump to the best balloon, you might think the following situation would establish the winner and jettison the loser.

Two theories make opposite predictions. You test the two to see which view of the world is more correct. (These kinds of studies are called **crucial experiments** and are highly respected.) Yet, even though crucial experiments are highly regarded, the "loser" of your study is not replaced by the winner. The loser has only lost a battle, not a war. There is usually enough vagueness in any theory for its arch-supporters to minimize the extent of the damage. They will either argue that your experiment was a near-miss (Their theory didn't really say that. You put words in its mouth or it mumbled something and you misunderstood it), or if they can, they may patch the theory up a little bit. Soon, at least in its supporters' eyes, the theory will be fully recovered from your blow.

Qualities of Preferred Theories

Why do crucial experiments rarely decide the fate of theories? One explanation is that most scientists choose to follow one theory over another on the basis of style as well as substance (in much the same way we choose one presidential candidate over another). Specifically, scientists prefer theories that are broad in scope, parsi-monious, and provocative.

Breadth

Popular theories are enormously broad in scope. For example, social learning theory can be applied to prisons, businesses, advertising, politics, schizophrenics, smokers, librarians, mad dogs, and Englishmen. Similarly, Freud's theory of the unconscious can be applied to virtually any situation.

Parsimony: There's Got to Be a Simple Explanation for All of This

Popular theories tend to be broad and **parsimonious** i.e., they explain a broad range of phenomena with a few principles. The value of having few rules is obvious when you consider that a major function of theory is to simplify our world. The parsimonious theory provides a few simple rules that summarize hundreds of observations. These "rules of thumb" make existing knowledge easier to understand, remember, and use. Therefore, scientists prefer theories with a few far-reaching principles to theories that require a different principle to explain each new phenomenon. Thus, it should be no surprise that two theories that have enjoyed great popularity (social learning theory and Freud's theory of the unconscious) possess only a few, broad-ranging principles (reinforcement and the unconscious).

Provocativeness

In addition to explaining a wide range of phenomena with a few basic principles, popular theories tend to explain things in a novel way. Popular theories provoke controversy by suggesting new ways of viewing the world. Thus, Darwin's theory of evolution had us look at apes as relatives, Einstein's theory of relativity had us look at matter and energy as being the same thing. Freud's theory had us look at ourselves as being motivated by forces we weren't aware of, and Watson's theory had us look at ourselves as a set of reflexes.

Are Scientists Too Loyal to Their Theories?

Understandably, many people are concerned with the fact that some scientists appear to resist letting go of pet theories and appear to be as concerned as much with a theory's form as with its accuracy. In fact, Thomas Kuhn (1970) argues that because of scientists' emotional involvement with their theories, theories don't evolve: Theories are merely replaced with more stylish theories.

Summary: Generating Research Ideas from Theory

Despite the fact that some scientists are too loyal to certain theories, theory is a very useful tool for developing research ideas. Not only does theory provide many research ideas, it also ties ideas into existing knowledge. Without research based on theory, psychology would move in every direction with little purpose, like an amoeba. In essence, the development of theory has helped psychology progress beyond what it was in 1892.

> a string of raw facts; . . . but not a single law in the sense in which physics shows us laws, not a single proposition from which any consequence can causally be deduced . . . This is no science, . . . (James, 1892, p. 468).

However, the fact that theory allows you to generate ideas that relate to previous knowledge doesn't mean that research based on hunches is worthless. Where would nuclear physics and nuclear medicine be without Madame Curie's serendipitously discovering radium; where would immunology be without Sir Alexander Fleming's accidentally discovering penicillin; where would psychology be without B.F. Skinner's fortuitously discovering schedules of reinforcement?

Obviously, there is room in psychology for both hunch-based and theory-based research. Furthermore, often hunch and theory can be combined. For example, suppose you had a hunch that consuming alcohol might make people more helpful under certain conditions. To determine what the "certain conditions" are, you might refer to theory on the effects of alcohol and theory on helping behavior. As a result, you might conclude that alcohol consumption might increase helpfulness if the helping situation entails a great deal of risk. If your results support your hypothesis, your results not only add to knowledge about the relationship between drinking and helpfulness, but support Latane's theory of bystander apathy—that people tend to weigh the risks of helping before they act. A series of studies supporting this hypothesis has already been published (Steele & Southwick, 1985).

Since hunches and theory are good sources of ideas, try to use both approaches for generating ideas. For now, don't worry about reading original sources of theory: textbook summaries will be fine. Once you have your five ideas, write them down. In the next section, we will tell you how to develop these ideas into research hypotheses.

CONVERTING YOUR IDEAS INTO A RESEARCH HYPOTHESIS

Qualities of a Research Hypothesis

Of course, some of your ideas may already be viable research hypotheses. To find out whether an idea is a research hypothesis, ask yourself these three questions: 1) Can my idea be tested?, 2) Can I test it?, 3) Should I test it?

Is My Idea Testable?

For your idea to be testable, it must satisfy the same basic criteria we required of a testable theory. First, you must be able to generate operational definitions of your key variables. For example, if you plan to measure the effects of attractiveness on liking, you must be able to objectively measure liking and you must be able to define attractiveness according to publicly observable criteria.

Second, your prediction must be specific and precise enough so that it can be disproven or supported. Ask yourself, "What kind of result would disconfirm my prediction?". Also, ask yourself, "What kind of result would confirm my prediction?".

By being precise, you can avoid making predictions that cannot be disproven. However, you must make sure that your idea is capable of being supported. In particular, you must be wary of the null hypothesis. The **null hypothesis** is a prediction that there is no relationship between your variables. No pattern of results can support the null hypothesis. To illustrate, suppose you hypothesize that there is no relationship between attraction and liking and you find none. Even so, you can't say that there isn't a relationship. You can only say that you didn't find the relationship. Failing to find an effect is hardly proof that an effect doesn't exist (If Columbus hadn't discovered America, it wouldn't mean that America didn't exist). As you will see in later chapters, the fact that the null hypothesis can't be proven has important implications for research design.

Ethical and Practical Considerations

If your hypothesis is testable, then you need to consider whether you can test it and whether you should test it. Not only must you question whether you have the knowledge, skill, and resources to test your research ideas, but, as a researcher, you have a serious obligation to make sure your study is ethical. You don't have the right to physically or psychologically harm another. Although reading Chapter 13 will help you decide whether your study can be done in an ethical manner, **never conduct a study without your professor's approval**!

Developing Your Idea into a Research Hypothesis

Chances are that most of your research ideas are not yet viable research hypotheses. In their present form, some of your ideas may be impractical, others may be unethical, and still others may be untestable. However, with a little ingenuity, most of your ideas can be converted into workable research hypotheses. Basically, most research ideas can be converted into research hypotheses by either studying the factors through passive observation, making the key variables more abstract, constructing a smaller scale model of the situation, toning down the strength of the manipulation, using animals as subjects, or finding ways to operationalize the critical variables.

To understand how these principles can turn even the most impractical, unethical, and untestable idea into a viable research hypothesis, consider the following: Receiving severe beatings causes one to be a murderer. How could we convert this idea into a research hypothesis?

Use Passive Methods

One possibility is simply to interview murderers and nonmurderers to see whether the murderers were more likely to have been beaten as children. Of course, even if

---

BOX 2-4   Qualities of a Good Hypothesis

TESTABLE

1. Key variables are operationalized.
2. The hypothesis makes specific and precise predictions.
3. The hypothesis does not make predictions that cannot be disproven.
4. The null hypothesis cannot be proved.

PRACTICAL

1. You have the skill and knowledge to test the hypothesis.
2. You have the physical and financial resources to carry out the study.

ETHICAL

Testing your hypothesis will not cause undue physical or psychological harm to your subjects.

you found that murderers were more likely than nonmurderers to have been beaten, your results wouldn't necessarily mean that the beatings caused the murders. Beatings may have no effect on murderers. Instead, murderers may only say they were beaten as children to get sympathy. Or, murderers may have been beaten more than nonmurderers because even as children, they were more aggressive and more disobedient than nonmurderers. Although a passive method like interviewing wouldn't allow you to discover whether beatings cause children to become murderers, it might allow you to address a related research hypothesis: "Are murderers more likely to have been beaten by their parents than nonmurderers?".

Making Variables More General

Another approach might be to make your key variables more abstract. That is, you might view murder as a more specific instance of aggression. Similarly, you might view beating as a specific instance of either aggression, pain, or punishment. Thus, you now have three research hypotheses that have been studied in controlled settings: "Aggression leads to more aggression", "Pain causes aggression", and "Punishment causes aggression."

Make Smaller-Scale Models of the Situation

Of course, you're not going to have human subjects hitting each other to measure aggression. Instead, you may give subjects an opportunity to destroy something that supposedly belongs to the other person, an opportunity to write a negative evaluation, an opportunity to press a button that supposedly (but doesn't really) delivers a shock to the other person, etc.

Smaller-scale models of the situation have not only ethical, but practical advantages. For example, if you're interested in the effects of temperature on aggression, you can't manipulate the temperature outside. However, you can manipulate the temperature in a room. Similarly, although you can't manipulate the size of a crowd at an N.B.A. game to see its effect on the performance of the players, you can manipulate audience size at a dart contest that you sponsor. By using the dart contest, your audience-size hypothesis is not only testable, but practical. That is, if audience size has an effect, you could probably find it by varying the size of the audience from zero (with you hiding behind a one-way mirror) to three (yourself and two friends). Once you have a small-scale model of a phenomenon, you can test all kinds of ideas that it previously seemed impossible to test. Can't you imagine using the dart contest situation to test the effects of factors such as audience involvement and size of reward on performance?

Use Less Extreme Manipulations

For ethical or practical reasons, you may want to use less extreme manipulations of your treatment. For example, if you were to use frustration to see its effects on aggression, you would want to use extremely low levels of frustration.

Carefully Screen Potential Subjects

In some research, you might decrease the ethical problems by choosing subjects who would be unlikely to be harmed by the manipulation. Therefore, if you were to do a frustration–aggression study, you might only use subjects who:

1. according to a recently administered personality profile, were well-adjusted and who—
2. were physically healthy,
3. volunteered after knowing about the degree of discomfort they would experience,
4. were fully aware that they could withdraw from the study at any time without any penalty,
5. will be fully informed about the purpose of the study immediately after they finish participating in the study.

Alternatively, you might use animal subjects rather than human beings to minimize harm. Using animals has the added advantages of allowing you to control aspects of their environment. For example, if you wanted to manipulate punishment in childhood, you could make sure that some rats received punishment beginning shortly after birth through adulthood. Such a manipulation would not only be unethical, but impossible with human subjects.

CHAPTER SUMMARY

In this chapter, you've learned how to generate research ideas from theory and intuition. You now have hypotheses about how two or more variables are related. However, before you can test these ideas, you must find a way to measure and/or manipulate your variables. To help you with this task, we wrote Chapter 3.

THE CASE OF THE USEFUL THEORY

"That fiend!" cried Holmes as he stared at the young woman's corpse. It was not a pretty sight.

I tried to console him. "Take comfort, Holmes. The police are hard at work on the case."

"The police will never solve this case, Watson. I know they have a new, energetic inspector—McGarrety—and he has a first-rate group of men working for him, but that's not enough. McGarrety's 'Book him, Slammo' approach won't work. They've interrogated almost everyone on this island, and what do they have—nothing. Absolutely nothing, except reams of notes. The murders continue," complained Holmes.

"But, they're collecting information. Facts decide cases, don't they?" I protested.

"Watson, you surprise me. Certainly, facts are necessary, but they mean nothing by themselves. Facts are only of value when you have some framework in which to interpret them. Pieces of a puzzle are only significant if you know where and how they fit. Thus, what may seem meaningless to others will often be a significant clue to me," boasted Holmes.

"I see what you mean. You're saying that McGarrety needs to formulate some kind of theory. A theory would help him make sense of the mountains of data he has collected."

"Precisely, Watson, precisely," complimented Holmes.

"But, how could he get such a theory?" I inquired.

"Well, he could use induction. He could look for patterns in his data. Surely, there must be some pattern. His men have interviewed hundreds of people and the fiend has claimed 36 victims. If only McGarrety would allow me access to his data, lamented Holmes.

"At least someone at Scotland Yard has a theory—Broughton." I offered.

"A theory," Holmes blustered, "more like common sense. He's simply looking for someone who resembles a crazed monster. He feels that the person who is killing these women must look like a monster. This theory, as you call it, has absolutely no evidence to support it. It is merely their own common sense. If they insist on following common sense, why doesn't he use the common sense notion that the killer is not going to be a raving maniac? After all, a person who has calmly killed victim after victim is necessarily cunning and unobtrusive. At least this kind of common sense has some basis in fact. History shows that mass murderers don't appear, on the surface, to be that different from the rest of mankind. That's how they remain unapprehended.

"What bothers me most about Scotland Yard is how they cling to this ridiculous theory. They refuse to follow other leads or to investigate other suspects. In addition, they ignore any evidence that contradicts the theory," bristled Holmes.

I tried to calm the master sleuth. "Bear in mind, Holmes, that Lestrade is not blindly following that theory. I've heard he has another that seems to have some merit."

Holmes glared at me for some time. Then, at last he spoke, icily "I suppose you are referring to Lestrade's grandiose assumptions, which he says account for all of the data. Have you read this so-called theory, Watson?"

I confessed that I had not.

"Why not?" pressed Holmes.

"Well," I mumbled, "It is rather long."

"Rather long is a gross understatement. To be precise, Lestrade's theory is 40 pages long. He devotes two pages to each murder. He has a different explanation for each of them and brilliantly deduces that there are 10 different murderers. In short, his theory lacks parsimony. I'll grant that Lestrade is well-meaning and thorough, but he doesn't think very deeply. He's too caught up with surface similarities between the murders. If the murders aren't exactly identical, he doesn't think the same killer was involved. I, however, am convinced that there are definite similarities among all 36 cases. Although some victims were stabbed, some were strangled, and some were clubbed, all the victims were attacked *from behind*. Furthermore, all the murders occurred on dark nights, when the victim was alone, and no men were seen by any subsequent passers-by. Yes, Watson, I am sure that all 36 victims died by the same hand."

"Very well, Holmes. Perhaps Lestrade's theory needs to be revised. But you must admit that it accounts for existing data," I replied.

"Nevertheless," protested Holmes, "A good theory doesn't merely account for existing data. It must make predictions about the future. A good theory would tell us when and where the murderer will strike next."

"Doesn't Lestrade's theory predict when and where the murders will occur?" I inquired.

"Yes," admitted my tall friend, "His theory predicts that 'the next murder will occur in London sometime within the next two years.' It's laughable! How is that theory going to help anyone catch the murderer? The only one that theory will help is Lestrade. He may get a promotion because the fools at Scotland Yard will be impressed that his theory hasn't been disproved. They don't realize that the theory is too vague to be disproved and consequently too vague to be useful. A useful theory would make specific predictions about the murderer's behavior—predictions that could be tested. If the predictions are wrong, the theory could be modified to be consistent with the facts. Eventually, we would have a theory that would allow us to trap the murderer."

"Why don't you develop such a theory?" I suggested.

"My dear Watson," he sighed, "I have done just that. I need only to refine it somewhat and I'll be able to lead this wretched villain into Lestrade's waiting arms. If you will but give me a few days leave, I will have this sorted out."

I returned to my surgery and left him to his theory.

Two days later I received a telegram, urging me to meet with Holmes at once. I cancelled my appointments, got my revolver, and was in Baker Street in a trice.

As I entered the sitting room, Holmes was speaking with a member of one of the most honorable families in England. I am sworn to secrecy as to her true identity, but I can tell you that she was the most beautiful woman I have ever seen.

"Come in, come in," said Holmes. "Madam, this is my colleague, Dr. Watson. And Watson you of course know this young lady. I was just discussing my new theory of the murders with her."

Our guest gasped, her eyes wide with fear, her hand over her mouth. Her mouth started to quiver and her skin turned a ghastly shade. Within seconds, she was dead. I rushed to her aid, but it was no use. The poison had done its work.

"I was afraid she might poison herself. Well, it is probably for the best. Her family could never have survived the publicity of a trial, much less her time in prison" reflected Holmes as he brought me a brandy.

As I sat stunned, Holmes explained the whole story to me. With each murder, he had refined his theory. At one point, he made a major revision so that it fit the facts. Eventually, he was able to pin down when and where the murderer would strike. He tried to convince the police of the validity of his theory, but, as was too often the case, their ignorance made them skeptical. Last night, he used his theory to trick the murderer into attacking him. He warded off the attacker and was able to identify her. He then arranged for her to meet him at Baker Street.

Thus ended the reign of terror of that most hideous villain, Jack the Ripper.

MAIN POINTS

1. The only purpose of research is to test ideas.
2. Research ideas may come from existing research, from intuition, or from theory.
3. To generate research hypotheses, first come up with an idea about behavior. Then, determine if you can convert this idea into a testable hypothesis.
4. Creative ideas are the product of persistence.
5. Analyzing literature, songs, tabloids, commercials, practical problems, honest differences of opinion, old sayings, and even your own difficulty in generating ideas are productive ways of developing research ideas.
6. Like intuition, theories are good sources of ideas. Unlike intuition, a theory is formally stated and internally consistent.
7. Hypothetical constructs are abstract variables that cannot be directly observed (love, learning, thirst, etc.). Researchers can deal with abstract constructs by devising operational definitions—concrete ways (recipes, if you will) of manipulating or measuring abstract constructs.
8. Testable theories make specific predictions and have variables that can be operationalized.
9. You can generate hypotheses from a theory by testing the theory's core assumptions, seeing how well it holds in extreme cases, checking its precision, applying the theory to novel or practical situations, or comparing two theories that make opposing predictions.
10. Scientists like theories that are broad in scope, parsimonious, and provocative.
11. The null hypothesis is that there is no relationship between two variables. Although it can be disproved, it can't be proved.
12. A research hypothesis must be testable and must be testable in an ethical manner.
13. Even the most impractical and unethical of ideas may be converted into a practical and ethical hypothesis if you use passive observational techniques, create models of the phenomenon rather than studying the phenomenon itself, make critical variables more abstract, tone down the intensity of your manipulations, or carefully screen your subjects.

KEY TERMS

hypothesis
deduction
induction
theory
operational definition

hypothetical construct
straw theory
crucial experiments
parsimonious
null hypothesis

EXERCISES

1. How are the qualities of a good theory similar to the qualities of a good answer to an essay test?

2. In terms of the null hypothesis, what's wrong with the following research conclusions:
There is no difference in outcome among the different psychological therapies
There is no difference in effectiveness between generic and name-brand drugs
Viewing television violence is not related to aggression
Nutrasweet® has no side effects when used by the normal population
There are no gender differences in emotional responsiveness

3. Using the "11 Ways to Tap Your Intuition," generate at least five research ideas.

4. As stated in this chapter, scientists are often reluctant to give up on a pet theory. Is this good or bad? Why?

5. Find an original statement of a psychological theory. Write out its propositions. Compare your list to a textbook summary of the theory's propositions. Are there any disparities? What conclusions do you draw about the advisability of relying exclusively on textbook summaries to learn about a theory?

6. Compare three textbook summaries of the same psychological theory. Are there any discrepancies? What implications would discrepancies between textbook summaries have for psychological research?

7. Is theory or intuition more valuable in generating useful research? Support your conclusions by listing the strengths and weaknesses of each.

8. What are the characteristics of a good hypothesis?

3

MEASURING AND MANIPULATING VARIABLES

OUTLINE

Science begins with measurement

—LORD KELVIN

OVERVIEW

In Chapter 2, we encouraged you to generate research hypotheses. If you took our suggestions to heart, you have several interesting research ideas. But before you can test any of these research ideas, you need concrete ways of measuring and manipulating your variables. In technical terminology, you need to know how to operationalize your variables.

Right now, you may feel that you need a magician to come up with objective, publicly observable ways to manipulate and measure your variables, especially if your research ideas involve constructs as abstract and subjective as love, motivation, shyness, religiousness, attentiveness, etc. Fortunately, as you will learn in this chapter, operationalizing variables is more a matter of logic than of magic.

MEASURING VARIABLES

Since all research involves measurement, no researcher can produce accurate information without adequate measures. Therefore, no matter what your research idea, one of the most important decisions you'll make is selecting a measure. As with any important decision, you should generate several possible solutions, evaluate the strengths and weaknesses of each possibility, and then choose the possibility or combination of possibilities that will best fit your needs. Therefore, we will devote the next few sections to showing you how to obtain measures, to evaluate the strengths and weaknesses of these measures, and to compare the measures with one another in light of the needs of your particular study.

Obtaining Measures
There are two basic ways to obtain a measure. You can use one that someone else developed or you can invent your own. Since inventing and refining a measure is a challenging task, your first step should be to see if any suitable measures exist. Even if you find that no suitable measures exist, what you learn about the strengths and weaknesses of existing measures may help you in developing your own. Listed below are some common dependent measures.

Number of bar presses
Time taken to run maze
Number of words recalled
Order in which words are recalled

Choice reaction time (Time it takes subject to choose between two or more alternatives.)
Respiration rate, heart rate, Galvanic skin response, blood pressure
Test scores (IQ, personality)
Amount of food consumed
Mirror tracing
Self-rating of attitude

Using a Previously Developed Measure

To find a previously developed measure, you should conduct a literature review of relevant books, journal articles, and other manuscripts. A good first step in conducting your review is to consult an introductory psychology textbook. For example, if you're interested in measuring love, turn to the back of your text and look up "love" in the index. The index will refer you to pages in the texts where love is discussed. You will find, embedded in these discussions, the names of researchers who have published research on love. Look up these researchers' names in your textbook's bibliography to find out where they published their articles. Next, go to the library and read their articles. In their articles, the researchers will describe, in great detail, how they operationalized love. The researchers may also explain why they chose to operationalize love the way they did.

After reading the bodies of these articles, you could track down the articles referenced in their bibliographies. Soon, you should have read enough to either:

1. learn about other well-accepted measures of love;
2. learn that their measure is fairly well accepted or;
3. learn that there are no well-accepted measures of love.

Although finding references through your textbook is a good way to start looking for measures, this technique will not guide you to the most recently developed measures. By the time most textbooks are published, their references are at least one year out of date. In addition, your text has probably not listed every relevant source. If you need to find more extensive or more current references, there are several library resources you can consult. Among the most useful are *Psychological Abstracts, Social Sciences Index, Social Science Citation Index, Current Contents,* and computerized searches. To learn more about these valuable library resources, consult "Appendix B: Library Resources."

Inventing Measures

Of course, in addition to copying someone else's measure, you could invent your own. To invent a measure you need a behavior that is a sign, a symptom, or an indicator of the presence of your concept. The behavior could be a verbal behavior (the answer to the question "How much do you love Mary?"), a nonverbal behavior (how long a subject gazes into Mary's eyes), or a physiological behavior (increases in blood pressure when Mary walks in the room). You can generate verbal, nonverbal, and physiological measures for virtually any construct if you take advantage of three important resources: definitions, theories, and intuition.

Definitions When trying to invent a measure, your first step should be to use a dictionary or an introductory textbook to look up the definition of your concept. Until you know what it is you want to measure, you'll have a hard time measuring it. Reading textbook and dictionary definitions may give you a clearer picture of what it is you want to measure. Just as importantly, reading definitions may give you a clearer picture of what you don't want to measure. For example, reading definitions of love might help you realize that you want to measure mature love and that you want to avoid unintentionally measuring concepts such as liking, or infatuation.

Besides helping you define exactly what it is you want to measure, ordinary

---

BOX 3-1 An Example of a Lovely Theory That Tells Us How to Measure Various Concepts

Rafael Frank's (1984) theory of love tells us that love can be measured in several ways, but it is not subjectively measurable. That is, you cannot ask a person how much they love someone because they do not know. However, you can measure love if the person loses their loved one. According to the theory, love can be assessed by determining how long it takes for the person's grief to become half as intense.

The theory also says that love can be assessed by the following formula:

Love = like × maturity/dependency × 20 (sexual attraction)/age.

From this formula, we see that if like, maturity, or sexual attraction equals zero, then love will equal zero because zero times any number is zero. Thus, if Bruno doesn't like Broomhilda, he doesn't love her. Likewise if Bruno is not at all mature, Bruno cannot love Broomhilda.

The theory tells us not only how to measure love but how to measure the other concepts in the formula. For example, the theory states that liking may be measured by simply asking people how much they like someone—by having them rate how much time they want to spend with the other person, rating how comfortable they feel with the other, how similar they perceive the other to be to themselves in terms of values, respect, and admiration, how many topics they can discuss, the number of activities they do together, and how favorably they rate the other person.

According to the theory, maturity can be measured by assessing the degree to which the person is concerned with people or things other than himself, an internal locus of control, and the ability to delay gratification.

Dependence, according to the theory, can be measured by the degree to which one could sleep alone, one's self-confidence, one's ability to do things alone, such things as approaching a stranger to talk, inviting people over for dinner, or going to a restaurant.

Sexual attraction, is easily measurable in physiological terms.

dictionaries, psychological dictionaries, and glossaries may provide hints about how to measure the concept. For instance, the *Random House Dictionary* defines love in several ways, including "sexual desire or its gratification" and "a feeling of warm personal attachment." These definitions suggest that measuring sexual desire, frequency of sex, or feelings of attachment may be promising methods for measuring love.

Theory   As you may remember from Chapter 2, a good theory suggests ways of measuring its constructs. Thus, if you are interested in measuring a concept, you should look at different theories of that concept. Careful questioning of these theories will give you ideas about what kinds of measures to use. For example, if you read a theory of love, you might determine whether, according to the theory, a person is aware of being in love. If people are unaware of being in love, asking people how much they love someone is useless. If, on the other hand, people are aware of how much love they feel, then asking them direct questions about the extent of their love might be useful. You might also determine whether the theory mentions any physiological or behavioral changes that accompany love. If you ask these questions of several theories, you will have several measures. In fact, as you can see from Box 3-1, we asked these questions of just one theory of love and came away with several measures.

Intuition   Of course, the same questions you ask of theory, you can ask of your intuition. Thus, if you were trying to measure love, you might ask yourself how someone in love would talk, act, and physiologically react.

TABLE 3-1   How Asking Questions of a Theory (Rafael Frank's Theory) of Love Can Give You Ideas about How to Measure Your Construct

Question	Theory's Answer
Can we use a self-rating scale to measure love?	No, because people are not consciously aware of the extent of their love.
Can we use a disguised measure to assess love?	Yes—if a person loses their loved one. Love can be assessed by determining how long it takes for the person's grief to become half as intense.
What other ways can you use to measure love?	By using this formula:
	Love = liking × maturity/dependency × 20/age

Note. From *A half-life theory of love* by R. Frank, 1984. Paper presented at the 92nd Annual Convention of the American Psychological Association. Adapted by permission of the author.

To help yourself articulate the behavioral signs or symptoms of love, think of three people: a person who is very much in love, a person who is slightly in love, and a person who is not at all in love. Then, act as though you are describing the behaviors of these different people to a skeptical stranger—a stranger who wants behavioral evidence that your perceptions of these people are correct. You might start by discussing how the person who is deeply in love is now bumping into things, spending three hours in the bathroom, smiling more, speaking to only one other person, singing songs, not eating, and not sleeping. Next, you might describe the person's verbal behavior: claiming to be in love, claiming that it's great to be alive, using "cute" words when in the presence of his partner. Finally, you might address physiological symptoms of his condition: increased heart rate, higher blood pressure, nervous stomach, etc.

PREREQUISITES FOR VALIDITY

After conducting a literature review and consulting definitions, theory, and intuition, you should have several potential measures. But how do you know if any of these measures are valid: measuring what you think they are measuring?

BOX 3-2 Theory Has Implications for Measures

WHAT IS SUCCESSFUL THERAPY?

Psychoanalytic Theory: Better memory for early childhood events, fewer errors of speech (Freudian slips), less self-destructive behavior, feeling less anxiety.

Rogers' Self Theory: Less of a difference between what the person thinks he or she is and what the person wants to be. A Q-sort is used to measure the difference between the ideal and the real self.

Maslow: Being less dependent on others, having a sense of humor, being concerned about other people, being able to laugh at oneself, having very close interpersonal relationships, being happy to be alive, feeling energetic.

Gestalt Psychology (Perles): Being more spontaneous, being more concerned about the present, being less inhibited by others.

Reality Therapy (Glaser): More accepting of society's norms, taking responsibility for your own behavior.

Behavior Therapy: Decreasing the undesired behavior, increasing the incidence of more desirable behavior.

> ### BOX 3-3   Measuring the Unmeasurable—the Unconscious
>
> How can we measure someone's unconscious mind, a mind they themselves do not know? Here are some measures of the unconscious. We will let you judge their validity. We should remind you, however, that for these measures to be valid, the unconscious must really exist.
>
> 1. Remembering events under hypnosis that you could not recall before.
> 2. Failure to recall important events, even under the influence of Sodium Pentothal.
> 3. Freudian slips.
> 4. Symbolism of dreams.
> 5. Inability to remember early childhood.
> 6. Having strong feelings toward therapist.
> 7. Having long pauses or quickly changing the subject while associating.
> 8. Unusual response to word association games. For instance, "Mother" to the word "sex" or not responding at all to the word "Father."
> 9. Analyzing self-destructive behavior.
> 10. Feeling anxiety for no apparent reason.

The first step to establishing validity is to show that your measure is not obviously inaccurate. Specifically, you must show that your measure is relatively free from three sources of contamination:

1. random error: unsystematic, chance error;
2. observer bias: bias due to observers seeing what they think subjects should be doing rather than seeing what subjects are actually doing; and
3. subject bias: bias due to subjects trying to impress or please the researcher rather than expressing their true thoughts or feelings.

Reliability: Freedom from Random Error

If you're measuring a stable characteristic (intelligence), you want your measurements to be reliable: stable, consistent. If your measurements are reliable, then you can be confident that your measurements are immune from **random error**: temporary, chance fluctuations. For example, if you were to weigh the same small amount of gold three times, you would expect to get the same measurement each time. If you didn't get the same results each time, you would take steps to correct the situation. You might move the scale inside, away from the gusts of winds that may be affecting your measurements. Intuitively, you realize that the more your measure is affected by the fickle winds of chance, the less accurate is its measure of your variable (gold).

Although getting reliable measurements does not guarantee accuracy (if your scale was stuck on a certain weight, you might consistently weigh any amount of gold at 10 pounds), getting inconsistent, unreliable measurements of a stable construct guarantees inaccuracy. Thus, the more reliable the measure, the greater the opportunity for validity. Therefore, if a junior-high student measures your I.Q. three times and measures it as 100 one day, 200 the next, and 150, the third day, you would know that the student's average measurement was off by at least 50 points. If, on the other hand, your I.Q. is measured by a professional as 155 one day, 145 the next, and 150 on the third day, the professional's measurements are more likely to be accurate to five points.

Sources of Unreliability

Clearly, you want your measurements to be affected by your construct rather than being bounced around by the erratic winds of chance. Therefore, if you find a measure, you want to know whether it is strongly contaminated by chance. If you invent a measure, you want to know how to assess and improve its reliability. To assess and to avoid unreliability, you need to understand its sources: random observer error, random changes in how the measure is administered, and changes in the subject.

Observer Error   One source of unreliability is random error due to human carelessness in making or recording observations. An obvious method of reducing random observer error is to simplify or eliminate the job of the human observer.

One way to simplify or eliminate the job of the human observer is to employ scientific measuring devices. To illustrate, let's examine how a series of increasingly sophisticated measuring devices can progressively reduce random error. Imagine that a researcher wants to record how long it takes a rat to run through a maze. At the least sophisticated level, the researcher's only instrument might be the clock on the wall. Certainly, to determine how long it took the rat to run the maze, using the wall clock is an improvement over having the researcher count aloud "one, two, three." However, the wall clock does not eliminate many sources of random error. For example, the researcher might make mistakes in reading the clock, might not always remember when the rat started the maze, might not always subtract the start time from the stop time correctly, and might not always look at the clock at exactly the moment the rat began and finished the maze.

At a slightly more sophisticated level, the researcher could use a stopwatch. The stopwatch would eliminate error due to the researcher forgetting when the rat started the maze and from incorrectly subtracting the stop time from the start time. In addition to the stopwatch eliminating some researcher errors, the stopwatch also reduces the chances of two other researcher errors. First, since the hand-held stopwatch would be easier to read than the distant wall clock, the researcher would be less likely to misread the rat's time. Second, since the researcher can look at the stopwatch and the rat at the same time, the researcher would be more likely to start and stop the stopwatch just as the rat entered the maze and goal box respectively.

Still, even with the stopwatch, there are at least three sources of human error. First, if the stopwatch wasn't digital, the researcher might still misread the stopwatch (Was that 6.05 or 6.06 seconds?). Second, even if the researcher read the time correctly, the researcher might misrecord the time. Third, the researcher might fail to start or stop the stopwatch at the right time.

To eliminate virtually every source of random observer error, the researcher could use a timer that automatically starts when the rat enters the maze and automatically stops when the rat reaches the goal box, displays the time on a digital read-out, and then prints out the time on a piece of paper. This most sophisticated measuring device would eliminate random human error involved in starting or stopping the stopwatch, misreading it, or misrecording the data. Because instruments can be such effective agents for removing random observer error, we have listed a representative sample of modern recording equipment in Box 3-4.

Using scientific equipment is not the only way to reduce human error. You can also reduce it by using measures that don't involve human judgment. If you want to reduce random observer error, use fixed-response items (multiple-choice, matching, fill-in-the-blank, etc.) rather than subjectively-scored items. Thus, if you want to measure love with a minimum of observer error, rather than having subjects write essays that must be subjectively scored for amount of love, give subjects a multiple-choice measure of love or have subjects circle a number on a rating scale.

Even if you have your observers make judgments, you could simplify the judgments they make. For example, rather than having them judge how deeply in love each subject is, define specific behaviors that indicate love (hand-holding, gazing into the other person's eyes, etc.), then have observers count how many of these "loving" behaviors each subject performed.

Of course, the strategy of having observers count the number of behaviors rather than categorizing behavior only increases reliability if observers can reliably determine whether or not a certain behavior occurred. Therefore, if you have observers count behaviors, you should clearly, specifically, and objectively define what constitutes an instance of the behavior. For example, if you were having observers count instances of hand-holding, you would have to define hand-holding in such a way that observers would never be in doubt about whether or not hand-holding occurred (hands were inter-locked below the waist for more than five seconds).

You may feel, however, that counting the instances of a certain, specific behavior won't give you the information you need. Instead, you may believe that you need an observer's judgment to categorize behavior (mildly affectionate, moderately affectionate, etc.). In this case you should take the following steps to reduce random observer error.

BOX 3-4 Common Instruments Used to Measure Behavior

laboratory computer
decibel meter
electromyograph: measures muscle tension
electroencephalogram: measures brain wave activity
galvanic skin response: measures sweating
tape recorder
videotape recorder
stopwatch
Skinner box cumulative behavior

First, if at all possible, permanently record each subject's behavior. If you have subjects write down their responses or if you tape, videotape, or photograph their behavior, observers can review their decisions. The capability of reviewing the behavior may prevent random errors due to attention lapses. (This is why some fans want football referees to use instant replays to make important calls.)

Second, define as precisely as possible what you mean by each rating category (e.g., mildly loving, moderately loving, extremely loving). A definition alone is not enough: Give a concrete example of each category. If your raters will be judging paragraphs, show them an example of a paragraph that expresses mild loving, another that expresses moderate loving, etc. If your raters will be judging behaviors, show them videotapes or photographs of each category of behavior.

If you don't combine clear-cut guidelines for scoring behavior with concrete examples, observers may not know how you want them to interpret behavior. As a result, each will interpret the behavior in his own way. If, on the other hand, all your observers know what you want, they are more likely to interpret behavior the same way (your way).

Third, conduct a training program for your raters. During the training sessions, have them rate several passages or videotapes and have them explain their ratings. More importantly, be sure to explain why a given passage or videotape should be rated a certain way. By explaining and defending your rating system to others, you will be able to form more objective, explicit guidelines about what constitutes each category. Near the end of the training session, you should give them new written passages, photographs, or videotapes to rate independently.

Training your raters has several advantages beyond letting them know how to interpret behavior. During training, raters make the inevitable rookie mistakes, but they learn from these mistakes and don't make them "on the job." Thus, a training program is an effective way of preventing contaminated data due to rater error. Furthermore, training shows raters that you take the task seriously and that you're concerned about accuracy. As a result, raters may also become more concerned about accuracy and therefore more motivated to be careful. Finally, training allows you to weed out bad raters. If, at the end of the training program, you find one or two individuals who still make ratings that differ both from your criteria and from the ratings made by the rest of the group you would conclude that they are very careless observers. Of course you won't let them observe actual subjects.

After you have carefully defined your categories, trained your raters, and eliminated the bad ones, there is one last step you can take to reduce random observer error. Take advantage of the fact that, in the long run, random errors even out. That means that although some of the individual ratings of a specific behavior could be dramatically affected by random error, the average of these ratings should not be. In a sense, random errors cancel themselves out. Therefore, to further reduce random error, have more than one rater judge each subject, then average the scores to determine each subject's final score. For example, if rater A gives the first subject a 3, rater B gives that subject a 4, and rater C gives that subject a 5, you would say that the first subject's score was a 4. Professional boxing takes advantage of the tendency for random observer errors to cancel themselves out by having three people judge a fight. (Note, however, that using multiple raters does nothing to reduce the effects of biased observers).

BOX 3-5 Ways of Reducing Random Observer Error

1. Eliminate human observers by using automation.
2. Eliminate demands on observers' memories and attention span by permanently recording behavior.
3. Eliminate the role of human judgment by simplifying the observer's task: limit them to recording readings from instruments, ratings from rating scales, or answers to fixed-response measures, or counting how many times a certain behavior occurs.
4. Prevent different observers from interpreting behavior differently by educating them about what you want them to do.
5. Prevent carelessness by motivating raters to do a good job.

Assessing Observer Error in Existing Measures We've discussed how you could decrease random observer error in a measure you invented. How could you assess whether an existing measure was free from random observer error? You could begin by determining the degree to which human judgment was involved. If all the observer had to do was score a multiple-choice test, you would not be worried about excessive random observer error. If the observer has to count behaviors, you'd want to make sure that you had clearly defined what constituted an instance of a behavior. If you defined the behavior so that the observer had only to count certain clear-cut behaviors (number of bar-presses, number of horn-honks, etc.), you wouldn't be overly concerned with random observer error, even if you didn't use recording devices (automated counters, videocameras, tape machines). However, if the observers had to categorize behavior (low, medium, high; good, bad), you'd want to know the measure's inter-observer reliability.

Interobserver reliability, also known as interjudge, interrater, scorer, and conspect reliability, is an index of the degree to which different raters give similar ratings. To obtain interobserver reliability, researchers have two or more observers independently (without talking to one another) rate the same behaviors. Researchers then compare how these different raters judged the same behavior (see Fig. 3-1). Finally, researchers calculate a correlation coefficient between the different rater's judgments of the same behavior. This **correlation coefficient** expresses the degree to which raters agree or disagree and is therefore called the interobserver reliability coefficient.

Interobserver reliability can range from -1 to $+1$. If the correlation coefficient is negative, the observers are judging the behavior oppositely: when one rates a behavior as high, the other will rate it as low (see Fig. 3-2). Usually, this much disagreement would be due to a misunderstanding about the scale. For example, one observer may think that the 1 to 5 scale goes from 1 (low) to 5 (high), whereas the other judge thinks the rating scale goes from 1 (high) to 5 (low).

An interobserver reliability coefficient around zero ($-.10$ to $+.10$) indicates that there is virtually no relationship between the observer's ratings. Knowing how one judge rated a behavior gives you no idea about how the other judge rated the same behavior (see Fig. 3-3).

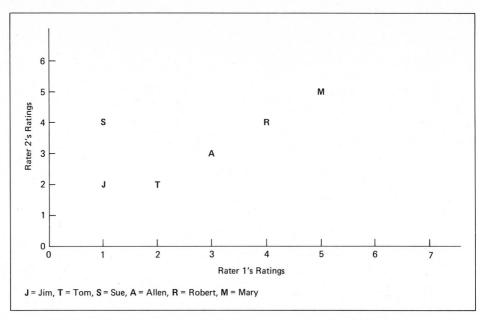

FIGURE 3-1   How Ratings of Six Subjects Compare for Raters 1 and 2

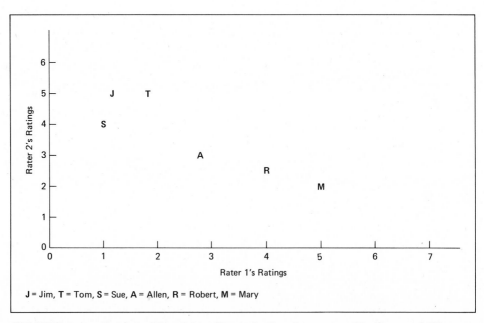

FIGURE 3-2   Strong Negative Correlation between Ratings of Six Subjects by Raters 1 and 2

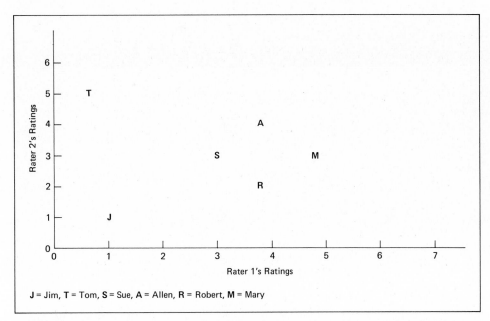

FIGURE 3-3   Near Zero Correlation between Ratings of Six Subjects by Raters 1 and 2

A positive correlation means that observers are agreeing to some extent: when one rates a behavior as high, the other will tend to rate the behavior as high (see Fig. 3-4). Since raters usually agree to some extent, you will almost never see a published study report an interobserver reliability coefficient below +.2. Therefore, when reading a study, your question won't be: "Did the observers agree?", but "To what extent did the observers agree?" Assuming the researchers report a positive interobserver reliability coefficient, you can find out the extent to which raters are agreeing by squaring the interobserver reliability coefficient and multiplying it by 100. If the correlation is 1.00, raters are in 100% agreement. If, on the other hand, the coefficient is only .5, there is only about 25% (.5 × .5 × 100 = 25%) agreement among raters. Put another way, 75% (100 − 25 = 75) of the difference between subject's scores might be due to random observer error.

Random Changes in Testing Environment as a Source of Unreliability

Random observer error is just one source of unreliability. Random changes in the testing environment may also contribute to measurement error. Fortunately, you can reduce error due to random fluctuations in the testing environment by administering the measure in the same way every time: standardization. To standardize administration of the measure, you might give the same instructions, use the same room, and otherwise make sure that you're administering it in the same way and under the same conditions.

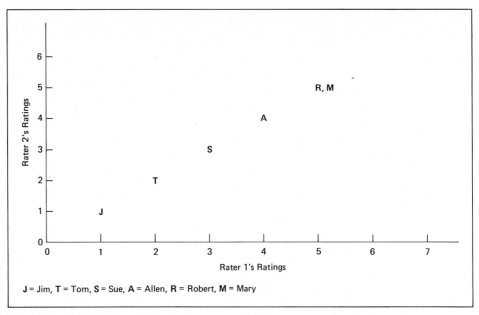

FIGURE 3-4   Strong Positive Correlation between Ratings of Six Subjects by Raters 1 and 2

Changes in Subjects as a Source of Unreliability

Finally, unreliability may stem from changes in the subject. If these changes reflect permanent changes, they don't threaten validity. For example, a subject's love score may change because she is no longer in love.

Assessing the Extent of Unreliability

Until now, we've focussed on the goal of increasing reliability. However, there will be times when you won't be interested in increasing your measure's reliability. If you're using a previously published measure, you probably wouldn't want to increase its reliability because that would mean changing the measure. If you changed the measure, you might ruin it. Even if your changes don't ruin the measure, they might prevent you from being able to compare your results with those obtained by researchers who used the original measure. If you're devising your own measure, you may have done all you could to reduce random error. In that case, you obviously wouldn't be interested in making your measure more reliable.

Of course, just because you aren't interested in increasing a particular measure's reliability, doesn't mean you aren't interested in reliability. In fact, you may decide on a measure based on whether it has an adequate degree of reliability or on how its reliability compares with that of your other measures.

You could get a sense of the measure's reliability by estimating how susceptible it would be to random changes in the observer, subject, or administration of the measure. Or, you could use a more formal technique by calculating a reliability coefficient. Perhaps the most obvious reliability coefficient to calculate would be the test-retest reliability coefficient. To compute your measure's test-retest reliability, give

---

BOX 3-6   Calculating a Correlation Coefficient

1. Calculate the mean and standard deviation for the first variable (X) and for the second variable (Y). (To calculate a standard deviation, see Table 5-1.) In this example, the mean of X is 3, the standard deviation of X is 1.41, the mean of Y is 2.4 and the standard deviation of Y is 1.02.
2. Set up a table in the following format

	Score for X	**Score for Y**	**X times Y**
1st pair of scores	1	1	1
2nd pr.	2	2	4
3rd pr.	3	2	6
4th pr.	4	4	16
5th pr.	5	3	15
	sum of X = 15	sum of Y = 12	sum of $X \times Y$ = 42

3. Multiply sum of X by sum of Y and divide by the number of pairs: $(15 \times 12)/5 = 180/5 = 36$
4. Subtract this term (36) from sum of $X \times Y$ (42): $42 - 36 = 6$
5. Finally, divide this term (6) by (number of pairs times the standard deviation of X and multiply by the standard deviation of Y). Correlation = $6/(5 \times 1.41 \times 1.02) = 6/(7.191) = .83$

---

your measure to the same subjects on two different occasions. Then, correlate the scores that each subject got the first time with the scores each subject got the second time (see Box 3-6).

If there are obvious reasons for not giving subjects the same test twice (subjects remembering the questions and their answers), you might use what people call parallel forms or alternate forms reliability. That is, you give subjects one form of the test, then give them another, and then correlate the two scores. Unfortunately, the difficulty with establishing parallel forms validity is the generating parallel forms. Imagine trying to devise two tests that are different, yet the same!

Understanding Published Reliability Coefficients

If you're examining a previously published measure, the reliability coefficient may have already been calculated for you. The measure's reliability coefficient may be cited in the original research report, in the test's manual, or in Buros' *Mental Measurements Yearbook*.

Unfortunately, comparing reliability coefficients is not as easy as it seems at first. For starters, different authors report different kinds of reliabilities and even when they report the same kind of reliability, they may use different terms for it (alternate forms versus parallel forms). Therefore, we designed Table 3-2 to help you discover what kind of reliability coefficient the authors are reporting.

TABLE 3-2 Evaluating the Reliability of Published Measures

Reliability coefficients that answer the question: Would a subject get the same score if she were tested a second time?

Procedure	Names	Comments
Give the same test at two different sessions.	Test-Retest	Subject may remember items from first time she took test.
Give two forms of test at two different sessions.	Alternate Forms Parallel Forms Delayed Equivalence	Have to develop two identical forms of the same test.

Reliability coefficients that only address the question: Would different raters make similar ratings?

Procedure	Names	Comments
Correlate scores given to same subjects by different observers.	Interobserver, Conspect, or Scorer Reliability	Even if measure has this kind of reliability, subjects may not get similar scores on a retest.

Reliability coefficients that only address the question: Are all the measure's questions measuring the same thing?

Procedure	Names	Comments
Split test in half. Correlate one half of test with the other half.	Split-Half Reliability	Even if measure has this kind of reliability, subects may not get similar scores on a retest.
Administer test once, calculate means of all possible split halves.	Kuder-Richardson	Same as above.

If you have different kinds of reliability coefficients for different measures, comparing them is like comparing apples and oranges. Obviously, subjects will tend to have retest scores closer to their original scores if the second test is the same as the original test (test-retest reliability), than if the second test is a different test (alternate forms reliability). Thus, if measure A's test-retest reliability is higher than measure B's alternate-forms reliability, you shouldn't automatically conclude that measure B is less reliable.

Even if you are fortunate enough to be comparing measures using the same reliability coefficients, you may still be comparing apples and oranges. For instance, measure C's test-retest reliability may have been obtained by giving subjects the retest a week after the first test, whereas measure D's may have been obtained by giving subjects the retest six months after the original test. Clearly, you would expect more changes in subjects over six months than over a single week. Thus, although a given measure might have a higher test-retest reliability coefficient than other measures, it is not necessarily the most reliable.

In short, when comparing the reliability coefficients of different measures, determine not only what kind of coefficients were calculated, but how they were calculated. A higher reliability coefficient does not necessarily mean a more reliable measure.

Reliability: Recognize Its Limits

Most importantly, when comparing measures, realize that the more reliable measure is not necessarily the more valid measure. For example, if you measure mood or some other construct that changes from day to day, you would not want a measure that has perfect reliability.

Even if you're measuring intelligence or some other construct that is presumed to be stable, reliability is important, but not all important. In a way, the relationship between random error and validity in a measure is similar to the relationship between ice and cola in a glass. Where there is ice, there can't be cola just as where there is random error, there can't be validity. Thus, if your glass is entirely full of ice, there can be no cola. That is, if you use a measure that is totally dominated by random error (measuring I.Q. by flipping a coin), then your measure will have no validity. In other words, reliability puts a ceiling on validity: When your measure is assessing chance, it can't be assessing your construct.

Note, however, that although reliability puts a ceiling on validity, low reliability, by itself, does not destroy validity. Just as the ice displaces and dilutes, but does not poison the cola, random error dilutes, but does not poison validity. Thus, as long as your measure has even the slightest degree of reliability, it can have some validity.

Finally, realize that reliability does not insure validity. Put succinctly: **A valid measure is reliable, but a reliable measure is not necessarily valid.** In other words, just as not having ice in your cola glass doesn't mean that you have cola in it, the absence of random error doesn't mean that you have validity. In fact, a reliable measure could be totally invalid. For example, a friend could reliably measure your heart rate at 60 beats per minute every time, but your friend might be listening to her watch rather than to your heart.

Since random error only dilutes validity and since many other factors poison validity, you should not use reliability coefficients as the only or even the primary means of determining whether a measure is valid. Only consider reliability when measures differ greatly in reliability, but are equal on all other dimensions.

Observer Bias: Seeing What We Hope or Expect to See

Even if a measure is reliable, it may be vulnerable to **observer bias.** Observers have a hard time being objective because their hopes and expectations may bias their perceptions.

To reduce observer bias, you can use many of the techniques you used to remove random observer error. You can eliminate human observer bias by replacing human observers with scientific recording devices.

If you can't eliminate the human observer, you may be able to reduce observer bias by decreasing the observer's role. Rather than having observers interpret open-ended responses, you could limit the observer's role to that of recording the subjects' answers to fixed-response items. If you can't eliminate, reduce or simplify the observer's role, you might be able to reduce bias by giving observers clear and objective criteria for judging behavior.

Even though these tactics should reduce observer bias by making subjects' behaviors less open to interpretation, they may not eliminate observer bias. To see why, suppose you were having observers judge essays in an attempt to find out whether men or women were more deeply in love. Even if you conducted a thorough training program for your raters, the raters might be biased if they knew whether the writer was a man or a woman. Therefore, instead of letting your raters know who wrote an essay, you should consider the benefits of **blind raters**: observers who are unaware of the subject's characteristics and situation.

In essence, the tactics you would use to reduce observer bias are the same tactics a professor would use to avoid favoritism in grading. The professor who is solely concerned with avoiding favoritism in grading would certainly not determine students' grades by sitting down at the end of term and trying to recall the quality of each student's class participation. On the contrary, this professor would give multiple-choice tests that were computer-scored. If he were to give an essay exam, the professor would establish clear-cut criteria for scoring the essays, follow those criteria to the letter, and not look at students' names while grading the papers.

Two Major Subject Biases

The professor's only concern is observer bias; however, the researcher must also be wary of **subject bias.** Psychologists have long been aware that subjects may change their behavior to please the observer. One of the earliest documented examples of this problem was the case of Clever Hans (Pfungst, 1911), the mathematical horse. Hans would answer mathematical problems by tapping his hoof the correct number of times. For example, if Hans's owner asked Hans what three times three was, Hans would tap his hoof nine times. Hans's secret was that he would watch his owner. His owner would stop looking at Hans's feet when Hans had reached the right answer.

Social Desirability Bias   Of course, if animals can produce the "right" answer when they know what you're measuring, so can humans. In fact, for humans, there are two kinds of "right" answers. The first kind is the **socially desirable** response: answers that make the subject look good. Subjects are quite willing to give socially desirable responses. For example, many studies have shown that people claim to be much more helpful (Latane and Darley, 1970) and less conforming (Milgram, 1974) than they really are.

Obeying Demand Characteristics   The second kind of "right" answer is the one that makes you, the researcher, look good by ensuring that your hypothesis is supported. Martin Orne (1962) believes that subjects are very willing to give a researcher whatever results she wants. In fact, subjects are so eager to please that they look for clues or hints as to how the researcher wants them to behave. According to Orne, if subjects find these hints, subjects follow the hints as surely as if the researcher had demanded that they follow the hint. Hence, Orne calls clues about the nature of the study **demand characteristics.**

The see how demand characteristics might come into play, suppose you have subjects rate how much they love their partner. Next, you give them fake feedback, supposedly from their partner, showing that their partner loves them intensely. Finally, you have subjects rate how much they love their partner a second time. In this loving study, subjects may realize that they're supposed to rate their love higher the second time. Therefore, if subjects reported that they loved their partner more the second time, you wouldn't know whether learning that their partner was devoted increased their love or whether they merely obeyed the study's demand characteristics.

How did subjects know what you wanted them to do? Your measure made it obvious that you were measuring love. Once subjects knew you were measuring love, they were able to guess why you showed them their partner's ratings. You gave them all the clues they needed to figure out what you would consider a ''good'' response.

If only there was a way you could measure subjects' love without their knowing it. Then, your study wouldn't be so vulnerable to subject biases. Fortunately, there are many ways to prevent subjects from knowing what you're measuring: You could prevent them from knowing they were being observed; prevent them from knowing what behavior you were observing; prevent them from knowing why you were observing that behavior; or you could choose a response that most subjects couldn't or wouldn't change.

Reducing Subject Biases

Measuring Subjects in a ''Nonresearch'' Setting
If subjects don't know that a researcher is observing them, they can't cooperate with the researcher. One way to observe subjects without their knowing it is to observe them in a nonresearch setting. For example, you may observe them in some real-world setting (library, restaurant, etc.) or while they're ostensibly in the study's waiting area. Although observing subjects in these settings may reduce demand characteristics, such observations raise ethical questions. We'll address these ethical concerns in Chapter 8 and again in Chapter 13.

Unobtrusive Observation
Even if subjects are observed in a research setting, they can be unobtrusively observed. For example, you might observe subjects' hand-holding behavior through a one-way mirror. Or, you might use a computer to unobtrusively record each subject's behavior. Without them knowing it, the computer could measure the number of error subjects made, how fast they responded, etc.

Unobtrusive Measures: Observing Subtle Behaviors or Physical Evidence of Behaviors
Even if subjects know they're being observed, they don't have to know what you're observing. That is, you could measure behaviors that were so subtle that subject's wouldn't think you would notice, much less be able to record. For example, your

measure might be some nonverbal behavior, such as posture, how close they sat to each other, or how long they gazed into each other's eyes.

Or, instead of directly measuring behavior, you might play detective by looking for the physical consequences of behavior. For instance, you might determine how close two people were sitting by measuring how far apart their chairs were; you might determine whether subjects read two pages by seeing whether they broke a seal you had placed between two consecutive pages; you might determine the popularity of a candidate by determining how many leaflets handed out in her behalf ended up in the nearest garbage can; you might compare the relative popularity of paintings at a museum by measuring how much the tile had eroded in front of each painting; you might assess the degree of communication between professors, staff, and administration by seeing how many classroom clocks kept accurate time.

"Unexpected Measures"

Rather than measuring subtle behaviors, you could use readily observable behaviors that appear so irrelevant to the study that subjects would never expect them to be measures. For example, you might measure how long it takes subjects to ask for help when their computer "unexpectedly" breaks down (Williams & Williams, 1983), whether subjects mail a lost letter (Milgram, 1966), how many peanuts a subject eats (Schachter, 1971), or whether the subject asks the researcher for a date (Dutton & Aron, 1974). If you wanted to use an "unexpected" measure to assess love, you might see if subjects would be willing to help repair some damage allegedly caused by their partner (picking up hundreds of data cards that the partner had knocked over or paying for some equipment the partner had broken).

Disguised Measures

Even if subjects know what behavior you're recording, you may be able to avoid subject biases if they don't know why you're recording it. That is, there's a difference between knowing what the measure is and knowing what construct it measures. For example, suppose you were measuring attitudes toward the president using the Hammond-Error Choice Technique (Hammond, 1948). In that case, you'd give your subjects a multiple-choice "knowledge" test. Unlike ordinary multiple-choice tests, subjects would have to choose between two or more wrong answers. If taxes had increased 20% during the president's first term, subjects might be given this test question:

At the end of the president's first term:

1. Taxes had increased by 10%.
2. Taxes had increased by 30%.

Subjects would know that you were interested in how they responded to this question. However, they would incorrectly assume that this was a knowledge test. Consequently, they would not realize that by choosing 1, they were indicating they liked the president and by choosing 2, that they disliked him.

If you were using a disguised measure to assess love, you might take advantage of one fact: If a subject loves a partner, the subject will overestimate how similar that partner is to him or her. Thus, you could have subjects rate their partners on a variety of characteristics. Subjects would probably think you wanted to know how accurately or how positively they rated their partner. Actually, you wouldn't be looking for either of those things. Instead, you'd be comparing their own self-ratings to their ratings of their partners. The more these ratings corresponded (the more subjects believed that they and their partner were similar), the higher the love score.

Overwhelming Subjects with Measures

Another way of confusing subjects about your purpose is to have them respond to many measures. If subjects respond to several measures, they may be less likely to guess what you're really interested in. For instance, even if you were interested in attitudes toward the president, you might give them questions about foreign affairs, mathematical principles, their mood, in addition to questions about the president. In fact, you could combine the strategy of disguising your measures and overwhelming subjects with measures by embedding your question about the president in the middle of some current events quiz or belief in democracy scale. Analogously, if you were measuring love through the disguised measure of perceived similarity, you could devise a "How Well do You Know Your Friends Quiz", in which you would embed the relevant questions such as, "What does your boyfriend or girlfriend think about gun

---

TABLE 3-3   Ways to Avoid Subject Biases

Technique	Example: Measuring Love
Measure subjects in nonresearch settings	Observe hand-holding in college cafeteria.
Unobtrusive observation	Observe hand-holding through one-way mirror in lab.
Unobtrusive measure (nonverbal)	Observe time spent gazing into each other's eyes.
Unobtrusive measures (physical traces)	Measure how far apart couple's chairs were.
"Unexpected measures"	Asking subject to repair damage "caused" by partner.
Disguised measures	Asking subjects to rate themselves and their partners, then seeing how similar they think their partner is to themselves.
Overwhelming subjects with measures	Asking subjects to rate several acquaintances (including their partner) on a wide number of dimensions.
Physiological responses	Pupil dilation, increased blood pressure in presence of partner.
Important behavior	Whether subject passes up opportunity to date very attractive other.

control?'' among irrelevant ones such as, "What does your best same-sex friend's think about gun control? How old is your boyfriend or girlfriend?''

Important Behaviors and Physiological Responses

Even if subjects know what you're measuring, there are two ways you can stop them from going along with your hypothesis or trying to seem nobler than they are. First, you can choose a response that is so important to your subjects that they'd be unwilling to cooperate with you or to lie for the sake of making a good impression. For example, rather than asking your subjects how likely they'd be to vote for the president or donate money to charity, use more personally involving criteria such as asking them to volunteer to work on the president's reelection campaign, or actually soliciting a donation to a charity. When subjects make a response that is personally involving, such as choosing which person to go out on a date with, or volunteering to go without food, they'll focus on what they need, rather than on what might impress you or on what you might want.

Second, you might choose a measure that subjects can't voluntarily control such as a physiological response (blushing, sweating, heart rate, brain wave activity). Therefore, if you were measuring love, you might measure the degree to which subjects' pupils dilate when they see their partner.

Making a Case for Construct Validity

If you've shown that your measure is reliable and isn't affected by observer or subject biases, it is probably assessing some construct. But it may not be measuring the construct you want to measure. How do you show that your measure is measuring the right thing, that it has construct validity?

Criterion Validity

One way to convince people that your measure is valid is to show that it correlates with existing (current) indicators (criteria) of the same construct, thereby establishing that the measure has **concurrent criterion validity.** The challenge of establishing concurrent criterion validity is finding criteria that relate to your construct. Basically, criteria fall into three categories: other measures of the same construct, group membership, and behaviors.

The most obvious criteria are other measures of the same construct. Thus, if you're measuring love, you might correlate your measure with other measures of love. Since all the measures are supposed to be measuring the same thing, the measures should correlate with one another.

Group membership is also an obvious and useful criterion. In fact, comparing groups that are known to have a certain characteristic with groups that are known not to have that characteristic is such a commonly used technique that it has its own name: the **known-groups technique.** Thus, in validating your love scale, you might give it to two groups—one that is known to be in love (dating couples) and one that is known to not be in love (friends). You would hope to find, as Rubin (1970) did when he validated his love scale, that the two groups score differently on your scale.

Finally, verbal and even nonverbal behavior may be useful criteria. Thus, you could correlate scores on the love scale with a behavior that lovers are supposed to do. For example, Rubin (1970) showed that his love scale correlated with how long the couples looked into each other's eyes.

Of course, you aren't limited to establishing concurrent criterion validity. You can also establish **predictive criterion validity** by correlating your measure with future criteria to show that your measure can be used to predict future behavior or future group membership. For instance, you might see if your measure could predict which dating couples would get engaged and which would soon split up (again, ala Rubin, 1970).

Discriminant Validity: Showing That You Aren't Measuring the Wrong Construct

Even if you show that your measure correlates with other criteria of love, critics may feel that you aren't measuring love but some other construct. For example, they might argue that you're measuring liking, empathy, intelligence, or extraversion instead. You might anticipate these attacks by correlating your measure with measures of liking, empathy, intelligence, extraversion, etc. Obviously, you'd hope that your measure wouldn't correlate strongly with unrelated constructs (intelligence) and that your measure would correlate more strongly with other measures of love than with measures of related constructs (liking). If you succeed in showing that your measure doesn't measure other constructs, you've established your measure's **discriminant validity.**

As you can imagine, formally establishing your measure's discriminant validity could take years. What if you have invented your own measure but don't have time to formally establish its discriminant validity? Then, try using this crude, informal way of determining whether your measure is measuring a construct that it shouldn't be measuring: Simply administer the measure to your friends and ask them what they think it measures. You may be surprised at their answers. Although your friends' responses are not as valid as a formally established discriminant validation study, their comments may alert you to other constructs that your measure is inadvertently measuring. If nothing else, your friends' comments may give you advance warning about what critics will dislike about your measure.

Internal Consistency: Are All Your Items Measuring the Same Thing?

Another way of supporting your belief that you are measuring the one construct you claim to be measuring is to show that you're measuring only one construct. Thus, if you were measuring sexual attraction with a 50-item test, you might assess your measure's validity by looking at its **internal consistency:** the degree to which each item is correlated with the overall test score. You would expect that if all your items were measuring the same unidimensional construct, all of the items should correlate with one another. Therefore, you would expect the measure to have a high degree of internal consistency.

But what if you were measuring a construct that was more complex than sexual attraction? For example, suppose you were measuring love and you believed that love had two dimensions (sexual attraction and willingness to sacrifice for the other). If love is made up of two separate constructs, then your love measure should be made up of two different subscales. Although the measure as a whole might have a low degree of internal consistency, each of the subscales should have a high degree

---

BOX 3-7   Validating a Love Measure—Rubin's Love Scale

Showing that measure was not excessively vulnerable to random error: Reliability of .85

Predictive Validity: Predicts how much two individuals will gaze at each other. Predicts probability that individuals will eventually get married.

Known-Groups Validity: Distinguishes friends from lovers.

Content Validity: All three dimensions of love are represented (predisposition to help, dependency, and possessiveness).

---

of internal consistency. All the responses to items related to sexual attraction should correlate with one another and all the responses to items related to sacrifice should correlate with one another.

Content Validity: Is Everything Represented?

Finally, you might try to make a case for your measure's validity by establishing its **content validity:** the extent to which it represents a balanced and adequate sampling of dimensions, knowledge, and skills. For example, if you defined love as "feeling sexual attraction toward a person and a willingness to make sacrifices for that person," then you would make sure your measure had both kinds of items.

Usually, content validity is a concern only when you are giving a knowledge or skills test, but for those kinds of tests, content validity may be extremely important. For example, a test to assess what you have learned about psychology should cover all areas of psychology, not just classical conditioning. Similarly, a test of oral communication skills should test not merely speaking skills, but listening skills, as well.

Summary of Construct Validity

As you can see, building a strong case for your measure's construct validity is several research projects in itself. Since validating a measure takes so much time and since most researchers are interested in finding out new things about a construct rather than finding new ways to measure it, most researchers don't invent their own measures. Instead, they use measures that others have already validated. (In fact, while reading about what it would take to validate your own love scale, you may have been saying to yourself "Let's use Rubin's scale instead.")

SENSITIVITY: THE ABILITY TO DETECT DIFFERENCES

Since establishing validity is so difficult and since validity is the degree to which a measure measures what it's supposed to measure, you might think that you should always choose the measure that appears to have the highest degree of construct

TABLE 3-4   Validating Empathy Measures

Criterion Validity (Known groups)	Child abusers score lower on empathy measures than nonabusers. Social workers with graduate training score higher on empathy than clerical employees. Prisoners who volunteer to help disadvantaged people score higher on empathy than prisoners who don't help. Medical students who score higher on empathy measures have more humanistic reasons for choosing medicine as a career than low scorers. Delinquents have lower empathy scores than nondelinquents.
Predictive Criterion Validity	High scorers are more likely to help people than low scorers. Therapists with high scores tend to have better success rates than therapists with lower success rates. High scorers tend to become more anxious when watching a speaker make a fool of himself.
Criterion Validity	Groups with low empathy scores have intense internal feuding. High scorers are better able to convey ideas during a charade performance. Higher scoring salespersons have better sales records. High scorers tend to have greater knowledge of leadership. Higher scorers are more extroverted and more self-disclosing than low scorers. Higher scorers are less aggressive than low scorers. Higher scorers have more affiliative urges than low scorers. Higher scorers are more anxious than low scorers. Studies have correlated empathy measures with one another.
Discriminant Validity	Studies have been done to show that empathy scores are not highly correlated with intelligence.
Content Validity	Experts have analyzed measures to see whether they tap two basic aspects of empathy: being able to take another's perspective and vicariously experiencing the emotion that another is feeling.

Note. Adapted from "Empathy: Review of Available Measures" by Bruce E. Chlopan, M.L. McCain, J. L. Carbonell, & R. L. Hagen, 1985, *Journal of Personality and Social Psychology, 48*, 635–653.

validity. But strangely enough, validity is not always the most important thing to look for in a measure. Depending on your research goals and your resources, you may value sensitivity, scales of measurement, ethics, or practicality over construct validity.

For example, if you're trying to find subtle differences between subjects, validity may not be as important as **sensitivity:** the ability to detect differences. A sensitive measure can help you find small differences so you can make discoveries; whereas an insensitive measure may lead you to fail to find these differences, thereby overlooking discoveries. Consequently, you may prefer using a sensitive measure that would allow you to find differences and then to debate what those differences mean (the validity question), rather than using a slightly more valid, but less sensitive measure that would fail to detect differences.

Whether or not you think sensitivity is all important, you will want your measure to be sensitive. But how do you know whether a measure is sensitive? How can you improve a measure's sensitivity? To see what affects sensitivity, imagine that you're trying to detect small changes in how much a man loves a woman. What flaws in your measure could stop you from detecting changes in the man's love?

Avoiding Insensitivity

Behaviors That Are Resistant to Change

One thing that could prevent you from detecting small changes in love is if you choose as your measure, a behavior that is very resistant to change. Important behaviors, such as getting married or buying a car, and well-ingrained habits, such as smoking or cursing, are resistant to change and therefore may not change as readily as the man's love changes. For instance, suppose you used as your measure of love the important behavior of the man asking the woman to marry him. Since the man would only ask the woman to marry him once his loved had reached a high level, this measure would be insensitive to the man's love changing from near zero to a moderate level.

So, if you're interested in sensitivity, stay away from measures that can't detect low levels of a construct. That is, don't use death as a measure of stress, tile erosion in front of a painting as a measure of the painting's popularity, or quitting smoking as a measure of love.

Measures Whose Scores Barely Vary

A second thing that could prevent you from distinguishing between subtly different levels of the man's love is if your measure didn't represent all these different levels. Therefore, a second reason why using "popping the question" is an insensitive measure is that there are only two scores he could receive (asked or didn't ask). You're trying to distinguish between numerous subtly differing degrees of love, but you're only letting your subject respond in two different ways. Clearly, if a measure is going to discriminate between many different degrees of love, subjects must be able to give many different responses.

1. ASK HOW MUCH INSTEAD OF WHETHER. One obvious way to allow subjects to get a variety of scores on a measure is to add scale points to your measure. Adding scale points to your measure may increase its ability to detect subtle differences just as adding inch-marks to a yardstick makes it more useful for detecting subtle differences in the length of boards. For instance, if you're measuring generosity, don't just record whether or not someone gave to charity. Instead, record how often (frequency of donating behavior) or how much they gave (amount), or how long you had to talk to them before they were willing to give **(response latency).** Similarly, if you are using maze running to measure motivation, don't simply record whether or not the rat ran the maze. Instead, time the rat to determine how fast (speed) it ran the maze.

Scientific equipment can help you add scale points to your measure. For instance, with the proper instruments, you can measure reaction time to the nearest ten thousandth of a second. Or, by using a sound meter to measure how loudly a person is speaking, you can go beyond saying that the person was speaking softly or loudly; you can specify exactly how many decibels the person produced.

2. ADD SCALE POINTS TO A SELF-RATING MEASURE. Of course, you can also add scale points to self-report measures. For example, don't measure love by asking the question: "Are you in love? (1-yes, 2-no)." Instead, ask (a la Johnny Carson), "How in love are you? (1-not at all; 2-slightly; 3-moderately; 4-extremely)."

Avoid Pseudo-Precision: Don't Add Too Many Scale Points

However, there are limits to adding scale points to a self-report measure. If you continue to add scale points, you'll reach a point where two things will happen to undermine your measure's sensitivity.

First, subjects will be so overwhelmed by the measure they won't use it as you intended. To take an extreme example, suppose you asked subjects to rate their love on a 10,000-point scale. Some subjects wouldn't respond at all; some would circle a series of numbers (5,000 through 7,000); some would circle one of the verbal labels you put under the numbers ("moderately in love") instead of a number; and some would write in their own verbal response ("a lot"). Others would simplify the scale by considering only the numbers 0, 1,000, 2,000, 3,000, 4,000, 5,000, 6,000, 7,000, 8,000, 9,000, and 10,000 acceptable responses. That is, they would mentally convert your 0 to 10,000 scale into a 0 to 10 scale.

Second, even if subjects try to use the scale as you designed it, their answers will be inaccurate. Since people aren't aware to the 10,000th degree the extent of their love, they can't accurately report it to that degree. Your measure's apparent precision would be an illusion. Because you're asking them to make a judgment they can't make, they will guess.

How to Avoid Pseudoprecision   Obviously, you don't want to reach the point where adding scale points undermines your measure's sensitivity. But what is that point?

According to conventional wisdom, the juncture at which you should stop adding scale points depends on the kind of question you're asking and the kind of subject you're asking. If you're asking about something that your subjects think about a lot and your subjects are intelligent, you might be able to use an 11-point scale. If you're asking about a feeling of which they're relatively ignorant (or apathetic toward) and they aren't very intelligent, you may want to use a 3-point scale. When in doubt, use a 5- or 7-point scale.

Don't Use an Impure Measure

Pseudoprecision dramatizes the third and last thing that could hurt your measure's sensitivity: using a very impure measure of the construct. If your love measure isn't measuring a construct, it won't be sensitive to changes in the man's love or to any other changes in him. No measure is pure, but some are unusually contaminated by other factors. If the measure is changing primarily because other irrelevant factors are changing, the measure will not be sensitive. In sum, to have a sensitive measure, you must have a measure that not only changes readily and has several scale-points but also changes because a construct changes.

Reliability as a Source of Impurities   One source of impurities is random error. Thus, if your love measure is changing because of random error, it isn't sensitive to changes in the man's love or to any other changes in him.

Unreliability is like static on your TV. With a little static, you can still enjoy your TV show. However, as the static increases, it becomes increasingly difficult to even make out what's happening on the screen. Similarly, with a lot of random error in your measurements, it becomes hard to discriminate between your data and the "background noise." If your measures are very unreliable, even a large difference between your groups may be due to random measurement error. Therefore, if you see that your groups score differently on a measure, you don't know if these differences are due to measurement error or actual differences. To illustrate this point, suppose you were measuring the time it took two different rats to run a maze. Suppose that rat A and rat B ran the maze four times. Their actual times were

	Trial 1	Trial 2	Trial 3	Trial 4
Rat A	6 s	6 s	6 s	6 s
Rat B	5 s	5 s	5 s	5 s

If you had obtained these data, you could clearly see that Rat B was the faster rat. However, suppose our measuring system was unreliable. For example, suppose you were having some problems with the stopwatch or you weren't always paying close attention. Then, you might record the rats' times as follows:

	Trial 1	Trial 2	Trial 3	Trial 4
Rat A	7 s	6 s	5 s	6 s
Rat B	8 s	4 s	6 s	2 s

Despite the random error in your measurements, you correctly calculated that Rat A runs the maze in an average of 6 seconds and Rat B runs it in an average of 5 seconds. Thus, random error doesn't bias your observations. However, because of the unreliable, erratic nature of your measuring system, it's hard to determine whether rat A is really the faster rat. That is, the unreliability of the measuring system causes static that makes it harder to clearly distinguish the picture the data are sending you.

Because too much random error in your measuring system can prevent you from detecting true differences between subjects, you should consider reliability when choosing a measure. Thus, you may want to calculate (for an invented measure) or look up (for an existing measure) each measure's reliability coefficient. If a measure's reliability coefficient is under .70, that means that more than half the variation in the score $(1.00 - (.70 \times .70) = .51)$ is due to random error. Therefore, you probably want to choose a measure that had a greater degree of reliability.

Of course, you don't necessarily have to know the reliability of an existing measure to know whether or not it's sensitive. If other investigators have used the measure, have been able to find differences, and been able to accept that those differences are not due to chance, the measure has some sensitivity. If any of the differences that investigators were able to accept as being reliable were relatively small, the measure probably has excellent reliability and sensitivity.

Inferences as a Source of Impurities   Unfortunately, even if your measure is reliable, it will not be a pure measure of a construct. You can only measure a construct by observing behavior, and no behavior is influenced exclusively by a single construct. For example, to measure love, you can't look inside someone's head (or heart). Instead, you can only infer a subject's love from the subject's behavior, and no matter what behavior you choose, the behavior will be affected by variables other than love. Yet, not all measures are equally likely to be influenced by irrelevant factors.

Some measures make fewer inferences than other measures and are therefore less influenced by irrelevant factors. For example, to assess the popularity of a painting by counting how many people saw the painting is an inference. Many factors other than popularity determine whether people will look at a particular painting (how close it is to a stairway, whether it is on the first floor or the fifth floor, whether it is near a restroom, etc.). However, counting the number of people involves less of an inference than assessing the painting's popularity by looking at how much the tile had eroded in front of a painting. Tile erosion is an indirect measure of how many people looked at the painting, and the number of people looking at the painting is an indirect measure of popularity. Thus, tile erosion would be affected by such irrelevant factors as how close the painting is to a stairway, what floor it's on, etc., and by factors such as the quality of the tile, what cleaning agents had been used on it, whether heavy machinery was dragged across it, etc.

Having subjects rate how much they love their partner also involves making some inferences (that subjects know the extent of their love, that they understand the question and are thinking about the question before responding, that they are honest, and that they are not responding on the basis of social desirability or demand characteristics). However, if you used as your measure whether they intended to buy roses for their partner, you're making all the above assumptions, and more. You're making the additional assumptions that each subject thinks sending flowers is what you do when you're in love and that each subject's partner wants to be sent roses.

Some measures are more sensitive not only because they make fewer inferences but also because they make safer ones. As a rule these measures tend to be simple, anonymous, and triggered by the researcher. The perfect example of such a measure is the anonymous self-rating scale. Because the response is triggered by the researcher handing out the scale, all subjects have an equal opportunity to respond to the scale in any way they wish. Because the scale is anonymous, subjects may respond the way they feel, rather than how they think other people want them to respond. Because filling out the scale is so easy, nothing prevents subjects from responding the way they wish. Therefore, if you measure love with a self-rating scale, you may have a relatively pure measure of love.

If, on the other hand, you used a complex, public, and totally unelicited behavior (how many roses they gave their partner) as your measure of love, your measure would probably be heavily contaminated by many factors. Since you didn't elicit the behavior, all subjects may not have equal opportunities to give roses: some may be approached by a flower vendor, others may not. Since the behavior is public, it may be affected not only by the subject's private feelings about giving roses but also by what the subject thinks other people (the partner, friends, acquaintances, relatives, the florist) would think. Finally, giving roses is a complex behavior, affected by factors such as the flower shop's distance from the subject, the price of roses, special holidays (Valentine's Day), etc.

Impurities Due to Not Having a Clear Idea of What You Want to Measure   Finally, you can often reduce the effect of irrelevant factors on your measure by clearly identifying what you want to measure and what you don't want to measure. For example, imagine that you're measuring love by how many roses subjects buy. You then become aware of one irrelevant factor determining this behavior: how much money subjects have. You might therefore account for this irrelevant factor by making your measure a proportion of income spent on roses (number of roses/monthly income).

To see how clearly identifying what you want to measure may allow you to eliminate a contaminating factor, consider the following memory experiment. Subjects are presented with facts about either an American or a Russian. The researchers believe that stereotypes about Russians will hurt subjects' memories for facts about Russians. Therefore, researchers initially think that their measure should be how many errors subjects make in recalling the words. However, after some reflection, the researchers realize that they aren't interested in just any kind of error, but in a certain kind of error. That is, they are interested in errors caused by forgetting favorable facts about Russians. Therefore, if they look at errors for favorable facts rather than total number of errors, their measure will be more sensitive to the kinds of differences they want to find.

Sensitivity: A Summary   You have seen that for a measure to be sensitive to differences between subjects, subjects must vary on the measure. Subjects are most likely to vary on relatively simple, innocuous behaviors that allow them to vary in terms of how much they feel, think, or behave rather than on only whether or not they think, feel, or behave. However, subjects should vary on these measures not simply for the sake of variation, but because they vary in the degree to which they possess the construct you are trying to measure. Subjects' scores should not vary because of random measurement error or because they differ on dimensions totally unrelated to the construct you're trying to measure. Thus, if you use simple, anonymous, elicited behaviors as measures (such as self-rating scales), you may be more likely to detect differences between subjects than if you observe complex, public, freely-performed behaviors.

SCALES OF MEASUREMENT

When you measure subjects, you assume that you're describing their behaviors or mental states. Although you could use words to describe subjects' behavior and mental states, you will usually employ numbers.

When you use numbers, you should remember two things. First, using numbers rather than words to describe subjects doesn't make your observations any more objective. Just as the belief that your verbal description of someone (very much in love) is an assumption that might be wrong, your assumption that a number (6) describes someone's love is an assumption that might be wrong.

Second, just as some words are more informative than others ("they're much more in love than the other couple" versus "they're in love to a different degree than the other couple"), some numbers are more descriptive than others. Rather than saying that some numbers provide more specific information than other numbers, psychologists say that different numbers represent different scales of measurement. In the next few sections, we'll see how some numbers are more descriptive than others, what the cost of getting more descriptive numbers is, the value of using more descriptive numbers, and how to get measures that will provide you with the kinds of numbers you need.

Nominal Numbers: Different Numbers Representing Different States

At the most basic level, you assume only that different numbers represent different states. That is, you assume that someone scoring a 1 on the love scale differs in their love from someone scoring a 3. At this most basic level, you are not presuming to know how subjects differ, only that they differ. You don't know whether or not the person scoring a 3 feels more love than the person scoring a 1. All you know is that they differ.

This most basic way of using numbers is perfect when you aren't interested in measuring different amounts but different kinds. For example, rather than finding out which couple is most in love, you might see whether different couples have different kinds of love. Thus, someone scoring a 1 might have companionate love, and someone scoring a 3 might have passionate love.

If you can assume that different numbers represent different states, your measure is producing at least **nominal scale data:** numbers that can front for words. However, since you can't directly measure love, your belief that someone scoring a 3 differs from someone scoring a 1 is an assumption. If your measure is invalid, this assumption is incorrect. For example, if you used the number of children the couple had as a measure of love, there may be absolutely no difference between the love possessed by couples having three children and the love possessed by couples having one child.

Ordinal Numbers: When Bigger Means More

Usually, you'll want to go beyond assuming that different numbers represent different levels or states of love. Instead of merely saying that subjects getting different numbers differ, you may want to say how they differ. For example, you may want to assume not only that 3 is different from 1, but that a score of 3 indicates more love than 1.

The Different Scales of Measurement

In other words, you may want to assume that there is a pattern or an **order** to your scores so that the higher the score, the more love the person feels. Thus, people scoring a 5 feel more love than people scoring 4, who feel more love than people scoring 3, etc. Obviously, your assumption that the numbers can be meaningfully **ordered** from lowest to highest, with higher numbers indicating more love, could be wrong. For instance, if you only had nominal data, 1 might indicate "passionate love" and 3 might indicate "companionate love." In that case, your numbers would not be representing different degrees of love, but different kinds of love. If, however, you can assume that higher numbers indicate more love than lower numbers, your measure is producing at least **ordinal scale numbers:** numbers that can be meaningfully ordered from lowest to highest.

Interval Scale Numbers: Knowing How Much More

But you may want to go beyond assuming that your measure produces ordinal scale numbers. You might assume not only that the numbers can be ordered but that the psychological distance between 1 and 2 is the same as the psychological distance between 2 and 3, which is the same as the psychological distance between any two consecutive whole numbers. In technical terminology, you're assuming that your numbers are on an **interval scale:** equal numerical intervals represent equal psychological intervals.

The assumption of equal intervals is not easy to defend, no matter what measure you use. If you use ranks, you probably don't have equal intervals. For example, suppose you successfully ranked 10 couples in terms of how much they loved each other. There might be little difference between the couple getting rank 1 and the couple getting rank 2, whereas there might be an enormous difference between the couple getting rank 9 and the couple getting rank 10.

If you use a behavioral measure, such as number of hugs, you could still fail to have equal intervals. Who would argue that the difference in love between a couple who gives 12 hugs and a couple who gives 11 hugs is the same as the difference between a couple who gives 1 hug and a couple who gives no hugs?

Even if you use a rating scale, the assumption of equal intervals might be hard to justify. For example, suppose you had people rate how they felt about their partner on a -30 (hate intensely) to a $+30$ (love intensely) scale. Would you be sure that someone who changed from -1 to $+1$ had changed to the same degree as someone who had changed from $+12$ to a $+14$?

Ratio Scales: Zeroing in on Perfection

Let's assume that your measure's numbers can be meaningfully ordered from lowest to highest and that equal intervals between numbers represent equal psychological distances. You may still want to make one last assumption: that your measure has an absolute zero. That is, you might assume that someone scoring a 0 on your measure feels absolutely no love. The assumption of having an absolute zero is not automatic even when measuring physical reality. For example, 0° Fahrenheit doesn't mean no temperature. If it did, we could make ratio statements such as 50° is half as warm as 100°. Similarly, if a score of 0 on your love measure represented absolutely no love (and you had equal intervals), then you could say that the couple who scored a 3 on the love measure was 3 times as much in love as the couple scoring a 1. Because measures that have an absolute zero and equal intervals allow you to make ratio statements, these measures produce **ratio scale data.**

Obviously, you'll have a hard time finding psychological measures that produce ratio scale numbers. Ratio scales demand that you have a perfect one-to-one correspondence between the numbers your measure produces and psychological reality. It's tough enough to have some degree of correspondence between scores on your measure and psychological reality, much less to achieve perfection.

BOX 3-8   Numbers and the Toll Ticket

Toll by Vehicle Class (in dollars)

Exit #	1	2	3	4	5	6	# Miles
1	0.25	0.35	0.60	0.35	0.50	0.40	3.0
2	0.40	0.45	1.00	0.60	0.90	0.70	10.0
3	0.50	0.60	1.35	0.80	1.25	0.95	40.0
4	0.80	0.90	2.15	1.30	1.95	1.50	45.0
5	0.90	1.10	2.65	1.55	2.40	1.85	49.0
6	1.45	1.65	3.65	2.15	3.30	2.55	51.0
7	3.60	4.15	9.95	5.85	9.30	7.15	117.0

The humble toll ticket shows us many kinds of numbers in action. For example, the numbers representing vehicle class (1–6) at the top of the ticket (under toll by vehicle class) are nominal numbers. The only reason the toll people used numbers instead of names is that numbers take less room. So, instead of writing car, truck, eight-axled truck, etc., they wrote 1, 2, 3, 4, 5, or 6. There's no particular order to these numbers as shown by the fact that a 3 is charged more than any other number.

The exits, when used as an index of distance, represent ordinal data. You know that if you get off at exit 4, you're going farther than if you get off at exit 5, but without looking at the miles column, you don't know how much farther. Thus, missing exit 4 isn't too bad, the next exit is only four miles away. Missing exit 6, on the other hand, is terrible—the next exit is 66 miles further down the road.

Money, as a measure of miles, is also an ordinal measure. That is, although it's true that the more money you spend, the farther you'll go, you can't predict how much farther you'll go merely by looking at how much money you spend. For example, if you are vehicle class number 1, it costs you 25 cents to go three miles, 10 cents more to go seven additional miles, and only 10 more cents gets you 30 additional miles. Thus, like behavioral measures, money spent and number of exits are only ordinal measures when they are used to indirectly measure another variable.

Why Our Numbers Don't Always Measure Up

But why don't you get ratio scale numbers from your measures? For example, why isn't the number of hugs a ratio scale measure? Isn't zero hugs the complete absence of hugs? Aren't three hugs three times as many as one hug? Yes and no. Yes, the number of hugs is a ratio scale measure if you're interested in knowing about hugging. But you aren't measuring hugs for hugging's sake. You are using hugs to measure love. You aren't trying to measure physical reality (hugs); you're trying to use physical reality to measure psychological reality (love). As an indirect, imperfect, reflection of love, the number of hugs is not a ratio scale measure. You can't measure love, or any other construct, directly. You can only measure constructs indirectly. As Box 3-8 shows, any indirect measure is unlikely to yield ratio scale numbers.

You have seen that there are four different levels of measurement: nominal, ordinal, interval, and ratio. As you proceed from nominal scale to ratio scale, you make progressively more assumptions about how informative your numbers are (see Tables 3-5 and 3-6).

Applying Different Scales of Measurement

Why should you be concerned about scales of measurement? Because the level of measurement you need depends on your research question (see Table 3-7) and the level of measurement you get depends on what kind of measure you use (see Table 3-8). Thus, you may find that you need to use a certain measure simply because it is the only one that can give you the kind of numbers you need to answer your research question.

When You Need Ratio Scale Numbers

Suppose you want to find out whether engaged couples are twice as much in love as dating couples who are not engaged. Since you're making a conclusion that requires a ratio, you need a measure that gives you ratio scale numbers. As Table 3-8

TABLE 3-5 Assumptions Made by Different Scales of Measurement

Nominal	Different scores represent differences on the construct (3 is a different kind of love from 1)
Ordinal	Higher scores represent more of the construct (3 is more love than 1)
Interval	Higher scores represent more of the construct and equal distances between numbers represent equal psychological differences (3 is more love than 1 to the same degree that 5 is more love than 3)
Ratio	Higher scores represent more of the construct and equal distances between numbers represent equal psychological differences and 0 means a complete absence of the construct. The numerical ratio between the higher and the lower score represents their relationship (3 is 3 times more love than 1)

TABLE 3-6   Degree of Correspondence between Different Scales of Measurement and Psychological Reality

Psychological reality	0	1	2	3	4	5	6
Ratio measurement	0	1	2	3	4	5	6
Interval measurement		0	1	2	3	4	5
Ordinal measurement		0		1	2		3

TABLE 3-7   Different Research Questions Require Different Levels of Measurement

Research Question	Minimum scale of measurement needed
Are members of group A more likely to be _____ **types** than members of group B?	Nominal
Is group A **more** _____ than another?	Ordinal
Is the difference between group 1 and group 2 **as much** as the difference between group 3 and group 4?	Interval
Did Group A change **as much** as Group B?	Interval
Is group A _____ **times** more _____ than another?	Ratio

TABLE 3-8   Measuring Instruments and the Kind of Data They Produce

Scale of Measurement	Measuring tactics commonly assumed to produce numbers that meet that scale
Ratio	Magnitude estimation
Interval	Rating scales (Magnitude estimation)
Ordinal	Behavioral measures Physiological measures Rankings (Rating Scales) (Magnitude estimation)
Nominal	Any valid measure

indicates, there are very few measures that you can use if you need ratio scale numbers.

Fortunately, you only need ratio scale levels of measurement if you're trying to make ratio statements such as "John is twice as attractive as Mike" or "Tim's joke is a third as funny as Tom's," "Married women are twice as happy as widows," or "Mary is four times smarter than Bob."

When You Need at Least Interval Scales

Since you will probably not be comparing groups to find out whether one group is twice as much in love as another group, you'll rarely need to assume that your measure has ratio properties. However, you may have to assume that your measure does have interval properties. For example, suppose you're trying to estimate the effects of therapy on relationships. Before relationship counseling is offered on your campus, you measure the degree to which couples are in love. Next, you observe who goes to counseling and who doesn't. Finally, at the end of the term, you measure the couples' love again. Let's say that you obtained the following pattern of results:

	Beginning of term	End of term
Didn't go to counseling	3.0	4.0
Went to counseling	5.0	7.0

(The higher the score, the more in love. Scores could range from 1 to 9).

Did the couples who went to counseling change more than those who didn't? Don't say yes too soon! If you say "yes," you're assuming that the psychological distance between 3 and 4 is the same as the distance between 5 and 6. However, it could be that the psychological distance between 5 and 7 is much less than the psychological distance between 3 and 4. Thus, to answer the question of which group changed more, you must assume that your data conforms to an interval scale. Therefore, to answer this research question, you would have to use a measure that has interval properties, such as a self-rating scale.

When Ordinal Data Is Sufficient

Suppose you don't care how much more in love one group is than the other, all you want to know is which group is most in love. For example, suppose you want to be able to order these three groups in terms of amount of love:

Didn't go to counseling at all	3.0
Went to counseling for 1 week	5.0
Went to counseling for 8 weeks	7.0

(The higher the score, the more in love. Scores could range from 1 to 9).

From these numbers, you may conclude that subjects who went to counseling for 8 weeks were most in love, those who went for 1 week were less in love, and those who didn't go to counseling were least in love. You can make these conclusions if you assume that you have data that is at least ordinal: higher numbers mean higher degrees of love.

When you assume that you have ordinal data, you're making a very simple assumption: the numbers are ordered. Note that you aren't assuming that the difference between 2 and 1 is the same as the difference between 3 and 2. You're assuming that 2 is bigger than 1 and 3 is bigger than 2, but you have no idea how much bigger 3 is than 2. Thus, if you only had ordinal data, you'd have no idea about how much happier the 8-week group was from the 1-week group. It could be that one week of counseling did an enormous amount of good and the additional seven weeks made a very small difference. Or, it could be just the opposite: one week of counseling did very little good, but an additional seven weeks made a big difference.

If you're only comparing two conditions, there's a good chance that you won't need to find out how much more one group is than the other. Instead, you may simply want to know which group is more and which group is less. In that case, all you need is ordinal data. And ordinal data is easy to obtain. As Table 3-8 shows, most measures are assumed to produce data that is at least ordinal.

When You Only Need a Nominal Level of Measurement

It's conceivable that you aren't interested in discovering which group is more in love. Instead, you might have the less ambigious goal of merely trying to find out whether or not the groups experience different levels or types of love. If that's the case, nominal data is all you need. Since you only need to make the least demanding and safest assumption about your numbers (that different numbers represent different things), any valid measure you choose will be sufficient.

Conclusions about Scales of Measurement

Your research question may dictate your choice of measures. If you need to make ratio statements, then you need a measure that produces ratio level data. If you need to make "how much more" statements, you need to use a measure that provides either ratio or interval data. If you need to make "more than" statements, you must use a measure that provides either ratio, interval, or ordinal data. Therefore, you may find yourself forced to choose the least valid of several measures if that measure is the only one that will give you the level of measurement your research question demands.

ETHICAL AND PRACTICAL CONSIDERATIONS

You should always be concerned about ethics when choosing a measure. You may decide against using disguised, unobtrusive, or unexpected measures because you feel subjects should be fully informed about the study before they agree to participate. Similarly, you may reject unobtrusive or field observation because you feel those tactics threaten subjects' privacy.

You should always be concerned about ethical issues, but you must often be concerned about practical issues as well. You may have to reject a measure because it's simply too time-consuming or expensive. Or, you might choose a measure primarily because it has high **face validity**: the extent to which it looks, on the face of it, to be valid. There is nothing scientific about face validity, but it may be important to the consumer (or the sponsor) of your research. For example, how loud a person yells and how many widgets a person produces may be equally valid measures of motivation. But, if you were going to get a manager to take your research seriously, which measure would you use?

SELECTING A MEASURE

Trade-Offs Involved in Using Different Types of Measures

Ideally, you would choose the most valid, sensitive, reliable, practical, and ethical measure. In actual practice, however, one measure will rarely be better than all the others on every dimension. The one that is highest in face validity may be the most vulnerable to subject biases because the subjects may know what the measure is assessing. The measure that is best at avoiding subject biases, may raise ethical questions, be low in face validity, have little evidence of construct validity, be impractical, be insensitive, or only provide ordinal data. To get a better idea of how a measure that is strong in one area may be in other areas, let's look at the strengths and weaknesses of four types of measures.

Self-Report Measures

Self-report measures are commonly used. However, there are several reasons why subjects' ratings may not reflect their true belief or feelings.

First, some subjects respond to all rating scales in the same way. Subjects who are set in their way of responding to a rating scale are said to exhibit a **response set.** Some have the response set of agreeing with every statement. These subjects are called "yea-sayers." Other subjects, the so-called "nay-sayers" are set on disagreeing with every statement. Still other subjects may be set in other ways, such as always picking the middle response, always picking the response that is furthest to the right, etc.

Second, subjects may intentionally distort their answers. Subjects may give you the answer they think you want (obeying demand characteristics), they may give you the answer that makes them look good (social desirability bias), or they may just plain lie.

Third, as Nisbett and Wilson (1977) have shown, subjects may not know their own minds. These researchers showed subjects five identical television sets. Subjects always preferred whichever TV set was furthest to the right. But did subjects say they liked the TV set because it was on the right? No, they said they liked it because it had a better picture. Numerous other investigators have done studies that confirm the finding that subjects often don't know their own minds very well—something psychoanalysts have been telling us for years.

Despite these three potential threats to the construct validity of self-rating scales, numerous self-rating scales have been shown to be valid. If you're comfortable assuming that rating scales won't be affected by subject biases, there are a host of good reasons for using them. Since rating scales involve asking subjects direct questions, they're easy to construct and have high face validity. Since self-rating scales allow subjects a variety of responses (strongly disagree, moderately disagree, etc.), since few things other than the subjects' beliefs affect how they'll respond, and since they're very reliable, they tend to be sensitive measures. Finally, they tend to provide interval level measurement.

Disguised Self-Report Measures

If, however, you feel that a rating scale's sensitivity and validity may be undermined by its susceptibility to social desirability and demand characteristics, you might consider a disguised, self-report measure: a question or set of questions that has no obvious relationship to the concept being measured. Clinical psychologists have developed some disguised measures such as projective tests (Rorschach Inkblot Test, the Thematic Apperception Test—TAT, etc.) and some well-known paper-and-pencil tests (the Minnesota Multiphasic Personality Inventory—MMPI).

Developing disguised, self-report measures is difficult. To develop such a measure, you have to know about a relationship between two variables that your subjects won't know. You may know about these relationships because of previous research or because of theory. For example, when asked to agree or disagree with the statement: "People are watching me," a subject would probably not guess that the paranoid response is to say no. But the researcher would know because past research has shown that paranoid schizophrenics are more likely to answer no to that quesion.

In the case of projective techniques, knowledge of theory gives the psychoanalyst an edge over the clients. Since most clients are ignorant of psychoanalytic theory, they probably don't realize that when they're talking about keyholes, they're really talking about sex. The psychoanalyst, on the other hand, will be keenly aware of the sexual symbolism. Of course, the psychoanalyst could be wrong.

The example of the projective test highlights the major advantages of and problems with disguised, self-report measures. What recommends disguised self-report measures is that they're so clever, so counter-intuitive. As a result, they're less susceptible to demand characteristics and social desirability biases. The regrettable aspect of disguised, self-report measures is that it's hard to find strong, documented relationships between such measures and other kinds of measures. More often than not, using a disguised, self-report measure means making a questionable assumption. For example, there is no documented evidence that talking about a keyhole means that the subject is discussing sex. Since it's hard to find disguised measures that strongly correlate with other measures, you may have difficulty developing or obtaining a useful, disguised self-report measure.

Aside from their questionable validity, disguised, self-report measures have other drawbacks. Because they're disguised, using them raises ethical questions. Do you have the right to deceive your subjects about what you're measuring? Because these measures are disguised, they may lack face validity. As a result, the general public may be less likely to think that your research is valid. Because subjects' responses are affected by more than the construct, disguised self-report measures tend to be insensitive. Finally, since they're so indirect, it's hard to assume that they provide more than ordinal data.

Behavioral Measures

Because of the weaknesses in verbal measures, you might wish to see a nonverbal measure. If you want to use a behavioral measure, you have many measures from which to choose. Your measure could be whether or not subjects left the room, donated to charity, kicked an inflatable doll, pressed a bar, recalled a word, slumped in a chair, etc. In addition to having a wide variety of behaviors you could observe, there are a wide variety of ways that you could record that behavior. To give only a few examples, you could measure the behavior's frequency: how many times the subject does the behavior, its duration: how long the subject does the behavior, its response latency: how long it takes before the subject begins doing the behavior, its rate: how many times the subject does the behavior in a certain period of time, its speed: how fast the subject does the behaviors, and errors: how many mistakes the subject makes while trying to do the behavior.

Using a behavioral measure may have several advantages. First, nonverbal behaviors can have higher face validity than self-report measures because actions speak louder than words. After all, what would be more convincing to a potential employer: A letter from your professor saying "I know ——— to be a motivated individual because he says he is" or "I know ——— to be a motivated individual because he has done enormous amounts of work in my classes?" Second, since actions often have more serious consequences than ratings, behavioral measures are sometimes less biased by demand characteristics and social desirability than are rating scales.

However, behavioral measures have several drawbacks. First, it's sometimes difficult to observe behavior objectively. Second, as we pointed out earlier, behavioral measures are unlikely to provide more than ordinal data. Third, behavioral measures may be unreliable not only because the observers recording the behavior may be unreliable, but also because subjects may behave in an inconsistent manner. Finally, because of unreliability and because overt behavior is affected by many factors other than your construct, behavioral measures may be insensitive.

Physiological Measures

If you're extremely concerned about subject biases, you may be concerned about the fact that both rating scales and behavioral measures involve voluntary behavior. That is, subjects can respond any way they please. So, if subjects want to please the researcher or make a good impression, they may. Therefore, rather than using a voluntary behavior, you might want to use an involuntary behavior, such as a physiological response.

There are several reasons to be enthusiastic about using physiological measures. First, they may be less influenced by subject biases than other measures.

Second, unlike some behavioral measures, physiological responses can be measured objectively. Third, physiological responses can now be used to measure a wide variety of constructs. In the past, no one used physiological measures for anything other than assessing the strength of emotional responses. Admittedly, there were many measures—perspiration rate, respiration rate, heart rate, muscle tension, pupil dilation, and alpha wave activity—but they were all measuring emotions. Currently, psychologists use physiological measures to measure constructs other than emotions. Thinking has been measured by assessing muscular tension in the face (Rinn, 1984), intelligence has been assessed by observing brain wave responses to stimuli (Eysenck & Eysenck, 1983), and self-consciousness has been assessed by looking at brain wave activity in the dominant relative to the nondominant hemisphere (Cohen, Rosen & Goldstein, 1985).

However, before rushing out to find physiological measures, realize that using them has its drawbacks. The most obvious drawback is a practical one. Because physiological measures can be very expensive, most schools don't own or give students access to the more sophisticated physiological measures.

The other drawbacks are less obvious but just as serious. First, physiological measures often have questionable validity. The relationship between physiological responses and mental states is often unclear. For example, recent research (Lykken, 1981) shows that lie detectors can detect emotional arousal but aren't too good at detecting whether someone is lying. Second, even if a physiological measure is valid, it's often insensitive. Third, physiological measures rarely provide more than ordinal scale data.

Selecting a Measure: Conclusions

Since you can't choose the ideal measure, you must choose the best measure for your particular study. In other words, you must know not only what trade-offs are involved in choosing a particular measure but what trade-offs you're willing to make. Therefore, you need to decide what concerns you most: validity, being able to detect differences, or practical considerations? If you're most concerned about validity, then you need to decide what threatens validity the most—demand characteristics, social desirability, observer error, or measuring the wrong construct?

Sometimes, you can easily determine what factors concern you and what factors don't. If you expect to find huge differences between your groups, then sensitivity will not be a high priority. If you're only trying to find out whether the groups differ, but not the extent to which they differ, then scales of measurement are not a concern. If your hypothesis is counterintuitive, subjects shouldn't be able to figure it out. Therefore, you wouldn't be concerned about demand characteristics.

Often, however, you can only determine your primary concerns about a measure after you know what design you'll use. You may find that your major measurement concern may be wiped out by using the proper design. For example, if you're concerned about social desirability, a two-group design may solve your problems. That is, if you're trying to find differences between two groups and both groups are just as influenced by social desirability, social desirability would not be a problem. Similarly, if sensitivity is your main concern you may be able to address this concern by using a very sensitive design.

The Case for Not Choosing among Measures: Multiple Operations

As you can see, choosing the "best" measure is very difficult. But, who says you have to choose between your measures? Why not use them all? If you use them all and they all give you the same pattern of results, you could be very confident that all your measures are accurately tapping the desired construct. The idea behind **multiple operations** is that you could be wrong with one measure, but it's unlikely you would be wrong with all of them.

The Case against Multiple Operations

However, critics point out that using multiple measures is not a perfect solution. One problem, as the following analogy illustrates, is how to combine the results from different measures. Suppose you aren't confident that you can correctly calculate correlation coefficients. You aren't even sure that the computer program will give you the right answer. Therefore, you want to check the computer by doing the problem by hand. To feel even more secure about your answer, you do it by hand four times, using four different formulas. If you get the same answer using all five methods (four times by hand, once by computer), you'll be happy. However, what if you get five different answers? Which method(s) would you use? Would you take an average of the five answers, would you turn in all five answers, or would you take the computer's answer?

Rather than take the average, you would probably take the computer's answer because it's more likely to be correct. The average would almost certainly be wrong. If you're going to accept the computer's analysis anyway, why do the other analyses? Similarly, if there is one method of measuring a construct that's clearly better than the rest, why use the other methods?

Of course, rather than handing in any single answer, you could give your professor all five of your answers. Let's assume the professor accepts your paper. How will she grade you? She couldn't totally ignore your wrong answers or your right answers. To give you a grade, she might be forced to generate some formula based on how many answers you gave, how close the answers were to the right answer, and how many answers were right. Obviously, grading your paper would be more complicated than grading a paper from someone who only turned in one answer per question. Analogously, if you use several measures, you have to consider how many variables you used and how many supported your hypothesis to decide whether your hypothesis was supported. More specifically, your statistics will have to decide whether the results supported the hypothesis. Clearly, the statistics you use will have to be more complicated than the ones used by someone who only used one measure. In fact, the statistical techniques for multiple measures are so complicated that most schools don't even offer courses on them.

If you use multiple measures, you not only complicate your statistics, you also multiply your practical and methodological headaches. For example, suppose you're assessing how much violence subjects watch on TV and are measuring their aggression with four different measures: punching a large, plastic, inflated doll; giving electric shocks to a confederate; tearing up a sheet of paper; and writing a negative evaluation of the researcher.

Using this many measures sets you up for several problems. First, your subjects may begin to suspect what you're trying to measure. (After all, you've *hit* them over the head with your measure four times.) So, demand characteristics may come into play. Second, the measures could have an effect on each other. For example, punching the doll might increase subjects' aggressiveness, or giving electric shocks might make them feel so guilty that they lost whatever aggressiveness they had. Even if the measures had little effect on one another, your subjects might have forgotten all about the TV program by the time they responded to the fourth measure (or they might be exhausted). Finally, simply fitting all those measures into the same room and having the subject respond to all of them in a short period could be a logistical nightmare.

So, according to critics of multiple operations, when it comes to measures, more is not always better. Many critics of multiple operations would rather have one good measure than a host of bad measures. Or, in the words of perhaps the first critic of multiple operations, Edgar Allen Poe:

> They make a vast parade of measures; but these are so ill-adapted to the objects proposed.

> —*The Murders in the Rue Morgue*, 1848

Converging Operations: A Compromise

Despite their objections, most critics concede that there are reasons for using a multiple operations approach. Critics realize that no one measure of a construct is perfect. Furthermore, they realize that if psychologists use only one measure of a construct, we may end up with a psychology of that measure (the psychology of punching inflatable dolls) rather than a psychology of the broader construct (aggression).

Although some critics find the logic of multiple operations appealing, they still believe that using a multiple operations approach is impractical. The proof of the impracticality of multiple operations, they say, lies in the fact that only a handful of studies have ever used them.

A solution that might satisfy both the advocates and critics of multiple operations is a **converging operations** approach. If you used a converging operations approach, you would conduct separate studies that differed only in terms of using a different measure each time. The converging operations approach would satisfy the need for multiple measures while avoiding the statistical, practical, and methodological problems attached with their use. The major drawback of a converging operations approach is that it requires doing several studies, which is, of course, more time-consuming than doing one.

Forgetting about Constructs: Behavior for Its Own Sake

You have seen that proving construct validity is impossible. Construct validity is always an inference—you can never see intelligence, aggression, love, etc. The only thing you can see is behavior. Because measuring constructs by observing behavior is so challenging and so speculative, many psychologists have decided to measure behavior for behavior's sake.

These psychologists are often called behaviorists because they aren't interested in behavior for what it represents, but for what it is. The behaviorist is interested in hand-holding, not as a measure of love, but for its own sake. Similarly, a behavior therapist may be concerned with a client's lack of eye-contact, not because the therapist feels that it's a sign of shyness, but because he's concerned about insufficient eye-contact. Obviously, many behaviors (smoking, drug abuse, blood pressure) are important in their own right.

Observing behavior for its own sake is all well and good, but there are problems. Most of these problems are the same one's you had when you measured behavior to assess a construct. For example, you still have to worry about observer bias, subject bias, and unreliable measures. Fortunately, scientific equipment and training can reduce these problems.

But perhaps the most serious problem with only being interested in measuring behavior is that behavior is not always, in itself, interesting. We aren't interested in intelligence test scores in their own right, we're interested in them because we believe they tap the construct of intelligence. Neither are we interested in bar pressing or maze running for their own sakes. At some point, most psychologists feel the need to bridge the gap between the specific tasks performed in a research study and real-life activities. More often than not, the vehicle that bridges that gap is a construct. Because constructs fulfill the useful function of allowing us to generalize our findings beyond the immediate research task, psychologists will continue to wrestle with such abstract and intangible constructs as learning, motivation, intelligence, thirst, and love.

MANIPULATING VARIABLES

To select a treatment, you follow many of the same steps as when you select a measure. You find both measures and treatments by doing a literature review. To invent your own manipulation, you consult the same sources you used to invent your own measure: intuition, theory, and definitions. When evaluating treatments, you have the same concerns as when you measure variables: random error, researcher bias, demand characteristics, providing evidence for validity, and detecting differences.

Concerns **Random Error**
Just as you want to measure a variable without random error, you want to manipulate variables (treatment) without random error. Therefore, just as you standardized the administration of your measure, you want to standardize the administration of your treatment. You want to administer it the same way every time.

Researcher Bias
Just as you were worried about researchers being biased in their observations, you will also be worried about **experimenter bias:** researchers being biased when they administer the treatment. For example, researchers may be more attentive and friendlier to the subjects they expect or want to do better on the task. As was the case with observer bias, the key is to use scientific equipment to administer the treatments, to use paper and pencil instructions, to standardize procedures, or to make the researcher blind to what condition the subject is in.

Subject Biases

Just as you were concerned that your measure might tip subjects off to how they should behave, you should be concerned that your treatment might tip subjects off as to how they should behave. One of the most frequently cited examples of how a treatment could lead to demand characteristics was a series of studies done in the 1920s at the Hawthorne Electric Plant. The investigators, Roethlisberger and Dickson, were looking at the effects of lighting on productivity. At first, everything seemed to go as expected. Increasing illumination increased productivity. However, when they reduced illumination, productivity continued to increase. It turned out that no matter what they changed or how they changed it, productivity increased. The researchers concluded that the treatment group was reacting to the special attention, rather than to the treatment itself. This effect became known as the Hawthorne Effect (Roethlisberger & Dickson, 1939).

Although many experts now believe that Roethlisberger and Dickson's results were not due to the "Hawthorne Effect," no one disputes that subjects may react merely to getting a treatment. Therefore, researchers use a wide variety of techniques to avoid the "Hawthorne Effect." Some of these techniques are similar to the techniques used to make a measure less vulnerable to subject biases. That is, just as with measures, researchers may manipulate the treatment in a nonresearch setting or use unexpected manipulations, such as a remark that the subject "accidentally" overhears.

In addition, researchers may make some subjects think they're getting a real treatment when they're really getting a **placebo:** a treatment that is known to have no effect. For example, in one drug study, some subjects were given a caffeine pill (the treatment), and the others received a sugar pill (the placebo).

Evidence for Validity

As with measures, you would like to provide evidence that your treatment is doing what you claim it is. The difference is that making a case for the validity of a treatment is less involved than making a case for the validity of a measure. The two most common ways of establishing validity are to do a manipulation check: a question that asks subjects what they're feeling, and to argue that your treatment is consistent with a theory's definition of the construct.

Consistency with Theory   For example, suppose you were manipulating cognitive dissonance: a state of arousal caused when subjects are aware of having two inconsistent beliefs. You would want to argue that your manipulation meets the three general criteria that dissonance theory says must be met for dissonance to be induced:

1. Subjects must believe they are **voluntarily** performing an action that is inconsistent with their attitudes (a smoker writing an essay about why people shouldn't smoke).

2. Subjects must feel that the action is public and will have consequences (before writing the essay, they must know that others will read their essay and know that they wrote it).

3. Subjects must not feel that they did the behavior for any reward (you didn't pay them for doing the behavior).

Manipulation Checks In addition to arguing that you obeyed the criteria set down by dissonance theory, you might do a manipulation check. You might ask subjects if they felt that their attitudes and behavior were inconsistent, if they felt they'd been coerced, if they felt that their behavior was public, whether they foresaw the consequences of their behavior, etc. Many researchers feel that you should always use a manipulation check, whether it be an informal one (what do you think I'm manipulating?) or a formal one (rating scales).

But what if giving people the manipulation check alerts them to the study? Then, manipulation check advocates would say to use the manipulation check, but only with practice subjects or after the subject has responded to your measure.

But what if your treatment is obvious (physical attractiveness, concrete versus abstract words, etc.)? Even then, manipulation check advocates would urge you to go ahead with a manipulation check for two important reasons. First, a manipulation check could establish the discriminant validity of your treatment. For example, wouldn't it be nice if you could show that your attractiveness manipulation increased perceptions of attractiveness but didn't change perceptions of age or fashion sense? Second, since you're doing research to test assumptions rather than make assumptions, you should be willing to check your own assumption that you know what you're manipulating.

Trade-Offs among Three Most Common Kinds of Manipulations

As with measures, there is no such thing as the perfect manipulation. Different manipulations have different strengths and weaknesses. Below, we will briefly highlight the strengths and weaknesses of three common kinds of manipulations: instructional manipulations, environmental manipulations, and stooge manipulations.

Instructional Manipulations

Perhaps the most common treatment manipulation is the **instructional manipulation:** presenting written or oral instructions. The advantage of an instructional manipulation is that you can standardize your manipulation easily. All you have to do is give each subject the same mimeographed instructions or play each subject the same tape. This standardization reduces random error and experimenter bias.

However, just because you can consistently present instructions to subjects, don't assume that your instructions will be perceived the same way every time. Subjects may ignore, forget, or misinterpret instructions. To reduce random error due to subjects interpreting your instructions differently, be sure to repeat and paraphrase your most important instructions. Many researchers advise you to be very blatant about your instructions. Thus, if you were manipulating anonymity, you would tell subjects in the anonymous condition that their responses would be anonymous, and confidential, and private, and that no one would know. Furthermore, you'd tell them not to write their names on the papers. In the public condition, however, you'd tell subjects that everyone would see their papers, that you were going to make xerox copies of their papers, and you'd make a big deal of their signing their names to the paper.

In addition to subjects not paying attention to or not understanding instructional manipulations, instructional manipulations have one other weakness. They tend to be vulnerable to subject biases. Subjects often know what you're trying to manipulate and can play along.

Environmental Manipulations

A tactic that may involve your subjects, thereby avoiding the problems caused by subject bias is to use an **environmental manipulation**: changing the subject's environment. Some environmental manipulations take the form of "accidents." For instance, smoke may fill a room, the subject may be induced to break something, or he may overhear some remark.

When considering an environmental manipulation, ask two questions. First, will subjects notice the manipulation? Even when manipulations have involved rather dramatic changes in the subjects' environment (smoke filling a room), a sizable proportion of subjects report not noticing it (Latane and Darley, 1970).

Second, can you present the manipulation the same way every time? Fortunately, many environmental manipulations can be presented in a consistent, standardized way. All animal research, for example, involves environmental manipulations that seem very real to the animal and can be consistently presented (food deprivation). Likewise, research in perception often involves environmental manipulations (presenting illusions or other stimuli). These manipulations vary from the routine—presentation of visual stimuli by computer, tachistoscope, memory drum, or automated slide projector—to the exotic. For example, Neisser (1984) has done studies where the manipulation consists of silently moving the walls of the subject's cubicle.

Manipulations Involving Stooges

Another way to involve subjects is to use **stooges:** confederates who pretend to be subjects but who are actually in league with the researcher. By using stooges, you may get subjects to respond openly, thus avoiding the demand characteristics that accompany instructional manipulations. The problem is that it's very hard to standardize the performance of a stooge. At best, inconsistent performances by stooges create unnecessary random error. At worst, stooges may bias the results. Some researchers try to get the advantages of stooges without any of the disadvantages by having subjects listen to tapes of actors rather than relying on stooges to give the exact same performance time after time. For example, both Aronson and Carlsmith (1974) and Latane and Darley (1968) had subjects believe they were listening to people talking over an intercom when they actually were only listening to a tape-recording.

As you can see, choosing manipulations usually means making compromises. To choose the right manipulation for your study, you must determine what your study needs most. Is experimenter bias your biggest concern? Then, you might use an instructional manipulation. Are you most concerned with demand characteristics? Then, you might use an environmental manipulation. But what if you can't decide on a "best" manipulation? Then you might decide to use a converging operations approach.

Converging Operations

Just as you can use converging measures to increase the chances that you are measuring what you think you are, you can use converging manipulations to increase the chances that you are manipulating what you want to. If you were to use a converging manipulations approach, you would conduct a series of studies that differed only in how you manipulated the treatment.

Manipulating Variables: A Summary

When manipulating variables, you have many of the same concerns you have when measuring them. However, when manipulating variables, you have one set of concerns that you don't have with measurement: How many levels of the treatment should you have and how different should your levels be? The choice of treatment levels may determine whether you find a difference between conditions and whether that difference is valid. We'll deal with the important decision of choosing treatment levels in Chapters 5 and 6.

CONCLUDING REMARKS

In Chapter 2, you developed a research idea: a prediction about how two or more variables were related. In this chapter, you learned how to operationalize these variables. Now that you have the raw materials to build a research design, you can take better advantage of the rest of this book.

THE CASE OF THE DISSOLVED SUICIDE PACT

(At the offices of attorney Mary Pason)

BOB MCATEE: Ms. Pason, you've got to help me. The police think that I killed Jim Jenson. But I didn't. Jim and I did have a suicide pact, but we called it off.

MARY PASON: Well, what did happen last night?

BOB MCATEE: I remember talking to Jim, then I blacked out. When I came to, Jim was dead. But I didn't kill him. We called it off. Besides we didn't plan to shoot each other, we planned to poison ourselves.

LT. BRAGG (standing in the doorway):   Very interesting. I'm sure Mr. Weiner will be interested in your suicide pact. As if he needed any help, with your finger prints on the murder weapon.

MARY PASON: How long have you been here, Lieutenant?

LT. BRAGG: Long enough. But don't worry counselor, I have an arrest warrant for Mr. McAtee.

(The next week)

STELLA RHODES: You haven't slept for days. You look awful, Mary. Get some sleep.

PASON: If I sleep, my client may hang.

STELLA RHODES: What were you doing all night?

PASON: Strange as it may seem, I was reviewing my college research design notes. I know there are some things about this case that I'm missing. And reviewing these notes has helped me to put my finger on some of them.

RHODES: Such as?

PASON: You'll see, Stella. You'll see.

Stella thought she saw a smile dart across her boss's face.

In court, Mary was an alert and active participant. Gone was the despondence and depressions she'd shown all too often in the first days of the trial.

For Weiner, the morning was a nightmare although it had started off pleasantly enough.

WEINER: And you told the police that you saw Jim Jenson enter the defendant's house at 9:15 A.M.

MR. FIG: Yes.

WEINER: And you then told the police that you heard arguing.

MR. FIG: Yes.

WEINER: Let the record reflect this witness's testimony that Jim Jenson argued with the defendant and left the house at 10:00 A.M. and that the coroner's report states that the victim died somewhere between 9:15 A.M. and 10:00 A.M.

JUDGE STURBRIDGE: Ms. Payson, you may cross-examine the witness.

PASON: Mr. Fig, isn't it true that you did not see the defendant leave the house at 10:00 A.M.?

MR. FIG: Yes.

PASON: And you did *not* hear the defendant and the victim arguing?

MR. FIG: Yes.

PASON: Would you explain to the court this apparent discrepancy in your testimony?

MR. FIG: I was just telling the officers what they wanted to hear. I wasn't trying to hurt nobody.

Mary Pason passed a slip of paper to Stella. On the paper were the words, "By changing the way you word questions, you can sniff out yea-sayers."

So Mr. Fig's testimony was not the gold mine that Weiner had hoped. To make up for Fig's testimony, Weiner called Miss Spencer to the stand. Miss Spencer was to testify that Bob McAttee had a motive for killing Jim Jenson.

WEINER: Please tell the court about Bob McAtee and Jim Jenson.

MISS SPENCER: Oh, Bob McAtee was very, very angry at Jim Jenson. Bob was mad enough to kill Jim.

PASON: Your honor, I object. The witness's statement that Bob McAttee was mad at the deceased calls for a conclusion from the witness. How can the witness know what is inside the mind of the defendant? Miss Spencer is not an expert in measuring psychological constructs. Therefore, I move that the witness's testimony be stricken from the record.

The judge sustained Pason's objections.

Weiner then called several eyewitnesses.

Unfortunately, Pason had found places where they disagreed with one another. One had said the defendant was angry, another had said the defendant was embarrassed, yet another had said he was afraid.

After thoroughly discrediting the witnesses, Pason said something to Weiner about complicated judgments lowering interobserver reliability and reliability putting a ceiling on validity. Weiner wondered whether Mary Pason was taunting him or just trying to confuse him.

Finally, out of desperation, Weiner had decided to present the physical evidence. The physical evidence revealed no sign of a struggle and no sign of the victim being poisoned, and thus suggested that a friend had killed Jim Jenson.

Yet, Pason had shot holes in this testimony also. Pason had experts admit that there could have been a struggle and there could have been poisoning, but that their tests might not have picked it up. "Insensitive tests," explained Pason.

And if that were not enough, Pason further discredited the expert testimony on the physical evidence. Mary Pason said, "Your honor, I would like to have these photographs entered as evidence."

Weiner objected, "Where did you get those photographs?"

Pason didn't answer Weiner's question and instead proceeded to point out that "These photographs contradict some of the expert witness's testimony. By the way, the D.A. should note that using instruments to avoid human error is a good idea."

Out of frustration, Weiner called his key witness, Mr. Erdberg, Jim's stepfather.

STEPFATHER: Bob McAtee and Jim Jenson had a suicide pact.

WEINER: I would like to mention to the court that the witness has made these statements during a lie detector test and passed.

PASON: Objection, your honor. As Mr. Weiner knows, the results of a lie detector test are not admissible as evidence. Lie detectors do not establish whether someone is lying, they measure changes in physiological signs. A person could be lying and his heart rate, blood pressure, or brain waves not reflect any change for a wide range of reasons—taking tranquilizers, being a pathological liar, etc. And your honor, the principal reason that lie detector tests are inadmissible as evidence is their vulnerability to observer bias on the part of the administrator.

Not only had the judge sustained Ms. Pason's objection, but she sternly warned Mr. Weiner. What was worse, Pason, by insinuating that the witness could be a drug fiend or psychopath, had totally discredited his testimony.

At the end of the day, both Weiner and Pason were in foul moods. Weiner because he had been humiliated repeatedly, Pason because she'd failed to do anything to prove her client's innocence. Pason hoped that private investigator Saul Drake had some good news for her.

SAUL DRAKE: Jenson's mother, Mrs. Erdberg, claimed that her son was not suicidal.

PASON: But that's what you'd expect her to say. That's the socially desirable response. Did you check on his behavior?

DRAKE: Yes, and there are signs that he may have been suicidal. He gave a friend his watch, saying "I won't need it anymore." And, Mary, he didn't buy another watch.

PASON: Well, that does support our client's story. But, I don't think that indirect evidence would hold up in court. However, I think I know who the murderer is.

The next day found Mary Pason in an exceptionally good mood. She greeted Stella Rhodes with, "I'm ready to go on the attack."

Mary recalled the witness who had passed the polygraph test, Erdberg, Jim Jenson's stepfather. Pason's questions were brutal.

PASON: Isn't it true that you will inherit more than one million dollars because of your stepson's death?

STEPFATHER: Yes, but that doesn't make me a murderer.

PASON: Isn't it true that you had access to the murder weapon.

STEPFATHER: Well, yes.

PASON: Isn't it true that you overheard Bob and Jim on the phone. You listened in on the line and found out that they had called off their suicide pact.

STEPFATHER: No.

PASON: I submit that you followed Bob to your stepson's house, having planned to fill the living room with nitrous oxide and kill them both. However, Jim began to wake up and you knew that the gas wouldn't work, so you took Bob's gun from his pocket and shot Jim.

STEPFATHER: No, besides they found no evidence of gas poisoning.

PASON: That was an insensitive test. Have you ever heard of the Crozier test of gas poisoning? That test will clearly show that Jim was exposed to nitrous oxide. Furthermore, I can call these two gentlemen who saw you purchase the gas. Need I call them?

STEPFATHER (screaming): They were two rich, spoiled brats who never worked a day in their lives. They would've ended it all, but that was too much work for them. I just tried to do it for them. Besides, Jim's money should have been mine.

(After the verdict)

WEINER: Mary, you know that the Crozier test checks for liver disease, not gas poisoning.

PASON: It does? Forgive me, I must have misunderstood. I guess I picked a measure with poor construct validity.

WEINER: Sounds more like a bluff to me. And about those two stooges you used, they didn't see the stepfather buy any gas.

PASON: I guess things are not always as they appear. Getting at the truth about what people really think and feel isn't as easy as it may seem at first. But, I guess after losing your 1,000th case in a row, you're beginning to learn that. You may want to consider another line of work.

MAIN POINTS

1. You may be able to use a measure or manipulation that someone has already published. Therefore, look for references in your textbook bibliographies, visit the library, or consider a computerized literature search.
2. Consulting a dictionary may help you be more precise about what it is you want to measure.
3. Both theory and intuition may suggest ways of measuring abstract concepts.
4. Sensitivity, reliability, and validity are highly valued in a measure.
5. Sensitivity is a measure's ability to detect small differences.
6. Validity refers to whether you're measuring what you claim.
7. A reliable measure is relatively free from random error.
8. Unreliability may stem from human error in making or recording observations, random changes in how the measure is administered, and changes in the subject.
9. An unreliable measure cannot be valid, but a reliable measure may be invalid.
10. An unreliable measure cannot be sensitive, but a reliable measure may be insensitive.
11. By asking how much rather than whether, by knowing what you want to measure, by avoiding unnecessary inferences, and by using common sense, you can increase the sensitivity of your measure.
12. A valid measure must have some degree of reliability and be relatively free of observer bias and subject biases.
13. Two common subject biases are social desirability (trying to make a good impression) and obeying demand characteristics.
14. By not letting subjects know what you're measuring, you may be able to reduce subject biases.
15. Establishing discriminant validity, criterion validity, and internal consistency are all ways of validating a measure.

16. Different kinds of measures produce different kinds of numbers.
17. Nominal numbers only let you say that subjects differ.
18. Ordinal numbers only let you say which subjects have more of a quality than others.
19. Interval and ratio numbers let you say how much more of a quality one subject has than another.
20. Ratio scales let you say how many times more of something (intelligent) one subject is than another.
21. Since no measure is perfect, choosing a measure involves trade-offs.
22. To avoid these trade-offs, some investigators use multiple operations or converging operations.
23. Choosing a treatment involves many of the same steps as choosing a measure.
24. You can use manipulation checks to make a case for your treatment's validity.

KEY TERMS

random error
interobserver reliability
correlation coefficient
observer bias
blind
subject biases
social desirability bias
demand characteristics
concurrent criterion validity
known-groups technique
predictive criterion validity

discriminant validity
internal consistency
content validity
sensitivity
response latency
nominal scale data
ordinal scale numbers
interval scale
ratio scale data
multiple operations
converging operations

EXERCISES

1. Define a concept you'd like to measure (memory, love, arousal, etc.)
2. Locate two published measures of that concept. (See Appendix B) How did you find these measures?
3. Develop a self-report measure, a physiological measure, and an overt behavior measure of your concept.
4. Take one of your measures and discuss how you could improve its sensitivity.
5. If you had a year to try to validate your measure, how would you go about it? (Hint: Refer to the different kinds of validities discussed in this chapter.)
6. What kind of data (nominal, ordinal, interval, or ratio), do you think your measure would produce? Why?
7. Why is reliability important?

8. What could you do to improve your measure's reliability?

9. How vulnerable is your measure to subject and observer bias? Why? Can you change your measure to make it more resistant to these threats?

10. Would there be an advantage to using a multiple operations approach to measuring your concept? Why or why not?

11. What factor would you like to manipulate? Define this factor as specifically as you can.

12. Find one example of this factor being manipulated in a published study. (See Appendix B.)

13. How would you manipulate that factor? Why?

14. How could you perform a manipulation check on the factor you want to manipulate? Would it be useful to perform a manipulation check? Why or why not?

15. Compare the relative advantages and disadvantages of using an instructional manipulation versus an environmental manipulation.

16. What would be the advantage of using a converging operations approach? If you used such an approach, what are the different manipulations you would use?

4

INTERNAL VALIDITY: WHY RESEARCHERS VALUE EXPERIMENTAL DESIGNS

OUTLINE

OVERVIEW

This chapter is about internal validity. As you may recall from Chapter 1, for a study to have internal validity, it must clearly demonstrate that a specific treatment causes an effect. Thus, if you establish that turning on blue lights in a room causes higher scores on a happiness questionnaire, your study has internal validity. However, demonstrating internal validity is not an easy task. There are several problems and obstacles that can distort the true relationship between variables. By studying this chapter, you'll know how to identify these threats.

THE LOGIC OF INTERNAL VALIDITY

The logic of establishing internal validity is simple. First, you determine that changes in a treatment (blue lighting) are followed by changes of another factor (increased happiness). Then, you determine that the treatment (blue lighting) is the only factor responsible for the effect (increased happiness). That is, you show that the results couldn't be due to anything other than the lighting. Or, as a psychologist would say, you rule out **extraneous factors:** factors other than the treatment.

ATTEMPTS TO ELIMINATE EXTRANEOUS VARIABLES

The most direct way to rule out the possibility that your results are due to the effects of extraneous factors is to eliminate all extraneous factors from your study. If there are no extraneous factors in your study, extraneous factors obviously can't be responsible for your results. In the abstract, there are two ways you can eliminate these extraneous factors:

1. get two identical groups, treat them identically, except that you only give one of the groups the treatment, then compare the treatment group to the no-treatment group;
2. get some subjects, measure them, make sure that nothing in their life changes except that they get the treatment, then measure them again.

In the next few sections, we'll try both of these approaches to see if either can successfully eliminate extraneous variables.

PROBLEMS WITH GETTING TWO IDENTICAL GROUPS

Suppose you get two groups of subjects and treat them identically, except that only one of the groups gets the treatment (blue lighting). Then, you give both groups the happiness scale and note that they have different levels of happiness.

What do you conclude? If the groups were identical before you introduced the treatment, you would correctly conclude that the treatment caused the groups to differ. However, if the groups were not identical, the effect could be due to **selection:** choosing groups that were different from one another before the study began.

Self-Assignment to Group as a Source of Selection Error

How can you avoid the selection error? That is, how can you get two identical groups? Obviously, one key to avoiding selection error is preventing subjects from choosing what condition they want to be in (self-selection). If your subjects choose their own conditions, then you know that the groups will differ on at least one dimension: one group chose the treatment, the other chose to avoid the treatment. Furthermore, the groups probably differ in ways that you don't know about. As a result, if you let subjects choose what condition they'll be in, you'll probably end up comparing apples and oranges.

Sometimes the effects of self-selection are obvious. For example, suppose you compare two groups—one group volunteers to stay after work to attend a seminar on "Helping Your Company", the other does not. If you find that the seminar group is more loyal to the company than the no-seminar group, you can't conclude that the effect is due to the seminar. The groups obviously differed in loyalty before the study began.

Sometimes the effects of self-selection aren't as obvious. For instance, what if you let subjects choose whether they get blue lighting or no lighting? If you find that the blue lighting group is happier than the no-lighting group, you can't conclude that the effect was due to the blue lighting. People who prefer blue lighting may be happier than people who prefer no lighting. You really don't know how subjects who choose one condition differ from those who choose another condition. But you do know that they differ. And these differences may cause the groups to differ at the end of the study.

Researcher Assignment to Group: An Obvious Source of Selection Bias

Obviously, letting subjects assign themselves to a group creates unequal groups. However, if you assign subjects to groups, you might unintentionally bias your study. For example, you might put all the smiling subjects in the blue light condition and all the frowning subjects in the no-treatment condition.

Arbitrary Assignment to Group as a Source of Selection Bias

To avoid the bias of "picking your own team", you might assign subjects to a condition on the basis of some arbitrary rule. For example, why not assign students on the right hand side of the room to the no-treatment group and students on the left side of the room to the treatment group? The answer is simple: "Because the groups are obviously not equal." At the very, very, least, the groups differ in that one group prefers the right side, and the other group prefers the left side. They probably differ in many other ways. For example, if the left side of the room is near the windows and the right side is near the door, we can list at least four reasons why left-siders might be happier or more energetic than right-siders:

1. People sitting on the left side of the room may be more energetic because they walked the width of the room to find a seat.

2. People sitting on the left side of the room may be early-arrivers (students who came in late would tend to sit on the right side so they wouldn't disrupt class by crossing the width of the room).

3. People sitting on the left side may be more interested in the outdoors since they chose to have access to the window.

4. People sitting on the left side may have chosen those seats to get a better view of the professor's performance (if the professor shows the typical right-hander's tendency of turning to the right, which, of course, is the student's left).

You can probably think of many other differences between "left-siders" and "right-siders" in a particular class. But the point is that the groups definitely differ in at least one respect (choice of side of room), and they almost certainly differ in numerous other respects.

What's true for the arbitrary rule of assigning subjects to groups on the basis of where they sit is true for any other arbitrary rule. Thus, any researchers who assign subjects on the basis of an arbitrary rule (the first subjects assigned to the treatment group, people whose last names begin with a letter between "A" and "L" in the treatment group, etc.) make their research vulnerable to selection bias.

Arbitrarily assigning subjects to groups doesn't work because you are assigning subjects to groups based on their differences. You are deliberately ensuring that they are different on some variable (preference for side of the room, etc.).

If you can assign subjects in a way that guarantees they are different, why can't you assign subjects in a way that guarantees they are identical? In other words, why not use **matching:** choosing your groups so that they have identical characteristics.

Matching: A Valiant, but Unsuccessful Strategy for Getting Identical Groups

The Impossibility of Perfectly Matching Subjects: Identical Subjects Don't Exist

In the abstract, matching seems like an easy, foolproof way of making sure that your two groups are equal. In practice, however, matching is neither easy nor foolproof. Imagine the difficulty of finding two people who match on every characteristic and then assigning one to the no-treatment condition and the other to the treatment condition. It would be impossible. Even identical twins would not be exactly alike—they have different first names and different experiences.

The Difficulty of Matching Groups on Every Variable: There Are Too Many Variables

Obviously, you can't create the situation where each member of the treatment group has a clone in the no-treatment group. But could you create a situation where, on the average, the treatment group and the no-treatment group matched? Although this task seems more manageable, it's still impossible because there are too many variables. Try as you might, there would always be some variable you had not matched on—and that variable might be important. Thus, even if you created two groups that had the same average age, same average intelligence, same average income, same average height, same average weight, there would still be thousands of variables on which the groups might differ. For example, the groups might differ in mood on the day of the experiment, how they were getting along with their parents, how many books they'd read, their overall health, etc.

Two Difficulties with Matching Groups on Every Relevant Variable

Clearly, you can't match your no-treatment and treatment groups on every single characteristic. However, making groups identical in every respect may be unnecessary. You only need them to be identical in respect to the factor you want to measure (happiness). Therefore, all you need to do is match your groups on characteristics that will influence their performance on your measure (the happiness scale).

Unfortunately, there are two problems with this "solution." First, matching only on those factors that influence the key variable may be impossible because there may be thousands of factors that influence the key variable (happiness). Second, you probably don't know every single characteristic that influences the variable you want to measure (happiness). If you knew everything about happiness, you probably wouldn't be doing a study to find out about it.

Instead of matching subjects on every characteristic that affects the factor you want to measure, why not match subjects on the factor you want to measure? In your case, why not match subjects on the happiness scores? That is, before you assign subjects to groups, test people on the happiness scale (what psychologists call a pretest). Next, match your groups so that the treatment group and no-treatment group have the same average pretest score. Finally, at the end of the study, test the subjects again, giving subjects what psychologists call a posttest. If you find a difference between your groups on the posttest, then you should be positive that the treatment worked, right? Wrong!

Even if the treatment had no effect whatsoever, there are two possible reasons why two groups that were the same at pretest could differ on the posttest: selection by maturation interactions and regression effects.

Problems with Matching on Pretest Scores

Selection by Maturation Interactions: Subjects Growing in Different Ways

The first reason is the **selection by maturation interaction:** the groups started out the same on the pretest, but afterwards developed at different rates or in different directions. That is, subjects that start out the same on a dimension may grow apart because they differ in other respects.

To visualize the strong impact that selection by maturation interaction can have, imagine you found a group of fourth grade boys and girls. You put all the boys in one group. Then, you had them lift weights. You saw that the average weight they could lift was 40 lb. You then picked a group of 4th grade girls who could also lift 40 lb. Thus, your groups are equivalent on the pretest. Then, you introduced the treatment: strength pills. You gave the boys strength pills for eight years. When both groups were in the 12th grade, you measured their strength. You found that the boys were much stronger than the girls. This effect might be due to the strength pills. However, the effect may also be due to the men naturally developing strength at a faster rate than the women. That is, the effect may be due to the failure to match on a variable (gender) that influences muscular maturation.

You have seen that groups may grow apart because of different rates of physical maturation. Groups may also grow apart because of different rates of social, emotional, or intellectual maturation. To illustrate this point, let's examine a situation where the two groups are probably changing in different ways on virtually every aspect of development.

For example, suppose you matched—on the basis of job performance—a group of 19-year-old employees with a group of 63-year-old employees. You then enrolled the 19-year-olds into a training program. When you compared the groups two years later, you found that the 19-year-olds were better than the 63-year-olds. Why? The difference may have been due to training. However, the difference may also have been due to the fact that 19-year-olds' productivity should increase even without training because they are just learning their jobs. The 63-year-olds' performance, on the other hand, might naturally decrease as this group anticipates retirement. Therefore, the apparent treatment effect may really be a selection by maturation interaction.

As you can see, matching on pretest scores is incomplete. Pretest scores are a good predictor of posttest scores, but not a perfect predictor. Many factors affect how a subject scores on the posttest. If the groups aren't matched on these other relevant variables, two groups that started out the same on the pretest may naturally grow apart.

If you were somehow able to match on pretest scores and all other relevant variables, you would be able to rule out selection by maturation. However, even then, your matched groups may not be equal.

The Regression Effect

How could your groups not be equal if you measured them and made sure that they were equal? The problem is that you can't measure them to make sure they are equal. In other words, measuring them as equal doesn't mean they are equal. Even though you tend to assume that measurement is perfect, it isn't. For example, if a police officer stops you for speeding, the officer might say "You were going 75." Or he might say, "I clocked you at 75." The officer's two statements are very different. You may have been going 40 and the radar mistimed you (radars have clocked trees at over 100 miles per hour) or you may have been going 95. In any event, you probably weren't going at EXACTLY the speed that the officer recorded. Even in this high technology age, something as simple as measuring someone's height is not immune from measurement error. In fact, one of the authors of this text regularly fluctuates between 5'5" and 5'8", depending on who measures her. Needless to say, if measurements of variables as concrete as height are contaminated with random error, measurements of behavior and constructs are probably similarly contaminated.

You can capitalize on measurement error to make two groups that are very different appear to be very similar and later appear to become very different. For example, suppose you were offered $1,000 to find and take pictures of a white sheep and a black sheep that are the same color. Then, you were asked to take another picture that would make the two sheep differ in terms of color. What would you do?

To get a photo of a black sheep that looks like a white sheep, you would take hundreds of pictures of white sheep and hundreds of pictures of black sheep. Eventually, due to some random measurement error (overexposure, underexposure, mistimed flash, error in developing film, etc.), you would get at least one photo of a white sheep that looks black, or a black sheep that looks white, or a black sheep and a white sheep that both look gray. You got the results you wanted by selectively taking advantage of measurements that had been heavily contaminated by random measurement error.

After you have a photo of a white sheep and a black sheep that appear to be the same color, making them "become" different colors is easy. You would simply rephotograph the two sheep. The second time you photograph the two sheep, the white one would probably look white and the black one would probably look black. The photographic illusion you created was temporary because extreme amounts of random measurement error rarely strike the same measurements twice in a row. In other words, to create the illusion of change, you took advantage of **regression to the mean:** the tendency for scores that are extremely unusual to revert back to more normal levels on the retest.

Regression toward the mean occurs because unusual scores tend to be unusually affected by chance. As a result, when subjects receiving unusual scores are retested, their scores tend to be affected by chance to a more usual (and lesser) degree the second time around.

In the example above, you intentionally took advantage of the erratic nature of random measurement error to "match" two groups on a factor in which they differ and then to make the groups appear to change on the posttest. Unfortunately, a researcher might unintentionally rely on measurement error to match two groups on a factor in which they differ. For instance, suppose a researcher working at an institution for the mentally retarded wants to see whether a specially developed training program can increase intelligence. The researcher wants to have two groups that are identical in intelligence, give one group the training program, and see whether the training program group does better on a second intelligence test than the no-training group. However, the researcher also wants both groups to have near normal intelligence. Unfortunately, after testing all the patients, the researcher only finds eight patients who score between 85 and 95 on the IQ test.

The researcher decides that eight subjects are only enough for the treatment group. Therefore, he still needs to find a no-treatment group, preferably one that has the same IQ as his treatment group. As he drives by your school, he has an idea: use some of your school's students as subjects. After clearing it with your school and taking precautions so that no one will be harmed by his procedures, he begins work. He sets up an office at your school and offers $25 to anyone who will take an IQ test.

After testing many people, he finds eight college students who score around 90 on the IQ test. He makes this group his no-treatment group. At the end of the study, he retests both groups. When he looks at his results, he's horrified. He finds that the eight college students score much higher on the second IQ test (the posttest) than the institutionalized people. On closer examination, he finds that the college students' IQ scores increased dramatically from the pretest to posttest, whereas the institutionalized patients' IQ scores dropped from pretest to posttest.

What happened? Did the true intelligence of the college students increase even though the researcher did nothing? Did the training program shrink the true intelligence of institutionalized patients?

What happened was that the investigator selected scores that were likely to be heavily contaminated with measurement error. To understand how this occurred, think about what would cause your classmates to score 90 on an IQ test. They certainly wouldn't score a 90 because that was their true level of intelligence. Instead, they must have scored so low because of some factors having nothing to do with intelligence. Perhaps pulling an all-nighter, being hung-over, or suffering from the flu would cause such a poor performance. If they did score a 90 on an IQ test because they were very ill, would it be likely that they would score a 90 the second time? No, chances are that they would not be as ill the second time they were tested. As a result, their second score should be higher because it would probably be a closer reflection of their true intelligence.

Likewise, the investigator chose those retarded patients' scores that were most likely to be loaded with measurement error. Consider how a retarded person could score 90 on the IQ test. What could account for a person scoring so far above his true score? Probably some form of luck would be involved. That is, just as you might have found yourself getting lucky on a multiple-choice test for which you were unprepared, a retarded person might get lucky the first time the test was administered. If you test 8,000 retarded people, eight might score fairly high due to chance. But would these same eight be as lucky the next time? It's a good bet that they wouldn't. Instead, their second score should be a more accurate reflection of their true score. Consequently, they would score lower than they did the first time.

Conclusions about Matching on Pretest Scores

In conclusion, there are two reasons why matching on pretest scores doesn't totally eliminate extraneous variables. First, since scores are flawed indicators of actual characteristics, matching does not eliminate the extraneous variable of measurement error. Because of measurement error, it's possible to get two groups that match on pretest scores but that are actually very different. That is, random error may create the mirage that two dissimilar groups are similar. As convincing as this mirage may be, it is only temporary. Often, the mirage will vanish on the posttest, as chance exerts less of an influence on scores so that the extremely deviant scores revert back to more typical levels (regression to the mean). If the mirage disappears during the posttest, two groups that appeared to be similar on the pretest may reveal their true differences during the posttest. Although the change in scores is only due to changes in measurement error, you can understand how people could mistakenly interpret these changes as a treatment effect.

Second, matching on pretest scores is incomplete. It is incomplete because the pretest performance is not a perfect indicator of posttest performance. Subjects change from pretest to posttest and many factors determine how they will change. Therefore, to predict a subject's posttest score, you need to match not only on the pretest score, but on every other variable that might affect how they will change. If you don't, you may have two groups that started out the same, but naturally grew apart—no thanks to the treatment. In other words, you may have what appears to be a treatment effect but is really a selection by maturation effect.

THE PRETEST–POSTTEST DESIGN

No matter how much we match, we can't form two identical groups of subjects. The only way we could get two identical groups of subjects would be to have the same subjects in both groups. That is, each subject could be in both the no-treatment group and in the treatment group. For instance, we might use a **pretest–posttest design,** where we give each subject the pretest, administer the treatment, then give the posttest. If we make sure that the subjects in the treatment group are the same subjects that were in the no-treatment group, we've eliminated the threat of selection.

**Advantages:
It Eliminates
Selection Bias**

Our solution seems perfect if we assume that the treatment is the only reason a subject's posttest score would be different from her pretest score. Unfortunately, there are two major reasons why this assumption is wrong. First, even without the treatment, subjects may change over time. For example, a subject's mood may change by the minute. Second, how subjects are measured, how accurately they're measured, and how many subjects are measured may change over time. Therefore, even if subjects don't really change between pretest and posttest, their scores may change because of changes in measurement.

**Two Basic
Problems with
Our Solution**

Maturation

A subject may change between the time of the pretest and the time of the posttest as a result of becoming more mature. For example, suppose you instituted a weight-lifting program for high-school sophomores. You find that—as seniors—they can lift 40 lb more than they could as sophomores. Your problem is that you don't know whether the weight training or natural development is responsible for the change. Similarly, if you give a baby 10 years of memory training, you'll find that her memory improves. However, this difference may be due not to the training but to **maturation:** changes due to natural development.

**How Subjects
May Change
between
Pretest and
Posttest**

History

A subject may change between pretest and posttest because the subject's environment has changed. These environmental changes are called **history.** To understand the effects of history, suppose two social psychologists have a treatment they think will change how Americans feel about space exploration. However, between pretest and posttest, a spacecraft explodes. Or, suppose an investigator was examining the effect of diet on maze-running speed. However, between pretest and posttest, the heat went off in the rat room and the rats nearly froze to death. Obviously, events that happen in a subject's life (history) between the pretest and the posttest can have a powerful effect on his posttest score.

Testing

One event that always occurs between the start of the pretest and the start of the posttest is the pretest itself. If the pretest changes subjects, you have what is known as the **testing effect.** For example, if your instructor gave you the same test twice, you'd score better the second time. However, your improvement might not be due to better studying habits, but rather to remembering some of the questions. People who've taken many intelligence tests (e.g., children of clinical psychologists) may score very high on IQ tests, regardless of their true intelligence.

The testing effect isn't limited to knowledge tests. It can occur with virtually any measure. To illustrate, let's choose a pretest that has nothing to do with knowledge. For instance, suppose we were to ask people their opinions about Greenland entering the world bank. Would we get another answer the second time we asked this question? Yes, because the very action of asking for their opinion may cause them to think about the issue more and to develop or change their opinion. In short, by measuring something, you may change it.

How Measurement May Change between Pretest and Posttest

Obviously, subjects' scores may change over time because subjects have changed. What is less obvious is that subjects' scores may change over time even if subjects haven't changed. Instead, their scores may change because of changes in how subjects are measured. Specifically, scores may change because of instrumentation, mortality, and regression.

Changes in How Subjects Are Measured: Instrumentation

An obvious reason for a subject's score changing from pretest to posttest is that the measuring instrument used for the posttest is different from the one used during the pretest. If the difference between pretest and posttest scores is due to changes in the measuring instrument, you have an **instrumentation effect.**

Sometimes, changes in the measuring instrument are unintentional. For example, suppose you're measuring aggression using the most changeable measuring instrument possible—the human rater. As the study progresses, raters may broaden their definition of aggression. Consequently, they may give subjects higher posttest scores on aggression, even though subjects' behavior hasn't changed. Unfortunately, there are many ways that raters could change between pretesting and posttesting. Raters could become more conscientious, less conscientious, more lenient, less lenient, etc. Any of these changes could cause an instrumentation effect.

Often, changes in the instrument occur because the researcher is trying to make the posttest better than the pretest. Thus, the researcher may correct typographical errors, eliminate bad questions, or make the scales neater, etc. Unfortunately, these changes, no matter how minor they may seem or how logical they may be, are changes. And these changes may cause instrumentation effects.

We're not saying that you shouldn't administer the best measure possible. Of course, you should. But you should refine the measure before beginning the study.

Changing the Extent to Which Measurement Is Affected by Random Error: Regression

Even if the measuring instrument is the same for both the pretest and posttest, the amount of chance measurement error may not be. In other words, with a pretest–posttest design, you still have to deal with regression toward the mean. To show that you don't get away from regression toward the mean by using the pretest-posttest design, think back to the researcher who was investigating the effects of a training program on intelligence. Suppose that he'd decided not to compare the eight highest-scoring patients with a group of college students. Instead, after having the eight highest-scoring patients complete the training program, he administered a second IQ test as his posttest. What would he observe?

As before, he'd have observed that the patients' I.Q. scores dropped from pretest to posttest. This drop is not due to the training program robbing patients of intelligence. Rather, the posttest scores more accurately reflect the patients' true intelligence. The posttest scores are lower than the pretest scores only because the pretest scores were inflated with random measurement error.

The pretest scores were destined to be inflated with measurement error because the investigators selected only those subjects whose scores were extreme. Extreme scores tend to have extreme amounts of measurement error. To understand why, remember that a subject's score is a function of two things: the subject's true characteristics and measurement error. Thus, an extreme score may be extreme because measurement error is making the score extreme. To take a concrete example, let's consider how a student might get a perfect score on a quiz. There are three basic possibilities for the perfect score:

1. the student is a perfect student;
2. the student is a very good student and had some good luck;
3. the student is an average or below average student but got incredibly lucky.

As you can see, if you study a group of people who got perfect scores on the last exam, you are probably studying a group of people whose scores were inflated by measurement error. If subjects were measured again, random error would probably be less generous (After all, random error couldn't be more generous. There's only one place for scores to go—down.). Therefore, if you were to give them a treatment (memory training) and then look at their scores on the next exam, you'd be disappointed. The group that averaged 100% on the first test might average "only" 96% on the second test.

In the case we just described, regression's presence is relatively obvious because it's taking advantage of a rather obvious source of measurement error—error in test scores. But regression may take advantage of less obvious sources of measurement error.

The subtlest form of measurement error seems more like an error in sampling than an error of measurement. For example, suppose you're trying to make inferences about a subject's typical behavior from a sample of her behavior. If the behavior you observe is not typical, you have measurement error. Even if you measured the behavior you observed perfectly, you have measurement error because you haven't measured the subject's typical behavior perfectly. This measurement error can, of course, lead to regression toward the mean.

To illustrate how a sample of behavior may be biased, let's look at a coin's behavior. Suppose you find a coin that comes up heads six times in a row. Although you have accurately recorded that the coin came up heads six times in a row, you might be making a measurement error if you were to conclude that the coin was biased towards heads. In fact, if you were to flip the coin ten more times, you probably wouldn't get 10 more heads. Instead, you would probably get something close to five heads and five tails.

Coins are not the only ones to exhibit erratic behavior. Virtually every behavior is inconsistent and therefore prone to atypical streaks. For example, suppose you watch someone shoot baskets. You accurately observe that she made 12 out of 12 shots. Based on these observations, you may conclude that she is a great shooter. However, you may be wrong. Perhaps if you had observed her shooting on a different day, you would have seen her make only 2 out of 12 shots.

To illustrate how this subtle form of measurement error can lead to regression toward the mean, suppose a person who's been happy virtually all of her life feels depressed. This depression is so unlike her that she seeks therapy. Before starting the therapy, the psychologist gives her a personality test. The test verifies that she's depressed. After a couple of sessions, she's feeling better. In fact, according to the personality test, she's no longer depressed. Who could blame the psychologist for feeling proud?

But has the psychologist changed the client's personality? No, the patient is just behaving in a way consistent with her normal personality. The previous measurements were contaminated by events that had nothing to do with her personality. Perhaps her depressed manner reflected a string of bad fortune: getting food poisoning, a friend dying, and being audited by the IRS. As this string of bad luck ended and her luck returned to normal, her mood returned to normal.

Regression toward the mean is such an excellent impersonator of a treatment effect that regression fools most of the people, most of the time. Many people swear that something really helped them when they had "hit bottom." Thus, the baseball player who recovers from a terrible slump believes that hypnosis was the cure, the owner whose business was at an all-time low believes that a new manager turned the business around, a man at an all-time emotional low feels that his new girlfriend turned him around, etc. What these people fail to take into account is that things are simply reverting back to the norm (regressing to the mean). When listening to stories about how people bounced back due to some miracle treatment, remember comedian Woody Allen's line: "I always get well, even without the leaches."

Changes in How Many Subjects Are Measured: Mortality
The last, and perhaps most obvious, reason that you could find differences between pretest and posttest scores would be if you were measuring fewer subjects at posttest than you were at pretest. In other words, your study may fall victim to **mortality:** subjects dropping out of the study before it's completed.

To illustrate how much of an impact mortality can have, imagine that you're studying the effect of diet on memory in older adults. You pretest your subjects, give them your new diet, and posttest them. You find that the average posttest score is higher than the average pretest score. Before concluding that you have an effect for the treatment (type of diet), you must not only rule out regression, instrumentation, testing, and history, but also mortality. A closer look at the data may show you that your results are due to mortality: the only reason posttest scores are higher than pretest scores is that the people who scored very poorly on the pretest are no longer around for the posttest.

Of course, you don't have to have subjects die to suffer mortality. In fact, mortality usually results from subjects deciding to quit the study, subjects moving away, or from subjects failing to follow directions.

CHAPTER SUMMARY

We tried to create a situation where we manipulated the treatment, while keeping everything else constant. However, nothing we tried worked.

When we tried to compare a treatment group versus a no-treatment group, we had to worry that our groups weren't identical before the study started. Even when we matched our groups, we realized that the groups might not be identical because:

1. we couldn't match on every single characteristic;
2. we couldn't match on subjects true characteristics, so we had to match based on imperfect measures of these characteristics.

Because of the problems with comparing a treatment group against a no-treatment group (see Box 4-1), we tried to measure the same group before giving them the treatment and after giving them the treatment. Although this before-after tactic eliminated some threats to validity, it created others. As Box 4-2 shows, subjects may change from pretest to posttest for a variety of reasons having nothing to do with the treatment. Subjects may change as a result of:

1. natural development;
2. other things in their lives changing; and
3. learning from the pretest.

Furthermore, subjects may appear to change from pretest to posttest as a result of:

1. the posttest measure being different from the pretest measure;
2. their pretest scores being unduly influenced by chance; and
3. subjects dropping out of the study so that the posttest group is smaller than the pretest group.

BOX 4-1   Questions to Ask When Comparing Two Groups

Selection: Were groups really equal before the study began?

Selection by maturation interaction: Would the groups have naturally grown apart, even without the treatment?

Regression effects: Even if the groups appeared equivalent before the study began, was this apparent equivalence merely a temporary illusion created by random measurement error?

BOX 4-2 Questions to Ask When Examining a Pretest—Posttest (Before—After) Study

Maturation: Could the pretest—posttest differences have been due to natural changes resulting from subjects becoming older?

History: Could other events in the subjects' lives have caused the pretest—posttest differences?

Testing: Could subjects score differently on the posttest as a result of the practice and experience they got on the pretest?

Instrumentation: Were subjects measured with the same instrument, in the same way, the second time?

Regression: Were subjects selected for their extreme pretest scores? Subjects who get extreme scores have a tendency to get less extreme scores the second time around.

Mortality: Did everyone who was given the pretest stick around for the posttest? Or, were the pretest group and the posttest group really two different groups?

Ruling out Extraneous Variables

Why couldn't we eliminate extraneous variables? Was it because we used improper designs? No. As you'll see in later chapters, matching subjects and testing subjects before and after treatment are useful research techniques. We failed because our strategy of trying to keep everything constant was flawed. Keeping everything the same is impossible. Imagine, in our ever-changing world, trying to make sure that only one thing (amount of blue lighting) in a subject's life changed!

Accounting for Extraneous Variables

Fortunately, you don't have to eliminate extraneous variables to rule out their effects. Instead of eliminating extraneous variables, you can rule out their effects. That is, you could try to track down a treatment's effect the way a detective tracks down a murderer. The detective is confronted with more than one suspect for a murder, just as you're confronted with more than one suspect for an effect. The detective can't make the suspects disappear, just as you can't eliminate extraneous factors. However, like the detective, you can use logic to rule out the role of some suspects and to implicate others.

Of course, before you can begin to account for the actions of every suspicious extraneous variable, you have to know "who" each of these variables are. At first glance, identifying all the thousands of variables that might account for the relationship between the treatment and the effect seems as impossible as eliminating all those variables.

Identifying Extraneous Variables

Fortunately, identifying the extraneous variables isn't as difficult as it first appears because every one of these thousands of factors fall into eight categories: the eight threats to validity. Thus, you really only have eight suspects (See Box 4-3). If you can show that selection, history, maturation, testing, regression, mortality, instrumentation, and selection by maturation were not responsible for the effect, then you can conclude that the treatment was responsible.

BOX 4-3   The Eight Threats to Internal Validity

Know THIS
CHART
←

History: Things other than the treatment that have changed in the subjects' environments.

Testing: Changes resulting from the practice and experience subjects got on the pretest.

Instrumentation: The way subjects were measured changed from pretest to posttest.

Regression effects: If subjects are chosen because their scores were unusual, these scores may be unusual because of extreme amounts of random measurement error. On retesting, subjects are bound to get more normal scores as random measurement error abates to more normal levels.

Mortality: Differences between conditions due to subjects dropping out of the study.

Maturation: Apparent treatment effects are really due to natural growth or development.

Selection: Treatment and no-treatment groups were different before the treatment was administered.

Selection by maturation interaction: Treatment and no-treatment groups were predisposed to grow apart.

The Relationship between Internal and External Validity

If you rule out these threats, you've established internal validity. That is, you have demonstrated that a factor causes an effect in a particular study. But you haven't demonstrated that you can generalize your results outside of your particular study. Internal validity alone does not guarantee that an investigator doing the same study, but with different subjects (depressed patients instead of college students), or a different setting (a library instead of a lab), or at a different time (300 years from now) would obtain the same results. If you want to generalize your results, you need external validity.

If internal validity doesn't guarantee external validity, why bother with establishing internal validity? The obvious answer is that you may not care about external validity. Some researchers don't care about generalizing their results; they may want only to show that a certain treatment causes a certain effect in a certain setting. For example, researchers may want to show that with their patients, in their hospital, giving the patients an exercise program reduces patients' alcohol consumption. The researchers may not care whether the treatment would work with other kinds of patients at other hospitals (external validity). They only care that they have a method that works for them.

Of course, few people are so single-minded that they're totally unconcerned with external validity. If you're concerned with external validity, why should you bother with internal validity? After all, in one sense, it seems that things you would do to improve your study's internal validity would reduce its external validity. For example, to reduce the problem of selection bias, you might use twins as your subjects. Although using twins (or clones) as subjects would increase internal validity by reducing differences between your treatment and no-treatment groups, it might hurt the generalizability of your study. Your results might only apply to twins. Similarly, you might reduce the threat due to history by testing your subjects in a situation (a lab or a vacuum) where they're isolated from nontreatment factors. Although this artificial situation may increase internal validity because the treatment was one of the only things to change during the study, you'd have to wonder whether the treatment would have the same effect outside this artificial situation. Would the results generalize to real life, where the factors you isolated your subjects from come into play?

Since the same procedures that increase internal validity may decrease external validity, some cynics say "Rigor times relevance equals a constant," meaning that if a study is rigorous (internally valid), it's not relevant (externally valid). Conversely, the cynics argue that if the study is relevant, then it's not rigorous.

Fortunately, the cynics are wrong: Internal validity and external validity are not incompatible. As you'll see in future chapters, you can have studies that have both internal and external validity. In fact, internal validity is often a prerequisite for external validity. Before you can establish that a factor causes an effect in every situation, you must show that the factor causes an effect in at least one situation (your study).

Thus, the first step to establishing external validity is often establishing internal validity. In the next chapter, you'll learn the easiest, most automatic way to take this step—the simple experiment.

 # THE CASE OF THE UNFINISHED NOTE

The dead man's body slumped over his desk. Next to his battered skull was a note. His last written words were: "I, Dr. Newdi, wish to inform our citizens of a terrible case of fraud. The guilty one ..."

The writer had been unable to finish. The dark black ink from the physician's pen had been lost in a sea of red blood. The blood-soaked page punctuated the importance of the note and the brutality of the crime. Beside the letter was the doctor's appointment book. During the day, he had made appointments with several important people: Dr. Lotz, Mr. Kline, Mr. Lendin, Dr. Oxnard, and Dr. Alpha. These persons were prime suspects.

HOLMES: "How do you see it, Watson?"

WATSON: "Obviously, Dr. Newdi had discovered that someone was not as successful as everyone believed. He was killed by the person he was going to expose."

HOLMES: "And who, pray tell, is the fraud turned murderer?"

WATSON: "Dr. Lotz is the murderer. Dr. Lotz cured only 30% of his patients. Dr. Newdi, who cured over 85% of his patients, discovered that Lotz was killing patients and threatened to expose him. Lotz killed Newdi to protect his reputation."

HOLMES: "You think so, Watson?"

WATSON: "Yes, look Newdi cured twice as many of his patients as Lotz did. Any fool can see that something was wrong with Lotz."

HOLMES: "Anyone who thinks that Lotz is a quack because his cure rates are lower than Dr. Newdi's is a fool. Dr. Newdi treated young, healthy patients suffering from nothing more than the common cold or boredom. I daresay Watson, most of his clients were having affairs with him. Dr. Lotz, on the other hand, treated the old and weak. His patients were ones that no other doctor would take. Considering this, his rate of cure is remarkable."

WATSON: "Good gracious, Holmes, you mean that selection bias could account for Lotz's patients doing worse than Newdi's?"

HOLMES: "Precisely."

WATSON: "Well, what about the other suspects. Surely, you don't suspect the eminent Mr. Kline. His training program for executives was truly remarkable. His success was not due to selection. Do you know that 70% of his trainees were promoted within five years?"

HOLMES: "Watson, did you know that 70% of ALL young managers are promoted within five years?"

WATSON: "Maturation!"

HOLMES: "Right."

WATSON: "Well, what about Mr. Lendin, the President of Crisis, Inc. Surely, you couldn't say his success was due to selection. Most of his cases were people under unusual stress. Many of his clients had had a run of bad luck and he took over and they were back on their feet. I've heard that his methods aren't very sound, but his success speaks for itself."

HOLMES: "But it's not HIS success. He is merely taking advantage of the way luck works. Watson, what happens when one has had an unusually bad run of luck?"

WATSON: "Well, this bad luck doesn't continue forever. Things usually return back to normal."

HOLMES: "The technical term is 'regression.' "

WATSON: "Well, it's regression to you, but it sounds like common sense to me."

HOLMES: "It should be, Watson. A pity that common sense is so uncommonly rare."

WATSON: "Well, Holmes, we are left with only two other suspects. Dr. Lotz's partner, Dr. Alpha doesn't seem to be suspect. He and Dr. Lotz both accepted patients who were equally sick. Yet, Dr. Alpha had a better success rate. I suppose you can explain that."

HOLMES: "Yes, they accepted patients who were equally sick, but Dr. Alpha's patients were always younger."

WATSON: "Selection by maturation, Holmes?"

HOLMES: "Right!"

WATSON: "That leaves us with Dr. Oxnard. He had a very good success rate. Of his regular patients, 90% are healthy. This is much higher than the London average of 60%. And before you say selection, may I remind you that he takes everyone."

HOLMES: "He does take everyone Watson, but he doesn't keep everyone. People tend to quit Dr. Oxnard. In fact, few people stay with him for more than two years. He takes summers off. During the rest of the year, he goes out of town frequently. As a result, people soon learn that if they do have health problems, they should change doctors."

WATSON: "Mortality, Holmes?"

HOLMES: "Exactly."

WATSON: "So, who is the murderer? They could all be suspects, except Lotz."

HOLMES: "They are all guilty, except Lotz."

WATSON: "But, the note says, the guilty one!"

HOLMES: "Precisely. That is why the note was left. Newdi was about to write the guilty ones, but he was stopped. Had he written, "guilty ones", they would have destroyed the note. However, the murderers thought that this deceptive clue would throw the police off the track. But they did not count on Sherlock Holmes being on the case."

WATSON: "But, maybe Dr. Newdi didn't know that they were all frauds."

HOLMES: "I'm sure he did. Dr. Newdi and I were in the same research design course. He did almost as well as I did. I'm sure he was aware of how misleading "facts" like cure rates can be. I'm also sure that the frauds felt that by providing each other with alibis, they would elude suspicion. They would take advantage of the fact that people assume that murder is always committed by a single person in order to frame Dr. Lotz."

WATSON: "Fortunately, you assumed nothing. You looked for all the possibilities. You looked for other possible reasons for these doctors' success rates and you looked for other possible explanations for the murder. The fact that you don't take things for granted sets you apart from the ordinary person."

HOLMES: "Precisely, my dear chap."

MAIN POINTS

1. If you observe an effect in a study that has internal validity, you know what caused that effect.

2. There are eight major threats to internal validity: selection, selection-maturation, regression, maturation, history, testing, mortality, and instrumentation.

3. When you compare a treatment group to a no-treatment group, beware of the selection bias: the groups being different before you administer the treatment.

4. To reduce selection bias, subjects should never get to choose what amount of treatment they get. In addition, subjects' characteristics, attitudes, or behaviors should have **nothing** to do with the group (treatment or no-treatment) in which they are put.

5. It is impossible to **match** two groups of subjects so that they are identical in every respect. Subjects simply differ in too many ways.

6. Even matching subjects on pretest scores is not perfect because of the problems of selection by maturation and regression.

7. Selection by maturation means that your two groups may mature at different rates or in different directions.

8. The fact that extreme scores tend to be a little less extreme the second time around is called regression toward the mean. Regression toward the mean can cause two groups that appear to be matched on a pretest to score differently on the posttest.

9. In the pretest–posttest design, you measure a group, administer the treatment, and measure the group again.

10. Using the pretest–posttest method is not as perfect as it first appears. It is vulnerable to testing, history, regression, maturation, mortality, and instrumentation biases.

11. Regression can occur in the pretest–posttest design because the person may have gotten the treatment when he most needed it. There was no place to go, but up. Many quacks take advantage of regression to the mean by using testimonials from people who would have gotten better anyway.

12. Maturation refers to biological changes that occur to people merely as a result of time. In some cases, becoming more mature, and not the treatment, accounts for pretest–posttest differences.

13. Events having nothing to do with the treatment that occur in a subject's life between pretest and posttest (history) can cause changes in a subject's posttest score.

14. Testing bias refers to the fact that taking a pretest may affect performance on a posttest.

15. The instrumentation bias occurs when the pretest is different from the posttest.

16. External validity is the degree to which the results from a study can be generalized.

17. Internal and external validity are not necessarily incompatible.

KEY TERMS

extraneous factors
selection
matching
selection by maturation interaction
regression to the mean
pretest–posttest design

maturation
history
testing effect
instrumentation effect
mortality

EXERCISES

1. What are the major reasons why a researcher does not want subjects to select the group in which they will be?

2. What are some of the problems associated with matching?

3. What is the selection by maturation effect? Give an example.

4. How can history affect research results?

5. Give an example of how history could affect research results.

6. What is the difference between history and maturation?

7. What is the regression effect? Give an example.

8. What is testing bias? Give an example.

9. What is an instrumentation bias? Give an example.

10. What is the difference between internal and external validity?

11. Can you have internal validity without external validity?

THE SIMPLE EXPERIMENT

OUTLINE

Overview

Causality: The simple experiment's purpose
The logic of causality

Basic terminology
Hypotheses
Administering the independent variable
The experimental and control groups
Collecting the dependent variable
The statistical significance decision
Summary of the "ideal simple experiment"

Errors in determining whether results are statistically significant
Type I errors
Type II errors
Summary of the effects of statistical considerations on designing the simple experiment

Nonstatistical considerations
External validity versus power
Construct validity versus power
Ethics versus power
Ethics versus the simple experiment

Analyzing data from the simple experiment
The problem: You can't know what you want to know
Estimating what you want to know
Comparing sample means
Inferential statistics: Judging the accuracy of estimates
Questions raised by results

Concluding remarks

The case of the blood-stained mansion

Main points

Key terms

Exercises

OVERVIEW

In this chapter, you'll learn the easiest way to establish that a treatment causes an effect—the simple experiment. You'll start by learning what a simple experiment is and how it works its magic. Next, you'll see why knowing how the simple experiment works will help you make intelligent decisions about how to conduct your experiment. Then, you'll examine the tough decisions involved in planning a simple experiment: making trade-offs among ethics, construct validity, external validity, and internal validity. Finally, you'll learn how to analyze the results of a simple experiment.

CAUSALITY: THE SIMPLE EXPERIMENT'S PURPOSE

The purpose of the simple experiment is to test whether a treatment causes an effect. The simple experiment's purpose is not to describe what happens but to explain why things happen.

The Logic of Causality

To determine that a treatment causes an effect, you must create a situation where you show that the treatment comes before the effect, that the effect occurs after the treatment is introduced, and that nothing but the treatment is responsible for the effect. If you were doing a chemistry experiment, you could show that heat caused a reaction by keeping everything except the heat constant, systematically varying the heat, and then observing a change in the behavior of the molecules after you increased the heat. The ideal for doing a psychological experiment to demonstrate causality would be to find two identical groups of subjects, treat them identically except that only one group gets the treatment, test them under identical conditions, and then compare the behavior of the two groups.

The Variability Problem

Clearly, you can't create this ideal situation. You can't find two identical groups of subjects. Furthermore, you can't test all your subjects under absolutely identical conditions. Because you give your treatment and no-treatment groups different instructions or manipulations, you usually have to test them separately—either in different rooms or at different times. But even if you could test them at the same time, in the same room, the two groups of subjects would still be sitting in different chairs.

What are the implications of the fact that groups can't be identical and different groups can't be tested under identical conditions? It means that if you see a difference between your treatment and no-treatment groups, you have to accept the possibility that this difference may be due to nontreatment factors.

If You Can't Eliminate Variability, Account for It

Since you can't completely eliminate the possibility that the difference between your groups is due to nontreatment factors, you'll have to settle for the next best thing: determining how unlikely this possibility is. If you could show that it's very unlikely that nontreatment variables are responsible for the group differences, then you could be confident that the difference between groups is due, at least in part, to the treatment. You might be wrong occasionally, but you'd have the percentages with you.

How can you set up a situation that allows you to determine the odds against the difference between groups being due to nontreatment factors? Use **independent random assignment:** randomly determining, for each individual subject, whether or not that subject gets the treatment. For example, you might flip a coin for each subject. If the coin comes up heads, the subject gets the treatment; if the coin comes up tails, the subject doesn't get the treatment.

The Advantages of Turning Variability into Random Variability What are the benefits of independent random assignment? First, by assigning subjects on the basis of a coin flip (or a random numbers table, see Box 5-1), you guarantee that treatment subjects and no-treatment subjects would differ systematically in only one way—the treatment.

BOX 5-1 Randomly Assigning Subjects to Two Groups

STEP 1: On the top of a sheet of paper, make two columns. Title the first "Control Group" and the second "Experimental Group." Under each group's name, draw a line for each subject you will need. Thus, if you were planning to use eight subjects (four in each group), you would draw four lines under each group name.

Control Group	**Experimental Group**
———	———
———	———
———	———
———	———

STEP 2: Turn to a random numbers table, like the one below. Roll a die to determine which column in the table you will use.

Random Numbers Table

line/ col.	1	2	3	4	5	6
1	10480	15011	01536	02011	81647	69179
2	22368	46573	25595	85393	30995	89198
3	24130	48360	22527	97265	76393	64809
4	42167	93093	06243	61680	07856	16376
5	37570	39975	81837	76656	06121	91782
6	77921	06907	11008	42751	27756	53498
7	99562	72905	56420	69994	98872	31016
8	96301	91977	05463	07972	18876	20922

STEP 3: Assign the first number in the column to the first space under Control Group, the second number to the second space, and so on. When you've filled all the spaces for the control group, place the next number under the first space under Experimental Group and continue until you've filled all the spaces. Thus, if you rolled a "5", you would start in the fifth column and your sheet of paper would look like this:

Control Group	Experimental Group
81674	06121
30995	27756
76393	98872
07856	18876

STEP 4: At the end of each control group score, write down a "C". At the end of each experimental group score, write down an "E". In this example, our sheet would now look like this:

Control Group	Experimental Group
81674C	06121E
30995C	27756E
76393C	98872E
07856C	18876E

STEP 5: Rank these numbers from lowest to highest. Then, on a second piece of paper, put the lowest number on the top line, the second lowest number on the next line, and so on. In this example, your page would look like this:

06121E
07856C
18876E
27756E
0995C
76393C
81647C
98872E

STEP 6: Number the top line, subject 1, the second line subject 2, and so on. The first subject who shows up will be in the condition specified on the top line, the second subject who shows up will be in the condition specified by the second line, and so forth. In this example, the first subject will be in the experimental group, the second in the control group, the third and fourth in the experimental group, the fifth, sixth, and seventh in the control group, and the eighth in the experimental group. Thus, our sheet of paper would look like this:

Subject Number 1 = 06121E
Subject Number 2 = 07856C
Subject Number 3 = 18876E
Subject Number 4 = 27756E
Subject Number 5 = 30995C
Subject Number 6 = 76393C
Subject Number 7 = 81647C
Subject Number 8 = 98872E

STEP 7: To avoid confusion, recopy your list, but make two changes. First, delete the random numbers. Second, write out experimental or control. In this example, your recopied list would look like this:

Subject Number 1 = EXPERIMENTAL
Subject Number 2 = CONTROL
Subject Number 3 = EXPERIMENTAL
Subject Number 4 = EXPERIMENTAL
Subject Number 5 = CONTROL
Subject Number 6 = CONTROL
Subject Number 7 = CONTROL
Subject Number 8 = EXPERIMENTAL

Second, you guarantee that the only other differences between groups are due to chance. Put another way, the groups are random samples of the same population: the total number of subjects who were in your study. Therefore, there are only two reasons why they might differ from one another: random sampling error and treatment. This is good news because you can use the science of random sampling error (inferential statistics) to determine the probability that the difference between your groups is due to chance. If, at the end of your study, the groups differ by more than would be expected by chance alone, then you can conclude that the difference is due to the one factor that varied systematically—the treatment. Since the science of chance is not an exact science, you can't be absolutely positive that the treatment had an effect. But you can be sure beyond a reasonable doubt.

If, on the other hand, the difference is less than would be expected by chance, you can't rule out the possibility that the difference between your groups is due to chance. Although the difference between your groups may be due to treatment, it could also be due to nontreatment variables. When the difference between your groups is less than could reasonably be expected by chance, your results are inconclusive.

BASIC TERMINOLOGY

Now that you understand the logic of random assignment, let's look at the simplest application of independent random assignment—the simple experiment. In the simple experiment, subjects are independently and randomly assigned to one of two groups, usually to either a treatment group or to a no-treatment group.

Hypotheses

Experimental Hypothesis

The simple experiment starts with an **experimental hypothesis:** a prediction that the treatment will cause an effect; that the treatment and no-treatment group will differ because of the treatment's effect. For example, you might hypothesize that full-spectrum lighting causes an improvement in mood, so that the group getting full-spectrum light will be happier than the group not getting full-spectrum light.

Null Hypothesis

The experimental hypothesis is pitted against the null hypothesis: the hypothesis that there is no evidence that the treatment has an effect, that any difference between the treatment and no-treatment groups is due to chance. Thus, the null hypothesis would be: "full spectrum lighting has no demonstrated effect on happiness."

If your experimental results show that the difference between groups is probably not due to chance, you can reject the null hypothesis. By rejecting the null hypothesis, you embrace the experimental hypothesis.

But what happens if you fail to demonstrate that the treatment has an effect? Can you say that there is no effect for full-spectrum lighting? No, you can only say that you didn't demonstrate that full-spectrum lighting causes a change in happiness. In other words, you're back to where you were before you began the study: you don't know whether or not full-spectrum lighting causes a change in happiness.

We cannot overemphasize the point that the failure to find a treatment effect doesn't mean there is no treatment effect. If you'd looked more carefully, you might have observed the effect (just as companies who conveniently fail to find a difference in quality between their brand and another brand may have found a difference had they looked more carefully). Put another way, the null hypothesis is a "maybe" hypothesis, stating that the difference between conditions may be due to chance. Obviously, saying that a difference may be due to chance is not the same as saying that a difference is not due to treatment.

Administering the Independent Variable

Once you have your hypotheses, your next step is to administer the treatment to some subjects and withhold it from others. In the experiment we've been discussing, you need to vary the amount of full-spectrum light people get. Furthermore, the amount of full-spectrum light a person gets should be independent of the individual's personal preferences. Since the level of full-spectrum light varies between subjects in the treatment condition and in the no-treatment (comparison) group, since the level of full-spectrum light varies independently of the subject's wishes, and since the level of full-spectrum lighting a subject gets is determined by independent random assignment, the level of treatment is called the **independent variable.**

The subjects who are randomly assigned to get the treatment (full-spectrum light) are called the **experimental group.** The subjects who are randomly assigned to get no treatment, the subjects who are compared with the experimental subjects, are called the **control group.**

As the terms experimental group and control group imply, you should have several subjects in each of your conditions. The more subjects, the more random assignment will thoroughly stir up and spread out nontreatment factors, making your two groups more similar before the study begins. If you are doing an experiment on a strength pill and only have two subjects—a 6'4", 280-pound offensive tackle and a 5'1", 88-pound weakling recovering from a long illness—randomization won't be able to make your groups equivalent. Thus, just as you'd want to flip a coin more than two times if you were trying to get approximately 50% heads and 50% tails, you'd use more than two subjects if you wanted to make your two groups equivalent before the study began.

The Value of Independence

Although we have noted that the experimental and control groups are groups in the sense that there are several subjects in each "group", that is the only sense in which these "groups" are groups. To conduct an experiment, you don't find two groups of subjects and then randomly assign one to be the experimental group and the other to be the control group. To see why not, suppose you were doing a study involving 10,000 janitors at a Los Angeles company and 10,000 managers at a New York company. You have 20,000 people in your experiment (one of the largest experiments in history). Then, you flip a coin and on the basis of that single coin flip, assign the L. A. janitors to no-treatment and the New York managers to treatment. Even though you have 10,000 subjects in each group, your treatment and no-treatment groups differ in a systematic way before the study begins. Your random assignment is no more successful in making your groups similar than it was when you had only two subjects. To get random assignment to equalize your groups, you need to assign each subject **independently:** individually, without regard to how previous subjects were assigned.

Even after you have assigned subjects to a condition, you don't want your control subjects to form a group nor do you want the experimental subjects to become a group. To prevent your "groups" from becoming groups, you don't test the control subjects in one group session and the experimental subjects in a separate group session. Instead, you'll probably test each subject individually.

To understand why you don't simply have two testing sessions (one for the control group and one for the experimental group), let's consider the consequences of that testing situation. First, it might allow the subjects to interact with one another. Instead of giving their own individual, independent responses, they might respond as a conforming mob. As a concrete example of the perils of letting subjects interact, imagine that you're doing an extrasensory perception (ESP) experiment. In the experimental group, all 50 subjects correctly guessed that the coin would turn up heads. In the control group, all 50 subjects incorrectly guessed that the coin would turn up tails. If each subject had made his or her decision independently, the results would certainly defy chance. However, if all the experimental group members talked to one another and made a group decision, they weren't acting as 50 individual subjects, but as one. In that case, the results wouldn't be as impressive: Since all 50 experimental subjects acted as 1, the odds of them correctly guessing the coin flip were the same as the odds of one person correctly guessing a coin flip: 50–50.

The previous example shows what can happen if subjects are tested in groups and allowed to freely interact, yet interaction can disturb independence even when group discussion is prohibited. Subjects may influence one another through inadvertent outcries (laughs, exclamations like ''Oh no!'') or through subtle nonverbal cues. In our happiness experiment, one sobbing subject might cause the entire experimental group to be unhappy. Consequently, we might falsely conclude that the unhappiness must be due to the treatment. If, on the other hand, we test subjects individually, the unhappy subject's behavior doesn't affect anyone else's responses. (For similar reasons, valid public opinion polls ask each person individually rather than asking a group of people for their opinions).

The second reason for not testing your groups as a group is that such testing causes the inevitable, random differences between testing sessions to become systematic effects. For example, suppose that when the experimental group was tested, there was a distraction in the hall, but there was no such distraction while the control group was tested. Like the treatment, this distraction was presented to all the experimental group subjects but to none of the control group subjects. As a result, if the distraction did have an effect, its effect might be mistaken for a treatment effect. However, if subjects were tested individually, it's very unlikely that only the experimental subjects would be exposed to distractions. Instead, distractions would have a chance to even out so that both groups would be affected by these factors to a similar extent.

But what if you're sure you won't have distractions? Even then, the sessions will differ in ways unrelated to the treatment. If you manage to test the subjects at the same time, you'll have to use different experimenters and different experimental rooms. If you manage to use the same experimenter and room, you'll have to test the groups at different times. So, if you find a significant difference between your two groups, is the effect due to differences on the treatment variable or due to differences in the two treatment sessions (an experimenter effect, a time of day effect, etc.)? To avoid these problems in interpreting your results, make sure that the treatment is the only factor that systematically varies. In other words, test subjects individually or in small groups so that random differences among treatment conditions can even out.

Collecting the Dependent Variable

After you have given your subjects varying levels of full-spectrum light and maintained each subject's independence, you now need to measure their happiness. You know that each person's happiness will vary depending on the individual's personality and you hope that their happiness will also depend on the level of light you gave them (the independent variable). Therefore, happiness is your **dependent variable.** Since the dependent variable is what the subject does that you measure, the dependent variable is often called the dependent measure. Using this term for the subject's behavior (dependent measure) may keep you from confusing it with the term for treatment (independent variable).

BOX 5-2   Key Terms of the Simple Experiment

Experimental Hypothesis: A prediction that the treatment will cause an effect.

Null Hypothesis: The hypothesis that there is no evidence that the treatment has an effect.

Independent Variable: The treatment variable.

Dependent Variable: The subject's behavior that is measured because the experimenter hopes it will be affected by the independent variable.

Experimental Group: The subjects who are randomly assigned to get the treatment.

Control Group: The subjects who are randomly assigned to get no treatment.

After measuring the dependent variable, you'll want to compare the happiness scores for the experimental group to the happiness scores for the control group. One way to make this comparison is to subtract the average of the scores for the control (comparison) group from the average of the scores in the experimental group.

The Statistical Significance Decision

Statistically Significant Results

Unfortunately, knowing how much the groups differ doesn't tell you how much of an effect the treatment had. After all, the entire difference between groups may be due to random sampling error. To determine the probability that the difference is not due exclusively to chance extraneous variables, you need to use statistics: the science of chance.

If, by using statistics, you find that the difference between your groups is greater than could be expected if only chance were at work, then your results are **statistically significant.** The term means that you're sure, beyond a reasonable doubt, that the results were not a fluke.

What is a reasonable doubt? Usually researchers want to be at least 95% sure that the treatment is responsible for the difference. In other words, they want less than a 5% chance that the results are due solely to random sampling error. Therefore, if you found a statistically significant effect in your lighting experiment, you'd conclude that your independent variable caused a change in the scores on your dependent variable and you'd be relatively confident that if you repeated your study, you'd get the same pattern of results.

Realize that statistically significant results are only significant in a statistical sense. Statistical significance does not mean that the results are significant in the sense of being large. Even a very small difference may be statistically reliable. For example, if you flipped a coin 5,000 times and it came up heads 52% of the time, this difference would be statistically significant (not due to chance).

Nor does statistical significance mean that the results are significant in the sense of being important. If you have a silly hypothesis, you may have results that are statistically significant but otherwise meaningless.

Null Results

But what if you can't reject the hypothesis that the difference between your groups is due to chance? Then, you have failed to reject the null hypothesis. Therefore, your results would not be described as not significant, or **null results.**

The terms "null results" and "not significant" accurately describe the inconclusiveness of these findings. With null results, you don't know whether the treatment has an effect that you failed to find or whether the treatment has no effect.

The situation is analogous to a "not guilty verdict": Is the defendant innocent or did the prosecutor present a poor case? Often, a person is acquitted more through lack of evidence against her than from any overwhelming proof of innocence.

Despite the fact that null results neither confirm nor deny that the treatment had an effect, people commonly abuse null results. They sometimes do this by arguing that null results secretly confirm their suspicions. For example, they may say "The difference between my groups shows that the treatment had an effect, (even though the difference is not significant)." Reread this statement because you're sure to hear it again: It's the most commonly stated contradiction in psychology. People making this statement are really saying "The difference is due to the treatment, even though I've found no evidence that the difference isn't simply due to chance."

Some people make the opposite mistake, believing that null results disconfirm their suspicions. That is, some people falsely conclude that null results definitely establish that the treatment had no effect. This is a mistake because it overlooks the difficulty of finding and proving that a treatment has an effect.

To emphasize that not finding something does not mean that it doesn't exist, let's consider null results in the context of a fingerprint investigation. In 70% of all fingerprint investigations, investigators don't find a single identifiable print at the murder scene—not even the victim's. Thus, the failure to find the suspect's fingerprints at the scene is hardly proof that the suspect is innocent. For basically the same reasons, the failure to find an effect is not proof that there is no effect.

Summary of the "Ideal Simple Experiment"

Thus far, we have said that the simple experiment gives you an easy way to determine "what causes it." If you can randomly assign subjects to either a treatment or no-treatment group (and you often can't for ethical or practical reasons), all you have to do is find out whether your results are statistically significant. If they are, then your treatment had an effect. No method allows you to account for the effects of nontreatment variables with as little effort as random assignment.

ERRORS IN DETERMINING WHETHER RESULTS ARE STATISTICALLY SIGNIFICANT

Unfortunately, however, you may make errors in accounting for chance. Although statistics will allow you to predict chance much of the time, you can't totally predict chance all of the time.

If you underestimate the role of chance, you may make a **Type I error:** mistaking a chance difference for a treatment effect. Examples of Type I errors in nonpsychology settings would include convicting an innocent person (mistaking a series of coincidences as evidence of guilt), or making a "false positive" medical diagnosis, such as telling someone she was pregnant when she wasn't or diagnosing someone as having AIDS when she doesn't.

Type I Errors

Preventing Type I Errors

What can you do about Type I errors? Although you can't completely eliminate them, you can decide what risk you're willing to take. Usually, experimenters decide that they're going to take a 5% risk of making a Type I error. They feel that 20 to 1 are great odds. But why take even that risk? Why not take less than a 1% risk?

To understand why not, imagine you're betting on someone who's flipping a coin. She always calls heads, you pick tails. She's winning most of the flips because she's cheating. Let's suppose that you continue betting until you have statistical proof that she's cheating. You don't want to make the Type I error of attributing her results to cheating when they're really due to luck. At what point would you stop betting? If you wanted to be absolutely 100% sure, you'd never stop because any kind of lucky streak is possible. If you wanted to be 99.9% sure, you'd bet for quite a while. But if you only wanted to be 90% sure, you wouldn't have to bet very long.

The point of this example is that in trying to be very, very sure that an effect is due to treatment and not to chance, you may make a **Type II error:** overlooking a genuine treatment difference because you think it might be due to chance. Examples of Type II errors in nonpsychological situations would include letting a criminal go free (mistakenly attributing the evidence as a set of coincidences because the jury wanted to be sure beyond **any** doubt), or making a "false negative" medical diagnosis, such as failing to detect that one person was pregnant or another had AIDS.

Type II Errors

As you can see, you may have to make trade-offs between the risk you're willing to take of a Type I and Type II error. You want to be cautious not to say that your two groups differed because of the treatment when in fact they differed only by chance. (Just as you wouldn't want to be so reckless as to accuse someone of cheating merely because 6 of 10 coin flips came up heads). However, you don't want to be so cautious that you fail to detect real treatment differences. In other words, you want your study to have **power:** the ability to find differences or, put another way, the ability to avoid making Type II errors.

Preventing Type II Errors by Increasing Power

Unfortunately, many undergraduate research projects are doomed from the start because they lack power. They're designed so that even if the treatment has an effect, the study won't find this effect significant. Fortunately, however, you can improve your study's power—and do so without increasing your risk of a Type I error.

To increase your study's power, you must reduce the likelihood that chance differences will hide your treatment effect. Two ways of doing that are

1. to reduce the effects of random error and
2. to increase the size of your treatment effect.

Reducing Random Error   One of the most obvious ways to reduce the effects of random error is to reduce the potential sources of random error. The major sources of random variability are differences (variations) among testing situations, unreliable dependent measures, differences (variations) among subjects, and sloppy coding of data.

1.   STANDARDIZE AND USE RELIABLE MEASURES. Since a major source of random error is variation in the testing situation, you can reduce it by standardizing your experiment—keeping the testing environment and the experimental procedures as constant as possible. Therefore, to improve power, you might want the noise level, illumination level, temperature, room, and time of day to be the same for each subject. Furthermore, you'd want to treat all your experimental group subjects identically and all your control group subjects identically. Finally, you'd also like to use a reliable and sensitive dependent measure. As we discussed in Chapter 3, some measures are less affected by random error than others.

The desire for standardization and reliable measures is responsible for some psychologists' love of instruments and the laboratory. In the lab's carefully regulated conditions, experimenters can create powerful and sensitive experiments.

Other experimenters (as you will see in Chapter 8), eschew the laboratory setting for real-world settings. The price they pay for leaving the laboratory is that variables they could control in the lab vary randomly in the field. These variables, free to vary wildly, create a jungle of random error that may hide real effects. Because of the variability in real-world settings, the difficulties of standardizing administration of the independent variable, and the difficulties of using sensitive, reliable measures in the field, even die-hard field experimenters may first look for a significant treatment effect in the lab before venturing out to find the treatment's effect in the field.

2.   USE A HOMOGENOUS GROUP OF SUBJECTS. Between subject differences may hide treatment effects. Even if the treatment effect is large, you may overlook it, mistakenly ascribing the difference between your groups to the fact that your subjects are years apart in age and worlds apart in terms of environment and genetic heritage.

To prevent the differences between subjects from obscuring treatment effects, select subjects who are similar to one another. For instance, select subjects who are the same sex, same age, and have the same IQ. Or, use rats as subjects. With rats, you can select subjects that have grown up in the same environment, have similar genes, and even have the same birthday. By studying homogeneous subjects under standardized situations, rat researchers can detect very subtle treatment effects.

3.   CAREFUL CODING. Obviously, sloppy coding of the data can sabotage the most sensitively designed study. Why do we mention this obvious fact? First, many undergraduates are guilty of sloppy coding. Although sloppiness doesn't necessarily bias the results, it will probably introduce random error that will rob you of power. Therefore, check and recheck the coding of your data. Second, careful coding is a cheap way to increase power. If you increase power by using animal subjects, you may lose the ability to generalize to humans. If you increase power by using a lab experiment, you may lose the ability to generalize to real-world settings. But careful coding costs you nothing except a little time.

Balancing out Random Error   Thus far, we've talked about the most obvious way to reduce the effects of random error—reduce the sources of random error. But there is another way. You can reduce the effects of random error by giving random error more chances to balance out. As you know, random error balances out in the long run. In the short run, you might get 5 heads in 6 coin flips, but in the long run, you'll end up with almost as many tails as heads.

To take advantage of the fact that random error balances out in the long run, use more subjects. If you use 5 subjects in each group, your groups probably won't be very equivalent before the experiment begins. However, if you use 40 subjects in each group, your groups will be fairly equivalent before the study begins. Consequently, a treatment effect that would be dismissed as due to chance in 5-subject groups, might be statistically significant if you used 30 subjects per group.

Bigger Effects are Easier to Find   Until now, we've talked about increasing power by making our experiment more sensitive to small differences. Specifically, we've talked about reducing the amount of random error or giving random error a chance to even out so that it won't obscure our treatment effect. We've left out the most obvious way to increase our experiment's power: increase the size of the effect.

Your best bet for increasing the size of the effect is to give the control group subjects a very low level of the independent variable and the experimental group a very high level of the independent variable. Your reasoning would be that if the treatment has an effect, the more treatment, the more effect you should get. Hence, to have adequate power in the lighting experiment, rather than giving the control group one hour of blue light and the experimental group two hours, you might give the control group no blue light and the experimental group 6 hours of blue light.

BOX 5-3 Ways to Increase Power

Use Standardized Measures.

Use Reliable Measures.

Use a Homogenous Group of Subjects.

Code Data Carefully.

Balance Out Random Error by Using Many Subjects.

Increase the Size of the Effect by Giving Your Experimental and Control Groups Very Different Amounts of the Treatment.

Summary of the Effects of Statistical Considerations on Designing the Simple Experiment

You've seen that statistical considerations dictate and influence virtually every aspect of the design process. Because you can't accept the null hypothesis (you can only reject it or fail to reject it), you can't do an experiment to find out that two treatments are identical or that a treatment has no effect. The only hypotheses you can hope to support are hypotheses that the groups will differ. Statistical considerations also mandate how you should assign your subjects (independent random assignment) and how you should treat your subjects (taking care to maintain their independence).

Even when statistics are dictating what you must do, they're suggesting what you should do. To avoid making Type II errors, statistics suggest that you standardize your procedures; use sensitive and reliable dependent measures; carefully code your data; use homogeneous subjects; use many subjects; and use extreme levels of the independent variable. Yet, statistical considerations are not the only things you should consider when designing a simple experiment.

NONSTATISTICAL CONSIDERATIONS

External Validity versus Power

Many of the things you can do to improve your study's power may hurt your study's external validity. By using a lab experiment to stop unwanted variables from varying, you may have more power to find an effect. However, by preventing unwanted variables from varying you may hurt your ability to generalize your results to real life—where these unwanted variables vary. By using a homogeneous set of subjects (18-year-old, Caucasian men with IQs between 120 and 125), you reduce between-subject differences, thereby enhancing your ability to find treatment effects. However, because you used such a restricted sample, you may not be as able to generalize your results to the average American as you could have had you used a more heterogeneous sample. Finally, although using extreme levels of the independent variable might help you detect a treatment effect, it may also prevent you from determining the effect of realistic, naturally occurring levels of the treatment variable.

Construct Validity versus Power

Not only may your efforts to improve power hurt external validity, they may hurt your experiment's construct validity. For example, you might use the most reliable dependent measure rather than one that has the most construct validity.

Or, you might compromise the validity of your independent variable manipulation. For instance, to maximize your chances of getting a significant effect for full-spectrum lighting, you might give the experimental group full-spectrum lighting and make the control group an **empty control group:** a group that doesn't get any kind of treatment. Unfortunately, if you found an effect in this study, you couldn't say that it was due to the effects of the full-spectrum lighting. It could be due to some other incidental effect of the manipulation: the treatment group getting a gift (the lights) from the experimenter; getting more interaction with and attention from the experimenter (as the experimenter checks subjects to make sure they're using the lights); adopting more of a routine than the controls (using the lights every morning from 6 A.M. to 8:00 A.M.); and having higher expectations of getting better (because they have more of a sense of being helped) than the controls.

To minimize these side-effects of the treatment manipulation, you might give your control group a **placebo:** a substance or treatment that has no effect. Thus, you might expose the control group to yellow light. Furthermore, you might reduce the chances of experimenters biasing the results if you made experimenters and subjects blind: unaware of which kind of treatment the subject was getting. The use of placebos, the use of **single blinds** (where either the subject or the experimenter is blind), and the use of **double blinds** (where both the subject and the experimenter is blind) all reduce the chances that you'll obtain a significant effect. However, if you use these procedures and find a significant effect, you can be relatively confident that the treatment itself, not some side effect of it, is the cause.

Ethical considerations may conflict with your desire for power. For example, suppose you want to use extreme levels of the independent variable (food deprivation) to ensure large differences in the motivation of your animals. In that case, you need to weigh the benefits of having a powerful manipulation against ethical concerns (see Appendix A).

Ethics versus Power

Finally, you must decide whether or not you can ethically conduct a simple experiment. Although the ethical ramifications of any research must be carefully considered before it's conducted (see Chapter 13), many feel that experimental designs require extra special consideration because experiments involve administering treatments to (doing something to) volunteer subjects.

Ethics versus the Simple Experiment

     Some feel that simple experiments require even more consideration than other experimental designs because simple experiments involve administering treatments to or withholding them from volunteer subjects on the basis of random assignment. In other words, it might be wrong to either administer a treatment or to withhold it (a cure for schizophrenia) on the basis of random assignment. In short, if you or your professor don't feel that it's ethical to randomly assign volunteers to different levels of your treatment, don't use a simple experiment.

ANALYZING DATA FROM THE SIMPLE EXPERIMENT

To understand how you're going to analyze your data, remember why you did the simple experiment. You did it to find out whether the treatment would have an effect on your subjects. More specifically, you wanted to know the answer to the hypothetical question: "If I had put all my subjects in the experimental condition, would they have scored differently than if I'd put all of them in the control condition?" To answer this question, you need to know the averages of two populations:

The Problem: You Can't Know What You Want to Know

1. what the average score on the dependent measure would have been if all your subjects had been in the control group and;
2. what the average score on the dependent measure would have been if all your subjects had been in the experimental group.

     Unfortunately, you can't directly measure both of these populations. If you put all your subjects in the control condition, then you don't know how they would have scored in the experimental condition; if you put all your subjects in the experimental condition, you don't know how they would have scored in the control condition.

Since you can't directly measure both of these populations, you estimate them by drawing two independent random samples from the total number of subjects participating in your study. One sample gets the treatment, the other doesn't. From the

Estimating What You Want to Know

sample that gets the treatment, you estimate what the average score would have been if all of your subjects had received the treatment. From the sample that did not get the treatment, you estimate what the average score would have been if all of your subjects had been in the control condition.

Calculating Sample Means

Even though only half your subjects were in the experimental group, you'll assume that the experimental group average is a good estimate of what the average score would have been if all your subjects had been in the experimental group. The same is true for the control group. Therefore, the first step in analyzing your data will be to calculate an average for each group.

Usually, the average you calculate is the **mean:** the result of adding up all the scores and then dividing by the number of scores. After you've collected your data, add up all the control subjects' scores on the dependent measure, then divide by the number of control group subjects to get the control group mean. Next, calculate the experimental group mean.

Comparing Sample Means

Once you have your two sample means, you can compare them. If the treatment had no effect, then your two sample means should be similar because they're samples from the same population. The two samples should resemble each other in the same way that two independent random samples of any other population (citizens of New York, white-collar workers, etc.) should resemble one another.

But even if your two samples come from the same population, your sample means will rarely be identical. One of the hazards of sampling a population rather than measuring the entire population is that you'll probably have some sampling error. For one reason or another, your sample may not perfectly represent the populations from which they were drawn. Perhaps if you'd started in a different place in the random number table, you would have drawn more accurate samples and your sample means would be identical. Because of the possibility of sampling error, you can't conclude that your population means differ simply because your sample means differ.

Inferential Statistics: Judging the Accuracy of Estimates

Anyone can tell you that two random samples of the same population may differ from one another because of sampling error. But you need to know more about sampling error than the mere fact that sampling error exists. You need to know enough to decide whether or not the difference between your sample means could easily be the result of sampling error. If you find that the difference is probably not due to sampling error, you can conclude that the sample means differ because the population means actually differ, i.e., your treatment had an effect.

To make this decision, you must rely on **sampling statistics** (also called **inferential statistics**): the science of inferring the characteristics of a population from a sample. Just as the science of anatomy allows an archaeologist to infer the characteristics of a dinosaur from a few bones, sampling statistics allows you to make inferences about a population mean from a sample mean.

Estimating the Accuracy of Individual Sample Means

Let's imagine that you want to know how close your sample means are to the true population means. If you knew how accurate each of your sample means were, you could decide whether or not the difference between your groups was due to sampling error. For example, suppose you knew that the control group mean was within one unit of its population mean and the experimental group mean was within one unit of its population mean. Then you'd know that if your groups actually differed by 10 units, the two populations differ. If, on the other hand, the groups differ by fewer than two units, the difference could easily be due to sampling error.

Consider Population Variability: The Value of the Standard Deviation   But how can you determine how close your sample means are to the true population means? Obviously, one factor that would affect how well a random sample reflects its population is the amount of variability in the population. If there is no variability in the population (everyone in the population scores a "5"), then all scores in the population will be the same as the mean. Consequently, there will be no sampling error because every random sample will always have a mean of 5.

However, if scores in a population vary considerably (e.g., ranging anywhere from 0 to 1000), then independent random samples from that population can be very inaccurate. Different samples may have very different sample means. Therefore, to know how accurate you can expect each of your samples to be (and thus how likely they are to vary due to sampling error alone), it would be nice to have an index of the variability of scores within a population.

The ideal index of variability is the population's **standard deviation:** a measure of the extent to which individual scores deviate from the population mean. Unfortunately, to get that index, you have to know the population mean (for the control condition, the average of the scores if all the subjects had been in the control condition; for the experimental condition, the average of the scores if all the subjects had been in the experimental condition). Obviously, you don't know the population mean for either the control or experimental condition—that's what you're trying to find out!

You can't calculate the population standard deviation, but you can estimate it by looking at the variability of scores within your samples. In fact, by following Table 5-1, you can estimate what the standard deviation would have been if everyone had been in the control group (by looking at variability within the control group) and what the standard deviation would have been if all your subjects had been in the experimental group (by looking at variability within the experimental group).

One reason the standard deviation is a particularly valuable index of variability is that many populations can be completely described simply by knowing the standard deviation and the mean. You probably already know that the mean is valuable for describing many populations. You know that, for many populations, most scores will be near the mean and that as many scores will be above the mean as below it.

What you may not know is that for most of these distributions, you can specify precisely what percentage of scores will be within a certain number of standard deviations from the mean. For instance, you can say that 68% will be within 1 standard

---

TABLE 5-1   How to Compute a Standard Deviation

	STEP 2	
STEP 1	**(subtract**	**STEP 3**
(calculate	**scores**	**(square**
mean)	**from mean)**	**differences)**

108	− 105 = 3	× 3 = 9
104	− 105 = − 1	× − 1 = + 1
104	− 105 = − 1	× − 1 = + 1
104	− 105 = − 1	× − 1 = + 1
(420/4 = 105)		

STEP 4: **Sum These Squared Differences to Get Sum of Squares (SS) (= 12)**

STEP 5: **Get Variance by Dividing SS (12) by One Less Than the Number of Scores (12/3 = 4)**

STEP 6: **Get Standard Deviation by Taking Square Root of Variance ($\sqrt{4} = 2$)**

---

deviation of the mean, 95% will be within 2 standard deviations of the mean, and 99% of the scores will be within 3 standard deviations of the mean. If the population's scores are distributed in this manner, the population is said to be normally distributed.

As the term "normally distributed" suggests, many populations are normally distributed: from grades on a class test to the heights of American men. Because normally distributed populations are common, plotting the distribution of scores in a population will often produce a **normal curve**: a bell-shaped, symmetrical curve that has its center at the mean (see Figure 5-1).

Obviously, it's handy to be able to summarize an entire distribution of scores with just two numbers: the mean, which gives you the center of a normal distribution and the standard deviation, which gives you an index of the width of the distribution. It's comforting to know that 68% of the scores will be within a standard deviation of the mean and that 95% of the scores will be within two standard deviations of the mean. But the standard deviation has more uses than merely describing a population.

You can use the standard deviation to make inferences about the population mean. For example, suppose you don't know the population mean, but you know that the population is normally distributed and that the standard deviation is 2.00. You know that the mean is within 1 standard deviation of 68% of the scores and within 2 standard deviations of 95% of the scores. Therefore, if you randomly selected a single score from that population, there'd be a 68% chance that the population mean

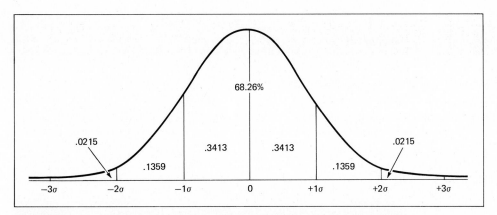

FIGURE 5-1 Different Proportions of Area under the Normal Curve within the Limits of the Various σ Units on the Base Line

would be within 2 units (1 standard deviation) of that score, and a 95% chance that the population mean would be within 4 units (2 standard deviations) of that score.

Consider Sample Size: The Role of the Standard Error Of course, to estimate your control group's population mean, you'd use more than one score. One obvious reason for using a sample mean based on several scores is that the bigger your independent random sample, the better your random sample will tend to be—and the better your sample, the closer its mean should be to the population mean.

Because you use more than one score to calculate the sample mean and because the number of scores you use affects the accuracy of your sample mean, the standard deviation is not an adequate index of your sample mean's accuracy. You need an index that includes the two factors that influence the degree to which a sample mean may differ from its population mean: population variability and sample size. Specifically, you need the **standard error of the estimate of the population mean:** an index of the degree to which random sampling error may cause the sample mean to be an inaccurate estimate of the population mean.

The standard error (of the estimate of the population mean) equals the standard deviation divided by the square root of the number of subjects in the sample. Thus, if the standard deviation was 40 and you had 4 people in your sample, the standard error would be 20 ($40/\sqrt{4} = 40/2 = 20$).

What does the standard error tell you? Clearly, the larger the standard error, the more likely a sample mean will misrepresent the population mean. But does this random error contaminate all samples equally or does it heavily infest some samples while leaving others untouched? Ideally, you'd like to know precisely how random error is distributed across various samples. You want to know what percentage of samples will be substantially biased by random error so that you know what chance your sample mean has of being accurate.

Using the Standard Error Fortunately, you can know how sample means are distributed. As statisticians have shown by drawing numerous independent random samples from known, normally distributed populations, the distribution of sample means will be normally distributed. Most (68%) of the sample means will be within 1 standard error of the population mean, 95% will be within 2 standard errors of the population mean, and 99% will be within 3 standard errors of the population mean. Therefore, if your standard error is 1.00, you know that there's a 68% chance that the population mean is within 1.0 point of your sample mean, a 95% chance that it's within 2.0 points of your sample mean, and a 99% chance that it's within 3.0 points of your sample mean.

You've seen that you can calculate the accuracy of your estimate of the population mean (your sample mean) when the population is normally distributed. You do this by taking advantage of the fact that sample means will follow a very well defined distribution: the normal distribution. But what if the population isn't normally distributed?

Even then, as the **central limit theorem** states: the distribution of sample means will be normally distributed if your samples are large enough (30 or more subjects). If you take numerous large samples from the same population, your sample means will not differ from one another because of the shape of the underlying population. The sample means will differ from one another for only one reason—random sampling error. Since random sampling error is normally distributed, your distribution of sampling means will be normally distributed—regardless of the shape of the underlying population. Consequently, if you take a large random sample from any population, you can use the normal curve to estimate how closely your sample mean reflects the population mean.

Estimating Accuracy of Your Estimate of the Difference between Population Means

Because you know that sample means are normally distributed, you can determine how likely it is that a sample mean is within a certain distance of the population mean. But in the simple experiment, you aren't trying to estimate whether a single sample is an accurate reflection of a certain population. Instead, you're trying to find out whether the two samples come from the same population or represent two different populations. Your focus is not on the individual sample means, but on the difference between the two means. Thus, rather than knowing how sample means from the same population are distributed, you'd like to know how differences between sample means (drawn from the same population) are distributed.

How Differences Are Distributed: The Large Sample Case   Fortunately, statisticians know how differences between sample means drawn from the same population are distributed. Statisticians have repeated the following steps thousands of times: take two random samples from the same population, calculate the means of the two samples (group 1 and group 2), subtract the group 1 mean from the group 2 mean. What do they conclude would happen in the long run (if these steps were repeated an infinite number of times)?

First, the average of all these differences would equal 0. This follows from what you know about estimating a single mean. You know that the mean of sample means would (in the long run) be the same as the population mean. Therefore, the mean of the group 1 means would be the same as the mean of the group 2 means:

Both would equal the population mean. Consequently, the average difference between them would be 0.

Second, the differences would be normally distributed. Since they're subtracting scores coming from one normal distribution (the distribution of sample means for a specific population) from scores that come from the same normal distribution (the distribution of sample means from the same population), it should not surprise you that your final distribution would have a mean of zero and be normally distributed.

Third, the standard for the distribution of differences between means is not the standard deviation or the standard error, but the **standard error of difference between means.** The standard error of the difference between means is larger than the standard error of the mean. This fact shouldn't surprise you because the difference between sample means is influenced by random sampling error that affects the control group mean and by the random sampling error that affects the experimental group mean. That is, the difference between sample means from the same population could differ because the first sample mean was inaccurate, the second sample mean was inaccurate, or both were inaccurate. The formula for the standard error of the difference reflects the fact that this standard error is the result of measuring two unstable estimates. Specifically, the formula is:

$$\sqrt{\frac{S_1^2}{N_1} + \frac{S_2^2}{N_2}}$$

where S_1 is the estimate of the population standard deviation for Group 1 and S_2 is the estimate of the population standard deviation for Group 2; N_1 is the number of subjects in Group 1 and N_2 is the number of subjects in Group 2.

We know that with large enough samples, the distribution of differences between means would be normally distributed. Thus, if the standard error of the difference were 1.0, we would know that 68% of the time, the true difference would be within 1.0 of the difference we observed; that 95% of the time, the true difference would be within 2.0 of the difference we observed; and that 99% of the time, the true difference would be within 3.0 of the difference we observed. Therefore, if we observed a difference of 5.0, we could be very confident that the difference between the group's populations was not 0. In other words, we could be confident that the groups are samples from different populations: that if all the subjects had received the treatment they'd have scored differently than if they'd all been in the control group. If, however, we observed a difference of 1.0, we realize that such a difference might well reflect random sampling error rather than the groups coming from different populations. Therefore, with a difference of 1.0 and a standard error of 1.0, we could not conclude that the treatment had an effect.

How Differences Are Distributed: The Small Sample Case   Although the distribution of differences would be normally distributed if you used large enough samples, your particular experiment probably won't use enough subjects. Therefore, you must rely on a more conservative distribution, especially designed for when you have small samples and don't know the population's standard deviation: the *t* distribution. Actually,

---

BOX 5-4 Terms to Keep Straight

Variance: The standard deviation squared.

Standard Deviation: A measure of the extent to which individual scores deviate from the population mean. Could also be used as an index of the extent to which **a** randomly selected **score** could be expected to differ from its population's mean.

Standard Error of the Mean: An index of the extent to which the mean of several randomly selected scores **(a sample mean)** could be expected to differ from its population's mean.

Standard Error of the Difference: An index of the degree to which **two sample means** representing the same population could be expected to differ from one another.

---

the t distribution is a family of distributions. The bigger your sample size, the more the t distribution you use will approximate the normal distribution.

The t distribution you'll use depends on how many degrees of freedom (df), you have. To calculate your degrees of freedom, simply subtract 2 from the number of subjects in your experiment. For example, if you had 32 subjects, your df would be 30 ($32 - 2 = 30$).

Executing the t Test   Now that you understand the basic logic behind the t test, you're ready to do one. Start by subtracting the means of your two groups. Then, divide this difference by the standard error of the difference. The number you get is called a t score. Thus, $t = $ Difference between means/standard error of the difference.

BOX 5-5 The *t*-Test for Equal Sized Groups

$$t = \frac{M_1 - M_2}{\text{Standard Error of the Difference}}$$

Where the standard error of the difference equals:

$$\sqrt{\frac{S_1^2}{N_1} + \frac{S_2^2}{N_2}}$$

Where S_1 equals the standard deviation for Group 1 and S_2 equals the standard deviation for Group 2.

Once you have your *t* score and your degrees of freedom, you refer to a *t* table to see whether your *t* score is significant. Thus, if you used 32 subjects, you'd look at the *t* table in Appendix E under the row labelled 30 *df*. If the number in the table is larger than the absolute value of your *t* score, your results are not statistically significant at the .05 level. If the number in the table is smaller than the absolute value of your *t* score, then your results are statistically significant at the .05 level: there's less than a 5% chance that the difference between your groups is solely due to chance. Consequently, you can be reasonably sure that your treatment had an effect.

Assumptions of the t Test   As with any statistical test, the *t* test requires that you make certain assumptions. First, because the *t* test compares the two sample means, it requires that you have data that allow you to compute meaningful means. You can't have ranked data because you can't meaningfully average ranks (two groups might have the same average rank on a test yet differ enormously in terms of their average score on the test). Nor can you have qualitative data. (Try averaging scores when 1 = nodded head, 2 = gazed intently and 3 = blinked eyes—what does an average of 1.8 indicate?) In short, to do the *t* test you must be able to assume that you have either interval scale or ratio scale data.

Second, since the *t* test is based on estimating random sampling error, it requires that you independently and randomly assigned each subject to a group. If this requirement is violated, the results of the *t* test are worthless.

In addition to these two pivotal assumptions, the *t* test makes some less vital assumptions. First, it assumes that the population from which your sample means was drawn is normally distributed. The reason for this assumption is that if the populations are normally distributed, then the sample means will tend to be normally distributed. This assumption is usually nothing to worry about for two reasons. First, most distributions are normally distributed. Second, as the central limit theorem states, with large enough samples, the distribution of sample means will be normally distributed, no matter what.

The second assumption is that scores in both conditions will have the same variances. This is not a very strict assumption. If you have unequal variances, it won't seriously affect the results of your *t* test, as long as one variance isn't more than 2½ times larger than the other.

BOX 5-6   Assumptions of the *t* Test

You have either interval scale or ratio scale data.

You independently and randomly assigned each subject to a group.

The population from which your sample means was drawn is normally distributed.

The scores in both conditions have the same variances.

Questions Raised by Results

Obviously, if you violate key assumptions of the *t* test, your results raise very serious questions. But even if you don't violate any of these assumptions, your results will raise questions—and this is true whether or not your results are statistically significant.

Questions Raised by Nonsignificant Results

Nonsignificant results raise questions because the null hypothesis can't be proved. Therefore, null results inspire questions about the experiment's power, questions such as:

1. Did you have enough subjects?
2. Were the subjects homogeneous enough?
3. Was the experiment sufficiently standardized?
4. Were the data coded carefully?
5. Was the dependent variable reliable enough?
6. Did you choose the wrong levels of the independent variable? In other words, would you have found an effect, if you had chosen two different levels?

Questions Raised by Significant Results

If the absolute value of your *t* score is greater than the tabled value, your effect is statistically significant. Since you found an effect for your treatment, you don't have to ask any questions about your study's power. But that doesn't mean that your results don't raise any questions. On the contrary, your significant effect raises many questions.

Some of these questions may be the result of making trade-offs to obtain adequate power. For example, if you used an empty control group or failed to use double-blind procedures, does your significant effect represent a placebo effect or an experimenter effect, rather than an effect of the treatment? Or, if you used an extremely homogenous group of subjects, do your results apply to other kinds of subjects? Or, if the experiment was very standardized, would the results occur in a less standardized, more naturalistic setting? Or, if you chose two extreme levels of your independent variable, would you have obtained the same pattern of results if you'd used more realistic levels of the independent variable?

Some questions raised by significant results are the inevitable results of the limits of the simple experiment—only being able to study two levels of a single variable. Therefore, with any simple experiment, you might ask to what extent do the results apply to levels of the independent variable that were not tested? To what extent could other variables modify the treatment effect?

CONCLUDING REMARKS

Clearly, the results of a simple experiment always raise questions. Results from any research study raise questions, but many of the questions raised by the results of the simple experiment are the direct or indirect result of the fact that the simple experiment is limited to studying two levels of a single variable. If the logic of the simple experiment could be expanded to designs that would study several levels of several independent variables at the same time, these designs could answer many of the questions raised by the simple experiment. Fortunately, as you'll see in the next two chapters, the logic of the results of a simple experiment can be extended to produce experimental designs that will allow you to answer several research questions with a single experiment.

THE CASE OF THE BLOOD-STAINED MANSION

WATSON: Strange business, eh, Holmes? What do you make of it? I'm referring to the ax murder at the Burruss mansion, of course. They found blood everywhere—blood of the victim and also blood of the assailant. The whole family is under suspicion by the police, pending the blood tests. Of course, the blood tests may clear the whole lot. What's your guess, old man?

HOLMES: My *hypothesis* is that the blood stains will be type O, the same blood type as the victim's wife.

WATSON: Why Holmes! What a dreadful thought, that poor sweet lady. She'd have to have flown into quite a rage to get the strength to have done all of that.

HOLMES: Quite! But what would it prove if the blood stains matched?

WATSON: Well, I should say that it's quite obvious. If the blood stains matched, then she would have the same blood type as the attacker. Therefore, . . . therefore, what? Holmes, I fail to understand what that means.

HOLMES: Why the confusion, Watson?

WATSON: Well, that would prove she had the same blood type as the assailant, but many people have the same blood type. Both you and I could have that blood type. My god, Holmes, millions people in this city could have that blood type!

HOLMES: Precisely, Watson. I have stated the null hypothesis.

WATSON: I don't follow, Holmes.

HOLMES: I've stated that I expect no difference between her blood and the blood at the scene. This is a meaningless hypothesis in itself because it can never be proved. Even if both her blood and that at the scene of the crime were type O, we would have no proof that her blood was at the scene of the crime.

WATSON: So far, I understand. But why state this nothing hypothesis?

HOLMES: Elementary, my dear Watson. Think. What happens if her blood type is O and the blood of the assailant is A? My null hypothesis has been disproved. We can be sure that Mrs. Evers was not the assailant. That is what I believed all the time. In fact, Mrs. Evers is our client.

WATSON: Honestly, Holmes, why didn't you say that in the first place.

HOLMES: And waste this opportunity to instruct you? My dear chap, you know my methods.

MAIN POINTS

1. The experimental hypothesis predicts that the treatment will cause an effect.
2. The null hypothesis, on the other hand, states that the treatment will not cause an observable effect.
3. With the null hypothesis, you only have two options: You can reject it or you can fail to reject it. You can never accept the null hypothesis.
4. The simple experiment is the easiest way to establish that a treatment causes an effect.
5. In the simple experiment, you administer a low level of the independent (treatment) variable to some of your subjects (the control group), and a higher level of the independent variable to the rest of your subjects (the experimental group).
6. Then, near the end of the experimental session, you observe how each subject scores on the dependent variable: a measure of the subject's behavior.
7. To establish causality with a simple experiment you must use independent random assignment to assign subjects to a group. The best way to do this is to use a random numbers table.
8. Your goal in using independent random assignment is to create two samples that accurately represent your entire population of subjects. You use the mean of the control group as an estimate of what would have happened if all your subjects had been in the control group. You use the experimental group mean as an estimate of what the mean would have been if all your subjects had been in the experimental group.
9. Does the treatment have an effect? In other words, would subjects have scored differently had they all been in the experimental group than if they had all been in the control group? This is the question that statistical significance tests ask.
10. If the results are statistically significant, the difference between your groups is greater than would be expected by chance (random sampling error) alone. Therefore, you reject the null hypothesis and conclude that your treatment has an effect.
11. There are two kinds of errors you might make when attempting to decide whether a result is statistically significant.
12. Type I errors occur when you mistake a chance difference for a treatment effect.
13. Type II errors occur when you mistake a genuine difference for a chance difference.
14. Because Type II errors can easily occur, nonsignificant results are inconclusive results.
15. To prevent Type II errors, reduce random error; use many subjects to balance out the effects of random error; and try to increase the size of your treatment effect.
16. If your experiment minimizes the risk of making Type II errors, your experiment has power. Technically, power is 1 minus the probability of making a Type II error. Less technically, power refers to your ability to find true differences as statistically significant.

17. Improving power may hurt your study's external and construct validity.
18. Using placebo treatments, single blinds, and double blinds can improve your study's construct validity.
19. Ethics may temper your search for power or even rule out doing an experiment.
20. Many distributions can be described by the normal curve.
21. The normal curve is a simple curve that can be described by two numbers: the mean and a standard term.
22. The standard deviation is an index of how much variation there is in your sample or population.
23. The standard error is an index of the variability of your sample means. It can be used to give you an idea of how much error has affected your estimate of the population mean.
24. The degrees of freedom for a t test are 2 less than the total number of subjects.
25. The formula for the t test is: Mean 1 − Mean 2/ standard error of the difference.

KEY TERMS

independent random assignment
experimental hypothesis
independent variable
experimental group
control group
independence
dependent variable
statistical significance
null results
Type I error
Type II error
power

empty control group
placebo
single blind
double blind
mean
sampling statistics
inferential statistics
standard deviation
standard error of the mean
central limit theorem
standard error of the difference
normal curve
normally distributed

EXERCISES

1. What is the purpose of the simple experiment? For what purposes (kinds of research ideas) would the simple experiment be inappropriate?

2. How does the simple experiment allow you to make causal statements?

3. Why is it important that subjects are assigned to a group through independent random assignment? What variables can't you study with a simple experiment because it requires independent random assignment? Why?

4. Why can't the null hypothesis be proved?

5. In what sense are the control group and experimental group really groups? In what sense, aren't they groups?

6. What do statistically significant results mean? What don't they mean?

7. What would you consider an acceptable risk for making a Type 1 error? Why?

8. How can Type 2 errors be prevented?

9. How do statistical considerations affect your design decisions?

10. What nonstatistical factors would you consider in designing an experiment? Which do you consider most important? Why?

11. What steps can a researcher take to increase an experiment's construct validity?

12. Under what situations do you think random assignment is unethical? (Hint: Think of situations where it would be unethical to randomly give a subject a treatment and think of situations where it would be unethical to randomly withhold treatment from a subject?)

13. What's the difference between the standard deviation, the standard error, and the standard error of the difference?

14. Calculate a *t* test for the following data:

Control Group	Experimental Group
5.0	7.0
4.0	5.0
3.0	6.0

15. In the example above, how many degrees of freedom do you have? Are the results statistically significant? If the results aren't statistically significant, list some possible reasons for that non-finding.

6

EXPANDING THE SIMPLE EXPERIMENT: MULTIPLE-GROUP EXPERIMENTS

OUTLINE

OVERVIEW

In Chapter 5, you learned how to perform a simple experiment. You now know that the simple experiment is internally valid and easy to do. However, you're also aware that the simple experiment is limited; with it, you can only study two values of a single independent variable.

In this chapter, you'll see why you might want to go beyond studying two values of a single variable and how the logic of the simple experiment (random assignment of subjects to groups) can be extended to accommodate your wishes. Specifically, you'll learn how and when to use random assignment to study the effects of three or more values of a single independent variable.

THE ADVANTAGES OF USING MORE THAN TWO VALUES OF AN INDEPENDENT VARIABLE

**Comparing
More than
Two Kinds of
Treatments**

The simple experiment is ideal if an investigator wants to compare two different kinds of treatments. But investigators are often interested in comparing three or more different kinds of treatments. For instance, Roedigger (1980) wanted to compare five kinds of memory strategies (rote rehearsal, imagery, method of loci, the link method, and the peg system). Clearly, he couldn't compare all five treatments in one simple experiment.

Therefore, instead of randomly assigning subjects to two different groups, he randomly assigned his subjects to five different groups. To learn how to randomly assign subjects to more than two groups, see Box 6-1.

Although Roedigger might have been able to compare the five treatments by using a series of simple experiments, using a single multivalued experiment has several advantages. Here are two of the most obvious ones.

First, by doing a single five-value experiment, Roedigger greatly reduced the number of experiments he had to perform. To compare all five treatments with one another, he'd have had to do 10 simple experiments. He'd have needed to do one experiment to compare rote rehearsal with imagery, another to compare rote rehearsal with the method of loci, another to compare rote rehearsal with the link method, and so on until he had compared each variable individually with each other variable.

Second, he reduced the number of subjects he had to test. If he'd done 10 simple experiments, he would've needed 20 groups of subjects. To have a reasonable degree of power, he'd need at least 15 subjects per group or 300 (15 × 20) subjects. With the five-group experiment, he could have the same **power with 75** (15 × 5) subjects.

BOX 6-1   Randomly Assigning Subjects to More Than Two Groups

STEP 1: Across the top of a piece of paper write down your conditions. Under each condition draw a line for each subject you'll need, like this:

Group 1	Group 2	Group 3
_____	_____	_____
_____	_____	_____
_____	_____	_____
_____	_____	_____

STEP 2: Turn to a random numbers table. Roll a die to determine which column in the table you'll use.

STEP 3: Assign the first number in the column to the first space under Group 1, the second number to the second space, and so on. When you've filled the spaces for Group 1, put the next number under the first space under Group 2. Similarly, when you fill all the spaces under Group 2, place the next number in the first space under Group 3.

STEP 4: Assign the first subject to the condition with the lowest random number. The second subject will get the second lowest number, and so on.

External Validity

Uncovering Relationships   In the simple experiment, you want to pick two levels of the independent variable that will allow you to find an effect. Intuitively, you realize that the greater the difference between how the two groups are treated, the greater the chances of finding a significant effect. Therefore, when choosing levels of the independent variable, you usually select two very different levels of the independent variable. Thus, if you were investigating the effects of exercise on depression, half of your subjects would exercise very little, and the other half would exercise a great deal. Your results might be as follows:

Group 1: Low amounts of aerobic exercise; High levels of depression
Group 2: High amounts of aerobic exercise; High levels of depression

Based on these results, you'd be tempted to conclude that there is no relationship between aerobic exercise and depression. However, this is a generalization:

Comparing More than Two Levels (Amounts) of an Independent Variable

You haven't tested other levels of the independent variable. Out of the many possible amounts of the independent variable you could have chosen, you've only sampled two. In this case, your generalization would be wrong if aerobic exercise had the following effects on depression:

Low amounts of aerobic exercise increase depression.
Medium amounts of aerobic exercise reduce depression.
High amounts of aerobic exercise increase depression.

The **U**-shaped relationship we've postulated between exercise and depression is fairly common in psychology. Psychologists often find **U**-shaped and upside-down, **U**-shaped relationships. Perhaps the most famous case is the Yerkes–Dodson Law, which states, in part, that with little motivation performance is poor, with medium motivation performance is good, and with too much motivation, performance is poor. You can probably think of many examples where (to paraphrase the littlest of the three bears) too little of some factor can be bad, too much can be bad, but a medium amount is just right.

If the relationship between aerobic exercise and depression is **U**-shaped and you pick extreme levels of your independent variable, you'll falsely conclude that the treatment has no effect. Therefore, you might be tempted to choose moderate levels of the treatment. However, if the relationship is not **U**-shaped and you use moderate levels, your levels may not be far enough apart to allow you to detect a treatment effect. Thus, as you can see, picking the right levels of your independent variable for a simple experiment is a tricky business.

To avoid making hard choices about what two levels to use, avoid simple experiments. Instead of choosing two levels, do experiments that use several levels of the independent variable so that you can choose three or more levels. Thus, if you'd used an experiment that examined three levels of aerobic exercise, you might have obtained the following pattern of results:

Group 1: Low aerobic exercise; High levels of depression
Group 2: Medium aerobic exercise; Low levels of depression
Group 3: High aerobic exercise; High levels of depression

Based on these results, you'd correctly conclude that aerobic exercise affects depression—regardless of whether the relationship between variables was like a straight line or **U**-shaped. In short, using multiple levels of an independent variable allows you to uncover effects that might not have been detected if you'd used a simple experiment.

Discovering the Nature of Relationships   You've seen that the researcher using the simple experiment may falsely conclude that a factor has no effect. Thus, in the worst case, the results from a simple experiment apply only to the two levels used in the experiment.

But what if the researcher using a simple experiment finds a significant effect? Even in that case, the researcher would have difficulty generalizing the simple experiment's results to unexplored levels of the independent variable. Why? Because to generalize results to unexplored levels of an independent variable, the researcher must not only know that a relationship exists, but she must also know the nature of that relationship. That is, the researcher must know the independent and dependent variables' **functional relationship:** the shape of the relationship. Simple experiments don't enable you to uncover the nature of a functional relationship.

To illustrate the weakness of the simple experiment in detecting functional relationships, let's reconsider our simple experiment investigating the effects of aerobic exercise on depression. Suppose the following results were obtained:

CONTROL GROUP:	0 min of exercise per day	1.0 self-rating of depression
EXPERIMENTAL GROUP:	100 min of exercise per day	10.0 self-rating of depression

Can you tell what the nature of the functional relationship is between aerobic exercise and depression? Perhaps the functional relationship is **linear** (like a straight line), as in Figure 6-1. However, the true relationship between exercise and depression might not resemble a straight line. Instead, it might be a nonlinear or **curvilinear** function, such as one of the curved lines in Figure 6-2.

Clearly, the simple experiment doesn't help you discover the functional relationship between two variables. Since you wouldn't know the functional relationship, you could do little more than guess if we asked you about the effects of 70 min of aerobic exercise. You might assume that the relationship is linear and therefore say that exercising 70 min a day would be better than no exercise and 70% as effective as exercising for 100 minutes a day. But if your assumption of a linear relationship is wrong—and it very well might be—your guess would be inaccurate.

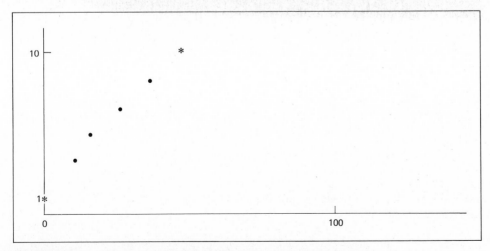

FIGURE 6-1   Linear Relationship between Two Points

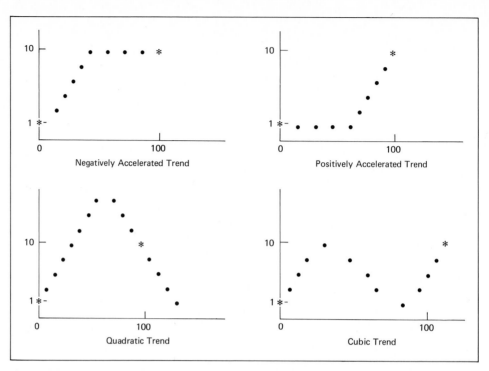

FIGURE 6-2   Some Possible Nonlinear Relationships

To get a line on the functional relationship between variables, you need to know more than two points. Therefore, if you expand the simple experiment into a multilevel experiment by adding a group that gets 50 minutes of exercise a day, you'll have a much clearer idea of the functional relationship between exercise and depression. As you can see in Figure 6-3, using three levels can give you a pretty good idea of the functional relationship among variables. If the relationship is linear, you should be able to draw a straight line through all three points. If the relationship is **U**-shaped, you'll detect that too.

Because you can detect the nature of the functional relationship when you use three levels of the independent variable, you can make accurate predictions about unexplored **levels of the independent variable.** Thus, if the functional relationship between aerobic exercise and depression were linear, you'd obtain the following pattern of results:

GROUP 1:	0 min of exercise per day	1.0 self-rating of depression
GROUP 2:	50 min of exercise per day	5.0 self-rating of depression
GROUP 3:	100 min of exercise per day	10.0 self-rating of depression

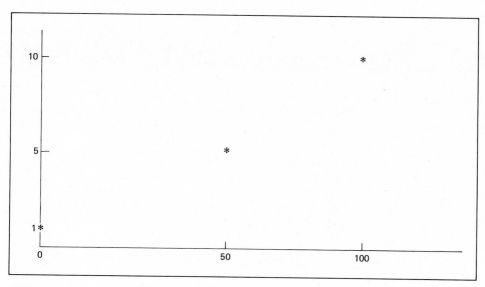

FIGURE 6-3   Possible Relationship between Three Points

In that case, you could confidently predict that 70 min of exercise would be 70% as beneficial for reducing depression as 100 min of exercise. If, on the other hand, the relationship was **S**-shaped, you'd get the following pattern of results:

GROUP 1:	0 min of exercise per day	1.0 self-rating of depression
GROUP 2:	50 min of exercise per day	10.0 self-rating of depression
GROUP 3:	100 min of exercise per day	10.0 self-rating of depression

In that case, you'd predict that a person who exercised 70 min would do as well as someone exercising 100 min a day.

Obviously, the more groups you use, the more accurately you can pin down the shape of the functional relationship. Yet, despite this fact, you don't have to use numerous levels of the independent variable because nature prefers simple patterns: Most functional relationships are linear and few are more complex than **U**-shaped functions. As a result, you'll rarely need more than four levels of the independent variable to pin down a functional relationship. In fact, you'll usually need no more than three carefully chosen levels to identify the functional relationship among variables.

Summary: Multilevel Experiments and External Validity   In summary, knowing the functional relationship between two variables is almost as important as knowing that a relationship exists. You want to be able to say more than: "If you exercise 100 min a day, you'll have less tension than someone who exercises 0 min a day." Who exercises exactly 100 min a day? You want to be able to generalize your results so that you can tell people what the effects are of exercising 50 min, 56 min, 75 min, and so forth. Yet, you have no intention of testing the effects of every single possible amount of exercise a person might do. Instead, you want to test only a handful of exercise levels. If these levels are chosen carefully, you'll be able to identify the functional relationship between the variables. Knowing the functional relationship will allow you to make educated predictions about the effects of exercise levels you haven't tested directly.

Using Multiple Levels to Improve Construct Validity of Experiments

You've seen that multilevel experiments have more external validity than simple experiments because of their ability to determine the functional relationship between two variables. In this section, you'll learn that multilevel experiments can also have more construct validity than simple experiments.

Confounding Variables in the Simple Experiment

Simple experiments are often contaminated by **confounding variables:** variables that are unintentionally manipulated. As we mentioned in Chapter 5, confounding variables are frequently a problem when you use an empty control group.

To understand the threat of confounding variables, let's take a hard look at our simple experiment on the effects of exercise on depression. You'll recall that the experimental group got 100 min of exercise per day, the control group got nothing. Clearly, the experimental group subjects are being treated very differently from the control group subjects. The groups didn't merely differ in terms of the independent variable (exercise). They also differed in terms of several other (confounding) variables: they got more attention and had more structured social activities than the control group.

Hypothesis Guessing in Simple Experiments

Furthermore, subjects in the experimental group knew they were getting a treatment, whereas subjects in the control group knew they were not being treated. If experimental group subjects suspected that the exercise program should have an effect (or if control group subjects felt bad because they weren't getting a treatment), the exercise program will seem as though it has an effect, even if it doesn't. In other words, the construct validity of the study might be ruined because subjects guessed the hypothesis.

Because of the impurities (confounding variables) of this manipulation, you can't say that the difference between groups is due to exercise. Although all manipulations have impurities, the most obvious source of impurities in this study stem from the empty control group. Thus, if you could eliminate or replace the empty control group, you could reduce the effect of confounding variables.

How the Multilevel Experiment Can Eliminate the Need for an Empty Control Group

If you wanted to do away with the empty control group, you could do a multilevel experiment. For example, you might have one group that gets 25 min of aerobic exercise, one group that gets 50 min, one group that gets 75 min, and a fourth group that gets 100 min. In such a study, the groups would be fairly similar to one another except for length of exercise session: All groups are being "treated" so hypothesis guessing shouldn't be a problem; all groups are having relatively equal opportunities to socialize with others; and all groups are setting and achieving goals (attending class and finishing the workout). Therefore, confounding is not as serious a problem as when you had an empty control group.

An added bonus of using this multilevel experiment is that it allows you to determine the functional relationship between exercise and depression. Because you know the functional relationship between amount of exercise and depression, you can estimate the effects of 0 min of exercise (see Figure 6-4). Thus, in this particular experiment, you can eat your cake (know how an empty control group would have scored) without having it.

How Multilevel Experiments Can Compensate for Empty Control Groups
If you insist on using an empty control group, the multilevel experiment may alert you if there are problems with this group. To illustrate, imagine that you have a four-level experiment where the first group gets no treatment, the second group gets 5 min of aerobic exercise, the third group gets 20 min, and the fourth group gets 80 min.

In this multilevel experiment, the three experimental groups are being treated almost identically. They only differ in terms of how much exercise they get. Consequently, any difference between the experimental groups is probably due to the amount of exercise, not to incidental, confounding variables (e.g., socializing with class members, setting goals).

The subjects in the three experimental groups would also have a hard time

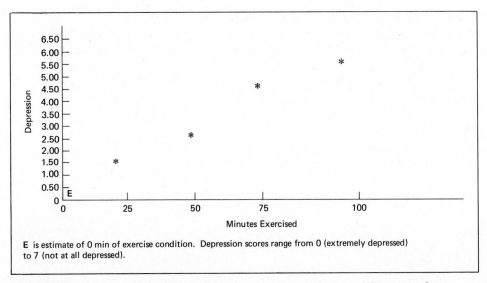

E is estimate of 0 min of exercise condition. Depression scores range from 0 (extremely depressed) to 7 (not at all depressed).

FIGURE 6-4   The Relationship between Exercise and Depression

figuring out the hypothesis and playing along with it. How can experimental subjects know which experimental group they're in? Experimental group subjects shouldn't be able to determine whether they're in the medium- or high-exercise group because: 1) 20 min could be a high level or a moderate level of exercise and 2) subjects may not even realize that there is more than one experimental group. Furthermore, even in the unlikely event that medium-exercise subjects correctly sensed that they were in the medium-exercise group, they would have a hard time figuring out how they could cooperate with the experimenter's hypothesis. How would they know how much depression they should report when given a medium level of exercise?

You've seen that subjects in a multilevel experiment would have a hard time figuring out the hypothesis and even a harder time playing along with it. Even if subjects guessed the hypothesis and tried to play along with it, they'd only be partially successful. More specifically, the experimental groups would behave differently from the control groups, but all the experimental groups would behave almost identically.

Consequently, you should be able to detect whether the results of a multi-level experiment are solely due to hypothesis guessing. To illustrate, look at Table 6-1. The results from one of these experiments are invalid because of hypothesis guessing. Do you think it's Experiment A or Experiment B. How do you know?

If you think Experiment B is the tainted experiment, you're correct! Why did you suspect Experiment B? Probably you assumed that if exercise has an effect, a high level of exercise will have more of an effect than a medium level of exercise. It's important to recognize that this is an assumption—and this assumption could be wrong. However, it's remarkable how often nature conforms to this assumption.

Increasing Validity through Several Control Groups

In the simple experiment, you're often forced to choose between control groups. You may have to decide whether to use a placebo group or an empty control group. Alternatively, you may have to decide between one kind of placebo group and another kind of placebo group. With a multiple-group experiment, you can have as many control groups as you need.

To see how difficult choosing between an empty control group and a placebo group can be, let's go back to the problem of examining the effects of aerobic exercise on depression. If you use an empty control group and an aerobic exercise group, the results could be due to hypothesis guessing or to any number of confounding vari-

TABLE 6-1 Results of Two, Multilevel Experiments

Experiment A		Experiment B	
Condition	Depression	Condition	Depression
No Exercise	8.0	No Exercise	8.0
Medium Exercise	9.5	Medium Exercise	11.5
High Exercise	11.5	High Exercise	11.5

ables (e.g., socializing with other students in the class, being put into a structured routine, etc.). If, however, you use a placebo group (e.g., meditation classes), your problems are not over. Suppose, for example, you find that the meditation group is less depressed than the exercise class. Would you conclude that exercise increases depression? No, because it might be that although exercise reduces depression, meditation reduces it more. To know whether exercise, as opposed to no treatment, increases or decreases depression, you'd need a no-treatment group. Thus, if you were interested in the effects of exercise on depression, you have two options: 1) Use a simple experiment and make some hard choices or 2) Use a multiple-group experiment so that you can include both control groups.

In the simple experiment, you're also faced with the difficult decision of what kind of placebo group to use because a single control group will almost always differ from experimental groups in ways that have nothing to do with the independent variable. For example, if an exercise group were less depressed than a meditation control group, we could be confident that this difference was not due to hypothesis guessing, engaging in structured activities, or being distracted from worrisome thoughts for a while. Both groups received a "treatment", both engaged in structured activities, and both were distracted for the same length of time.

However, the groups may differ in that the exercise group may have engaged in a more social activity, listened to louder and more upbeat music, or been exposed to a more energetic and enthusiastic instructor. Therefore, the exercise group may be less depressed for several reasons having nothing to do with exercise: feeling part of a group, interest and positive mood induced by music; and being exposed to a nondepressed model.

To rule out all these possibilities, you might use several control groups. For example, to control for the "social activity" and the "energetic model" explanations, you might add a group that went to a no-credit, acting class taught by a very enthusiastic professor. To control for the music explanation, you might add a control group that listened to music or perhaps even watched aerobic dance videos.

In summary, the multivalent experiment can be used to reduce the effects of hypothesis guessing and confounding variables. You can reduce these threats to validity by using multiple experimental groups, multiple control groups, or both.

ANALYSIS OF MULTIPLE-GROUP EXPERIMENTS

In the next few sections, you'll learn the logic behind analyzing the results of a multiple-group experiment. Obviously, understanding this logic will be useful if you plan to do a multiple-group experiment. But even if you don't plan to conduct a multiple-group experiment, understanding the logic and the vocabulary used in analyzing multiple-group experiments is necessary if you're to understand research articles that report data from such experiments.

An Intuitive Overview

As a first step to understanding how multiple-group experiments are analyzed, let's look at data from three experiments that compared the effects of no-treatment, meditation, and aerobic exercise on happiness. All of these experiments had 12 subjects rate their feelings of happiness on a 1 (not at all happy) to 10 (very happy) scale. Here are the results of Experiment A:

	No-Treatment	Meditation	Exercise
	5.01	5.02	5.03
	5.01	5.02	5.03
	5.01	5.02	5.03
	5.01	5.02	5.03
GROUP MEAN	5.01	5.02	5.03

Compare these results to the results of Experiment B:

	No-Treatment	Meditation	Exercise
	4.00	6.00	8.00
	4.00	6.00	8.00
	4.00	6.00	8.00
	4.00	6.00	8.00
GROUP MEAN	4.00	6.00	8.00

Are you more confident that Experiment A or Experiment B found a significant effect for the treatment variable? If you said "B", why? Because the group means for Experiment B are farther apart than for Experiment A. Intuitively, you realize that although it's easy for chance to account for small differences among group means, it's more difficult for it to account for large differences. In other words, the more variability there is among group means, the more likely that at least some of this variability is due to treatment.

Now, compare Experiment B with Experiment C. The results of Experiment C are listed below:

	No-Treatment	Meditation	Exercise
	1.00	1.00	10.00
	8.00	9.00	8.00
	6.00	6.00	6.00
	1.00	8.00	8.00
GROUP MEAN	4.00	6.00	8.00

Do you think the results from Experiment B or Experiment C are more likely to indicate a real treatment effect? Both experiments have the same amount of variability between group means, so you can't choose one over the other on that basis. Yet, once again, you'll pick Experiment B. Why?

Because you're concerned about one aspect of Experiment C—the extreme amount of variability within each group. You realize that the *only* reason that the scores within a group vary is because of random error. Thus, you see that Experiment C is more affected by random error than Experiment B. The large amount of random error in Experiment C (as revealed by the within-groups variability) disturbs you because you realize that this random error might be the reason the groups differ from one another. In Experiment B, on the other hand, the lack of any within-group variability indicates that there is virtually no random error in your data. Therefore, in Experiment B, you feel fairly confident that random error is not causing the group means to differ from one another. Instead, you believe that the means differ from one another because of the treatment.

Intuitively then, you understand the three most important principles behind analyzing the results of a multiple-group experiment. First, you realize that between-group variability alone is not an adequate measure of treatment effects. Although treatment effects should cause the groups to differ from one another, random error will also cause the groups to differ from one another (even if no treatment was administered, the group means would probably differ). In other words, between-group variability is not a pure index of treatment effects because it also contains an estimate of random error. Second, you realize that within-group variability is due solely to random error. Third, you know that if you compare between-group variability (the effects of random error plus treatment) to within-group variability (the effects of random error), you'll be able to determine whether or not the treatment had an effect.

You now have a general idea of how to analyze data from a multiple-group study. To see how to perform an analysis, look at Box 6-2. To more fully understand the logic and vocabulary used in these analyses—a must if you're to understand an author's or a computer's report of such an analysis—read the next few sections.

A Closer Look

Assessing Within-Group Variability

As you already know, within-group variability reflects the amount of random error in the data. The only reason subjects in the meditation group would differ from one another is random error. Since they all got the same treatment and since subjects are randomly assigned to the group, the only reason they would vary from one another is due to random error caused by factors such as individual differences, unreliability of the measure, lack of standardization, etc. Similarly, the only reason subjects in the no-treatment group would differ from one another is random error. The same is true for the exercise group subjects.

To measure this within-group variability, we first calculate the variance of the scores within each group. Since we have three groups, we have three measures of within-group variability—or three estimates of random error. Since we only need one estimate of the variability due to random error, we average all these within-group variances to come up with the best estimate of the degree to which individual scores are affected by random error—the within-group variance. Since the **within-group**

BOX 6-2 Analyzing Data from a Multiple-Group Experiment

To analyze data from a multiple-group experiment, most researchers use analysis of variance. To use analysis of variance, your observations must be independent, your scores should be normally distributed, each of your groups should have the same variance, and you must have interval data.

In analysis of variance, you set up the F ratio: a ratio of the between-group variance to the within-group variance. Or, to use proper terminology, you set up a ratio of mean square between (MSB) to mean square within (MSW).

To calculate mean square within groups, you must first calculate the sum of squares for each group. You must subtract each score from its mean, square each of those differences, and then add up all those squared differences. If you had the following three groups, your first calculations would be as follows:

	Group 1	Group 2	Group 3
	5	6	14
	4	5	12
	3	4	10
GROUP MEAN	4	5	12

Sum of squares for Group 1:
$(5 - 4)^2 + (4 - 4)^2 + (3 - 4)^2 = 1^2 + 0^2 + 1^2 = 1 + 0 + 1 = 2$

Sum of squares for Group 2:
$(6 - 5)^2 + (5 - 5)^2 + (5 - 6)^2 = 1^2 + 0^2 + 1^2 = 1 + 0 + 1 = 2$

Sum of squares for Group 3:
$(14 - 12)^2 + (12 - 12)^2 + (10 - 12)^2 = 2^2 + 0^2 + 2^2$
$$= 4 + 0 + 4 = 8$$

To get the sum of squares within groups, you add all of these sums of squares together $(2+2+8 = 12)$.

To get the mean square within groups, you divide the sum of squares within by the number of degrees of freedom. The number of degrees of freedom in a multiple-group experiment equals the number subjects minus the number of groups. Since you had 9 subjects and 3 groups, your within-group degrees of freedom are 6 $(9-3=6)$. So, your mean square within is 2 $(12/6 = 2)$. Note that you would have obtained the same mean square if you'd calculated the variance for each of your groups $(1+1+4)$ and averaged those variances $(6/3)=2$.

To get the mean square between groups, calculate the variance of the group means, as shown below:

Calculate mean of group means: $(4+5+12)/3 = 21/3 = 7$. Subtract each group mean from the overall mean and square each difference:

$$4-7 = -3; \quad -3 \text{ squared} = 9$$
$$5-7 = -2; \quad -2 \text{ squared} = 4$$
$$12-7 = 5; \quad 5 \text{ squared} = 25$$

Add up all these squared differences: $25 + 9 + 4 = 38$. Divide this term by one less than the number of groups. Since you have three groups, divide by 2. So, your variance among groups is 19 ($38/2 = 19$).

To transform your variance among groups to a mean square between, multiply it by the number of subjects in each group. In this case, you have three subjects per group, so you multiply 19×3 and get 57.

Since the *F* ratio, is just the ratio of mean square between to mean square within, your *F* ratio is 57/2 or 28.5.

At this point, this is how your ANOVA summary table would look:

Source of Variance	Sum of Squares	Degrees of Freedom	Mean Square	*F* Ratio
TREATMENT			57	28.5
ERROR	12	6	2	

To fill in the rest of the table, you need to know the sum of squares treatment and the degrees of freedom for the treatment. The degrees of freedom for the treatment is one less than the number of groups. Since you have three groups, your *df* treatment are 2. To get the sum of squares for the treatment, simply multiply the *df* treatment by the mean square treatment ($2 \times 57 = 114$). This is your completed ANOVA summary table:

Source of Variance	Sum of Squares	Degrees of Freedom	Mean Square	*F* Ratio
TREATMENT	114	2	57	28.5
ERROR	12	6	2	

To determine whether the *F* of 28.5 is significant, you would look in the *F* table for the critical value for 2 *df* in the numerator and 6 *df* in the denominator. If 28.5 is larger than that value, the results would be statistically significant.

variance is an estimate of the amount of random error in your data, it is also referred to as **error variance.**

Assessing Between-Group Variability

Once you have a measure of within-group variability, the next step is to get an index of the degree to which your groups vary from one another. It is at this step where it becomes obvious that you can't use a *t* test to analyze data from a multiple-group experiment. When using a *t* test, you determine the degree to which the groups differ from one another in a very straightforward manner—you subtract the average score of Group 1 from the average score of Group 2. Subtraction works well when you want to compare two groups but doesn't work well when you have more than two groups. You can only subtract two scores at a time. So, if you have three groups, which two groups do you compare? Group 1 from Group 2? Or, Group 2 from Group 3? Or, Group 1 from Group 3?

You might answer this question by saying "all of the above." That is, you might argue that the way to adapt the *t* test to a multiple-group situation is to perform more *t* tests. Thus, with three groups, you should do three *t* tests: one comparing Group 1 against Group 2, a second comparing Group 1 against Group 3, and a third comparing Group 2 against Group 3. However, that's not cricket.

An analogy will help you understand why you can't use multiple *t* tests. Suppose a stranger comes up to you with a proposition: "Let's bet on coin flips. If I get a 'head,' you give me a dollar. If I don't, I give you a dollar." You accept the proposition. He then proceeds to flip three coins at once and then makes you pay up if even one of the coins comes up heads. Why is this unfair? This is unfair because he misled you: You thought he was only going to flip one coin at a time, so you thought he had only a 50% chance of winning. But since he's flipping three coins at a time, his chances of getting at least one head are much better than 50%.

When you do multiple *t* tests, you're doing basically the same thing as the coin hustler. You start by telling people the odds that a single *t* test will be significant due to chance alone. For example, if you use conventional significance levels, you would tell people that the odds of getting a statistically significant result for a particular *t* test by chance were less than 5 in 100.

Then, just as the hustler gave himself more than a 50% chance of winning by flipping more than one coin, you give yourself a more than 5% chance of getting a statistically significant result by doing more than one *t* test. The 5% odds you quoted would only hold if you had done a single *t* test. If you're using *t* tests to compare three groups, you'll do three *t* tests. If you do three *t* tests, the odds of at least one turning out significant is much more than 5%.

Of course, the more groups you use in your experiment, the greater the difference between the significance level you report and the actual odds of at least one result being significant by chance. Just to give you an idea of how great the difference between your stated significance level and the actual odds can be, suppose you had six levels of the independent variable. To compare all six groups with one another, you'd need to do 15 *t* tests. If you did 15 *t* tests and used a .05 significance level, the probability of getting at least one significant effect by chance would be more than 50%!

As you've seen, the t test is not useful for analyzing data from the multiple-group experiment because it measures the degree to which groups differ by using subtraction—and you can only subtract two group averages at a time. To calculate the degree to which more than two group means differ, you need to calculate a variance.

The variance you want to calculate should do more than indicate the extent to which the group means differ. You want this variance to be equivalent to the within-group variance when there is no treatment effect, and to be larger than that variance when there is a treatment effect. That is, the between-group variance, like the within-group variance, should be an estimate of the degree to which individual scores are affected by random error. But unlike the within-group variance, the between-group variance should also be an estimate of treatment effects. In other words, the **between-group variance** should be the sum of two quantities: an estimate of the degree to which individual scores are affected by random error + treatment effects. (To calculate the between-group variance, see Box 6-2.)

Comparing Variances

Once you have your between-group variance (an estimate of random error plus any treatment effects) and your within-group variance (an estimate of random error), the next step is to compare your variances. If the between-group variance is bigger than the within-group variance, then some of the between-group variance may be due to a treatment effect. Because you'll determine whether the treatment had an effect by comparing (analyzing) the between-group variance with the within-group variance, this statistical technique is called **analysis of variance (ANOVA)**.

But how do you compare your two variances when doing an ANOVA? You might think that you'd compare your two variances by subtracting them from one another. That is, you might hope to do something like this:

Between Groups Variance   − Within Groups Variance = Treatment Effect
(Random Error + Possible Treatment Effects) −   (Random Error)   = (Treatment Effect)

However, in analysis of variance (ANOVA) you compare your two indices by dividing rather than by subtracting. Specifically, you set up the following ratio:

$$\frac{\text{Between-Group Variance}}{\text{Within-Group Variance}}$$

In technical terminology, the index of between-group variance is called **mean square between subjects** (abbreviated MS between) or **mean square treatment** (abbreviated MST); the index of within-group variance is called **mean square within** (MSW) or **mean square error** (MSE) and the ratio of two variances is called the F ratio. Thus, when reading articles, you may see tables resembling the one below:

SOURCE	MS	F RATIO
Treatment (T)	10	2
Error (E)	5	

Conceptually, the F ratio can be portrayed as follows:

$$F = \frac{\text{Random Error} + \text{Possible Treatment Effect}}{\text{Random Error}}$$

By looking at the formula, you can see that the F ratio will rarely be much less than 1. If there is no treatment effect, the formula reduces to random error/random error, and if you divide anything by itself (5/5, 8/8), you'll usually get 1. In that case, the between-group variance and the within-group variance should be roughly equivalent because both are measuring the same thing—random error in individual scores.

You would not reject the null hypothesis if the F ratio was approximately 1.00. You would figure that:

$$F = \frac{\text{Random Error}}{\text{Random Error}} = 1.00$$

But what would happen if the treatment had an effect? Again, Group 1's scores differ from one another only because of chance. The same is true of Group 2's scores differing from one another, and Group 3's scores. In other words, within-group variance is still due only to random error.

But what about the variance among the three group means? Will they vary from each other merely because of chance? No, the groups differ from each other because they received different levels of the treatment. Thus, the variance among group means would be due not only to random error, but also to the treatment causing real differences among groups. Therefore, the between-group variance would be larger than the within-group variance because it isn't only estimating random error (the only thing within-group variance is doing) but also measuring the treatment effect. Consequently, you'd expect the ratio of between-group to within-group variances to be greater than 1.

$$F = \frac{\begin{array}{c}\text{Between-Group Variance}\\ (\text{treatment } + \text{ random error})\end{array}}{\begin{array}{c}\text{Within-Group Variance}\\ (\text{random error})\end{array}} > 1, \quad \text{when the treatment has an effect.}$$

If you saw such an F ratio, how would you know whether it was significant? Clearly, it's larger than 1, but is it significantly larger?

Using an F Table   To determine whether an F ratio is large enough to indicate a difference between your groups, you need to consult an F table, like the one in Appendix E. Just as the t table told you how big a t score had to be to reach significance, the F table tells you how big an F ratio has to be to be statistically significant. As was the case with the t scores, how large a ratio has to be to reach significance depends on the number of degrees of freedom.

Calculating Degrees of Freedom   To use the F table, you need to know two degrees of freedom: one for the top of the F ratio (between-group variance, MST) and one for the bottom of the F ratio (within-group variance, MSE).

Calculating the degrees of freedom for the top of the F ratio (between-group variance) is simple. It's just one less than the number of values of the independent variable. So, if you have 3 values of the independent variable (no-treatment, meditation, and exercise), you have 2 df. If you had four values of the independent variable, (no-treatment, meditation, archery, aerobic exercise), then you would have 3 df.

The second degrees of freedom, the degrees of freedom for the bottom part of the F ratio (within-group variance) is equal to one less than the number of subjects minus the degrees of freedom for the treatment. Thus, if you're doing an F test with three groups (df treatment = 2) and 36 subjects, your second df would be 33 (i.e., 35 − 2). If you use the same number of subjects (36), but have six groups (df treatment = 5), your second df would be 30 (i.e., 35 − 5).

Once you know the degree of freedom, you simply look in the table under that number. If your F ratio is larger than the values listed, then the results are statistically significant at the .05 level.

The Meaning of Statistical Significance

What does it mean if your results are statistically significant? As you know, statistical significance means that the null hypothesis has been rejected. In the multiple-group experiment, the null hypothesis is that all the differences among your group means are due to chance (all your groups are the same). Rejecting this hypothesis means that, because of treatment effects, all your groups are not the same. In other words, you can conclude that at least two of your groups differ. But which ones? Even in a three-group experiment, there are numerous possibilities: Group 1 might differ from Group 2 and/or Group 2 might differ from Group 3 and/or Group 1 might differ from Group 3. A significant F ratio doesn't tell you which groups differ. Therefore, once you have performed an F test to determine that your groups differ, you need to do additional tests to determine which of your groups differ from one another.

Pinpointing a Significant Effect

Post Hoc t *Tests among Group Means: Which Groups Differ?*   You might think that all you'd have to do to determine which groups differ is compare group means. However, some group means may differ from one another solely as a result of chance. To determine which group differences are due to treatment effects, you need to do additional tests. These additional tests are **post-hoc** t tests.

Before you chastise us, saying you wanted to do t tests all along, please hear our two-pronged defense. First, you can only do **post-hoc tests** after you get a significant F test. That is why post-hoc tests are called post hoc (after the fact). To do otherwise is considered statistical malpractice. Just as a physician wouldn't do a biopsy on the liver unless she had done more general tests that indicated liver trouble, a psychologist doesn't ask which groups differ from one another unless he has found out that some groups differ. Second, post-hoc tests are not the same as conventional t tests. Unlike conventional t tests, post-hoc t tests are designed to correct for the fact that you're doing more than two comparisons.

At this point, there's no reason for you to know how to do post-hoc tests. You should simply be aware that if you choose to do a multiple-group experiment, you should be prepared to do a post-hoc analyses. You should also be prepared to encounter post-hoc tests if you read a journal article that reports a significant F for a multiple-group experiment. If you read about a Bonferroni t test (Dunn test), Tukey test, Scheffé test, Dunnett test, Newman–Keuls test, Duncan, or LSD test, don't panic. The author is merely reporting the results of a test to determine which means differ from one another. (If you want to know more about post-hoc tests, see Appendix E.)

Post Hoc Trend Analysis: What Is the Shape of the Relationship? If you're interested in generalizing your results to unexplored levels of the independent variable, you may not be interested in determining which groups differ from one another. Instead, you may be interested in determining the shape of the relationship between the independent and dependent variable. If so, instead of following up a significant main effect with post-hoc tests between group means, follow up the significant effect with post-hoc **trend analyses**.

But why should you do a trend analysis to determine the shape of a relationship between your independent and dependent variable? Can't you see this relationship by simply graphing the group means? Although graphing allows you to see the pattern in the data from your experiment, only by using statistics can you tell whether the pattern is a reliable one. Therefore, if you want to know whether the pattern you observe in your data (a straight line, a curved line, a combination of a curve and a straight line, etc.) would occur if you repeated the experiment, you must do a post-hoc trend analysis. Refer to Appendix E to see how to do a post-hoc trend analysis.

Obviously, to plan an experiment, you don't need to know how to do a trend analysis. However, if you want to do such an analysis on your data, there are three things you should know before you test your first subject. First, you must have selected levels of your independent variable that increase proportionally, (e.g., 10, 20, 30 mg., or 10, 100, 1000 mg.). Second, you must have an interval scale measure of your dependent variable. Third, the more levels of the independent variable you have, the more trends you can look for. Specifically, the number of trends you can examine is one less than the number of levels you have. If you have three groups, you can test for straight lines (linear component), and for a U-shaped curve (quadratic component). With four levels, you can test for straight lines, U-shaped curves, and double U-shaped lines (cubic component). Thus, if you're expecting a double U-shaped curve, you must use at least four levels of the independent variable.

BOX 6-3   Requirements of a Post-Hoc Trend Analysis

1. Your independent variable must have a statistically significant effect.
2. Your independent variable should be quantitative and the levels used in the experiment should vary from one another by some constant proportion.
3. The number of trends you can look for is one less than the number of levels of your independent variable.
4. Your dependent variable must yield interval or ratio scale data.

SUMMARY OF THE MULTIPLE-GROUP EXPERIMENT

You have seen that you can expand a simple experiment by using more than two values of the independent variable. You have seen that by expanding the simple experiment in this way, you can increase the external validity of your experiment (by increasing your ability to generalize your results to unexplored values of the independent variable), and you can increase the construct validity of your experiment (by ruling out confounding variables).

MAIN POINTS

1. As compared with the simple experiment, the multiple-group experiment's sensitivity to nonlinear relationships makes it more likely to obtain significant treatment effects and to detect the functional relationship between your independent and dependent variables.
2. Knowing the functional relationship allows more accurate predictions about the effects of unexplored levels of the independent variable.
3. To use the multiple-group experiment to discover the functional relationship, you must carefully select your levels of the independent variable, and your dependent variable must be measured on an interval scale.
4. Multiple-group experiments may have more construct validity than a simple experiment because they can have multiple control groups or multiple experimental groups.
5. To analyze a multiple-group experiment, you first have to conduct an F test.
6. An F test is the ratio of between-group variance to within-group variance.
7. The following summarizes the mathematics of an F table.

Source of Variance (SV)	Sum of Squares (SS)	Degrees of freedom (df)	Mean Square (MS)	F
Treatment (T)	SST	levels of T minus one	SST/df T	MST/MSE
Error (E)	SSE	Subjects — df T − 1	SSE/df E	
Total	SS Total	Subjects − 1		

8. If you get a significant F, you know that the groups are not all the same. To find out which groups are different, you need to do post-hoc tests.

KEY TERMS

functional relationship
linear
curvilinear
levels of the independent variable
confounding variables
within-groups variance (mean square within, mean square error, error variance)

between-groups variance (mean square treatment, mean square between)
analysis of variance (ANOVA)
post-hoc test
trend analysis

EXERCISES

1. A simple experiment finds that subjects who wear sunglasses with rose-tinted lenses are more optimistic than subjects who do not wear sunglasses. Refute the validity of this claim based on what you know about using multiple groups.

2. Improve the study in exercise 1 by designing an experiment with three levels.

3. Make a case for the superiority of your multiple group-study.

4. What statistic would you use to analyze your data? Why?

5. Use Box 6-1 to randomly assign 30 subjects to 3 conditions.

7

EXPANDING THE SIMPLE EXPERIMENT: FACTORIAL DESIGNS

OVERVIEW

In Chapter 5, you learned that the simple experiment is internally valid and easy to do. However, you also learned that it was limited: With it, you can only study two values of a single independent variable.

In Chapter 6, you learned that by extending the logic of the simple experiment to studying three or more values of a single variable, you could design experiments that possess impressive internal, external, and construct validity. In this chapter, you'll see why you might want to extend the logic of the simple experiment to study the effects of two or more independent variables in a single experiment.

THE 2 × 2 FACTORIAL DESIGN

How One Experiment Can Do as Much as Two

To illustrate how you can study two independent variables in a single experiment, suppose you wanted to know the effect of both caffeine and exercise on appetite. You want to use two levels of caffeine (0 mg and 20 mg) and two levels of exercise (no exercise and 50 min exercise). To examine these variables with one experiment, you'd randomly assign subjects to four groups: a no-exercise, no-caffeine group; a no-exercise, 20 mg caffeine group; a 50 min exercise, no-caffeine group; and a 50 min exercise, 20 mg caffeine group. In technical terminology, you'd be using a **factorial experiment**: an experiment that examines two or more independent variables (factors) at a time. Specifically, since the exercise factor has 2 levels and since the caffeine factor has 2 levels, you have a 2 (no-exercise/exercise) × 2 (no-caffeine/caffeine) factorial experiment.

Of course, if you wanted to study the effects of exercise and caffeine on appetite, you wouldn't have to do a factorial experiment. Instead, you could do two simple experiments. One experiment would look at the effects of caffeine on appetite. The other would look at the effects of exercise on appetite. To visualize the difference between your two options, doing one 2 × 2 factorial experiment or doing two simple experiments, look at Table 7-1.

As you can see by looking at Table 7-1, the 2 × 2 experiment has every group that the two simple experiments have and one group that the simple experiments don't have. The factorial experiment's Group 1 is the same as the control groups used in both simple experiments. The factorial experiment's Group 2 is the same as the first simple experiment's experimental group. The factorial experiment's Group 3 is the same as the second simple experiment's experimental group. Because of Groups 1, 2, and 3, you'd expect that the 2 × 2 experiment could do everything that the two simple experiments do—it can. If you compare Group 1 (the no-exercise, no-caffeine group) with Group 2 (the no-caffeine, 50 min exercise group), you'd get a **simple main effect** for exercise—just as you would if you did Simple Experiment #1. If you compare Group 1 (the no-exercise, no-caffeine group) with Group 3 (the no-exercise, 20 mg caffeine group), you'd get a simple main effect for exercise—just as you would if you did Simple Experiment #2.

TABLE 7-1   Two Simple Experiments versus a 2 × 2 Experiment

	Two Simple Experiments	
	Experiment 1 (on exercise)	**Experiment 2 (on caffeine)**
CONTROL GROUP	no exercise	no caffeine
EXPERIMENTAL GROUP	50 min exercise	20 mg caffeine
	A 2 × 2 Factorial Experiment	
	No Exercise	**50 min Exercise**
NO CAFFEINE	1 Control Group (same as E1 and E2 control)	2 (same as E1 experimental)
20 MG CAFFEINE	3 (same as E2 experimental)	4

If the 2 × 2 experiment can do everything two simple experiments can do with only three groups, why do you have Group 4? You have group four so that you can find out things that you couldn't had you used two simple experiments.

How One Experiment Can Do More than Two

The most obvious difference between having four groups and having two simple experiments is that you can calculate more simple main effects with four groups than with two experiments. You can compare Group 3 (the no-exercise, 20 mg caffeine group) with Group 4 (the 50 min exercise, 20 mg caffeine group) to get a simple main effect for exercise. You can also compare Group 2 (the 50 min exercise, no-caffeine group) with Group 4 (the 50 min exercise, 20 mg caffeine group) to get a simple main effect for caffeine. Consequently, with four groups, you can calculate four simple main effects: a simple main effect for caffeine when exercise is held constant at 0 min, a simple main effect for caffeine when exercise is held constant at 50 min, a simple main effect for exercise when caffeine is held constant at 0 mg, and a simple main effect for exercise when caffeine is held constant at 20 mg.

There are two primary advantages to having two pairs of simple main effects (a pair of caffeine simple main effects and a pair of exercise simple main effects). First, you can average each pair of simple main effects to find the average effect for that variable in your study—what psychologists refer to as the variable's **overall main effect**. In the caffeine–exercise study, you could average your two caffeine simple main effects to get an overall main effect for caffeine and you could average your two exercise main effects to get an overall main effect for exercise.

Second, by comparing each variable's two simple main effects, you can determine the effects of combining variables. You can see whether the effect of caffeine is the same in the no-exercise condition as it is in the 50 min exercise condition. If the simple main effect for caffeine differs *depending* on the level of exercise, you have an **interaction** between your variables.

In short, if you were to do this 2 × 2 experiment, you'd look for three different kinds of effects: the average or main effect of caffeine; the average or main effect of exercise; and the interaction between caffeine and exercise. A significant main effect for caffeine would mean that caffeine had an effect, a significant main effect for exercise would mean that exercise had an effect, and a significant interaction would mean that the **combination** of exercise and caffeine produce an effect that is not simply the sum of their two separate effects.

How Interactions Limit the Generalizations Scientists Can Make

Significant interactions force scientists to answer such questions as, "Does caffeine increase calorie consumption?", by saying "Yes, but it depends on . . .", or "It's a little more complicated than that." Psychologists don't give these kinds of responses to make the world seem more complicated than it is.

Psychologists would love to give simple answers. Like all scientists, they love parsimony. Therefore, they'd love to report main effects that aren't complicated, qualified, or interfered with by interactions. They'd like to say that exercise is always good, drinking caffeine is always bad. However, if interactions occur, scientists have the obligation to report them—and in the real world, interactions abound. Only the person who says, "Give me a match, I want to see if my gas tank is empty" is unaware of the pervasiveness of interactions. Time and time again, you learn that when variables combine, the effects are different from what you'd expect knowing only their independent effects.

Thus, the complexity of the world may compel you to do complicated experiments. But how would you describe the results from a complex study?

Potential Results of a 2 × 2 Experiment

There are eight basic patterns of results you could obtain with a 2 × 2 experiment:

1. a main effect for your first independent variable, no main effect for your second independent variable, and no interaction;
2. no main effect for your first independent variable, a main effect for your second independent variable, and no interaction;
3. a main effect for your first independent variable, a main effect for your second independent variable, and no interaction;
4. a main effect for your first independent variable, a main effect for your second independent variable, and an interaction;
5. no main effect for either independent variable, but an interaction;
6. a main effect for the first independent variable, no main effect for the second independent variable, and an interaction;
7. no main effect for the first independent variable, a main effect for the second independent variable, and an interaction; and
8. no main effects or interactions.

The first step to finding out which of these patterns you have is to calculate the mean response for each group and make a table of these means.

A Main Effect and No Interaction

Suppose you obtained the results displayed in Table 7-2. From the first row, you can see that when there was no caffeine, exercise had no effect on appetite. Obviously, this finding could have been discovered by doing a simple experiment. Looking at the next row, you see that exercise had no effect in the 20 mg caffeine group. Again, this effect could have been discovered by doing a simple experiment. Averaging the effect of exercise over both the 0 mg and 20 mg caffeine conditions, you find that exercise's average (overall) effect (the overall main effect of exercise) was 0. Thus, there was no main effect for exercise.

Looking at the columns tells you about the effect of caffeine. You see that when there is no exercise, the subjects consume 200 more calories in the 20 mg caffeine condition than in the no-caffeine group. This simple main effect of caffeine could have been discovered by using a simple experiment. Looking at the second column, you learn that in the 50 min condition, the 20 mg caffeine group consumes 200 more calories than the no-caffeine group. Thus, it appears that there is a main effect for caffeine.

You also know that there is no interaction because the effect of caffeine is unaffected by the level of exercise. As Table 7-2 demonstrates, the effect of caffeine is independent of the amount of exercise.

Instead of having no interaction and a main effect for caffeine, you could have no interaction and a main effect for exercise. This pattern of results is shown in Table 7-3. From the first row, you can see that when there was no caffeine, exercise increased calorie consumption by 500. Looking at the next row, you see that exercise also increased calorie consumption by 500 in the 20 mg caffeine conditions. Averaging the effect of exercise over both the 0 mg and 20 mg caffeine conditions, you find that exercise's average (overall) effect (the overall main effect of exercise) was 500.

Looking at the columns tells you about the effect of caffeine. You see that when there is no exercise, the subjects in the 0 mg caffeine condition consumed the same number of calories as subjects in the 20 mg caffeine condition. Looking at the

TABLE 7-2   Main Effect for Caffeine, No Interaction

	No Exercise	50 min Exercise
NO CAFFEINE	(1) 2,000 cal	(2) 2,000 cal
20 mg CAFFEINE	(3) 2,200 cal	(4) 2,200 cal

Simple effect of exercise (no caffeine): 2,000 − 2,000 = 0 (no effect).
Simple effect of exercise (20 mg caffeine): 2,200 − 2,200 = 0 (no effect).
Overall main effect of exercise: (0 + 0)/2 = 0 (no effect).

Simple main effect of caffeine (no exercise): 2,200 − 2,000 = 200 (effect).
Simple main effect of caffeine (50 mm exercise): 2,200 − 2,000 = 200 (effect).
Overall main effect of caffeine: (200 + 200)/2 = 200 (effect).

TABLE 7-3 Main Effect for Exercise, No Interaction

	No Exercise	50 min Exercise
NO CAFFEINE	(1) 2,000 cal	(2) 2,500 cal
20 mg CAFFEINE	(3) 2,000 cal	(4) 2,500 cal

Simple main effect of exercise (no caffeine): 2,500 − 2,000 = 500 (effect).
Simple main effect of exercise (20 mg caffeine): 2,500 − 2,000 = 500 (effect).
Overall main effect of exercise: (500 + 500)/2 = 500 (effect).

Simple main effect of caffeine (no exercise): 2,000 − 2,000 = 0 (no effect).
Simple main effect of caffeine (50 min exercise): 2,500 − 2,500 = 0 (no effect).
Overall main effect of caffeine: (0 + 0) 2 = 0 (no effect).

second column, you learn that in the 50 min exercise condition, the 0 mg caffeine group consumes the same number of calories as the no-caffeine group. Thus, it appears that there is no main effect for caffeine.

You also know that there is no interaction because the effect of exercise is unaffected by the level of caffeine. As Table 7-3 demonstrates, the effect of exercise is the same regardless of the amount of caffeine consumed.

Although making tables of means is a useful way to summarize your data, perhaps the easiest way to interpret the results of your experiment is to graph the data. Get a piece of paper and plot your four means. Then, draw a straight line between the means of Group 1 and Group 3. Draw a second line between the means of Group 2 and Group 4. Your graph should look something like Figure 7-1:

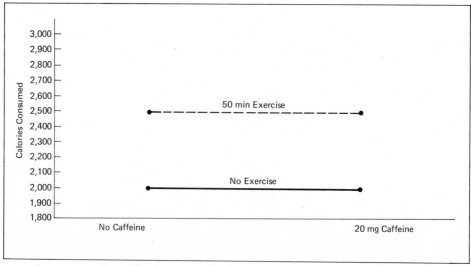

FIGURE 7-1 Main Effect for Exercise, No Interaction

The graph confirms what you saw in the table. Exercise increased calorie consumption as shown by the 50 min of exercise line being above the no-exercise line. Caffeine did not increase calorie consumption as shown by the fact that both lines stay perfectly level as they go from no caffeine to 20 mg caffeine. Finally, there's no interaction between exercise and caffeine on calorie consumption, as shown by the fact that the lines are parallel. The lines are parallel because exercise is having the same effect on the no-caffeine groups as on the 20 mg groups. Thus, if you've graphed your data, you only need to look to see whether your lines are parallel to see whether you have an interaction.

Two Main Effects and No Interaction

Another pattern of effects you might get are reflected in Table 7-4. From the first row, you can see that when there was no caffeine, exercise increased calorie consumption by 500. Looking at the next row, you see that exercise increased calorie consumption by 500 in the 20 mg caffeine group. Averaging the effect of caffeine over all caffeine conditions, you find that the overall main effect of exercise was to increase calorie consumption by 500.

Looking at the columns tells you about the effect of caffeine. You see that when there is no exercise, the subjects consume 200 more calories in the 20 mg caffeine condition than in the no-caffeine group. Looking at the second column, you learn that in the 50 min exercise condition, the 20 mg caffeine group consumes 200 more calories than the no-caffeine group. Thus, it appears that in addition to the exercise main effect, you have a caffeine main effect.

Finally, you also know that there is no interaction because the effect of caffeine is unaffected by the level of exercise. As Table 7-4 demonstrates, the effect of caffeine is independent of the amount of exercise and the effect of exercise is independent of the amount of caffeine consumed.

TABLE 7-4 Main Effects for Caffeine and Exercise, No Interaction

	No Exercise	50 min Exercise
NO CAFFEINE	(1) 2,000 cal	(2) 2,500 cal
20 mg CAFFEINE	(3) 2,200 cal	(4) 2,700 cal

Simple main effect of exercise (no caffeine): 2,500 − 2,000 = 500 (effect).
Simple main effect of exercise (20 mg caffeine): 2,700 − 2,200 = 500 (effect).
Overall main effect of exercise: (500 + 500)/2 = 500 (effect).

Simple main effect of caffeine (no exercise): 2,200 − 2,000 = 200 (effect).
Simple main effect of caffeine (50 min exercise): 2,700 − 2,500 = 200 (effect).
Overall main effect of caffeine: (200 + 200)/2 = 200 (effect).

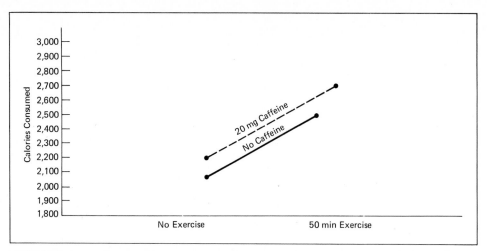

FIGURE 7-2   Main Effects for Caffeine and Exercise, No Interaction

If you graph your means, your graph should look something like Figure 7-2:
The graph confirms what you saw in Table 7-4. The caffeine increased calorie consumption as shown by the 20 mg caffeine line going above the no-caffeine line. Similarly, exercise increased calorie consumption as shown by the fact that both lines slope upward as they go from no exercise to exercise. Finally, the graph tells you that there is no interaction between exercise and caffeine on calorie consumption because the lines are parallel.

Two Main Effects and an Interaction

Now imagine that you got a very different set of results from your study. For example, suppose you found the results in Table 7-5.

TABLE 7-5   Main Effects for Caffeine and Exercise with an Interaction

	No Exercise	**50 min Exercise**
NO CAFFEINE	(1) 2,000 cal	(2) 2,200 cal
20 mg CAFFEINE	(3) 2,200 cal	(4) 3,000 cal

Simple main effect of exercise (no caffeine): 2,200 − 2,000 = 200 (effect).
Simple main effect of exercise (20 mg caffeine): 3,000 − 2,200 = 800 (effect).
Overall main effect of exercise: (200 + 800)/2 = 500 (effect).

Simple main effect of caffeine (no exercise): 2,200 − 2,000 = 200 (effect).
Simple main effect of caffeine (50 min exercise): 3,000 − 2,200 = 800 (effect).
Overall main effect of caffeine: (200 + 800)/2 = 500 (effect).

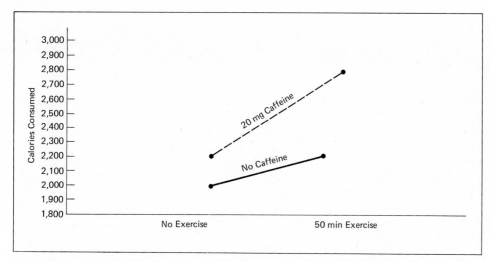

FIGURE 7-3   Main Effects for Caffeine and Exercise with an Interaction

As Table 7-5 shows, you have main effects for both exercise and caffeine. The average effect of caffeine is to increase calorie consumption by 500 and the average effect of exercise is to increase calorie consumption by 500. However, the effect of caffeine varies depending on how much exercise subjects get. In the no-exercise condition, caffeine increases calorie consumption by 200. In the exercise condition, on the other hand, caffeine increases consumption by 800 calories. Since the effect of caffeine varies depending on the amount of exercise, you have an interaction. This interaction is revealed in Figure 7-3, by the fact that the lines are no longer parallel.

Interaction without Main Effects

You've seen that you can have main effects without interactions, but can you have interactions without main effects? Consider the data in Table 7-6 and Figure 7-4.

TABLE 7-6   No Main Effects for Caffeine or Exercise with an Interaction

	No Exercise	**50 min Exercise**
NO CAFFEINE	(1) 2,000 cal	(2) 2,500 cal
20 mg CAFFEINE	(3) 2,500 cal	(4) 2,000 cal

Simple main effect of exercise (no caffeine): 2,500 − 2,000 = 500 (effect).
Simple main effect of exercise (20 mg caffeine): 2,000 − 2,500 = − 500 (effect).
Overall main effect of exercise: (500 + (−500))/2 = 0 (no effect).

Simple main effect of caffeine (no exercise: 2,500 − 2,000 = 500 (effect).
Simple main effect of caffeine (50 min exercise): 2,000 − 2,500 = −500 (effect).
Overall main effect of caffeine: (500 + (−500))/2 = 0 (no effect).

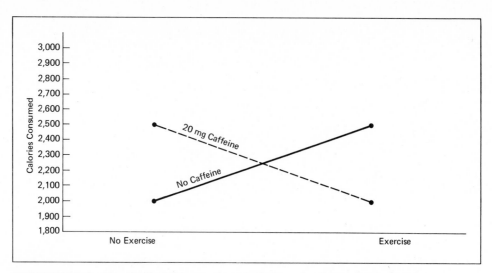

FIGURE 7-4 No Main Effects for Caffeine or Exercise with an Interaction

In this figure, you notice that the lines are not parallel. Therefore, you have an interaction. But note you don't have a main effect for caffeine or exercise: On the average, there is no effect for exercise or caffeine on calorie consumption. However, you wouldn't say that either caffeine or exercise are unrelated to hunger. Instead, you'd say either that caffeine has an effect, but its effect depends on the level of exercise; or, if you prefer to emphasize exercise, you'd say that exercise has an effect, but that effect depends on the amount of caffeine consumed.

TABLE 7-7 Main Effect for Exercise Only and an Interaction

	No Exercise	50 min Exercise
NO CAFFEINE	(1) 2,000 cal	(2) 2,500 cal
20 mg CAFFEINE	(3) 2,250 cal	(4) 2,250 cal

Simple main effect of exercise (no caffeine): 2,500 − 2,000 = 500 (effect).
Simple main effect of exercise (20 mg caffeine): 2,250 − 2,250 = 0 (no effect).
Overall main effect of exercise: (500 + 0)/2 = 250 (effect).

Simple main effect of caffeine (no exercise): 2,250 − 2,000 = 250 (effect).
Simple main effect of caffeine (50 min exercise): 2,250 − 2,500 = −250 (effect).
Overall main effect of caffeine: (250 + (−250))/2 = 0 (no effect).

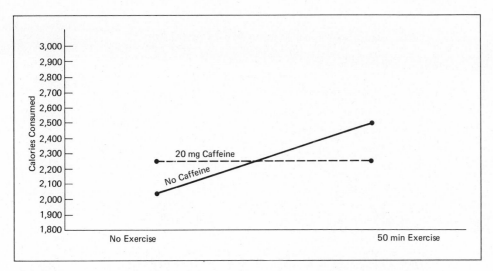

FIGURE 7-5   Main Effect for Exercise only and an Interaction

One Main Effect and an Interaction

Of course you could have one main effect and an interaction, as in Table 7-7.

As this table shows, there is no effect, on the average, for caffeine. There is an average effect of 250 calories for exercise. However, the effect for exercise is uneven. In the no-caffeine condition, exercise increases consumption by 500 calories. In the 20 mg caffeine conditions, exercise has no effect on calorie consumption. Thus, the effect of exercise is qualified by caffeine level. You can see in Figure 7-5 that the same conclusion would be reached if you looked at a graph of the data.

As you can see from the graph, the interaction is indicated by the fact that the lines are not parallel. If you mentally combine the two lines, you would see that the lines slope upward, indicating a main effect for exercise. You can also see that the midpoint of both caffeine lines is at the same place (2,250), indicating that there is no main effect for caffeine.

No Main Effects and No Interaction

Finally, you could have no effect for caffeine, no effect for exercise, and no interaction. An example of such dull findings is shown in Table 7-8 and in Figure 7-6.

ANALYZING THE RESULTS FROM A 2 × 2 EXPERIMENT

You can now graph and describe the eight possible patterns of results from a 2 × 2 experiment, but how do you analyze your results? How do you know whether a main effect or an interaction is significant?

TABLE 7-8   No Main Effects and No Interaction

	No Exercise	50 min Exercise
NO CAFFEINE	(1) (2,500)	(2) (2,500)
20 mg CAFFEINE	(3) (2,500)	(4) (2,500)

Simple main effect of exercise (no caffeine): 2,500 − 2,500 = 0 (no effect).
Simple main effect of exercise (20 mg caffeine): 2,500 − 2,500 = 0 (no effect).
Overall main effect of exercise: (0 + 0)/2 = 0 (no effect).

Simple main effect of caffeine (no exercise): 2,500 − 2,500 = 0 (no effect).
Simple main effect of caffeine (50 min exercise): 2,500 − 2,500 = 0 (no effect).
Overall main effect of caffeine: (0 + 0)/2 = 0 (no effect).

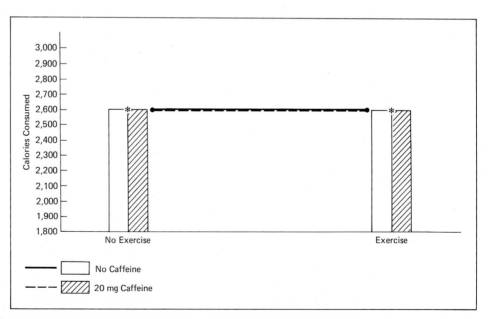

FIGURE 7-6   No Main Effects and No Interaction

As you did with the multiple-group experiment, you would use analysis of variance. Of course, instead of testing for one main effect, you'll be testing for two main effects and an interaction. Thus, your ANOVA summary table might look like this:

Source of Variance	Sum of Squares	df	Mean Square	F
EXERCISE MAIN EFFECT (A)	900	1	900	9.00
CAFFEINE MAIN EFFECT (B)	200	1	200	2.00
INTERACTION (A × B)	100	1	100	1.00
ERROR TERM	3600	36	100	
TOTAL	4800	39		

Despite the fact that this ANOVA table has two more sources of variance than an ANOVA for a multiple-group experiment, most of the rules that apply to the multiple-group ANOVA table apply to the table for a factorial design. Thus, from Chapter 6 (or by consulting Box 7-1), you realize that the table above reveals that we have two levels of the exercise variable, two levels of the caffeine variable, and 40 subjects (since you know that the total of the degrees of freedom is one less than the number of subjects).

BOX 7-1 The Mathematics of an ANOVA Summary Table for Between-Subjects Factorial Designs

1. Degrees of freedom (df) for a main effect equals one less than the number of levels of that factor. If there are three levels of a factor (low, medium, high), that factor has 2 df.
2. Degrees of freedom for an interaction is the product of the degrees of freedom for the factors making up that effect. If you have an interaction between a factor that has 1 df and a factor that has 2 df, that interaction has 2 df: (1 × 2 = 2).
3. To get the degrees of freedom for the error term, add up the degrees of freedom for all the main effects and interactions, and subtract that number from one less than the total number of subjects.
4. To get the mean square for any effect, get the sum of squares for that effect, then divide by that effect's degrees of freedom. If an effect's sum of squares was 300, and its df was 3, its mean square (ms) would be 100.
5. To get the F for any effect, get its mean square and divide it by the mean square error. If an effect's ms was 100 and the mse was 50, the F for that effect would be 2.

The only new thing you need to calculate is the first degree of freedom for the interaction term. To do that, multiply the degrees of freedom for the main effects. For a 2 × 2 experiment, that would be 1 (*df* for first main effect) × 1 (*df* for second main effect) = 1.

Interpreting the Results of an ANOVA Table

To determine whether your effects were significant, you compare the F for each effect with the F table under the appropriate number of degrees of freedom. If you have a significant main effect, you'll want to know whether this main effect was qualified by an interaction.

Main Effects without Interactions

If the interaction was not significant, your conclusions are simple and straightforward. Having no interactions means there are no "ifs" or "buts" about your results. For instance, if you have a main effect for caffeine and no interactions, that means that caffeine had the same kind of effect throughout your experiment—no matter what the level of exercise was.

Interactions

If you find a significant interaction, your results are not as easy to interpret. Having an interaction means that caffeine has a different effect depending on the level of exercise the subject expended. So, before you can interpret your main effects, you'll need to understand the nature of the interaction.

The easiest way to understand an interaction is to graph it. If the lines in your graph cross each other, a variable has one kind of effect in one condition, and the opposite kind of effect in another condition. This kind of interaction is called a **cross-over** or a **disordinal interaction**. You'd have a cross-over interaction if caffeine increased the number of calories consumed in the no-exercise condition, but decreased calorie consumption in the 50 min exercise condition (as in Figure 7-4).

If the lines don't cross, you have an **ordinal interaction**. An ordinal interaction reflects the fact that a factor appears to have more of an effect in one condition than in another condition. An ordinal interaction would occur if caffeine subjects consumed 500 more calories than no caffeine subjects in the no exercise condition, but only consumed 200 more calories than no-caffeine subjects in the exercise condition.

We say appears to have more of an effect because you're assuming that you can accurately compare conditions to determine whether a variable had more of an effect in one condition than in another. In other words, you must have interval data so that you can say, for example, that the difference between 2,000 calories and 2,200 calories is less than the difference between 5,000 calories and 5,500 calories.

Obviously, in this case, you have interval data—if you are interested in number of calories consumed. However, if you're using calories consumed as a measure of how hungry people felt, then your measure may not be interval. You may not have a one-to-one correspondence between number of calories consumed and degree of hunger. It may take the same increase in perceived hunger to make a person who normally eats 2,000 calories eat 2,200 calories as it does to get someone who would eat 5,000 calories to eat 5,500 calories. The ordinal interaction may reflect a problem with your measure of perceived hunger rather than an interaction between caffeine and exercise on perceived hunger.

Thus far, we've suggested that ordinal interactions may be due to a lack of interval data. Let's now turn our attention to two cases in which a lack of interval data definitely leads to ordinal interactions.

Ceiling Effects

Suppose we look at how information about a target person affects how that person is rated using a 2 (information about a target person's traits [no information versus extremely positive information]) × 2 (information about a target person's behavior [no information versus extremely positive information]) experiment. As our dependent measure, we have subjects rate the target person's character on a 3-point scale (1 = below average 2 = average 3 = above average).

We obtain an ordinal interaction. The interaction suggests that getting information about a target person's behavior has less of an effect if you already have information about the target person's traits. In fact, the interaction suggests that if subjects already know about the target person's traits, information about the person's behavior is worthless.

The problem in interpreting this interaction is that the results could be due to a ceiling effect. Although getting additional favorable information about the target person should raise the subject's estimation of him, the subject can't show this increased respect. If, after getting positive trait information, subjects rate the person above average, their rating is at the ceiling. Getting more positive information about the target person may improve subjects' impression of the target, but it can't improve their rating. Subjects may feel the person is a four, but the highest they can rate is three. This is an example of the **ceiling effect**: the effect of a treatment or combination of treatments is underestimated because the dependent measure is not sensitive to psychological states above a certain level. The interaction is due to the dependent measure placing an artificially low ceiling on how high a response can be.

Floor Effects

Conversely, floor effects can also account for ordinal interactions. If instead of using no information and extremely positive information, we'd used no information and extremely negative information, we might again obtain an ordinal interaction. This time, however, the interaction could be due to the fact that subjects couldn't rate target persons lower than 1 (below average). We'd have a **floor effect**: the effect of the treatment or combination of treatments is underestimated because the dependent measure places too high of a floor on what the lowest response can be.

As floor and ceiling effects show, an ordinal interaction may reflect a measurement problem rather than a true interaction. So, be careful when interpreting ordinal interactions.

PUTTING THE 2 × 2 EXPERIMENT TO WORK

You now understand the logic behind the 2 × 2 design. In the next sections, you'll see how you can use the 2 × 2 to get research that is more interesting and has greater construct validity, external validity, and power than a simple experiment.

Adding a Replication Factor to Increase Generalizability

The generalizability of results from a single simple experiment can always be questioned. Critics ask questions such as "Would the results have been different if a different experimenter had performed the study?" and "Would the results have been different if a different manipulation had been used?" The researcher's answer to these critics is to do a **systematic replication**: a study that varies from the original only in some minor aspect, such as using different experimenters or different manipulations.

For example, Morris (1986) found that students learned more from a lecture presented in a rock-video format than from a conventional lecture. However, he only used one lecture and one rock video. Obviously, we'd have more confidence in his results if he'd used more than one lecture and one rock-video lecture. Morris plans to replicate his experiment using another lecture and another rock-video.

As you can see, he'd have benefited from doing a 2 × 2 experiment. Since the 2 × 2 factorial design is like doing two simple experiments at once, he could have obtained his original findings and replicated them in a single 2 × 2 experiment. Specifically, in addition to manipulating the factor of presentation type, he could also have manipulated the factor of **stimulus sets**: the particular stimulus materials used in the experiment. Thus, he could have done a 2 (presentation type [conventional lecture versus rock video format]) × 2 (stimulus sets [material about Shakespeare versus material about economics]) study. Because psychologists often want to show that the manipulation's effect can occur with more than just one particular stimulus set, experimenters routinely include stimulus sets as an experimental factor.

Similarly, it's not unusual to have more than one experimenter run a study and use the experimenters as a factor in the design. Some investigators use experimenters as a factor to show the generality of their results. Specifically, they want to show that certain experimenter attributes (gender, attractiveness, status) don't affect the outcome of the experiment. Other investigators use experimenters as a factor to ensure that experimenters are not intentionally or unintentionally influencing the results. For example, Ranieri and Zeiss (1984) did an experiment in which subjects rated their mood by filling out a self-rating form. They were concerned that experimenters might unintentionally influence the subjects' responses so they used three experimenters and randomly assigned subjects to an experimenter. If they'd found that different experimenters achieved different patterns of results, they'd suspect that the results might be due to experimenter effects rather than to the manipulation itself.

Using an Interaction to Find an Exception to the Rule

Thus far, we've discussed instances where the investigator's goal in using the factorial design was to increase the generalizability of the experimental results. Often, however, you read a research report and say "But I bet that wouldn't happen under——— conditions." In that case, you should do a study in which you essentially repeat the original experiment, except that you add what you believe will be a mediating factor.

To see how this might work, let's look at a study by Jackson and Williams (1985). These researchers were aware of the phenomenon of social loafing: people are less productive in tasks when they work in groups than when they work alone. But they felt that social loafing wouldn't occur on extremely difficult tasks. They therefore did a study, which, like most social loafing studies, manipulated whether or not subjects worked alone or in groups. In addition, they added what they thought would be a mediating factor: whether the task was easy or difficult.

As expected, and as other studies had shown, social loafing occurred. However, social loafing only occurred when the task was easy. When the task was difficult, the reverse of social loafing occurred: subjects worked better in groups than alone. This interaction between task difficulty and social loafing confirmed their hypothesis that task difficulty mediated social loafing.

Using Interactions to Create New Rules

We've discussed looking for an interaction to find an exception to an existing rule. Some interactions, however, do more than complicate existing rules: they reveal new rules. Consider Barbara Tversky's (1973) 2 × 2 factorial experiment. Dr. Tversky randomly assigned students to one of four conditions: 1) expected a multiple-choice test and received a multiple-choice test; 2) expected a multiple-choice test and received an essay test; 3) expected an essay test and received a multiple-choice test; 4) expected an essay test and received an essay test. She found an interaction between the test expected and the test received.

Her interaction showed that subjects did better when they got the same kind of test they expected. Similarly, a researcher might find an interaction between mood (happy, sad) at the time of learning and mood (happy, sad) at the time of testing. The interaction might reveal that recall was best when subjects were in the same mood at the time of testing as at the time of recall. As you can see, the 2 × 2 experiment may be useful for you if you're interested in the effects of similarity.

Using Interactions to Pinpoint What You're Manipulating

Similarity isn't the only construct that interactions help you tap. Often, interactions can help you get a more specific idea of what constructs you're manipulating. For example, suppose you manipulated negative ion concentration and found that the higher the concentration of negative ions, the better mood people were in. You might conclude that negative ions improve mood. However, this conclusion would be wrong. A study by Baron, Russell, and Arms (1985) shows that although higher negative ion concentrations improve mood for people who haven't been provoked, higher negative ion concentrations cause negative shifts in moods for people who have been provoked. Thus, the interaction between provocation and negative ion concentration suggests that negative ions intensify mood rather than improve it.

Similarly, Johnson (1985) looked at the effects of smell on sexual arousal (You can bet the perfume companies were interested!). In his experiment, female subjects viewed slides of men. He found that when subjects smelled androstenol, their brain wave reaction to the photographs was stronger than when they didn't smell androstenol. But how did he know that androstenol was really increasing sexual arousal? Couldn't the brain-wave pattern simply reflect the fact that subjects were aroused by androstenol?

Johnson anticipated this question, and he not only manipulated androstenol but whether the pictures were of men or of women. He found that when women smelled androstenol while viewing a picture of a female subject, androstenol didn't increase the brain-wave activity. In fact, in this condition, androstenol actually reduced the brain wave activity.

The interaction between photo (same sex or opposite sex) and androstenol (no androstenol/androstenol) shows that androstenol didn't merely increase arousal. Because of this interaction, Johnson can make a convincing argument that androstenol increases **sexual arousal**.

Studying Nonexperimental Variables

Rather than converting a simple experiment into a 2 × 2 experiment by adding a second experimental factor, you could convert a simple experiment into a 2 × 2 design by adding a nonexperimental factor: a factor that you can't randomly assign, such as age, sex, or personality type. In that case, you'd have a 2 × 2 study in which half the study is an experiment and the other half isn't. In this kind of study, you could make causal statements about the effects of the experimental factor, but you couldn't make any causal statements regarding the nonexperimental factor.

If you can't make causal statements about the nonexperimental factor, why would you want to add one to your simple experiment? The most obvious and exciting reason is because you're interested in that nonexperimental variable. To see how adding a nonexperimental variable (age of subject, sex of subject, introvert–extrovert, etc.) can really spice up a simple experiment, consider the following simple experiment: Subjects are either angered or not angered in a problem-solving task by a confederate who poses as another subject. Later, subjects get an opportunity to punish or reward the confederate. Obviously, we'd expect that subjects would punish the confederate more when they had been angered. This simple experiment, in itself, wouldn't be very interesting.

Holmes and Will (1985) added a nonexperimental factor to this study—whether subjects were Type A or Type B personalities. The results of this study were intriguing: If subjects hadn't been angered, Type A subjects were more likely to punish the confederate than Type B subjects. However, if subjects had been angered, there was no difference between Type A and Type B subjects.

You can add a nonexperimental variable to a simple experiment for most of the same reasons you'd add an experimental variable: to increase the generalizability of the findings, to look for a similarity effect, and to look for a mediating factor. In addition, you can use a nonexperimental variable to improve your study's power.

Generalizability

You could increase the generalizability of a simple experiment that used only men as subjects by using men and women and making the sex of subject a factor in your design. This design would allow you to determine whether the effect held for both men and women.

Similarity

If you were interested in similarity, you might include some subject characteristic (sex, status, etc.) as a factor in your design, while manipulating the comparable experimenter or confederate factor. For example, if you were studying helping behavior, you could use style of dress of the subject (dressed-up/casual) and style of dress of the confederate as factors in your design. You might find this interaction: dressed-up subjects were more likely than casually dressed subjects to help confederates who were dressed-up, but that casually dressed subjects were more likely than dressed-up subjects to help confederates who were dressed casually. This interaction would suggest that similarity of dress influences helping behavior.

Mediating Variables

If you thought that intelligence would be a mediating variable for the effectiveness of programmed instruction, you might use intelligence as a factor in your design. To do this, you'd first give your subjects an IQ test and then divide them into two groups (above average intelligence and below average intelligence). Next, you'd randomly assign the high-intelligence group so that half of them were in programmed instruction and half were in group instruction. You would do the same for the low-intelligence group. This study might reveal some interesting findings. For instance, suppose you found that programmed instruction vastly improves learning for low-IQ children but slightly decreases learning for high-IQ children. If you'd only done a simple experiment, you might have found a significant positive effect for the new teaching technique. On that basis, you might have recommended using this technique with all school children. What a terrible mistake!

Power: The Blocked Design

The only difference between blocked design and other 2 × 2 studies that include a nonexperimental factor is its purpose. In the **blocked design**, you aren't interested in the nonexperimental variable. You only include it to improve the power of your design.

To see why you might use a blocked design, suppose you want to find out whether the programmed learning method is more effective than the lecture method. Your subjects are 60 fourth graders at a local elementary school. As you're planning your study, you discover that the students vary widely in terms of intelligence. Half of the students seem to be well above average, the other half seem to be well below average.

This wide range of individual differences, this heterogeneity of your sample, concerns you because this means you'll have a great deal of error variance. This error variance may prevent you from detecting a genuine treatment effect. That is, with all these individual differences in learning ability, it will be hard to detect the effect of different instructional techniques. Specifically, your mean square error may be so large that only enormous treatment effects will reach significance.

What can you do? You might eliminate the intelligent students from the experiment. That would give you a more homogeneous group and would reduce error variance due to individual variability.

However, the costs of this solution are high. You're obeying one rule of increasing power (reduce error variance) by breaking another rule (increase the number of subjects). Put another way, although eliminating the extreme subjects should reduce the amount of random error variance in your data, reducing the number of subjects reduces the opportunities for random error to balance out. In a sense, "you're robbing Peter to pay Paul." Also, by limiting who can be in the experiment, you're limiting the generalizability of your results. Obviously, your results wouldn't apply to extremely intelligent children.

Fortunately, there is a solution that allows you to use all your subjects and reduce error variance at the same time. Before the experiment starts, divide your subjects into two groups (or blocks)—the high-IQ group (block) and the low-IQ group (block). Next, randomly assign each member of the high-IQ group to instruction condition, thus ensuring that half the high-IQ subjects are assigned to the pro-grammed instruction group and half are assigned to the lecture instruction condition. Then randomly assign each member of the low-IQ block to instruction condition. In other words, the solution is to do exactly the same study we discussed under the mediating factor study.

The difference between doing this blocked design and the mediating factors study we described earlier is not what you're doing, but why you're doing it. If you're doing a blocked design, you don't care about intelligence and you don't care about the interaction between intelligence and instruction. You only care about getting enough power to find a significant instruction effect.

To see how the blocked design can improve your study's power, let's look at an analysis of variance summary table for this experiment. As you can see, you have a 2 × 2 study, where instructional technique is the experimental factor and intelli-gence is the nonexperimental factor.

	SS	df	MS	F
INSTRUCTION CONDITION (C)		1		
INTELLIGENCE (I)		1		
INTERACTION (C × I)		1		
ERROR		56		
TOTAL		59		

Note how this analysis differs from a table of a 60-subject experiment on the effects of memory technique that doesn't include intelligence as a factor:

	SS	df	MS	F
INSTRUCTION CONDITION (C)		1		
ERROR		58		
TOTAL		59		

The most obvious difference between the two tables is that the error term in the blocked design has 56 df, whereas the error term in the regular experiment has 58 df. What's the significance of losing those 2 df?

The loss of 2 df in the error term may increase your mean square error. It might increase because $MSE = SSE/df$ error. Obviously, if your SSE is 58 in both experiments, your MSE will be greater than 1 in Experiment 1 (58/56 = 1.04), and equal to 1 in Experiment 2 (58/58 = 1.00).

Why do you care that losing those 2 df could increase your mean square error? Because the reason you decided to use a blocked design was to reduce mean square error. You knew that the larger your estimate of random error, the larger the differences would have to be among your groups to reach significance. With a large estimate of random error, even a moderate treatment effect could be shrugged off as being due to random error. Conversely, with a small estimate of random error, even a small difference between your groups might be significant. In short, you were concerned about reducing mean square error because you knew that a large mean square error would shrink your F ratio (because $F = MST/MSE$).

Therefore, if the blocked design does increase the size of your mean square error, then using the blocked design could backfire, hurting your chances of finding a significant difference. This point will become clear if you compare the ANOVA in Table 7-9.

TABLE 7-9 When Blocking Backfires

Blocked Design

Source	SS	df	MS	F
INSTRUCTION CONDITION (C)	5	1	5	2.5
INTELLIGENCE (I)	0	1	0	0
INTERACTION (C × I)	0	1	0	0
ERROR (S/CI)	112	56	2	

Simple Experiment

Source	SS	df	MS	F
INSTRUCTION CONDITION (C)	5	1	5	2.6
ERROR (S/CI)	112	58	1.9	

In this case, the loss of 2 df hurt power—the blocked design gave us a smaller F than the simple experiment. Usually, however, blocked designs will increase the size of your F ratio by reducing error variance.

To understand how blocked designs reduce error variance, remember what error variance is—variability that can't be accounted for. In a simple experiment, there's no way to account for individual differences in intelligence. This variability is therefore one factor that makes up error variance. By making variability due to individual differences in intelligence a factor in your design, you're removing that variability from your error term. You're absorbing that variability, accounting for it, as part of your intelligence main effect. As a result, you'll end up with a smaller error term. Consequently, as you can see in Table 7-10, you've made your treatment effect easier to spot.

In this case, the F for intelligence is much higher in the blocked analysis ($F = 25$) than in the simple design. The larger F is due to a sum of squares error

TABLE 7-10   When Blocking Improves Power

Simple Experiment

Source	SS	df	MS	F
INSTRUCTION CONDITION (C)	5	1	5.0	2.6
ERROR (S/CI)	112	58	1.9	

Blocked Design

INSTRUCTION CONDITION (C)	5	1	5	25
INTELLIGENCE (I)	84	1	84	168
INTERACTION (C × I)	0	1	0	0
ERROR (S/CI)	28	56	0.5	

(SSE) of 28 in the blocked case versus 112 in the simple case. Why was the SS error 84 units smaller in the blocked case? Those 84 units were soaked up by the blocking factor—intelligence.

You've seen that blocking can increase or decrease your study's power. If the blocking variable accounts for enough variance, the loss of error degrees of freedom will be justified. How much variance is enough? Traditionally, statisticians have argued that the correlation between the blocking variable and the dependent variable should be at least .30 (a small to moderate relationship). Otherwise, you've not only wasted time and energy in pretesting but decreased your chance of finding an effect for the experimental factor. Therefore, if the correlation between the blocking variable is not at least .30, you shouldn't use a blocked design. Remember, the term "blocked design" is a technical one meaning that you're only using the design to increase power and you've no interest in the blocking variables. In the blocked design, you know there is a main effect of the nonexperimental variable. But you aren't interested in this main effect in its own right. You're only using it to siphon off extraneous variance so that you can find an effect for the experimental factor.

Expanding the 2 × 2 Experiment

Obviously, you can make the 2 × 2 more complex. We've already alluded to the fact that you can expand a 2 × 2 by adding more levels to one or both variables. For instance, if you were examining the effects of exercise and caffeine on hunger, you could use three levels of exercise and three levels of caffeine. This 3 × 3 factorial experiment would combine the advantages of a factorial experiment (looking at more than one variable at a time), with the advantages of a multilevel experiment (having more than two levels of each variable).

In addition, you can expand the 2 × 2 by adding one or more variables. You could do a 2 × 2 × 2 or even a 2 × 2 × 2 × 2. Imagine, you could study four variables at once! Unfortunately, as you add factors, you complicate your statistics. For instance, if you have a 2 × 2, looking at the effects of exercise and caffeine on hunger, your F table would look like this:

	SS	df	MS	F
EXERCISE		1		
CAFFEINE		1		
INTERACTION OF EXERCISE AND CAFFEINE		1		
ERROR		36		

But, if you had a 2 × 2 × 2, looking at the effects of exercise, caffeine, and temperature on hunger, your F table would look like this:

	SS	df	MS	F
EXERCISE		1		
CAFFEINE		1		
TEMPERATURE		1		
INTERACTION OF EXERCISE WITH CAFFEINE		1		
INTERACTION OF EXERCISE WITH TEMPERATURE		1		
INTERACTION OF CAFFEINE WITH TEMPERATURE		1		
INTERACTION OF EXERCISE WITH CAFFEINE WITH TEMPERATURE		1		
ERROR		72		

Even without doing the calculations, you realize that the analysis for the 2 × 2 × 2 is much more complicated than the 2 × 2. Graphs of 2 × 2 × 2 designs also dramatize the 2 × 2 × 2's complexity. You need not one, but two graphs to depict a 2 × 2 × 2, such as in Figure 7-7.

Of course, you can also expand the 2 × 2 by adding both levels and variables. If you wanted to, you could do an 8 × 2 × 4 × 3 × 6 experiment. But, as you can imagine, the more complex your design, the more difficult it is to interpret. You must

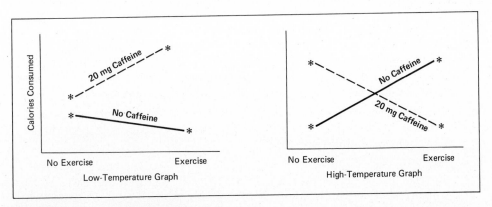

FIGURE 7-7   Graphing a 2 × 2 × 2

walk the fine line between getting a lot of useful information from an experiment and getting a lot of uninterpretable information. For most novice experimenters, that fine line is the 2×2 experiment.

CONCLUDING REMARKS

In this chapter, you've seen the benefits of using the factorial experiment. Your awareness of this design opens up new possibilities for research. Just as importantly, your understanding of this commonly used design increases your ability to read, understand, and evaluate the research of others. You now have the ability to discover new paths for research that radiate from the research of others. In the next two chapters, you'll refine this ability.

WATSON SOLVES A CASE

LESTRADE: The reason I called on you, Mr. Holmes, is so that you can reassure my superiors that Sir Edward died of natural causes.

HOLMES: I'm not sure I can do that, Inspector. From examining the body, I think that Sir Edward was poisoned.

LESTRADE: Initially, I was under the same impression, Mr. Holmes. However, the coroner found no trace of poison in the body. That's when I thought of you. Could there be some rare poison that we wouldn't have detected?

HOLMES: There are a few oriental poisons with which London coroners are not familiar. But before conjecturing further on this point, tell me, were there any needle marks on the body?

LESTRADE: I see what you're getting at Mr. Holmes. If Sir Edward were poisoned, how was it administered? My thoughts exactly. The coroner swears there were no needle marks on the body. We are therefore sure that the poison had to be in something he ate or drank—and there's the problem. Sir Edward died at a party. He drank from the punch bowl and ate from the buffet table, just as everyone else did. If his food were poisoned, why weren't any of the other guests sick? If his drink were poisoned, why didn't we find any traces of poison in Sir Edward's glass? It's a mystery to me, Mr. Holmes.

HOLMES: What you say is very puzzling, indeed. It's very tempting to just assume that Sir Edward died a sudden death. Why are your superiors so bent on thinking he was murdered?

LESTRADE: Well, he'd been acting very strangely of late. He also had many enemies. In fact, just before going to the party, he met with one of his worst enemies, James Moriarty, at Moriarty's club. But Moriarty couldn't have poisoned him because Sir Edward and Moriarty both ate the same thing—

some canapés from a plate that the waiter brought in. Professor Moriarty suffered no ill effects from them.

HOLMES: Intuitively, I know that Moriarty is behind his death. But, I'm afraid I have no concrete evidence. What do you make of this, Watson?

WATSON: It reminds me of one of the first patients I had when I was in India. Things were very chaotic during the war and inadequate records were kept. I took over the private's case because his physician had died earlier in the day. I administered a perfectly safe drug to the young private—perfectly safe, unless the patient has been given quinine. The combination (or interaction, if you will) of the two drugs is invariably lethal. Unfortunately, unbeknownst to me, the soldier's previous doctor had been treating the lad for malaria with quinine, so when I administered my drug, he died. I'll never forget that.

HOLMES: Brilliant, Watson! You've solved the case. We've only been looking at the main effects of drugs. That's where we went wrong. The main effect of the drug Moriarty gave Sir Edward must be negligible, and the main effect of what Edward consumed at the party—probably alcohol—is also nonlethal. But the interaction between the two drugs must be fatal. What fiendish brilliance! But we have him now, Watson. I have a list of drugs that interact with alcohol to produce death. I'll have the coroner look for the presence of these drugs in the body and in the sample of the canapés from Moriarty's club. It's a pity, we didn't discover this earlier. We could have offered Moriarty a brandy.

MAIN POINTS

1. Factorial experiments allow you to look at more than one variable or factor at a time.
2. The simplest factorial experiment is the 2 × 2 experiment.
3. The 2 × 2 allows you to study two independent variables in one experiment, and it lets you see the effects of combining different levels of those two independent variables.
4. Whenever independent variables combine to produce an unexpected effect, you have an interaction.
5. Interactions can most easily be observed by graphing your data. If your two lines aren't parallel, you have an interaction.
6. When you graph your data and your lines cross, you probably have a cross-over (disordinal) interaction. If the lines aren't parallel but they don't cross, you have an ordinal interaction.
7. Ordinal interactions may be the result of ceiling effects or floor effects. That is, they may reflect a measurement problem rather than the fact that two variables combine in an unexpected manner.
8. A significant interaction usually qualifies main effects. Thus, a significant interaction means that you can't talk about your main effects without referring to the interaction.

9. Sometimes the interaction in the 2 × 2 represents another variable. For instance, in a 2 × 2 experiment with place of learning and place of testing as factors, an interaction may reveal that it's best to be tested in the same place you learned the information.

10. You can use the 2 × 2 to refine a simple experiment by adding a replication factor to increase generality, adding a potential mediating factor, or examining the effect of a personality variable.

11. You can also improve the power of a simple experiment by using a blocked design. Your hope is that the blocked factor will absorb enough random error to make an otherwise nonsignificant result statistically significant.

12. Factorial designs can be as complicated as you desire. However, the more complex the design, the more difficult it is to analyze and interpret its results.

KEY TERMS

factorial experiment
simple main effect
overall main effect
interaction
cross-over (disordinal) interaction

ordinal interaction
ceiling effect
floor effect
stimulus set
blocked design

EXERCISES

1. Define an interaction.

2. Graph the following data from an experiment on the effect of lighting and color of glasses on mood.

Color of glasses

Lighting level		Transparent	Rose-colored
	DIM	5	10
	BRIGHT	10	5

Scores reflect mood based on a scale of 1 (bad mood) to 10 (great mood). Is there an interaction? How do you know?

3. How many subjects were used in the following study? How many levels of lighting were used? How many levels of glasses were used? Complete the table.

	SS	df	MS	F
glasses	10	1	—	—
lighting	—	2	20	—
interaction	400	2	200	—
error	540	54	?	
Total	990	59		

4. A professor doing a simple experiment finds that students who are given lecture notes but don't attend the lecture, perform better than those who do attend the lecture. Would there be any advantages to refining this study using a 2 × 2 design?

8

FIELD EXPERIMENTS AND WITHIN-SUBJECTS DESIGNS OR, HOW TO PROSPER DURING THE UPCOMING SUBJECT SHORTAGE

OUTLINE

OVERVIEW

If you want to use randomization to perform an internally valid experiment, there are several designs from which you can choose. You aren't limited to the situation we've so far discussed, where you independently and randomly assign subjects to condition in a laboratory setting.

In this chapter, you'll learn about other options. You'll begin by learning about the field experiment. In the field experiment, you let many nonexperimental variables vary freely: leaving randomization and statistics to account for them. By not controlling nonexperimental variables, you often obtain findings that have impressive external validity.

After learning about field experiments, you'll learn about matched pairs and within-subjects designs. In these designs, you try to either reduce (by matching pairs of subjects in the matched pairs design) or eliminate (by using subjects as their own controls in the within-subjects design) between-subject differences. Then, you let randomization take care of the effects of the few remaining uncontrolled variables. By limiting the nonexperimental variables that randomization has to account for, you can detect effects that might be overlooked by other investigators.

Finally, you'll learn how to compare these designs. By the end of this chapter, you'll be able to choose the best experimental design for your research problem.

THE FIELD EXPERIMENT

When most people think of the typical psychological experiment, they probably envision a sterile laboratory stocked with subjects and fancy equipment. But you realize that a well-stocked laboratory does not an experiment make. What makes an experiment is random assignment.

Obviously, you don't need a lab to randomly assign subjects to groups. Therefore, if you don't want to do your experiment in a lab, you could conduct a **field experiment**: an experiment performed in a natural setting.

Advantages of Doing the Field Experiment

Why would you want to leave the comfort of the lab to do a field experiment? There are four major reasons for leaving the lab: 1) the desire for more power, 2) the desire to generalize your results to different settings, 3) the desire to generalize your results to a different group of people, and 4) the desire to ensure that subjects are reacting to the treatment rather than feigning the reaction they think will please you.

External Validity

First, you might want to generalize your results beyond the laboratory setting. The controlled, isolated lab is a far cry from the chaotic, crowded world that we live in. Consequently, some people question whether an effect found in a lab would hold in a real-world setting. The field experiment lets you find out.

Second, you might want to generalize your results to people other than those who volunteer to be in psychology experiments. In most lab experiments, subjects are students in introductory psychology courses. These students are probably not "typical" of the average person. In the field experiment, on the other hand, your subjects can be anyone at all.

Construct Validity

Third, you might want to avoid lab experiments because volunteers for these experiments know they're in an experiment. Because they know the treatments aren't "real," their responses may be more of an act than an honest reaction to the treatment. Thus, rather than reacting to the treatment as they naturally would, they may act the way they think you want them to act. In other words, they may act to confirm your hypothesis.

To field experiment subjects, on the other hand, the treatment is real. These subjects aren't trying to confirm your hypothesis. In fact, they don't even know you're doing an experiment on them. Because of their naïveté, they're more likely to give natural responses.

Power

Fourth, you might leave the lab because you don't have enough volunteer subjects. As you may remember from Chapter 5, the more subjects you have, the more able you are to find significant effects. When confronted with having only a few people who might agree to come to the lab for your experiment, and a world of potential subjects waiting for you outside the lab, you may decide to go where the subjects are.

Limitations of the Field Experiment

Although the field experiment may give you more power, more construct validity, and greater external validity, the field experiment is not a panacea. The field experiment may lack external, construct, or internal validity. Furthermore, field experiments may lack power, be unethical, or demand more time and energy than you would ever suspect.

Is It Ethical?

The first problem to consider is an ethical one. According to the American Psychological Association's Code of Ethics (1981a), all subjects for an experiment should be volunteers. Not only should subjects be volunteers, but you should get their **informed consent** prior to their participation. That is, subjects should have a good idea of what's going to happen to them and should give their written permission before the experiment begins. Furthermore, after the experiment, subjects should be **debriefed**: informed about what they've just done and why.

These ethical guidelines may conflict with your research goals. You may not want to use volunteers because volunteers are atypical, but the guidelines urge you to use them. If you were forced to use volunteers, you might not want to tell them what the experiment was about so they wouldn't play along with your study. However, the guidelines recommend that human subjects know for what they're volunteering. Finally, you may not want to debrief your subjects for fear they might tell other potential subjects about the study. The ethical guidelines, on the other hand, stress that you debrief subjects so they get some benefit from their participation and so you can remove any harm you may have inadvertently caused.

What's the solution to these thorny ethical issues? Unfortunately, there are no easy answers. Your desire for valid information must be weighed against your subjects' rights to privacy. Since you may not be able to fairly weigh subjects' rights against your desires, you should consult informed individuals (e.g., your research design professor) before doing a field experiment. In addition to consulting with your professor, you may also have to get your experiment approved by your institution's ethics committee.

Perhaps the easiest way to deal with ethical problems is to avoid violating the guidelines. For example, you might do a field experiment, but ask for volunteers, give informed consent, and debrief your subjects. Under these conditions, you've lost some advantages of field experimentation, but you may still get subjects that are more "typical" than laboratory subjects, and you do get to see whether your results generalize to a real-world setting.

A more controversial approach is to perform a field experiment on unsuspecting volunteers while they think they're waiting for an experiment to begin. For example, Latane and Darley (1968) had subjects witness a theft while they were in a waiting room ostensibly waiting to start a laboratory experiment.

The "experiment in the waiting room" is a compromise between ethical principles and research goals. When you meet the ethical guidelines requesting the use of volunteer subjects, you lose the ability to get subjects who are more like "real people" and you lose access to a larger pool of potential subjects.

When you try to meet the research goals of seeing whether the effect would occur outside the lab and whether it would occur with naïve subjects, you violate the ethical guidelines for informed consent. Because subjects signed up for one experiment but ended up in another, you've raised serious ethical questions.

External Validity Is Not Guaranteed

If you think that by doing a field experiment you'll get subjects who represent the average person, you may be disappointed. In the "waiting room" study we just described, the subjects are the same college sophomores would participate in a lab study. Even doing an experiment in the field (e.g., a shopping mall), won't ensure that your subjects will represent "the average person." In fact, in many field experiments, you may not know who your subjects represent, other than saying, for example, that they "represented people who used the telephone booth at the Tarfield Mall between 2:00 P.M. and 4:00 P.M. during March 1989."

Construct Validity Is Not Guaranteed

Similarly, if you want to study naïve subjects, the field experiment may let you down. Former subjects, or nosey bystanders, may talk about the experiment to potential subjects and ruin everyone's naïveté. To illustrate this point, consider a field experiment conducted by Shaffer, Rogel, and Hendrik (1975) in the Kent State University Library. A confederate of the researcher sat down at a table occupied by a naïve subject. After several minutes of studying, the confederate walked away from the table leaving behind several personal items. Sometimes the confederate asked the naïve subject to watch his belongings (request condition) other times he said nothing (no-request condition). Shortly after the confederate left the table a "thief" appeared, went through the confederate's belongings, discovered a wallet, and quickly walked away with it. The dependent variable was whether subjects tried to stop the thief. Results showed that 64% of the subjects in the request condition tried to stop the thief, compared to only 14% of the subjects in the no-request condition.

Put yourself in the place of one of Shaffer, et al.'s subjects. You've seen a thief steal a man's wallet, and perhaps you've even tried to foil the robbery attempt. Wouldn't you tell someone about it? Let's say you told a friend about the incident and that friend says she's heard of a similar incident. One night she goes to the library to study. Shortly after she sits down, she finds herself approached by the same victim she's heard about, and witnesses the very crime about which you told her. Not only has she lost her naïveté, but very soon the whole school will know about the experiment.

Or, put yourself in the place of a curious bystander, say the reference librarian. You're working at the reference desk and out of the corner of your eye you observe two students sitting at a table. One gets up and walks away leaving behind his books and several personal items. You go about your work. But then you notice a different man go up to the pile of belongings, rummage through them, pocket a wallet, and walk hurriedly away. What would you do? As a responsible employee, you'd try to stop the thief and report the incident to the authorities. The campus police arrive to get your statement, perhaps even to make an arrest. To stop the police investigation, the researcher explains that it's only an experiment. Students in the library strain to overhear the conversation and question you endlessly about the incident. Soon, everyone on campus knows about the experiment.

Thus, a field experiment may end up having no more construct validity than a laboratory study unless you take appropriate precautions. Therefore, if you were doing Shaffer et. al.'s study, you'd try to collect all the data in one night to reduce the chances of subjects talking to potential subjects. Furthermore, to reduce the chance of innocent bystanders destroying subjects' innocence, you might inform the library staff about the experiment.

Internal Validity Is Not Guaranteed

If not carefully conducted, the field experiment may not only lack external and construct validity, but internal validity as well. Although all field experiments should have internal validity, some don't because of failure to randomly assign subjects to groups and because subjects drop out of the study (mortality).

Failure to Randomly Assign All the designs we have discussed so far rely on independent random assignment for their internal validity. Unfortunately, random assignment is much more difficult in the field than in the laboratory. Random assignment is especially difficult when you're manipulating an important, real-life treatment. Often real-world subjects and their representatives don't believe that people should be randomly assigned to important treatments. Instead, they believe that people should be able to choose their own treatment.

To imagine the difficulties of random assignment in the field, suppose you wanted to study the effects of television violence on children's behavior. You approach parents and tell them that you want some children to watch certain nonviolent television programs (e.g., "Mr. Rogers Neighborhood," "Sesame Street") and other children to watch violent television programs (e.g., "Prime Time Wrestling," "The A-Team," "The Smurfs"). You may find that some parents would be willing for you to assign their children to nonviolent fare, but few are going to let you randomly assign their child to either condition. If you say, "I want to be able to assign your child to either one of these conditions," many parents will object. Some will say, "You can show my child 'Sesame Street,' but you're not going to make her watch violence and trash!" Other parents will say, "You can make my kid watch wrestling. I watch it all the time anyway. But not those other shows. They're on the same time as my shows. You're not going to make me sit around and watch kiddie junk!" Of course, the hassles with the parents may be nothing compared with the hassles of getting the children themselves to agree to random assignment.

Yet, with enough persistence (and enough money), you could probably get people to agree to random assignment. But once you've done that, you face a huge problem—How do you know that subjects will watch the television shows you assigned? You can't go to everyone's house. You can't trust young children to carry out your instructions. You can't trust parents to supervise the children because they may be busy with other tasks. Therefore, the prospect of using random assignment to determine children's television diets seems intimidating.

In fact, the idea of randomly assigning children to television viewing seems so intimidating that most investigators researching the effects of TV have avoided field experiments even though such experiments would provide the strongest evidence about whether viewing violence on television causes aggressive behavior.

But have these researchers given up too soon? Cook and Campbell (1979) claim that researchers often give up on random assignment faster than they should. Cook and Campbell argue that random assignment can often be used in the field—if the researcher is creative.

In the case of researching the impact of television on children's behavior, researchers may have given up too soon. Perhaps researchers should approach a nursery school. If the nursery school would cooperate and get informed consent from the parents and children, the television viewing could take place at the school as part of the children's ordinary routine. In this way, you would know that subjects were getting the treatment to which were assigned.

Mortality   Unfortunately, even after you assign your subjects to condition, they may not stay assigned. Mortality may raise its ugly head: That is, subjects may drop out of your experiment before you have collected the dependent measure. For example, suppose you're doing the television violence experiment with nursery school children. As the study progresses, you find that subjects are dropping out of the violent television condition (perhaps the kids are getting too violent or the parents are having second thoughts). But subjects are not dropping out of the nonviolent condition. The fact that subjects in one group are more likely to quit than subjects in the other group seriously damages the study's internal validity.

Power May Be Inadequate

Not only is it easier to create an internally valid experiment in the lab than in the field, but it's also easier to create a powerful experiment in the lab than in the field. In the lab, you can have impressive power by reducing random error and by using sensitive dependent measures. By leaving the lab, you may lose your ability to reduce random error and to use sensitive measures.

Random Error In the laboratory, you can reduce random error by minimizing the degree to which irrelevant variables vary. You can reduce unwanted variation due to individual differences by using a homogeneous group of subjects. You can reduce unwanted variation in the environment by testing subjects under identical conditions. You can reduce unwanted variation due to subjects being distracted, by putting subjects in a soundproof, simple, virtually distraction-free environment. You can reduce unwanted variation in your procedures by rigidly standardizing your experiment. Thus, if you do your study in the laboratory, you can use many tactics to stop irrelevant variables from varying.

By leaving the lab, you may lose your ability to stop these variables from fluctuating. Sometimes you willingly give up the opportunity to control these variables so that you can generalize your results to the real world. For example, you may do a field experiment to get access to a heterogeneous group of subjects. The advantage of having a wide range of subjects is that you can generalize your results to a wide range of people. The disadvantage is that you're giving individual differences a chance to account for a sizeable difference between your groups. Therefore, your treatment's effect might be obscured by these individual differences.

Sometimes, however, you unwillingly give up the ability to control irrelevant variables. For instance, you always want to standardize your procedures, but if you have to conduct your study on the run ("Excuse me, may I talk to you for a moment?"), without the benefit of equipment, in a noisy, crowded environment, it's hard to follow the same procedure every time. Similarly, although you always want subjects to pay attention to your manipulation, field subjects may not even notice it: The real world is much more distracting than the lab.

Problems in Using Sensitive Dependent Measures One reason you may lose power by doing a field experiment is that it's harder to reduce random error in the field than in the lab. You may also lose power by doing a field experiment because you may have to use less sensitive measures in the field. To illustrate, let's say you're interested in whether getting an unexpected gift will increase happiness. In the lab, you'd probably measure happiness by having subjects rate how happy they are on a 1-to-7 scale. Even if you were to use a more indirect behavioral indicator of happiness, such as helping, you'd measure helping with a high degree of precision. For example, you'd either measure exactly how long it took subjects to help a person, or how much they helped the person.

In the field, measuring happiness is much more difficult. You probably won't be able to have subjects fill out a rating scale. Therefore, you'll probably have to use a less sensitive behavior measure, such as helping. Furthermore, you may not even be able to measure helping with any degree of precision. Unlike in the lab, you can't merely sit in your chair, gaze through a one-way mirror, and record how much or how long subjects help. Instead, you must inconspicuously peer around the corner, filter out the dog barking, the traffic sounds, and other people to see whether your subjects help. Under these conditions, you're lucky to see whether subjects help at all—much less see how much they help. Thus, in the field, you may be too busy to collect anything other than dichotomous (two-valued) variables. Clearly, asking whether someone responded gives you less information than asking how long it took the person to respond or to what extent he responded.

But you don't have to settle for less sensitive measures when you go the field. One way to avail yourself of more sensitive measures is to use a second experimenter who does nothing but record data. This leaves you free to put quarters (unexpected gifts) in phone booths, hide until a subject finds it, and make yourself a convenient person "in need" for your unsuspecting subjects to demonstrate their good will. This second experimenter could observe and record things like how quickly subjects responded and to what extent they responded.

If you don't have a second experimenter, let such equipment as videotape cameras, tape recorders, and stopwatches, do the recording for you. For example, Milgram, Bickman, and Berkowitz (1969) had confederates look up at a tall building. Their independent variable was how many confederates looked up at the building. Their dependent measure was the proportion of people walking by who also looked up. Actually, the confederates were looking up at a videotape camera. After the experiment was over, Milgram et al. were able to count the number of people looking up by playing the videotape.

Failure to Establish and Maintain Independence

Some field experimenters try to regain the power lost due to having high levels of random error and insensitive measures by using a large number of subjects. To get large numbers of subjects, some researchers do field experiments on intact groups (e.g., work groups, classes). Unfortunately it's hard to independently assign subjects from intact groups, and once they're assigned, it's hard to maintain independence. For example, suppose a nursery school was willing to help you out with your study on the effects of watching prosocial television. Then you would have a large, convenient sample. However, there might be a catch: the nursery school might insist that you keep the classes intact. Thus, although you might want to assign each student independently, you may have to assign one class to one condition and another class to the other condition. Consequently, no matter how many people are in your study, you only have two independent units—the two classes. Because any two classes will obviously differ from one another in many ways, your experimental and control groups would be very different before the experiment began.

Even if you're able to independently assign subjects, you may be unable to maintain independence because subjects interact with one another, thereby influencing each other's responses. If the children in the group influence each other, you don't have independent responses from 60 individuals. Instead, you have responses from two mobs. For example, suppose there is one very aggressive child in the control group. As any teacher knows, one misbehaving child can cause virtually everyone in the group to misbehave.

Special Problems with Doing Field Experiments with Intact Groups

Violation of independence, whether due to faulty assignment or failure to maintain independence of responses, can have one of two consequences—bad and worse. The worst consequence happens if the researcher doesn't realize that independence has been violated. In that case, she would conduct her statistical tests as if she had more individual units than she has. She would think that since each group is made up of 30 randomly assigned subjects, the groups should be fairly equivalent. She would believe that since she has so many independent units, chance differences between groups should be minimal. However, since she really has only two independent units, chance could easily be responsible for substantial differences between groups. Therefore, she is very likely to misinterpret a difference that's due to chance as a treatment effect.

The bad consequence occurs if the researcher realizes that she has only two independent units. In that case, the good news is that since she realizes that even large differences might be due to chance, she probably won't mistake chance differences for treatment differences. However, the bad news is that she'll tend to dismiss real treatment effects as being due to chance. In other words, her study will be powerless.

Threats to Construct Validity

You can remedy the problem of too few independent units by using more classes. For example, you might have 10 classes in one group and 10 classes in the other. But violation of independence is only one problem with using intact groups. Using intact groups exposes your study to three serious threats to construct validity: demoralization, compensation, and diffusion of treatment.

Demoralization   Your study's construct validity starts to erode the moment the classes talk to each other and find out about their differential treatment. Don't be surprised if the no-television group becomes **demoralized**. They may vent their frustration about missing out on television by being violent. As a result, the television-watching group may be better behaved, even though watching television didn't improve their behavior. In this case, it's not that watching television reduces violence, it's that feeling deprived increases violence.

Compensation   On the other hand, upon learning of the experimental group's good fortune, **compensation** could occur. That is, the no-television class might pull together and behave well so that they'd be allowed to watch television. As a result of their efforts, the no-television group might behave better than the television group. Again, you would see a difference between your groups, but the difference wouldn't be due to the effects of watching television.

Diffusion of Treatment   Finally, you might not observe any effect for treatment because of **diffusion of treatment**: both your groups are getting the treatment. In your television study, members of the no-television class might be watching television just like the television class. For example, their teacher may borrow the television from the other teacher (their teacher may succumb to their begging to "watch television like the other class"). Or, if the classes are held in the same room, pupils in the no-television group might watch or overhear the other class's television shows. Consequently, the impact of the television shows would diffuse to the no-television group.

Minimizing Threats to Construct Validity

How can you minimize demoralization, compensation, and diffusion of treatment? The steps to take are obvious once you realize that these threats usually result from subjects finding out that their treatments differ. With this in mind, the first step is to make your conditions resemble one another as much as possible. Never use a treatment group and a no-treatment group. Instead, use a treatment group and a placebo treatment group, or two different kinds of treatment.

In the television study, you could have one group watch one kind of television program (e.g., violent) while the other watched another kind of program (e.g., non-violent). Or, you could be even sneakier and show both groups the same shows—the only difference being that in one condition you've edited out some of the violence. In this way, subjects won't notice that their conditions differ.

The second step is to give subjects fewer opportunities to talk. For example, shorten the time between giving the treatment and collecting the dependent measure. Obviously, the longer the time between introducing the treatment and collecting the dependent measure, the more likely the groups are to talk. Therefore, you might conduct the entire study in one day rather than having it last for several months.

If you want to look at long-term effects of treatment, you could reduce opportunities for subjects to talk to one another by using subjects who won't run into one another. Thus, in the television study, rather than assigning different classes in the same schools to different conditions, you could assign different schools to different conditions. The chances of a toddler from Busy Bee Day Care comparing curriculum with a child from Lazy Linda's Day Camp are remote.

THE MATCHED PAIRS DESIGN

If you don't have enough subjects to do a powerful simple experiment, you have two basic alternatives. Your first alternative is to get access to more subjects by doing a field experiment; your second is to use a design that requires fewer subjects than a simple experiment, such as a matched pairs design. The matched pairs design will be the focus of this section. As you will see, the **matched pairs design** combines the best aspects of matching and randomization: it uses matching to reduce irrelevant variables and it uses randomization to establish internal validity.

Procedure

In the matched pairs design, you first measure your subjects on a variable that's related to the dependent measure (e.g., pretest scores). Then, you form **matched pairs**: pairs of subjects who have similar scores on this measure. Thus, if you were doing a memory experiment using a matched pairs design, you'd first give all your subjects a memory test. Next, you'd rank their scores on this memory test from lowest to highest. Then, you'd pair the two highest scorers, the next two highest scores, and so on. This would give you pairs of subjects with similar scores. Finally, you'd randomly assign one member of each pair to the control group and the other to the experimental group.

**Considerations
in Using
Matched
Pairs Designs**

Power

You'll recall that researchers using simple experiments or other between-subject designs lose power because individual differences obscure treatment effects. With between-subject designs, researchers often don't know whether a difference between groups is due to the treatment or to the groups being different before the experiment began.

To reduce the risk that between-subject differences may obscure a treatment effect, some experimenters try to reduce differences between their subjects by using a homogenous group of subjects. For example, one researcher may use only subjects who are 18 years old, white, American, male, and have IQs between 115 and 120. Another researcher may use only female lab rats that are between 180 and 210 days of age.

Rather than reducing random error by limiting who can be in the experiment, the matched pairs researcher uses matching. If matching succeeds in reducing random error, the matched pairs design will usually give you more power than the simple experiment. The same difference that would not be statistically significant with a simple experiment may be significant with a matched pairs design.

How is this possible? Because your t value will be higher with the matched pairs design. Remember, the t value is the difference you observe divided by an estimate of random error (the standard error of the difference). With less random error, the t value becomes larger. For example, if the standard error of the difference for a simple experiment is 6, then a difference of six seconds between conditions would yield a nonsignificant t value of 1.00 (6/6). However, if a matched pairs design reduced random error so much that the standard error was only one, then that same difference of six seconds would yield a highly significant t value of 6.00 (6/1).

But what if matching fails to reduce random error? Then, the matched pairs design may be less powerful than the simple experiment. Why? Because by using a matched pairs design instead of a simple experiment you lose half your degrees of freedom. For instance, if you used 20 subjects in a simple experiment, you would have 18 df (2 less than the number of subjects). But in a 20 subject, matched pairs design, you have only 9 df (1 less than the number of pairs). Losing degrees of freedom can hurt your power. As you know from looking at the t table in Appendix E, the fewer degrees of freedom you have, the larger your t value must be to reach significance. In our example, with 18 df (what you'd have if you tested 20 subjects in a simple experiment), you'd only need a t value of 2.101 for your results to be statistically significant. On the other hand, with 9 df (what you'd have if you tested 10 pairs of subjects in a matched pairs experiment), your t value would have to be at least 2.262 to be statistically significant.

Thus, if you got the same t value with the matched pairs design as you would have with a simple experiment, you would lose power by using the matched pairs design. However, if your matching is any good, you should get a larger t value when you use a matched pairs design, and the increase in the size of the t value will more than compensate for the degrees of freedom you will lose.

External Validity

Power is not the only consideration in deciding to use a matched pairs design. You may either use or avoid matching for reasons of external validity.

For example, a matched pairs design may have more external validity than an equally powerful between-subjects design. Why? Because the between-subjects design may get you power by limiting what type of subject can participate (male, albino rats between the ages of 180 and 185 days), whereas the matched pairs gets you power without limiting the kind of subject you can have. Since you can reduce random error by matching subjects rather than limiting the kinds of subjects you have, the matched pairs design may allow you to generalize your results to a broader population.

However, if subjects drop out of the study between the time they're tested on the matching variable and the time they're to perform the experiment, matching will reduce the generalizability of your results. For instance, you might start off with 24 subjects (12 pairs), but end up with only 10 pairs of subjects. Although you're not losing enough subjects to seriously damage your study's power, you're hurting your experiment's external validity: you can't generalize your results to individuals resembling the subjects who dropped out of your experiment.

Whether or not subjects drop out, matching reduces the ability to generalize your results to individuals who were not pretested. To illustrate, suppose an experimenter uses a matched pairs design to examine the effect of caffeine on anxiety. In the experiment, the subjects receiving caffeine become more anxious than those not receiving caffeine. Can the investigator generalize her results to people who haven't taken an anxiety test before consuming caffeine? No, it may be that caffeine only increases anxiety if it's consumed after taking an anxiety test: taking the anxiety test makes subjects so concerned about their level of anxiety that they interpret any increase in feelings as an increase in anxiety. Because of the anxiety test, the stimulation produced by caffeine, which might ordinarily be interpreted as invigorating, is interpreted as anxiety.

Construct Validity

In the caffeine study we just discussed, taking the anxiety test before and after the treatment might make subjects aware that the experimenter was looking at the effects of a drug on anxiety. However, the fact that subjects are guessing the hypothesis doesn't, in itself, ruin the experiment's construct validity.

For example, if you used a treatment condition and a placebo condition, it doesn't matter if subjects think the drug is supposed to increase anxiety. Since both groups have the same hypothesis ("The drug I took will increase my anxiety"), knowing the hypothesis wouldn't cause the treatment group to differ from the placebo group. A significant difference between groups would have to be due to the treatment.

If, on the other hand, your independent variable manipulations have low construct validity, matching will make those weaknesses more damaging. For instance, if, in the caffeine study, an empty control group was used (nothing was given to control subjects), matching might seriously threaten construct validity. In this case, the two groups would have different hypotheses. The experimental group subjects would hypothesize that the drug should affect their anxiety level. Since control subjects were not given anything resembling a drug, they wouldn't form such a hypothesis. Consequently, a significant effect might be due to the two groups acting on different hypotheses.

Analysis   If you have interval or ratio data, you can analyze the results of a matched pairs design by using the dependent groups t test. Although you must use several steps to compute the **dependent groups t test**, the simplicity of the steps makes this one of the easiest tests to do. To learn how to do this simple statistical test, look at the example in Box 8-1.

BOX 8-1   Calculating a Dependent Groups t Test in Seven Easy Steps

STEP 1: Subtract Condition 1 score from Condition 2 score for each subject or for each matched pair.

Pair or Subject	Condition 1 Score	Condition 2 Score	Difference
1	3	2	1
2	4	3	1
3	5	4	1
4	2	1	1
5	3	2	1
6	5	2	3
7	5	2	3
8	4	3	1
9	3	4	-1
10	5	6	-1

STEP 2: Sum up the differences, then divide by the number of pairs of scores to get the average difference.

Pair or Subject	Condition 1 Score	Condition 2 Score	Difference
1	3	2	1
2	4	3	1
3	5	4	1
4	2	1	1
5	3	2	1
6	5	2	3
7	5	2	3
8	4	3	1
9	3	4	-1
10	5	6	-1
		Total difference =	10

Average Difference = 10/10 = 1

STEP 3: Calculate the variance for the differences by subtracting each difference from the average difference. Square that difference and divide by 1 less than the number of pairs of scores.

Pair or Subject	Average Difference (AD)	Observed Difference (D)	AD − D	AD − D Squared
1	1	1	0	0
2	1	1	0	0
3	1	1	0	0
4	1	1	0	0
5	1	1	0	0
6	1	3	− 2	4
7	1	3	− 2	4
8	1	1	0	0
9	1	− 1	2	4
10	1	− 1	2	4
			Total Sum of Squares =	16

Variance of differences = 16/9 = 1.77

STEP 4: Take the square root of the variance of the differences to get the standard deviation of the differences

$$SD = \sqrt{1.77} = 1.33$$

STEP 5: Get the standard error of the difference by dividing the standard deviation of the differences by the square root of the number of pairs of scores

$$\frac{1.33}{\sqrt{10}} = .42$$

STEP 6: Set up the t ratio by dividing the average difference by the standard error of the difference

$$t = \frac{1}{.42} = 2.38$$

STEP 7: Calculate the degrees of freedom by subtracting 1 from the number of pairs of scores. Then, look up the t value in the t table in Appendix E.

Summary of the Matched Pairs Design

The matched pairs design's weaknesses stem from matching. If matching alerts subjects to the purpose of your experiment, it can cost you the naïveté of your subjects.

If subjects drop out of the experiment between the time they're measured on the matching variable and the time they're to be given the treatment, matching costs you the ability to generalize your results to the subjects who dropped out. No matter what, matching costs you time and energy.

Although matching has its costs, it offers one big advantage: power without restricting your subject population. Matching makes the matched pairs design very powerful, whereas random assignment makes the matched pairs design internally valid. Because of its power and internal validity, this design is hard to beat when you can only study a few subjects.

PURE WITHIN-SUBJECTS DESIGNS

The **within-subjects design** is very similar to the matched pairs design. In fact, if you conduct both kinds of experiments, you'll end up doing very similar things for the same reasons. Although the "nuts and bolts" and the logic behind both designs are very similar, the similarities are most apparent when you look at those "nuts and bolts," such as how you carry out the two kinds of studies.

Procedure The procedural differences between the two conditions, within-subjects experiment and matched pairs experiment stem from the fact that in the within-subjects experiment, you are getting two scores from a single subject rather than from a pair of subjects. The matched pairs researcher randomly determines, for each **pair**, who will get what treatment. In some pairs, the first member will get Treatment A; in other pairs, the first member will get Treatment B.

The within-subjects researcher randomly determines, for each **individual**, when subjects will get each treatment. For some individuals, the first treatment will be Treatment A; for other individuals, the first treatment will be Treatment B. Whereas the matched pairs experimenter randomly assigns members of pairs to treatments, the within-subjects experimenter randomly assigns individual subjects to orders of treatments.

Considering a Within-Subjects Design

Power
Like the matched pairs design, one of the main reasons for using the within-subjects design is power. The within-subjects design increases power in two ways.

The first way is similar to the matched pairs design—reducing random error. As you'll recall, the matched pairs experimenter tries to reduce random error by reducing individual differences. Therefore, the matched pairs experimenter compares similar subjects with one another. Within-subjects experimenters are even more ambitious: they want to eliminate random error due to individual differences. Therefore, they don't compare one subject with another subject; instead, they compare each subject's score under one condition with that same subject's score under another condition.

The second way the within-subjects design increases power is by increasing how many observations you get. As you know, the more observations you have, the more random error will tend to balance out, thus giving you more power. With the designs we've discussed up to now, the only way to get more observations was to get more subjects. With those designs, you can only get one score per subject. But in a within-subjects experiment, you get at least two scores out of each subject. In the simplest case, your subjects serve double duty by being in both the control and experimental conditions. In more complex within-subjects experiments, your subjects might do triple, quadruple, or even octuple duty.

The Order Problem

Although getting more observations per subject improves power, this tactic has drawbacks. To get a general sense of these drawbacks, imagine being a subject in a within-subjects experiment where you take a drug, play a videogame, take a second drug, and play the videogame again.

If you perform differently on the videogame the second time around, can the experimenter say that the second drug has a different effect from the first drug? No, because the experimenter didn't compare how you performed after taking Drug 1 with how you performed after taking Drug 2. Instead, he compared how you performed after taking Drug 1 with how you performed after taking Drug 1, playing the videogame once, and then taking Drug 2. Put another way, the only treatment you got before you played the videogame the first time was Drug 1. But before you played the videogame the second time, you were exposed to three "treatments": the first drug, playing the videogame, and the second drug.

In the next few sections, you'll see how these "treatments" can hurt the validity of a within-subjects experiment. You'll start by examining how the effects of playing the videogame after the first treatment could linger and affect your performance when you play the videogame after the second treatment. Next, you'll see how the effects of the first drug might linger and affect your performance while you're playing the videogame after the second treatment. Finally, you'll see how being exposed to all three treatments can affect your second game performance by making you aware of the experimental hypothesis. Thus, by the end of the next few sections, you'll understand how the order in which you get the treatments may affect the results. Specifically, you'll know how Treatment A may appear to have one kind of effect when it comes first but appear to have a different kind of effect if it comes second.

Practice and Fatigue Effects   If you perform better after the second treatment than you did after the first, your improvement may simply reflect the effects of **practice** on the videogame. Subjects often perform better as they warm up to the experimental environment and get used to the experimental task.

Even if your performance isn't affected by practice, it may be affected by **fatigue**. You may do worse on later trials merely because you're getting tired or less enthusiastic as the experiment goes on. Unfortunately, a researcher might interpret your fatigue as a treatment effect.

Carry-over Effects   A third factor that might cause you to perform differently after the second treatment is **carry-over**: the effects of an earlier treatment lingering to affect responses in later trials. For example, suppose that on Trial 1, the researcher first gave you marijuana, then measured your videogame performance. On Trial 2, she gave you alcohol and measured your videogame performance. On Trial 3, she gave you a placebo and measured your videogame performance. Your performance might be worst in the placebo condition. Although the researcher might think that the drugs improved your performance, she could be wrong. Your poor performance in the placebo condition may be due to carry-over (hang-over?) effects from the previous treatments.

Sensitization   A fourth factor that might cause you to perform differently after the second treatment is **sensitization**: after getting several different treatments and performing the dependent variable task several times, subjects may realize (become sensitive to) what the independent and dependent variables are. Consequently, during the latter parts of the experiment, you might guess the experimental hypothesis and play along with it. Certainly, by the third trial, you should realize that the experiment had something to do with the effects of drugs on videogame performance. Thus, the results from the third trial would probably have no construct validity.

Dealing with the Order Problem
You've seen that because of fatigue, practice, carry-over, and sensitization, the order in which subjects get the treatments could affect the results. Practice effects might cause a subject to do better on the last trial, even though none of the treatments had an effect. Alternatively, fatigue effects might cause a subject to do worse after the last treatment condition, even though none of the treatments had an effect. If carry-over occurs, a subject could appear to be affected by Treatment C, a treatment that has no effect, because the subject is still being affected by a previous treatment.

Finally, you've seen how sensitization could cause an order effect because the subject is most naïve about the experimental hypothesis when receiving the first treatment, least naïve when receiving the last treatment. Thus, the ability of the subject to play along with the hypothesis increases as the study goes on.

Minimizing Each of the Individual Threats

Obviously, there are steps you can take to minimize these threats. To minimize the effects of practice, you can give subjects extensive practice before the experiment begins. For example, if you're studying maze running and you have the rats run the maze 100 times before you start administering treatments, they've probably learned as much from practice as they can. It's therefore unlikely that the rats will benefit greatly from the limited practice they get during the experiment. You can reduce fatigue effects by making the experiment interesting, brief, and not too taxing.

You can reduce carry-over effects by lengthening the time between treatments. For instance, if you were looking at the effects of drugs on maze-running performance, you might space your treatments a week apart (e.g., marijuana, wait a week, alcohol, wait a week, placebo).

You can reduce sensitization by using treatments that seem so similar to one another that subjects won't notice that you're varying anything (Greenwald, 1974). For example, suppose you were studying the effects of different levels of full-spectrum light on typing performance. Your different treatments could seem similar because they actually are similar (you use slightly different amounts of full-spectrum light), because you change the level of the treatment so slowly that subjects don't notice (between trials you change lighting level watt by watt until it reaches the desired level), or because you use good placebo treatments (rather than using darkness as a control condition you use light from a normal bulb as the control condition).

You can also reduce order effects by reducing the number of experimental conditions: the fewer conditions, the fewer opportunities for practice, fatigue, carry-over or sensitization. To illustrate this fact, compare a within-subjects experiment that has 11 conditions with one that has only 2. In the 11-condition experiment, subjects have 10 opportunities to practice on the dependent measure task before they get the last treatment; in the 2-condition experiment, subjects only have one opportunity for practice. In the 11-condition experiment, subjects have 11 conditions to tire them out; 2-condition subjects only have 2. In the 11-condition experiment, there are 10 treatments that could carry-over to the last trial; in the 2-condition experiment there is only 1. Finally, in the 11-condition experiment, subjects have 11 chances to figure out the hypothesis; in the 2-condition experiment, they only have 2 chances.

Randomization

Although you can take steps to reduce the effect of order, you can never be sure that you have eliminated its effect. Therefore, if a subject scores differently after receiving the second treatment than he did after receiving the first treatment, you'll never know whether this difference is due to differences in the treatment or to differences in the order in which the treatments were given.

Since the order of treatments will probably affect your results, you shouldn't give each subject the treatment in the same order. Instead, you should assign subjects to get the treatment in different orders. You can do this by randomly determining, for each subject, which treatment they get first, which treatment they get second, and so on. Randomization should ensure that subjects get the treatments in different orders.

Unfortunately, randomization doesn't always balance out the effects of order. For example, if you randomly assign each of 24 subjects to a different order, you probably won't find that 12 subjects got Treatment A first and 12 subjects got Treatment B first. In fact, you may find that 16 of the 24 got Treatment A first.

The within-subjects design and the matched pairs design are very similar. In terms of procedures, the only real difference is that the matched pairs experimenter randomly assigns members of pairs to treatments, whereas the within-subjects experimenter randomly assigns individual subjects to orders of treatments. In terms of analysis, the two designs are virtually identical. In fact, to analyze data from the two-condition, within-subjects design, you can use the same dependent groups t test (see Box 8-1) that you used to analyze matched pairs designs. The only difference is that instead of comparing one member of a pair against the other, you compare each subject with him or herself. Specifically, instead of comparing, for each pair, the member who got one treatment with the member who got the other treatment, you compare, for each subject, the subject when he or she got the first treatment with the same subject when he or she got the other treatment.

Summary and Analysis of Pure Within-Subjects Designs

The two designs share similar strengths. They both have impressive power because they reduce the effects of between-subject differences. Because of the power of these two designs, both should be seriously considered if subjects are scarce.

The unique strengths and weaknesses of the within-subjects design stem from the fact that it collects more than one observation per subject. Because it uses subjects (rather than matched pairs) as their own controls, the within-subjects design is the more powerful of the two. Because it uses subjects as their own controls, the within-subjects design is also more useful if you want to generalize your results to real-life situations in which individuals get more than one "treatment." Thus, if you were studying persuasion, you might use a within-subjects design because a person is likely to be exposed to many types of persuasive messages (Greenwald, 1976).

Although there are benefits to collecting more than one observation per subject, there is one big drawback: you have to contend with order effects. To deal with order effects, you can try to minimize the effects of practice, fatigue, carry-over, and sensitization and then hope that randomization will balance out the order of your treatments.

COUNTERBALANCED WITHIN-SUBJECTS DESIGNS

Instead of hoping that chance might balance out the order of your treatments, why not make sure? That is, why not use a counterbalanced design? In a **counterbalanced** design, like the within-subjects design, each subject gets more than one treatment. However, unlike the within-subjects design, subjects are randomly assigned to systematically varying orders of conditions in a way that ensures that routine order effects are balanced out. Thus, if you were studying two levels of a factor, the counterbalanced design would ensure that half your subjects got Treatment A first and that half got Treatment B first. Now that you understand the main objective of counterbalancing, let's look at an example to see how counterbalancing achieves this goal.

Procedure If you were to use a counterbalanced design to study a two-level factor, you would randomly assign half your subjects to receive Treatment A first and Treatment B second, whereas the other half would receive Treatment B first and Treatment A second. By randomly assigning your subjects to these counterbalanced orders, most order effects will be neutralized. For example, if subjects tend to do better on the second trial, this will not help Treatment A more than Treatment B because both occur in the second position equally often.

The Advantages and Disadvantages of Counterbalancing By using a counterbalanced design, you have not merely balanced out routine order effects. You have also added another factor to your design—a counterbalancing factor. Adding this factor has one disadvantage and several advantages.

The disadvantage of adding the two-level between-subjects factor of counterbalancing is that you now need more subjects than you did when you were planning to use a pure within-subjects design. You need two groups of subjects to test your two-level between-subjects factor of counterbalancing; you only needed one group when you were using a pure within-subjects design. In effect, by going from a within-subjects design to a counterbalanced design, you are going from having zero levels of a between-subjects factor to having two levels of a between-subjects factor. As you recall from our discussion of multilevel experiments, the more levels of a between-subjects factor you have, the more subjects you need.

The advantages stem from the fact that by adding the two-level factor of counterbalancing, you have converted the two-condition experiment into a 2 × 2 experiment. The treatment is a within-subjects factor (all subjects get all levels of the treatment) and counterbalancing is a between-subjects factor (different subjects get different sequences of treatments). This 2 × 2 experiment gives you more information than the simple two-condition experiment. With the two-condition experiment, you only obtain a single main effect (treatment main effect) so you can discover only whether the treatment had an effect.

With the 2 × 2, you obtain two main effects and an interaction. As a result, you find out three things. First, you find out whether the treatment had an effect (treatment main effect). Second, you determine whether subjects getting the treatments in one sequence did better than the subjects getting the other sequence (counterbalancing main effect). Finally, you determine whether a treatment has one effect for one group of subjects, but another effect for the other group (the treatment by counterbalancing interaction).

To understand what these three effects represent, let's look at a rehearsal strategy experiment. In this study, subjects learned lists of words using two different rehearsal strategies. In one condition, they made a sentence out of the list; in the other, they formed mental images. Subjects performed the tasks in two different, counterbalanced orders. Half the subjects formed sentences for the first list, then formed images to recall the second list. The other half formed images to recall the first list, then formed sentences to recall the second list. The means for that study are listed in Table 8-1 and the results of the analysis of variance is summarized in Table 8-2.

Table 8-1 Table of Means

Memory Strategy

Group's Sequence	Images	Sentences	Average Effect for Strategy
Group 1 (images first, sentences second)	8.0	7.0	+1.0
Group 2 (sentences first, images second)	7.0	8.0	−1.0
Average Effect of Group	+1.0	−1.0	Strategy Main Effect = 0

Group's Sequence Main Effect = (1 + 1)/2 = 0

Table 8-2   Analysis of Variance Table

Source	SS	df	MS	F	p
Group Sequence (counterbalancing)	0	1	0	0	not significant
Error Term for Between-Subjects Factor	44	22	2		
Memory Strategy	0	1	0	0	not significant
Memory Strategy Times Group Sequence (effect or order—1st versus 2nd)	10	1	10	10	p<.01
Within-Subjects Error Term	23	23	1.0		

By looking at Table 8-2, we see that the main effect for counterbalancing is not significant. As Table 8-1 shows, both groups recalled about the same amount. Next, we see that the memory strategy factor also failed to reach significance. Thus, we have no evidence that one strategy is superior to the other. Finally, we find that we have a significant interaction of memory strategy and group sequence. By looking at Table 8-1, we see that this interaction is caused by the fact that Group 1 does best using images, whereas Group 2 does best by making sentences. In other words, subjects do better on the first list than on the second.

Thus, the memory strategy by group sequence interaction tells us not only that there is an order effect, but also what kind of order effect we have. In this case, the order effect is such that the first list is better recalled than the second.

What does this order effect mean? If the researchers were not careful in their selection of lists, the order effect could merely reflect that the first list was composed of words that were easier to recall than the second list. But if the researchers chose lists that were of equal difficulty, the order effect must reflect either the effects of practice, fatigue, carry-over, or sensitization. In this case, it probably reflects the fact that recalling the second list is impaired by the practice the subjects got on the first list. This negative practice effect is not considered a nuisance by psychologists. On the contrary, it is one of the most important and most widely investigated facts of memory—interference.

Now that you understand the three effects that you find with a counterbalanced design, let's look at an experiment where all three effects are of interest to the researcher. A politician produces two commercials (an emotional commercial and a rational commercial). She hires a psychologist to find out which commercial is most effective so she'll know which one to give more air time. The researcher uses a counterbalanced design to address the question.

By looking at the treatment main effect, the researcher is able to answer the original question: "Which ad is more effective?". By looking at the counterbalancing main effect, he is able to determine whether one sequence of showing the ads is better than another. He is able to answer the question: "should we show the emotional ad first or the rational ad first?". Finally, by looking at the ad by counterbalancing interaction, the researcher is able to determine whether there is an order effect. He is able to answer the question: "in terms of increasing the candidate's popularity, do the two ads seem to build on one another?". Obviously, he would expect the ads to build on one another. Therefore, he would expect that voters would rate the candidate higher after seeing the second ad than they did after the first.

But what if he doesn't find an order effect? Then, since there is no obvious benefit of showing both ads, he might suggest that the candidate only show one ad. Or, what if he got an order effect demonstrating that people always rated the candidate worse after the second ad? In that event, he'd take a long, hard look at the ads. It may be that both ads are making people dislike the candidate or it may be that the combination of these two ads doesn't work. Seeing both ads may reduce liking for the candidate by making her seem inconsistent. For example, one ad may suggest that she is for increasing military spending, whereas the other suggests that she is against it.

Thus, if order or sequence effects are of interest to you, the counterbalanced design is your best bet. Perhaps order effects are of most interest to you when you can control the order of real-life treatments. In that case, you'd like to know how to order the treatments to your advantage. Thus, you might be interested in using a counterbalanced design to find out whether it's best to be the first or the last person interviewed for a job. Or, if you want to do well in one particular course, you might like to know whether you'd do better if it were the first subject you studied or the last. To find out about these order effects, you'd need to rely on a counterbalanced design.

Similarly, sequence effects will probably be of the most interest if you can control the sequence of real-life treatments. There are probably many situations in which you may ask yourself, "If I do these tasks in one sequence, will that lead to better outcomes than if I do them in a different sequence? For instance, will studying your courses in one sequence give you a 2.8 G.P.A. whereas if you studied them in a different order you'd get a 3.2? Or, if you're going to compliment and criticize a friend, would you be better off to criticize, then praise or to praise, then criticize?

In conclusion, the counterbalanced design not only balances out routine order effects, but also tells you about the effects of order and sequence. Knowing what kind of order and sequence effects exist are sometimes of interest because real life is often a series of treatments (Greenwald, 1974).

CHOOSING DESIGNS

If you want to compare two levels of an independent variable, you have several designs you can use: matched pairs, within-subject designs, counterbalanced designs, and the simple between-subjects design. To help you choose among these designs, we'll briefly summarize the ideal situation for using each design.

The matched groups design is ideal when: 1) you can readily obtain each

Choosing Designs: The Two-Condition Case

subject's score on the matching variable without arousing their suspicions about the purpose of the experiment, 2) the matching variable correlates highly with the dependent measure, and 3) subjects are scarce.

The pure within-subjects design is ideal when: 1) sensitization, practice, fatigue, or carry-over are not problems; 2) you want a powerful design; 3) subjects are hard to get; and 4) you want to generalize your results to real-life situations, and in real-life, individuals tend to be exposed to both levels of the treatment.

The 2×2 counterbalanced design is ideal when: 1) you want to balance out the effects of order or you're interested in learning the nature of any order or sequence effects; 2) you have enough subjects to meet the requirement of a counterbalanced design; and 3) you aren't concerned that being exposed to both treatment levels will alert subjects to the purpose of the experiment (sensitization).

The simple experiment is ideal when: 1) you think fatigue, practice, sensitization, or carry-over could affect the results; 2) you have access to a relatively large number of subjects; 3) you want to generalize your results to real-life situations, and, in real-life, individuals tend to receive either the first level of the treatment or the second, but not both.

Choosing Designs: When You Have More than Two Levels of the Independent Variable

You are now thoroughly familiar with the advantages and drawbacks of using within-subjects designs and counterbalanced designs to study two levels of an independent variable. You can see how both designs could be extended to incorporate three or more levels of an independent variable. Furthermore, you realize that if you wanted to study three or more levels of an independent variable, you have three basic options: a multilevel between-subjects design, a matched group design (matched trios, matched quartets, etc.) or a multilevel within-subjects design.

You may even think you know how to decide which of these designs to use. Intuitively, it would seem that you would use the same criteria you used when studying the two-condition case. Therefore, if you'd picked a within-subjects or counterbalanced design when investigating two levels of the factor, you might think you should use the same design if you were studying more than two levels of the factor. However, this isn't the case. In fact, there are three reasons why you may not want to go beyond studying two levels of a variable with either a totally within-subjects design or with a counterbalanced within-subjects design at this point in your career.

First, the two-condition within-subjects design is the design least vulnerable to order effects. As you add levels, you multiply the risk that practice, fatigue, carry-over, or sensitization will contaminate your results. Order effects can be so tricky that even counterbalancing may not totally control for them.

Second, after you go beyond two levels, you can't use the dependent groups t test. Instead, you must use a within-subjects analysis of variance. The computations for this kind of analysis of variance are so complex that you really should use a computer program—and not all statistical packages will do it. Furthermore, by using multiple levels, you're setting yourself up for doing post-hoc tests—and the majority of computer programs won't do post-hoc tests on within-subjects designs.

Third, by adding levels you complicate counterbalancing, and that leads to problems. Ironically, one thing that isn't a problem is actually figuring out the correct counterbalancing. As you can see from Box 8-2, counterbalancing complex designs is simple. The problems are that:

1. With more than two conditions, you need more subjects because you have more groups.
2. With more than two conditions, your counterbalancing is less likely to include every possible order. Consequently, you may have difficulty generalizing your results to individuals who get the treatments in an order you didn't test.
3. With more conditions, order and sequence effects are harder to interpret. To find out the effect of order when you have two levels of an independent variable, you need to interpret a 2×2 interaction. To determine the effect of order when you have four levels of a factor, you have to interpret a 4×4 interaction.

With more levels, you not only have to interpret more complex interactions, you also allow more complex effects to occur. With four levels of a factor, for example, you can have very complex order and sequence effects. You could have any combination of linear, quadratic, and cubic interactions and sequence main effects. (If you're having trouble understanding these terms, you probably want to stick to a two-condition experiment.) With two conditions, on the other hand, you can only have two kinds of order effects (first better than second, or second better than first) and only two kinds of sequence effects (Sequence 1 where subjects get Treatment A then Treatment B is best, or Sequence 2 where subjects get Treatment B then Treatment A is best).

In conclusion, if you want to study several levels of an independent variable, you may be better off—at this point—using a between-subjects design or a matched group design (matched trios, matched quartets, etc.) instead of using a within-subjects design. However, if you have a computer program or statistical consultant (preferably both), you may decide to use a within-subjects or counterbalanced design if:

1. You need power.
2. You want to generalize your results to real-life situations where people are bound to get more than two levels of the treatment.
3. You feel that order effects aren't a problem, or you want to study order effects.

Thus far, we've discussed studying the effects of a single variable. Often, however, you may want to investigate the effects of two or more variables. To investigate more than one independent variable, you could use a multifactor within-subjects design, a multifactor between-subjects design, or a **mixed design**: a design where one factor is between and the other is within. (You are already familiar with one special kind of mixed design—the counterbalanced design.)

Choosing between a two-factor within-subjects design and a two-factor between-subjects design is similar to choosing between a multilevel within-subjects design and a multilevel between-subjects design. Specifically, if you can handle the statistics; if sensitization, practice, fatigue, and carry-over aren't problems; and if

Choosing Designs: When You Have More than One Independent Variable

BOX 8-2   The A, B, Cs of Counterbalancing Complex Designs

You've seen an example of the simplest form of counterbalancing in which one group of subjects gets Treatment A followed by Treatment B (A–B) and a second group gets Treatment B followed by Treatment A (B–A). This simple form of counterbalancing is called A–B, B–A counterbalancing. Note that even this simple form of counterbalancing guarantees that every condition occurs in every position, equally often. Thus, in A–B, B–A counterbalancing, A occurs in both the first and last position. The same is true for B. Furthermore, each condition precedes each condition the same number of times that it follows that condition. This is **balance**. Thus, in A–B, B–A counterbalancing, A precedes B once, and follows B once.

Achieving these two objectives of counterbalancing is easy with only two conditions; with more conditions, counterbalancing becomes more complex. For example, with four conditions (A,B,C,D) you'd have four groups. To determine the order in which groups will go through the conditions, you'd consult the following 4 × 4 Latin square.

The 4 × 4 Latin Square

Position

	1	2	3	4
GROUP 1	A	B	D	C
GROUP 2	B	C	A	D
GROUP 3	C	D	B	A
GROUP 4	D	A	C	B

In this 4 × 4 Latin square, Treatment A occurs in all four positions (1st, 2nd, 3rd, and 4th), as do Treatments B, C, and D. In addition, the square has balance. As you can see from looking at the square, every letter precedes every other letter twice and follows every other letter twice. For example, if you just look at Treatments A and D, you see that A comes before D twice (in Groups 1 and 2) and follows D twice (in Groups 3 and 4).

Balance is relatively easy to achieve for 2, 4, 6, 8 or even 16 conditions. But, what if you have three conditions? Immediately, you recognize that with a 3 × 3 Latin square, A can't precede B the same number of times as it follows B. At best, Condition A can either precede B twice and follow it once, or precede it once and follow it twice. Thus, with an uneven number of conditions, you can't create a balanced Latin square.

Perhaps the easiest solution to trying to achieve balance when you have an uneven number of treatment levels is to add a level so you have an even number of levels. However, if you insist on using an uneven number of treatment levels, you can achieve balance by using two Latin squares. For instance, consider the 3 × 3 Latin squares in the following table.

Two 3 × 3 Latin Squares

	Square 1 Position				Square 2 Position		
	1	**2**	**3**		**1**	**2**	**3**
GROUP 1	A	B	C	GROUP 4	C	B	A
GROUP 2	B	C	A	GROUP 5	A	C	B
GROUP 3	C	A	B	GROUP 6	B	A	C

If you randomly assign subjects to six groups, as outlined in the 3 × 3 Latin square table, you assure balance. See for yourself that if you take any two conditions, one condition will precede the other three times, and will be preceded by the other condition three times.

you're concerned about power or about generalizing your results to real-life situations where people will tend to be exposed to several levels of the treatment, then you should use a within-subjects design. If you're worried about the statistics of a complex within design, if you're worried about order effects, if you aren't worried about power, and if you're only interested in how subjects getting one treatment differ from subjects getting another treatment, use a totally between-subjects design.

Sometimes, however, you'll find choosing between a totally within and a totally between design difficult. For example, consider the following two cases.

Case #1: You're studying the effects of brain-lesions and practice on how well rats run mazes. On the one hand, you don't want to use a totally within-subjects design because you consider brain damage to occur "between subjects" in real life. On the other hand, you don't want to use a totally between-subjects design because you think that practice occurs "within subjects" in real life.

Case #2: You're studying the effects of subliminal messages and marijuana on creativity. You expect that if subliminal messages have any effect, it will be so small that only a within-subjects design could detect it. However, you feel that oral ingestion of marijuana shouldn't be studied in a within design because of huge carry-over effects.

In these and similar cases, the mixed design is the ideal solution. Instead of trading off the needs of one variable for the needs of another variable, you're able to give both variables the design they need.

CONCLUDING REMARKS

You're now familiar with most of the basic experimental designs. You know what they are, how to perform them, how to analyze them, how to interpret their results, and how to choose among them. Therefore, you should be very comfortable reading the report of any kind of experiment. If you're not, you will be by the time you finish reading the next chapter.

BOX 8-3   Making Sure the Computer Understands Your Design

If you use a two-factor design, you will probably have a computer analyze your data for you. Fortunately, most computers can analyze data from any kind of design: totally between subjects, totally within subjects, or mixed design. Unfortunately, if you're not careful, the computer may analyze data from your design as if it were from another kind of design. To ensure that the computer understands your design, check your printout carefully.

If you used a totally between-subjects design, your printout should include only one error term. If you take the MS for any treatment or interaction and divide it by your one and only MS error, you'll get the F for that effect.

If, on the other hand, you used a totally within-subjects design, your printout will contain several error terms. Specifically, each main effect and each interaction will have its own error term. Thus, if you have three effects (two main effects and an interaction effect), you'll have three error terms.

The degrees of freedom for an effect's error term will equal the degrees of freedom for the effect multiplied by one less than the number of subjects. Thus, if you used 21 subjects in a 4×3 design, it's easy to correctly match the error term to the effect. The four level factor has 3 df (remember, the formula for all main effects is number of levels minus one). So, its error term will be the one that has 60 df (3×20). The three-level factor has 2 df so its error term has 40 df (2×20). The interaction term will have 6 df (remember, you calculate the interaction degrees of freedom by multiplying the degrees of freedom of the factors that make it up. In this case, $3 \times 2 = 6$.). Therefore, the error term for the interaction will have 120 df ($6 \times 20 = 120$). (It's no accident that the procedure for determining the error term degrees of freedom seems similar to the way you calculate degrees of freedom for an interaction. The error term is the interaction between subjects and the effect you're testing).

Rarely, would the computer analyze a within design as a between design or vice versa. The computer most often gets mixed up when you use a mixed design. It sometimes fails to realize which factors are within-subjects factors and which are between subject. So, if you do a mixed design, scrutinize your computer printout carefully.

Start with the between factors. All between factor main effects should be tested against a single error term. This error term is also used to test any interactions that involve between factors **only.** To make sure that this is the case, divide the MS for each between-factor main effect or exclusively between-factor interaction by the MS for the between-subjects error term. In every case, you should get the same F that's reported in the print-out.

To double-check that the computer correctly identified all the between-subjects variables, add up the degrees of freedom for all the between-subjects main effects plus the degrees of freedom for the interactions that involved only between subjects plus the degrees of freedom for the between-subjects error term. The total should be one fewer than the number of subjects.

Next, check the within factors. As in the within-subjects design, each within-subjects main effect and each interaction that involves only within-subjects factors should be tested against a different error term.

Finally, look at interactions involving both within and between factors. To find the appropriate error term for these interactions, ignore the between-subjects factor. Attend only to the within-subjects factors. If A is a within factor and B is a between factor and you see an A $\times$ B interaction, this interaction should be tested against the same error term that A is tested against. If A is a within factor and B and C are between factors, the error term for the A $\times$ B $\times$ C interaction should still be the same error term that was used for testing A. If it isn't, the computer doesn't understand your design.

MAIN POINTS

1. Not all experiments occur in a laboratory.
2. A field experiment is performed in a natural setting.
3. Field experiments can be useful when you want to: 1) increase power, 2) generalize your results to different settings or subjects (external validity), and 3) increase construct validity.
4. The field experiment is not a cure-all and may: 1) lack power, 2) be unethical 3) and demand more time and energy than you anticipate. In addition, the field experiment doesn't guarantee external, construct, or internal validity.
5. Although random assignment is more difficult in the field, many researchers abandon its use too soon.
6. Field experiments that use intact groups often fail to either establish or maintain independence, and may be vulnerable to three threats to construct validity: 1) demoralization, 2) compensation, and 3) diffusion of treatment.
7. The matched pairs design uses matching to reduce random error and uses randomization to establish internal validity.
8. Because the matched pairs design gives you power without limiting the kind of subject you can use, you may be able to generalize your results to a broader population (i.e., it may have greater external validity) than a simple experiment.
9. The matched pairs design's weaknesses stem from matching. Matching may sensitize subjects to your hypothesis and they may drop out of the study between the time of the matching test and the time the experiment is performed.
10. The two-condition within-subjects design gives you two scores per subject.
11. The within-subjects design increases power by: eliminating random error due to individual differences, and by increasing the number of observations.
12. Because of the effects of practice, fatigue, carry-over, and sensitization, the order in which a subject gets the treatments may affect the results.

13. To reduce the effects of order, you should randomly determine the order in which each subject will get the treatments.

14. In the counterbalanced design, subjects are randomly assigned to systematically varying orders of conditions to ensure that routine order effects are balanced out. Counterbalancing tells you about the effects of order and of sequence.

15. Because you must include the between-subjects factor of counterbalancing in your analyses, counterbalanced designs need more subjects than pure within-subjects designs.

16. In counterbalanced designs, subjects will be exposed to several treatments. Consequently, they may be sensitized to the hypothesis.

17. If you want to compare two levels of an independent variable you can use: matched pairs, within-subjects designs, counterbalanced designs, and simple between-subjects designs.

18. Mixed designs have both a within- and a between-subjects factor.

KEY TERMS

field experiment
informed consent
debrief
demoralization
compensation
diffusion of treatment
matched pairs design
dependent groups *t* test

within-subjects designs
practice effects
fatigue effects
carry-over
sensitization
counterbalanced
mixed designs

EXERCISES

1. On a sheet of paper list the advantages and disadvantages of each of these designs: field experiment, matched pairs, pure within-subjects design, and counterbalanced within-subjects design.

2. Under what circumstances would you use each of the designs?

3. Develop a field experiment that employs one of the other designs discussed in this chapter (i.e., matching, pure within-subjects design, counterbalanced within-subjects design). Why did you select the design you did? Would another design be as effective in testing your research question? Explain.

4. If you were to examine several levels of a factor, would you use a between- or a within-subject design? Why?

5. What is a mixed design? Construct a research question that would best be answered through a mixed design. Explain how you decided which factor should be the between-subjects factor and which should be the within-subjects factor.

6. Design a matched pairs experiment. Is this design superior or inferior to other designs for testing your hypothesis? Why?

9

DEVELOPING IDEAS: CRITICALLY READING RESEARCH

"The best way to get a good idea is to steal one"

—HOW TO SUCCEED IN BUSINESS WITHOUT REALLY TRYING

OVERVIEW

In this chapter, you'll learn how to benefit from reading other people's research. You'll start by learning how to make sense of a research article. Then, you'll learn how to spot flaws and limitations in research. Finally, you'll learn how you can get research ideas by reading research. Thus, the aim of this chapter is to make you an intelligent consumer and producer of research.

READING ARTICLES

Before You Go On

You wouldn't find a "how to" manual about how to fix a Volkswagen very useful unless you were reading it while you were fixing a Volkswagen. Similarly, you'll find this "how to read an article" chapter little more than a review of what you already know, unless you read it while you're reading an article. Therefore, before you go on to the next section, get an article.

But don't get just any article. Since critically evaluating means actively applying what you've learned about research design, get an article that will motivate you to do just that. Specifically, choose an article that uses a design you're familiar with and that you find interesting.

To start your quest for such an article, you could:

1. Glance at the table of contents of journals, looking for titles that sound interesting;
2. look at sections of books that you find particularly interesting and look up the articles they reference;
3. consult some of the resources described in Appendix B—for example, *Psychological Abstracts, Social Sciences Citation Index,* etc.

Once you've found an interesting title, find the article and look at the first page. Directly beneath the title you'll see a paragraph that stands apart from the rest of the article. Although unlabeled, this one-paragraph summary of the study is called the abstract.

Read the Abstract

By reading the abstract, you'll get an idea of what the researchers were trying to discover, what design they used, and what they found. But most importantly (and the reason the authors wrote the abstract), you'll get an idea about whether you want to read the article. Once you find an article that has an interesting title and abstract, you're ready to start reading for understanding.

Reading the Introduction

The best place to start reading an article is at the beginning. The beginning of the article is called the introduction, and it is the most difficult and the most important part of the article to understand. You must understand the introduction because it's where the authors tell you how they developed their hypothesis, why the hypothesis is important, and why their method of testing the hypothesis is the best. If you understand the introduction, you should be able to anticipate what will be said in the rest of the paper.

The main reason the introduction may be hard for you to understand is that the authors are not writing it with you in mind. Instead, they're writing it to other experts in the field. Their belief that the reader is an expert has two important consequences for how they report their research. First, they don't think that they have to describe other published studies in depth. In fact, authors often assume that just by mentioning the authors and the year of work (e.g., Miller & Smudgekins, 1956), the reader will instantly recall the essentials of that article. Second, because they assume that the reader is an expert, they don't think they have to define concepts or theories in their field.

Since you're not an expert in the field, the authors failure to fully describe studies and define concepts may make it difficult to fully understand what they're trying to say. Fortunately, you can compensate for not having the necessary background by doing two things. First, read the articles to which the authors refer. Second, look up unfamiliar terms or theories in a psychological dictionary or textbook.

Once you've done this background reading, you should reread the introduction until you understand it. How will you know if you understand it? One test is to try to describe the logic behind the hypothesis in your own words. A more rigorous test is to design a study to test the hypothesis, and then describe the impact of those results for current theory and further research. As you can see, a thorough understanding of the introduction takes more than a few minutes.

Reading the Method Section

After you understand the introduction, read the method section. The method section should be easy to understand for two reasons. First, the only thing the method section does is tell you what happened in the study—who the subjects were, how many subjects there were, and how they were treated.

Second, the method section should be easy to understand because the introduction should have said how the author planned to test the hypothesis. Therefore, the only trouble you may have in understanding a method section is if you're unfamiliar with some task (e.g., a Stroop task) or piece of equipment (e.g., tachistoscope) that the researchers used. If you run into unfamiliar apparatus, perhaps the best thing

Reading for Understanding

to do is to look it up in a laboratory equipment catalog or ask your professor. If you run into an unfamiliar measure, find an article that describes the measure in detail (such an article should be referenced in the study's bibliography) or get a copy of the measure.

After reading the method section, take a few minutes to think about what it would've been like to be a subject in each of the study's conditions. Then, think about what it would've been like to be the researcher. Don't go on to the results section until you understand what happened well enough that you could act out the roles of both researcher and subject.

Reading the Results Section

Now turn to the results section and find out what happened. Depending on the study, the authors will usually report anywhere from one to three kinds of results.

Results of the Manipulation Checks   If the researchers used a manipulation check, they'd put the findings relating to it at the beginning of the results section. Usually, these results will be statistically significant and unsurprising. For example, if a study manipulates attractiveness of defendant and seriousness of crime, the researchers will probably report that subjects rated the "attractive" defendant as more attractive than the "unattractive" defendant and that subjects rated the "serious" crimes (e.g., assault, murder) as more serious than the "less" serious crimes (e.g., prostitution, embezzlement). Once they've shown you that they manipulated the factors they said they were going to, they're ready to discuss the effects of these factors.

Results Relating to Hypotheses   The next findings the authors would discuss are those relating to the hypotheses. The authors try to clearly connect the results to the hypotheses so that the reader can easily tell how the hypotheses fared. For example, if the hypothesis was that attractive defendants would receive lighter sentences than unattractive defendants, the author would report what the data said about this hypothesis: "The hypothesis that attractive defendants would receive lighter sentences was not supported. Attractive defendants received an average sentence of 6.1 years whereas the average sentence for the unattractive defendants was 6.2 years. This difference was not significant, $F(1,32) = 1.00$, n.s."

Other Significant Results   After reporting results relating to the hypotheses (whether or not the results are statistically significant), authors will dutifully report any other statistically significant results. Even if the results are unwanted and make no sense to the investigator, significant results must be reported. Therefore, you may read things like: "There was an unanticipated interaction between attractiveness and type of crime. Unattractive defendants received heavier sentences for violent crimes whereas attractive defendants received heavier sentences for nonviolent crimes, $F(1,32) = 18.62$, $p < .05$." Or, you may read: "There was also a significant four-way interaction between attractiveness of defendant, age of defendant, sex of subject, and type of crime. This interaction was uninterpretable." Typically, these results will be presented last: Although an author is obligated to report these unexpected and unwelcomed findings, she is not obligated to emphasize them.

Reading the Discussion

Finally, read the discussion. The discussion should hold a few surprises. In fact, before reading the discussion, you could probably write a reasonable outline of it if you jotted down the main findings, related them to the introduction, and speculated about the reasons for any surprising results. Thus, if the authors get the results they expect, the discussion is mostly a reiteration of the highlights of the introduction and results sections. If, on the other hand, the results are unexpected, the discussion section is usually an attempt to reconcile the introduction and results sections.

Looking for Weaknesses

Now that you understand the notions the authors are trying to sell, you're ready to challenge their claims. Engage your powers of critical reasoning by thinking about how you would've studied the same problem. Once you're in a critical frame of mind, systematically scrutinize each section of the article, starting with the introduction.

Critiquing the Introduction

Read the introduction with the same skepticism with which you'd read an advertisement—because the introduction is an ad. It's an unusual ad, but an ad nonetheless. Instead of using emotional appeals or endorsements from famous people, the introduction tries to get you to buy through using arguments that appear logical and by making the authors seem to be experts. Instead of trying to get you to buy hamburgers, the introduction is trying to get you to buy several ideas:

1. Testing the hypothesis is vital.
2. The hypothesis follows logically from theory and intuition.
3. The authors have found the perfect way to test the hypothesis.

Obviously, you can question all of these notions. The first idea, that testing this particular hypothesis is vital, is certainly a matter of opinion. What one scientist feels is important, another may feel is worthless.

The second notion, that the hypothesis follows logically from theory or intuition, is slightly less open to interpretation. If you've become familiar with the theories, concepts, and articles the authors mention, you're now in a position to decide whether the authors' interpretation of these studies or theories are accurate. Beware: Authors may occasionally twist or oversimplify theories or studies.

The third notion, that the authors have found the perfect way to test their hypothesis, is definitely open to question. Since measures aren't perfect, and since executing a study involves making a series of decisions, all of which involve trade-offs, no study is perfect. Therefore, when reading the introduction, a healthy dose of skepticism is vital.

Critiquing the Method Section

When you get to the method section, you can begin your critiquing in earnest. The method section gives you enough specific information so you can critique the study's construct, external, and internal validity.

Evaluating the Study's Construct Validity   Start by questioning the construct validity of the treatment. Remember, no manipulation is perfect. One way to find weaknesses in a manipulation is to imagine that you're a subject and think about how you might misinterpret a manipulation. In the defendant study we've been discussing, put yourself in the place of a subject judging an attractive defendant versus an unattractive defendant. By looking at the picture of the defendants, you may find that you'd have perceived the attractive defendants as not only more attractive, but also better dressed and more affluent than the unattractive defendants. Thus, the "attractiveness" manipulation might really be a status manipulation. Or, you might find that the unattractive defendants seem bigger and stronger than the attractive defendants.

When thinking about the validity of a manipulation don't overlook the control condition. Often, the weakness of the manipulation is in the control conditions. Playing the role of subject will help you spot these inadequate control groups. For instance, suppose the researchers used a photo of an attractive person in the attractive conditions, but used a no-photo condition as their control group. By playing the role of subject, you'd immediately be aware that the results might not be due to level of attractiveness, but to the presence or absence of attractiveness information— knowing what a person looks like, might influence the length of sentence imposed.

Pretending to be a subject might be even more helpful when questioning the dependent measure's validity. Think about what factors would influence your response on your measure. If the authors argue that the length of sentence is a measure of forgiveness, think about what things other than forgiveness might lead you to give a very short or a very long sentence. You might decide that subjects might give lenient sentences because they're uncertain about the defendant's guilt; they don't want the defendant to appeal the sentence; they think the defendant is too frail to survive a long sentence, etc.

Evaluating Whether Subjects Played along with the Hypothesis   Finally, think about whether the results were obtained because subjects guessed the hypothesis and played along with it. Imagine being a researcher and ask yourself how you might have unintentionally influenced subjects or tipped them off to the hypothesis. Next, pretend to be a subject, and ask yourself whether you could have guessed the hypothesis. Then ask yourself these specific questions:

1.   Did the study have **experimental realism**?: subjects were involved in the task, rather than merely playing a role.
2.   Was an empty control group (a group that got no treatment at all, not even a placebo treatment) used? Subjects in such a group might guess they were in the control group.
3.   Were double-blind procedures used? If the experimenter is not blind to knowing what condition the subject is in, then she might overtly or covertly influence the subject to behave in a manner that supports the hypothesis.
4.   Was the study standardized to avoid researcher bias?
5.   Was the dependent measure an obtrusive or unobtrusive measure? If the subject is unaware of the behavior being recorded, he probably won't fake the behavior.
6.   Was the dependent measure a behavioral measure? Subjects may be less likely

to play along with the hypothesis when it involves changing their behavior than when it involves making a mark on an anonymous rating scale.

7. Were subjects exposed to pretesting, several levels of treatment, or any other factor that would make them aware of the hypothesis?

8. Were subjects debriefed and asked not to tell other people about the study?

9. Was a cover story used so subjects wouldn't guess the researcher's hypothesis?

Evaluating the Study's External Validity You can also scrutinize the method section to question the study's external validity. For example, would the treatment have the same effect in a study that used different subjects? To address this question, look at the characteristics of the subjects. Do they represent the "average person"? More importantly, do they fail to represent some group of people for whom you feel the results wouldn't hold? For example, what if the jury study had used only male subjects? The method section will also help you get an idea to what extent the results would hold in other settings. Is the experiment high on **mundane realism**? That is, is it similar to real life? More importantly, does the researcher setting differ in specific ways that you believe will nullify or reverse the treatment's effect?

You can also question whether the findings would generalize to different levels of the treatment. For example, if the authors used two levels of an independent variable (e.g., very attractive/very unattractive), you might wonder whether a defendant who was extremely attractive would fare better than a defendant who was slightly above average.

Finally, you could ask whether the results would hold if other factors had been varied. For instance, you may have noticed that all the defendants were female. Would the results hold for male defendants?

Evaluating the Study's Internal Validity Looking at the method section can also help you in critiquing a study's internal validity. If you find that subjects were independently and randomly assigned to condition, you have a randomized experiment and you don't have to worry about internal validity, unless:

1. independence wasn't established or maintained;

2. mortality was a problem (e.g., many subjects dropped out of the experiment, and more dropped out of some conditions than other conditions).

If you don't have independent and random assignment, you don't have a randomized experiment. As a result, the study's internal validity is probably threatened by at least one of the threats to internal validity discussed in Chapter 4.

Critiquing the Results Section

The first thing to check in the results section is whether the correct tests were done. For example, if three groups were used, t tests should not have been used. Instead, analysis of variance should have been used. Next, determine whether the data conform to the assumptions of the test. For example, if analysis of variance was used, was the data at least interval scale data? Then, try to determine whether significant results might have been due to data fishing. That is, did they perform so many statistical tests that some were bound to be significant by chance?

Finally, question the interpretations of the test results. In particular, question null results. As you know, nonsignificant results are inconclusive. Therefore, if the authors obtained null results, you should question the experiment's power. Determine whether a more powerful statistical test (parametric rather than nonparametric) could have been used. Then go back to the method section and find out whether:

1. The different conditions were different enough on the independent or predictor variable.

2. The dependent measure was as sensitive as it could have been.

3. The study was sufficiently standardized.

4. Enough subjects were used.

5. The subjects were homogeneous enough that random individual differences wouldn't have obscured a genuine effect.

6. The most sensitive design was used.

7. The length of time between treatment and measurement was short enough so that the effect of the treatment wouldn't wear-out by the time it was being measured.

Critiquing the Discussion

In rereading the discussion, think about three things. First, in light of the weaknesses you found, is the authors' way the only way to interpret the predicted results? Second, think of a way to explain any of the findings the authors can't explain, then think of a way to test your explanation. For example, suppose the authors couldn't explain why attractive defendants got stiffer penalties for minor crimes. You might say that for the minor crimes used in the study (e.g., prostitution, embezzlement), subjects might be very likely to believe that an attractive person committed these crimes but doubt whether an ugly person could pull them off. Third, note any weaknesses or limitations that the authors concede. If you haven't already found those weaknesses, chide yourself and then add them to your list.

BOX 9–1   Questions to Ask of a Study

QUESTIONS ABOUT CONSTRUCT VALIDITY

1. Was the manipulation valid?

2. Was the measure valid?

3. Did the subjects play along with the hypothesis?
  a. Did the experiment lack experimental realism?
  b. Was an empty control group used?
  c. Did the researcher fail to make the study double-blind?
  d. Did the lack of standardization make it easy for researchers to bias the results?
  e. Was the dependent measure too obtrusive?
  f. Was the dependent measure a rating scale measure?
  g. Were any procedures used that might sensitize subjects to the hypothesis (matching on dependent variable, a within-subjects design, etc.)?
  h. Was a cover story used?
  i. Could subjects have learned about the study from former subjects?

QUESTIONS ABOUT EXTERNAL VALIDITY

1. Would results apply to the average person?
   a. Were subjects human?
   b. Are subjects distinct in any way?
   c. Is there any specific reason to suspect that the results wouldn't apply to a different group of subjects?
2. Would the results generalize to different settings?
   a. Was the study done in a lab?
   b. Did the study have mundane realism?
   c. Can you pinpoint a difference between the research setting and a real-life setting and give a specific reason why this difference should prevent the results from applying to real life?
3. Would the results generalize to different levels of the treatment variable?
   a. What levels of the treatment variable were included?
   b. What levels of the treatment variable were excluded?
   c. How many levels of the treatment variable were used?

QUESTIONS ABOUT INTERNAL VALIDITY

1. Was an experimental design used? If so, internal validity should not be a problem unless:
   a. Independence was not established or maintained?
   b. Mortality a problem?
   c. A within-subjects design was used and order effects posed a serious threat?
2. If a nonexperimental design was used, were history, maturation, mortality, instrumentation, testing, selection, selection by maturation interactions, or regression threats?

QUESTIONS ABOUT POWER

1. If null results were obtained, ask whether:
   a. measures were sensitive enough?
   b. the study was sufficiently standardized?
   c. enough subjects were used?
   d. conditions differed enough on treatment or predictor variable?
   e. subjects were homogenous enough?
   f. design was sensitive enough?
   g. length of time between treatment and measurement of effect was too long? too short?

TURNING LEAD INTO GOLD: DEVELOPING RESEARCH IDEAS

As you can see, any study can be questioned. To document or destroy a study's findings, additional studies must be done. Thus, familiarity with research breeds more research.

Direct Replication

Whenever you read a study, one obvious research idea always comes to mind—to repeat the study. That is, do a **direct replication.**

But isn't repeating a study fruitless? Isn't it inevitable that you'll get the same results the author reported? Not necessarily. A direct replication may turn out differently from the original study because of Type I errors, fraud, or because the effect doesn't generalize to different times or places.

Suspicion of Type I Error

The original study's results may have been significant because of a Type I error. To understand how Type I errors can get published, imagine that you're a crusty journal editor who only allows simple experiments that are significant at the .05 level to be published in your journal. If you accept an article, the chances are less than 5 in 100 that the article will contain a Type I error. Thus, you're appropriately cautious. But what happens once you publish 100 articles? Then, you may have published five articles that have Type I errors.

In fact, you may have many more Type I errors than that. How? Because people don't send you nonsignificant results. They may have done the same experiment eight different times, but it only came out significant the eighth time. Thus, they only send you the results of the eighth replication. Or, let's say 20 teams of investigators do the same experiment, only the team that gets significant results (the team with the Type I error) will submit their study to your journal. For example, while serving as editor for the *Journal of Personality and Social Psychology*, Dr. Anthony Greenwald received an article that found a significant effect for ESP. Since Dr. Greenwald was aware that many other researchers had done ESP experiments that were not significant, he asked for a replication. The authors could not replicate their results.

Suspicion of Fraud

Although fraud is very unusual, it does occur. Researchers may cheat for personal fame or simply because they believe their ideas are right even though their results fail to reach the .05 level of significance.

Since thousands of researchers want to be published and since many are under great pressure to do so, why is cheating so rare? Because if other scientists can't replicate your results, you're in trouble. Thus, the threat of replication keeps would-be cheats in line. However, some scientists are beginning to worry that science's fraud detectors are not as effective as they once were because people aren't doing replications as often as they used to (Broad & Wade, 1982). By doing direct replications, you can help to discourage cheating.

Because of Type I errors and fraud, some findings in the literature probably are inaccurate (Broad & Wade, 1982). Psychologists are concerned with the fact that some findings may not be replicable. As a result, they've tried to provide an incentive for people to replicate studies by establishing a journal to publish the results of direct replications. If you do a direct replication, you may want to submit your article to *The Journal of Replications*.

Changing Times

You may get different results if you do a direct replication because times have changed. For example, a study done in the 1930s about the effects of the race and sex of the defendant on jury verdicts may not hold today. Although psychologists believe that certain classic findings will hold today, tomorrow, and forever, we have a duty to test this assumption.

Different Locations

Finally, you may get different results because the study's results don't generalize to your subjects. For example, a study done at a French University may turn out differently at your university or college.

Rather than repeating the study, you could do a **systematic replication**: A study that varies in some systematic way from the original study. Because the systematic replication is similar to the original study, the systematic replication, like the direct replication, can help verify that the results reported by the original author would hold today. Because the systematic replication varies in a systematic way from the original study, it may have more power, more external validity, or more construct validity than the original.

Systematic Replication

Lack of Power

If a study obtains null results, you may want to repeat it but add a few minor refinements to increase power. You might standardize the study to a greater degree by having researchers follow a very detailed script or use instruments (such as a computer) to present stimuli. You might improve power by using more homogeneous subjects, more subjects, a more sensitive measure, or more extreme levels of the treatment or predictor variable. Or, you might replicate the experiment using a more sensitive design. For instance, if the authors used a simple experiment and found no effect for a mnemonic strategy on recall, you might replicate the experiment with a blocked design (blocking subjects by IQ), or you might use a within-subjects design.

External Validity

If the study has adequate power, it may lack external validity. Note that many of the things you were doing to improve power reduce the generalizability of the results. If the researcher uses a homogeneous group of subjects to reduce power, she may not be able to generalize the results to other kinds of subjects. What applies to this particular group of subjects (e.g., white, middle-class, first-year college students) may not apply to other groups of people (e.g., poor, uneducated, elderly).

If a study was done in a laboratory to reduce error variance, you don't know that the results would generalize outside of this artificial environment. If you measure the dependent variable immediately after the subject gets the treatment to maximize your chances of obtaining a significant effect, you don't know whether the treatment's effects last.

To increase a study's generalizability, there are at least four things you can do. First, you can systematically vary the kinds of subjects used. If the study used all male subjects, you might use all female subjects. Second, you can change a lab experiment into a field experiment. By moving the defendant study to the field you might be able to use real jurors as subjects rather than college students. Third, you can wait a while before collecting the dependent measure to see whether the effects last. Fourth, you can use different levels of the independent variable to see whether the effects would generalize to different levels of the independent variable. In the defendant study, researchers only compared attractive versus unattractive defendants. You might replicate the study to see whether extremely attractive defendants have an advantage over moderately attractive defendants.

Construct Validity

Finally, you might do a systematic replication to improve a study's construct validity. Often, you can make some minor changes that will reduce the threat of hypothesis guessing.

To illustrate, imagine a two-group experiment where one group gets caffeine (in a cola), and the other group gets nothing. You might want to replace this empty control group with a placebo treatment (a caffeine-free cola). Or, you might keep the empty control group, but add a treatment condition in which subjects get a very small amount of caffeine. This will give you three levels of the treatment variable. If both treatment conditions differ from the control group but don't differ from one another, you might suspect that subject and experimenter expectancies were responsible for the treatment effect. Because of the advantage of using three levels of the treatment variable, you may wish to replicate a 2×2 study as a 3×2 or a 3×3 study.

Besides adding or improving levels of the independent variable, there are three other minor alterations you can do to make it harder for subjects to discern the hypothesis. First, you could replicate the study, making it a double-blind experiment. Second, you could mislead the subjects regarding the purposes of the study by giving them a clever cover story. Third, you could do the study in the field: If subjects don't know they're in a study, they probably won't guess the hypothesis.

Conceptual Replication

If you think there were problems with the original study's construct validity and that these problems can't be solved by making minor procedural changes, you should perform a **conceptual replication**: a study that is based on the original study, but uses different methods in order to better assess the true relationships between the treatment and dependent variables. In a conceptual replication, you might use a different manipulation of the treatment variable or a different measure.

Because there is no such thing as a perfect measure or manipulation of a construct, virtually every study's construct validity can be questioned. Since the validity of a finding is increased when the same basic result is found using other measures or manipulations, virtually any study can benefit from conceptual replication. Therefore, you should have little trouble finding a study you wish to conceptually replicate.

There are many ways to go about a conceptual replication. One way is to use another way of manipulating the treatment variable. Remember, the more manipulations, the better. In fact, you might use two or three manipulations of your treatment variable and use the type of manipulation as a factor in your design. Ideally, one of the manipulations might be the one used in the original study. For instance, suppose a study used photos of a particular woman dressed in either a "masculine" or "feminine" manner to manipulate the variable "masculine versus feminine style." You might use the original photos for one set of conditions but also add two other conditions, using your own photos. Then, your statistical analysis would tell you whether your manipulation had a different result than the original study's manipulation.

Instead of manipulating "masculine" versus "feminine" by dress, you might manipulate "masculine" versus "feminine" by voice (masculine versus feminine sounding voice) or by writing style.

Although varying the treatment variable for variety's sake is worthwhile, changing the manipulation to improve it is even more worthwhile. One way of improving a treatment manipulation is to make it more consistent with the definition of the construct. Thus, in our previous example, you might feel that the original picture manipulated "fashion sense" rather than "masculine versus feminine style." Therefore, your manipulation would have two photos of a woman who was fashionably dressed in a feminine way versus a woman who was fashionably dressed in a masculine manner. You might also want a manipulation check to get more evidence of the validity of the manipulation. Thus, you might ask subjects to rate the masculine and feminine photos in terms of attractiveness, fashion sense, and masculinity versus femininity.

Because no manipulation is perfect, replicating a study using a different treatment manipulation is valuable. Similarly, because no measure is perfect, replicating a study using a different measure is valuable. Often, you can increase the construct validity of a study by replicating it with a measure that is more behavioral or less obtrusive than the measure used in the original study.

Replications: A Summary

Replications are important to the advancement of psychology as a science. Direct replications are essential for guaranteeing that the science of psychology is firmly grounded in fact. Systematic replications are essential in making psychology a science that applies to all people. Conceptual replications are necessary for psychology to go beyond knowing about the effects of specific operations on specific measures to knowing about broad, universal constructs.

Extending Research

Systematic and conceptual replications extend previous research. Consider, for a moment, the conceptual replication that reveals that the original investigators weren't measuring the constructs they thought they were measuring, the conceptual replication that uses more relevant behavior as the dependent variable, the systematic replication that shows the finding occurs in field settings or in other countries, the systematic replication that determines the duration of the effect, or the systematic replication of a simple study by using a multilevel experiment that illuminates the functional relationship between the treatment and dependent variables. Clearly, conceptual and systematic replications can transcend the original research.

In addition to the replications we discussed, there are two other ways of extending published research. You could replicate and extend research by repeating the study while adding a variable that you think might mediate the observed effect.

For instance, if you think that being attractive would hurt a defendant if the defendant had already been convicted of another crime, you might add previous convictions as a factor. Finally, you could extend the research simply by doing the follow-up studies that the authors suggest in their discussion section.

CONCLUDING REMARKS

You know not only how to criticize research but how to improve it. Thus, every time you read an article, you should get at least one research idea.

Once you have a research idea, you have a good idea of how to test it. You know how to operationalize variables and how to choose a randomized experimental design. If you want to do an experiment, you can skip ahead to Chapter 13—Putting It All Together. If you aren't sure that randomized experimental designs are the best way to address your research question, read the next three chapters to learn about other approaches to research.

BOX 9–2   Replications: Why and How

Direct replication: To verify results.

1. Repeat study.

Direct replication: To establish external validity.

1. Replicate a study done many years ago.
2. Replicate a study done in a foreign land.

Systematic replication: To improve power.

1. Improve standardization of procedures.
2. Use more subjects.
3. Use more homogenous subjects.
4. Use more extreme levels of treatment or predictor variable.
5. Use a more sensitive dependent measure.
6. Use a more powerful design (within or blocked design rather than simple between-groups design).

Systematic replication: To improve external validity.

1. Use more heterogeneous group of subjects or use a subject group (e.g., females) that was not represented in the original study.
2. Repeat as a field study.

3. Delay measurement of the dependent variable to see whether treatment effect persists over time.
4. Use more levels of the independent or predictor variable.

Systematic replication: To improve construct validity.

1. Replace an empty control group with a placebo treatment group.
2. Use more than two levels of the independent variable.
3. Alter study so it's double-blind.
4. Add or improve cover story.
5. Replicate as a field study.

Conceptual replication: To improve construct validity.

1. Use different manipulation of treatment variable and add manipulation check.
2. Use different dependent measure.
   a. More behavioral.
   b. Less obtrusive.

Other ways of extending research.

1. Replicate the research but add another factor to the design.
2. Conduct studies suggested by authors in their discussion section.

MAIN POINTS

1. In the introduction the authors tell you what the hypothesis is, how they arrived at it, why it's important, and they justify their method of testing it.
2. To understand the introduction you need to refer to theory and previous research.
3. The method section tells you who the subjects were, how many subjects there were, and how they were treated.
4. Three kinds of results may be presented in the results section: results of manipulation checks, results of hypothesis, and other statistically significant results.
5. The discussion section either reiterates the introduction and results sections or tries to reconcile them.
6. When you critique the introduction, question whether testing the hypothesis is vital, whether it follows logically from theory and intuition, and whether the authors have found the best way to test it.
7. When you critique the method section, question the construct validity of the independent and dependent variables, determine if subjects may have played along with the hypothesis, and evaluate external and internal validity.

8. When you look at the results section, question any null results.
9. In the discussion section, question the authors' interpretation of the results, try to explain results that the authors have failed to explain, find a way to test your hypothesis, and note any weaknesses the authors concede.
10. The possibility of Type I error or fraud or lack of generalizability may justify doing a direct replication.
11. You can do a systematic replication to improve power, external validity, or construct validity.
12. Conceptual replications are mandated when problems with a study's construct validity cannot be ameliorated through minor changes.
13. Replications are vital for the advancement of psychology as a science.
14. Reading research should stimulate research ideas.

KEY TERMS

experimental realism
mundane realism
direct replication

systematic replication
conceptual replication

EXERCISES

1. Complete your critique of the journal article you selected.
2. What are the major sections of a journal article? What information is usually contained in each section?
3. What weaknesses should you look for in each section? What weaknesses did you find in your article?
4. Design a direct replication based on the article you critiqued. Do you think your replication will yield the same results as the original? Why?
5. Design a systematic replication based on the article you critiqued. What problems in the original study does your systematic replication correct? How?
6. Design a conceptual replication based on the article you critiqued. What problems in the original study does your conceptual replication correct? How?

10

CAUSALITY WITHOUT RANDOMIZATION: SINGLE-SUBJECT AND QUASI-EXPERIMENTS

OUTLINE

OVERVIEW

In this chapter, you'll learn how the experimental designs presented in Chapters 5, 6, and 7 allow you to make causal statements. Then, you'll be introduced to two other categories of designs that allow you to infer causality: single-subject experiments and quasi-experiments.

INFERRING CAUSALITY IN RANDOMIZED EXPERIMENTS

Whether you use a randomized experiment or any other technique, you must satisfy three criteria if you are to infer that one variable (smiling at others) causes a change in another variable (others helping you).

Establishing Covariation

First, you must establish **covariation**: that the cause and effect change together. Therefore, to show that smiling causes people to help you, you must prove that people are more helpful to you when you smile than when you don't.

In the randomized experiment, you establish covariation by comparing the average scores for your different conditions. If your conditions are significantly different from one another, then you know that changes in the independent variable are accompanied by changes in the dependent variable: covariation. Thus, in a randomized experiment involving smiling and helpfulness, you'd compare the amount of help you got when you smiled with the amount you got when you didn't smile.

Establishing Temporal Precedence

Second, you must show that the causal variable comes before the effect: **temporal precedence**. That is, you'd have to show that you smile at others before they help you. Otherwise, it may be that you smile after people help you.

In a randomized experiment, you automatically establish that the cause comes before the effect (temporal precedence) by manipulating the independent variable. You always present the independent variable (smiling) before you present the dependent measure task (giving subjects an opportunity to help).

Establishing Ceteris Paribus

Third, you must show that the causal factor is the only thing that is varying, that everything else is the same. In scientific jargon, you must show that there is **ceteris paribus**: all other things equal. Therefore, to show that your smiling causes others to be nice to you, you must show that everything is the same during the times that you smile and the times that you don't smile, except for your smiling.

It's difficult to prove that the only difference between the times when you smile and times when you don't is your smile. But without such proof, you cannot say that your smiling causes people to be more helpful. Why? Because you might be smiling more when the weather is nicer, when things at school are more relaxed, or when you're with your friends. These same conditions (being with friends, nice weather) may be the reason you're getting help—your smile may have nothing to do with it. If you can't be sure that everything else was the same, then the relationship between smiling and helpfulness may be **spurious**: due to other variables.

Approximating Ceteris Paribus

In the randomized experiment, you don't establish ceteris paribus by keeping everything except the treatment variable(s) constant. Instead, you approximate ceteris paribus by using random assignment to convert systematic error into random error and by using statistical tests to subtract out the random error.

As you learned in Chapter 5, random assignment ensures that uncontrolled variables don't vary systematically. Your conditions will be equivalent except for the effects of the independent variable and the chance effect of random variables. Therefore, as a result of randomization, only random variables stand in the way of ceteris paribus.

If you could remove those random variables, you'd achieve ceteris paribus. But, of course, you can't remove them. However, you can use statistics to estimate their effects: If the difference between groups is greater than the estimated effects of random error, the results are statistically significant. If you find a statistically significant effect for your independent variable, you can argue that your independent variable causes a change in the dependent variable. However, you may be wrong. You may have underestimated the amount of random error and falsely identified a chance difference as a treatment effect (i.e., Type I error).

AN ALTERNATIVE TO RANDOMIZATION AND STATISTICAL TESTS: THE SINGLE-SUBJECT EXPERIMENT

All experimental designs establish that the cause comes before the effect by manipulating the independent variable (smiling) before presenting the dependent measure task (helping). All experimental designs establish covariation by comparing the different treatment conditions (e.g., comparing smiling versus no-smiling conditions). But not all experimental designs use randomization to approximate ceteris paribus.

Establishing Ceteris Paribus

The single subject experiment, for example, strives to achieve, rather than to approximate, ceteris paribus. Instead of letting nontreatment variables vary and then accounting for the effects of those variables, single-subject experimenters stop nontreatment factors from varying.

What is the single subject experiment and how does it stop nontreatment factors from varying? In the **single-subject design**, as the name implies, the experimenter studies a single subject. Then, the experimenter makes sure that the subject's behavior on the dependent measure task (pecking) occurs at a consistent rate. This is called establishing a **stable baseline**. Finally, the experimenter introduces the treatment. This design establishes ceteris paribus by eliminating the two basic threats to ceteris paribus: nontreatment effects due to between-subject variability and nontreatment effects due to within-subject variability.

Between-subject variability is obviously not a problem for the single-subject design. Differences between individuals can't account for differences between conditions because the same subject is in all conditions. Experimenters using between-subject designs have to be concerned that differences between conditions may be due to the fact that different individuals are in the different conditions. In other words, between-subject experimenters worry that individual difference variables may be responsible for the differences between treatment conditions. The single-subject experimenter has no such worries.

But the single-subject experimenter does have to deal with random within-subject variability. With or without treatment, a subject's behavior may vary. How does the single-subject experimenter know that the treatment is responsible for the change in the subject's behavior?

She is confident that the difference between no-treatment and treatment conditions is not due to random within-subject variability because she's collected a stable baseline. The baseline shows that the subject's behavior is not varying.

But how does a single-subject experimenter obtain a stable baseline? After all, behavior is variable. To obtain a stable baseline, the experimenter must control all relevant environmental variables (the variables that might affect the subject's responses).

If the experimenter doesn't know what the relevant variables are, she tries to keep the subject's environment as constant as possible by performing the experiments under highly controlled conditions (soundproof laboratories). If the experimenter knows which are the relevant variables, then she only needs to control those relevant variables. Thus, if an experimenter knew that parental praise was the only relevant variable in increasing studying behavior, she'd only need to control that one variable. However, the experimenter usually doesn't know what variables can be safely ignored. Psychology has not advanced to the state where we can catalog which variables affect and which don't affect every possible response.

After attempting to control variables, the experimenter checks to see whether she's succeeded by looking at the baseline. If the baseline isn't stable, she continues to control variables until the behavior becomes stable.

But what if a researcher can't achieve a stable baseline? Then, she can't use a single-subject design. This is often the case. If the organism is complex and therefore affected by many variables, if the behavior is complex and therefore affected by many variables, or if the environment is extremely complex, the researcher usually can't control all the relevant variables. Consequently, you'll rarely see a single-subject experiment investigating the creativity of an executive in a business setting. More often, single-subject experimenters have a simple organism (pigeon, rat, planarium, neuron) perform a rather simple behavior (pecking) in a simple environment (Skinner boxes).

Thus far, we've seen how the single-subject experimenter can hold individual difference variables and relevant environmental variables constant. But how does she know that the difference between conditions isn't due to the organism maturing?

The single-subject experimenter may hold maturation constant by choosing an organism that she knows won't mature during the course of the study. Thus, she might use a pigeon or a rat because those organisms don't mature very much during their lifespans and the extent of their maturation as it relates to certain tasks (bar pressing and pecking) is well documented.

Or, as you'll soon see, the experimenter may use a design that will allow her to account for maturation. But before examining that kind of design, let's look at an example of the purest and simplest single-subject designs.

Howard Blough (1957) wanted to study the effect of LSD on the threshold for visual perception in a pigeon. His first step was to place the pigeon in a highly controlled environment, a Skinner box, equipped with a light that could illuminate a spot on the stimulus panel at different intensities. On the wall of the Skinner box were two disks—"1" and "2". As an index of visual threshold, the pigeon was conditioned to peck at Disk 1 when the spot was visible and to peck at Disk 2 when the spot was not visible.

Before Blough began to manipulate his independent variable (LSD), he had to make sure that no other variables were influencing the pigeon's behavior. To do this he had to keep all the relevant variables in the pigeon's environment constant. Therefore, he placed the pigeon in the Skinner box and carefully observed the pigeon's behavior while it performed the visual perception task. If he'd succeeded in eliminating all irrelevant variables the pigeon's behavior would be relatively stable—the relationship between pecking and illumination would be constant. If he'd failed, he would observe fluctuations in the pigeon's behavior (e.g., erratic increases and decreases in pecking).

Once the pigeon's behavior was stable, Blough was ready to introduce the independent variable, LSD. After administering the LSD, Blough compared the pigeon's behavior before the treatment (A), to its behavior after the treatment (B). Blough found that after taking the LSD, the pigeon's threshold for visual perception decreased as indicated by pecking at Disc 2 (can't see spot) under a level of illumination that prior to treatment lead to a peck at Disc 1. Because Blough had insured that irrelevant variables were not influencing the pigeon's behavior, he concluded that the LSD was the sole cause of the decrease in visual threshold.

Blough's study was exceptional because he knew that the pigeon's behavior wouldn't change much over time. However, other kinds of subjects, human beings, for instance, might change, or develop over time. Therefore, most experimenters aren't so confident that they've controlled all the important variables. They know that two potentially important nontreatment variables have changed from measurement at baseline (**A**) to measurement after administering the treatment (**B**).

First, because the posttest comes after the pretest, subjects have had more practice on the task when performing the posttest. Thus, their performance may have improved as a result of the practice they got on the pretest (i.e., testing). Second, time has passed from pretest to posttest. Consequently, changes in behavior from pretest to posttest may reflect changes due to maturation, such as fatigue, boredom, development, etc. Because psychologists realize that the effects of testing and maturation may threaten internal validity, single-subject experimenters rarely use the **A–B design**.

The Reversal Design

Instead, psychologists prefer to use designs such as the reversal design. In the **reversal design**, also known as the **A–B–A design**, the experimenter measures the behavior three times: before the treatment is introduced (A), after introducing the treatment (B), and after withdrawing the treatment (A).

To see why the A–B–A design is superior to the A–B design, consider one in a series of single-subject experiments performed by Ayllon and Azrin (1965, 1968).

Variations on the Single-Subject Design

They worked with a group of psychotics in a mental hospital to see if a token economy was an effective way of increasing socially desirable behavior. In a typical experiment, Ayllon and Azrin first identified a desirable behavior (e.g., feeding oneself) to be associated with a reinforcer—a token that could be used to buy such unconditioned reinforcers as candy, movies, social interaction, or privacy. Next the experimenters collected baseline behavior for a patient (A); then administered the treatment (gave the patient tokens for each instance of the socially desirable behavior) and measured the behavior (B). They found that the patient performed more socially desired behaviors once the tokens were introduced. Great! A token economy increased socially desirable behavior. Right?

If Ayllon and Azrin's study had ended here, they couldn't be confident in their answer. Remember, with an A–B design, you don't know whether the increase in socially desirable behavior is due to maturation, testing, or the treatment.

However, by expanding the A–B design to an A–B–A design, by withdrawing the treatment and continuing to observe their patient's behavior, they were able to determine that the treatment (tokens) increased socially desirable behavior. If, after withdrawing the treatment, socially desirable behavior had continued to increase, they would've concluded that the increase in socially desirable behavior was not due to the treatment. Instead, they would've concluded that the increase was due to maturation and/or testing.

What made them conclude that the treatment was responsible for the effect? They found that socially desirable behavior increased when they introduced the tokens and fell back to near-baseline level when the tokens were withdrawn.

But if tokens caused the effect, shouldn't their withdrawal cause the behavior to fall to baseline rather than near baseline? Although you'd like to see the dependent measure (socially desirable behavior) fall back to baseline level, don't insist on this pattern of results before you're willing to make a causal inference. Chances are, you won't get it. Most behaviors won't return to baseline after you withdraw the treatment because of:

1. maturation effects,
2. testing effects, and
3. carry-over effects.

Because of these effects, you can infer causality as long as there is a substantially higher (or lower) level of the dependent variable during treatment than during both pretreatment and posttreatment baselines.

Certainly, you can be logically justified in inferring causality if treatment behavior is substantially different from both pretreatment or posttreatment behavior. Unfortunately, justified or not, you could be wrong if you infer causality based on such an apparent treatment effect.

How could you be wrong? You'd be wrong if the effects of practice and/or maturation are cyclical. For instance, suppose performance was affected by menstrual cycles. Performance might therefore be good during the pretreatment phase (before menstruation), poor during the treatment phase (during menstruation), and good during the posttreatment phase (after menstruation). Although such an unsteady effect of maturation or testing would be unlikely, it's possible.

To rule out the possibility that your apparent treatment effects are due to some simple cyclical pattern involving either maturation or practice, you might extend the A–B–A design to make it an A–B–A–B design. Ayllon and Azrin did this, and found that reintroduction of the token rewards led to an increase in the socially desirable behavior. By adding even more measurements, you could use an A–B–A–B–A design to rule out the possibility of an even more complicated maturational or practice cycle. Obviously, the more measurements you collect, the less likely it is that time or practice can explain apparent treatment effects. Imagine trying to explain how maturation or testing effects could explain apparent treatment effects in an A–B–A–B–A–B–A–B–A–B design!

Multiple-Baseline Design

Another single-subject experimental design that rules out the effects of maturation and testing is the multiple-baseline design. In a typical multiple-baseline design, you would collect baselines for several behaviors. For example, you might collect baselines for a child making her own bed, putting her toys away, washing her hands, and vacuuming her room. Then, you'd reinforce one of the behaviors. If the behavior being reinforced increases (putting her toys away), you'd suspect that reinforcement is causing the behavior to increase.

But the effects might be due to being observed or to the child becoming more mature. To see whether the child's improvement in behavior is due to maturation and/or testing, you'd look at her performance on the other tasks. If those tasks are still being performed at baseline level, then maturation and testing are not improving performance on those tasks. Since maturation and practice have no effect on the other behaviors, they probably aren't increasing the particular behavior you decided to reinforce. Therefore, you'd be relatively confident that the improvement in putting toys away was due to reinforcement.

To be even more certain that the reinforcement is causing the change in behavior, you'd reinforce a second behavior (washing hands) and compare it against the other nonreinforced behaviors. You'd continue the process until you'd reinforced all the behaviors. If you observed increases in every behavior after you reinforced that behavior but didn't observe increases in behaviors that were not being reinforced, you'd be very confident that reinforcement was responsible for the increase in behavior.

Internal Validity

The single-subject experimenter uses a variety of strategies to achieve internal validity. Like the physicist, the single-subject experimenter keeps many relevant variables constant. For example, he holds individual difference variables constant by studying a single subject and holds environmental variables constant by placing that subject in a highly controlled environment (Imagine a rat in a soundproof Skinner box!).

Like the within-subjects experimenter, the single-subject experimenter must worry that subjects may have changed as a result of being measured or as a result of time passing. Thus, both kinds of experimenters may adapt similar strategies to

Evaluation of Single-Subject Experiments

deal with these threats. Both experimenters may try to reduce maturation by shortening the length of their study. Both may try to reduce the effects of practice (testing) by giving subjects extensive practice on the task prior to beginning the study. By giving extensive preexperimental practice on the task, they reduce the likelihood that subjects will benefit from any additional practice they get during the experiment. Single-subject experimenters, in particular, like to make sure the subject's response rate is stable before the treatment is introduced.

Although both experimenters may sometimes adapt similar strategies to eliminate threats to validity, their basic methods for attacking these problems are fundamentally different. Whereas the within-subjects experimenter relies primarily on randomization to rule out practice and fatigue effects, the single-subject experimenter relies on introducing and removing the treatment in a systematic order.

Both experimenters must also be concerned about carry-over effects. Because of carry-over, investigators using an A–B–A design frequently find that subjects don't return to the original baseline. Of course, the problems of carry-over multiply when you use more levels of the independent variable or when you use more than one independent variable. To minimize complications from carry-over, most single-subject experimenters use only two levels of a single independent variable.

Construct Validity

The single-subject researcher and the within-subject experimenter have even more in common when they attack threats to construct validity. For both researchers, sensitization poses a serious problem and both researchers use the same solution. Specifically, both can reduce the effects of sensitization by making the difference between the treatment conditions so subtle that subjects don't even realize that anything has changed (e.g., gradually varying the loudness of a stimulus), using placebo treatments, and/or using very few levels of treatment. Researchers' concerns about sensitization may account for the popularity of the A–B–A design over more complicated single-subject designs such as A–B–A–B–A–B–A–B–A–B.

External Validity

At first glance, the single-subject experiment seems to have less external validity than other designs. How can the results from one subject be generalized to others? Furthermore, how can the results from an experiment conducted in such a highly controlled setting be generalized to other settings? Although it seems that other designs must have more external validity than the single-subject experiment, things are not always as they seem.

Whether you use one subject or 1,000 subjects, you can only infer that your results will apply to individuals that weren't in your study. In other words, you're assuming than no other iniviudal difference variables interact with your treatment to reverse or negate its effects. Since single-subject experiments tend to investigate processes that are well understood and known to occur in all organisms, the results of such experiments may be generalized to other members of the same species. Thus, the results of psychophysical and operant conditioning experiments performed on a single member of a species can often be generalized to other members of that species.

In addition to having strong generalizability because they study universal processes (such as reinforcement), single-subject experiments may have strong generalizability because they only study a single subject. To see why this apparent weakness could be a strength, consider the situation in which you have a treatment that makes half your subjects get better and half your subjects get worse. On the surface, it would seem that this situation would be tailor-made for a randomized experiment that used many subjects. After all, if you do a single-subject experiment, the results would only generalize to half the population.

But, what if you did a traditional between-subjects design? Then, the positive effects from subjects who improved would be cancelled out by the negative effects from subjects who got worse. As a result, the average treatment effect would be zero. You'd conclude that the treatment had no effect even though it had an effect for every single subject. Your results, based on many subjects, wouldn't generalize to anybody (just as national surveys show that the average American family has 2.3 children, although no American family has 2.3 children). Thus, the single-subject experiment, although only generalizing to half the population, would apply to many more people than the between-groups experiment. Furthermore, whereas replicating the between-groups experiment would just give you the same results every time, replicating the single-subject experiment would alert you to the fact that the treatment sometimes harms and sometimes helps subjects. As a result of continued replications of the single-subject experiment, you might be able to isolate the variable that determines whether subjects are harmed or helped by the treatment.

You've seen that results based on a highly controlled study of a single subject can often be generalized to other subjects. But can the results of an experiment conducted under such controlled conditions be generalized to other settings? Yes, especially when the single-subject experiment investigates universal phenomena that are relatively unaffected by setting (e.g., sensation). Even when the results can't be generalized to all settings, single-subject investigators can often be specific about which settings their results would generalize to because of their detailed knowledge of the phenomenon.

Conclusions about Single-Subject Experiments

Not coincidentally, the single-subject experiment bears a close resemblance to physics and chemistry experiments. As is the case with experiments in the physical sciences, the single-subject experiment is most easily interpreted when the potential causal variables have been identified and controlled. Furthermore, just as universal physical laws (e.g., gas laws) allow the results of chemistry experiments done on a few hydrogen molecules to be generalized to all hydrogen molecules, universal psychophysical laws (e.g., laws of operant conditioning) may allow experiments done on a single member of a species to be generalized to all members of the species. Finally, like physics or chemistry experiments, when much is known about the variables that affect a given phenomenon, scientists can accurately predict the extent to which the results of a highly controlled study can be applied to other settings.

But is it good that the single-subject design resembles natural science experiments? The answer to that question depends entirely on who you ask.

According to supporters of the single-n design, the answer is a resounding "yes." They claim that there are no basic differences among various scientific disciplines and so the same methods that lead to the discovery of physical laws can reveal the laws of human behavior. As evidence of their progress toward discovering these laws and that this progress has allowed them to study behavior outside of highly controlled environments, they proudly point to the many single-n experiments published in the *Journal of Experimental Analysis of Behavior* (JEAB) and the *Journal of Applied Behavioral Analysis* (JEAB) that study behaviors in real-life settings.

Opponents, however, feel that the single-n design has not adapted to the unique problems of studying the behavior of complex organisms. Some even believe that it doesn't adequately deal with the threats to internal validity so it doesn't merit being called an experimental design. These psychologists think that the single-n design is an historical relic from a time when psychology tried to emulate "true" sciences. They feel that psychology has now progressed enough to make its own way with its own methods.

Are the single-n researchers using a time-tested technique that will insure great success? Or are they, like the sorcerer's apprentice, playing with a technique that isn't appropriate for their problem? Only time will tell.

QUASI-EXPERIMENTS

Another popular alternative to the randomized experiment is the quasi-experiment. According to the authorities on quasi-experimental design, Cook and Campbell (1979), **quasi-experiments** are, "experiments that have treatments, outcome measures, and experimental units, but do not use random asignment to create the comparisons from which treatment-caused change is inferred" (p. 6).

Like experiments, quasi-experiments establish temporal precedence because the treatment comes before the outcome. Like experiments, quasi-experiments assess covariation by comparing treatment versus nontreatment conditions. However, unlike the experiments, quasi-experiments are unable to establish ceteris paribus through either randomization or control.

Thus, the challenge in quasi-experiments is inferring ceteris paribus without the aid of random assignment or control of relevant variables. The first step to meeting this challenge is to be aware of all the variables that might account for a relationship between the treatment and the effect. Once you've identified these variables, you'll try to demonstrate that these variables didn't account for the relationship.

The Spurious Eight   To be aware of all the variables that might account for the relationship between the treatment and the effect is a tall order. Fortunately, however, all possible threats to ceteris paribus fall under the eight threats to internal validity that you learned about in Chapter 4, namely, apparent treatment effects being due to:

1. **HISTORY:** events in the outside world that are unrelated to the treatment.
2. **MATURATION:** natural biological changes.
3. **MORTALITY:** subjects dropping out of the study. For instance, subjects might drop out shortly after entering the treatment condition.
4. **TESTING:** subjects having experienced the pretest.
5. **INSTRUMENTATION:** changes in the measuring instrument.

6. **SELECTION:** comparing groups that are different (comparing apples and oranges).

7. **STATISTICAL REGRESSION:** regression to the mean (the tendency for subjects who receive extreme scores on the pretest to receive less extreme scores on the posttest).

8. **SELECTION-MATURATION INTERACTION:** the groups naturally maturing at different rates. In other words, just because two groups scored similarly at the beginning of the study, you can't assume that they would've scored identically at the end of the study.

Once you've identified the threats to internal validity, you must determine which threats are ruled out by the design and which threats you can eliminate through logic. Experimental designs rule out threats to validity automatically, but quasi-experimental designs vary in their ability to do this. Yet, even with a quasi-experimental design that doesn't automatically rule out threats, you may be able to infer causality.

Using Logic to Combat the Spurious Eight

The pretest–posttest design is very similar to the single-subject A–B design. But rather than compare one subject's behavior before treatment with that subject's behavior after treatment, you include several subjects in your comparison. In a pretest–posttest experiment you'd test one group of subjects, administer a treatment, and then retest them.

The Pretest–Posttest Design

This design doesn't rule out many threats automatically. However, since you're testing individuals against themselves, you don't have to worry about selection or selection-maturation interactions.

Although you do have to worry about mortality, instrumentation, regression, maturation, history, and testing, you may be able to rule out these threats on the grounds that they're extremely improbable. If nobody dropped out of your study, mortality isn't a problem. Similarly, if you were careful enough to use the same measure and administer it in the same way, instrumentation isn't a problem. You might be able to rule out regression by arguing that people were not in the study because their scores were extreme. To support your argument, you might discuss the reasons subjects were in the study and you might show that their pretest scores were not extreme. If there is a very short time between pretest and posttest, maturation is unlikely. About the only maturation that could occur in a short period of time would be boredom or fatigue. Obviously, you could rule out boredom and fatigue, and thus maturation if performance was better on the posttest than on the pretest. If there were only a few minutes between the pretest and posttest, then history is unlikely to be a problem.

Thus far, in this particular study, you've been able to rule out every threat except testing. And, you might even be able to rule that out. For instance, if your measure was an unobtrusive one, testing might not be a problem. Or, if you used a standardized test, you might know how much people tend to improve when they take the test the second time. If your subjects improved substantially more than these norms, you could rule out the testing effect as an explanation for your results.

In summary, you can infer causality from experiments and quasi-experiments. The key is to establish temporal precedence, covariation, and to rule out the spurious eight. Experiments and quasi-experiments automatically establish temporal precedence and covariation. But, whereas experiments automatically rule out the spurious eight, quasi-experiments do not. Thus, to infer causality with a quasi-experiment, you must use your wits to rule out some of the threats to validity. Box 10-1 gives some examples of how you might use logic to disarm the spurious eight.

The pretest–posttest design doesn't automatically eliminate most threats to validity. However, you can extend it into a quasi-experiment that can: the time series design.

Time Series Designs

The **time series design** is an extension of the basic pretest–posttest design. It uses several pretests and/or posttests. For this reason, you might call time series designs pre-pre-pre–post-post-post designs. Like the pretest-posttest design, a major advantage of the time series design is that it isn't threatened by selection.

To illustrate the differences between the pretest–posttest design and the time series design, suppose you are interested in seeing if disclosing a professor's marital troubles affects evaluations by her students. With a pretest–posttest design, you'd have a class evaluate the professor before she tells them about her marital problems, then have them rate her afterward. If you observed a difference between pretest and

---

BOX 10—1   Preventing Threats to Validity

THREATS   PRECAUTIONS

History: Isolate subjects from external events. Short time between start and end of study.

Maturation: Short time between start and end of study. Use subjects who are maturing at slow rates.

Testing: Only test subjects once. Give subjects extensive practice on task prior to collecting data so they won't benefit substantially from practice they obtain during the study. Know what testing effects are (from past data) and subtract them out. Use different versions of same test.

Instrumentation: Administer same measure, same way, every time.

Mortality: Use rewards, innocuous treatments, and brief treatments so that subjects don't drop out of study. Use placebo treatments and/or subtly different levels of the treatment so that more subjects don't drop out of one condition than out of another. Make sure subjects understand instructions so they aren't thrown out for not following directions.

Regression: Don't choose subjects on basis of extreme scores. Don't match groups on variables on which they're fundamentally different.

Selection: Random assignment. Extensive matching

Selection Interactions: Reduce the effect of variables that might interact with selection. For example, could you reduce history by isolating subjects from external events or reduce maturation by keeping length of study brief, etc.

posttest ratings, you'd be tempted to say that the difference was due to the disclosure. However, the "treatment" effect might really be due to history, maturation, testing, mortality, instrumentation, or regression. Since you have no idea how much of an effect history, maturation, testing, mortality, and instrumentation may have had, you can't tell whether or not you had a treatment effect.

Estimating the Effects of Threats of Validity with a Time Series Design

But what if you extended the pretest–posttest design? That is, what if you had students rate the professor after every lecture for the entire term, even though the professor wouldn't disclose her marital problems until the sixth week? Then, you'd have a time series design.

What do you gain by all these pretests and posttests? From plotting the average ratings for each lecture, you know how much of an effect maturation, testing, instrumentation, and mortality tend to have. In other words, when you observe differences from week to week during the pretest, you know those differences aren't due to the treatment. Instead, those differences must be due to maturation, testing, history, instrumentation, or mortality. Thus, if there is a steady improvement in the professor's ratings from week one to week six (the predisclosure period), you wouldn't claim that a similar difference from week six to seven (when the marital disclosures were introduced) is a treatment effect. Instead, you'd view such a difference as being due to the effects of history, maturation, mortality, testing, or instrumentation. If, on the other hand, you found a much greater increase in ratings from week six to week seven than you found between any other two consecutive weeks, you'd suspect that the professor's disclosures about her marital problems improved her student evaluations.

Yet, your suspicions could be wrong. That is, you're assuming that you can correctly estimate the effects of history, maturation, mortality, testing, and instrumentation during the time that the treatment was administered because you have measurements from other periods of the same length. This assumption is only correct if the effects of history, maturation, mortality, instrumentation, and testing are relatively consistent over time. In other words, your suspicions could be wrong if there is a sudden change in any one of these variables.

Inconsistent Instrumentation Effects   Obviously, sudden changes in these variables are possible. Variables that have had no effect or only small, consistent effects can suddenly have large effects. Suppose you administered the same rating scale in the same way for the first six weeks. Your measurements from weeks one through six wouldn't be affected by instrumentation. As a result, your estimate for the amount of change to expect between week six and week seven wouldn't include any effect for instrumentation. However, this estimate would be incorrect if you changed your rating scale at the same time the professor started telling her class about her marital problems. In that case, you could mistake an instrumentation effect for a treatment effect.

Inconsistent Mortality Effects   Likewise, if mortality doesn't follow a consistent pattern, you might mistake mortality's effects for treatment effects. For example, suppose that the last week to drop the course was the same week that the professor started to tell the class about her problems. In that case, a disproportionate number of students who didn't like the professor might drop out during that week. Consequently, the professor's ratings might improve because of mortality, rather than because of her disclosures. Although you can discount some of this mortality effect because mortality was gradually improving ratings from weeks one through six, the sudden rash of mortality will create an effect much greater than the data from weeks one through six would lead you to expect. Consequently, you might believe you have a treatment effect, when you really have a mortality effect.

Inconsistent Testing Effects　Whereas the effect of testing should be gradual and consistent in this study, the effect of testing will not be consistent in every study. For example, in some studies, subjects might develop insight into the task. As a result of discovering the rule behind the task, their performance may increase dramatically. Even when subjects aren't aware of having insight, practice doesn't always lead to steady improvement in performance. As you know from experience, you may practice at a task for weeks with little evidence of improvement and then, almost overnight, your performance will improve dramatically.

Inconsistent Maturation Effects　Similarly, maturation's effect may sometimes be discontinuous. For instance, suppose you measure young children every three months on a motor abilities test. Then, you expose them to an enriched environment and measure them again. Certainly, you'll see a dramatic change. But is this change due to the treatment, or due to the children jumping to a more advanced developmental stage (e.g., learning to walk)?

　　　Unfortunately, you can't escape sudden, sporadic maturation by studying adults. Even in our teacher evaluation study, subjects might mature at an inconsistent rate. That is, first-year students might mature rapidly after getting their first exams back, students might suddenly develop insight into the professor's lecturing style, or the professor might suddenly develop insight into how the students like to have the class conducted. If this sudden development occurred the same week the professor started to disclose her marital problems, maturation could masquerade as a treatment effect.

History　Although you can often reasonably assume that the effects of testing, instrumentation, mortality, and maturation are consistent across time, history is less predictable. There are many specific events that could affect performance on the posttest. For instance, ratings of the professor might change as a result of students getting the midterm back, the professor getting ill, the professor reading a book on teaching, etc. Unlike the single-subject design, the time series design doesn't control all these history effects. Indeed, you could argue that the time series design's lack of control over history, and thus its vulnerability to history, prevent it from reaching experimental design status.

　　　History is the one threat to which the time series is vulnerable, but you can try to reduce its effects. One strategy is to have a very short interval between testing sessions. With an extremely short interval, you give history fewer opportunities to have an effect.

In addition to reducing the effects of history, you can try to do a better job of estimating its effects. Thus, following the idea that you can best predict the future by intimately knowing the past, you might collect an extensive baseline. Ideally, you'd collect baseline data for several years before having the professor disclose her marital problems. This baseline will help you identify any historical events or patterns that tend to repeat themselves regularly. For instance, your baseline would alert you to cyclical patterns in student evaluations, such as students being very positive toward the professor during the first two weeks of the term, being more negative after the midterm examination, and then becoming more favorable during the last week of the term. As a result, your baseline would prevent you from mistaking these cyclical fluctuations for a treatment effect.

Regression   To this point, we've discussed threats to validity that might be expected to change steadily from week to week or from test to test. But, what about regression? Since regression is due to chance measurement error, it won't change steadily from week to week or from test to test. Therefore, you can't use a time series design to measure regression's effect. However, you can use time series designs to determine whether regression is a likely explanation for your results. Specifically, you should suspect regression if:

1.   the ratings immediately before the treatment are extremely high or extremely low relative to the previous ratings, and
2.   the posttreatment ratings, although very different from the most immediate pretreatment level, aren't substantially different from earlier pretreatment ratings.

Eliminating, Rather than Estimating Threats to Validity
You've seen that the time series design can rule out certain threats to validity by estimating the effects of those threats. When using these designs, however, don't overlook the possibility of eliminating threats to validity rather than simply estimating their effects. That is, try to eliminate the threat of instrumentation in time series designs by using the same measuring instrument each time and administering it the same way. For our teacher evaluation study, we'd give students the same rating scales and the same instructions each time. In addition, try to eliminate mortality whenever possible. So, if you had students sign their rating sheets, eliminate mortality by only analyzing data from students who had perfect attendance. (If the ratings were anonymous, you could eliminate mortality by only analyzing ratings from days where attendance was perfect.)

Furthermore, try to reduce the effects of maturation and history by keeping the interval between pretest and posttest short. Finally, minimize the likelihood of regression occurring by choosing the time that you'll administer the treatment well in advance—don't administer the treatment as an immediate reaction to extremely bad ratings.

Types of Time Series Designs
Now that you're familiar with the basic logic behind the time series design, you're ready to consider extensions of it. One simple way of extending a time series design

is to increase the number of pretest and posttest measurements you take. The more measurements you take, the easier it'll be to estimate the combined effects of maturation, history, mortality, testing, and instrumentation. In addition, the more measurements you have, the less likely that an unusual history, maturation, mortality, testing, or instrumentation effect will occur at the same time you administer the treatment. That is, if you only measure student evaluations on the fifth, sixth, and seventh weeks, it won't be too much of a coincidence for an unusual history, maturation, mortality, testing, or instrumentation effect to occur between the sixth and seventh weeks, but not between the fifth and sixth weeks. However, if you have students evaluate the teacher from week 1 to week 12, it would be quite a coincidence for a threat to have an extraordinarily large effect between the sixth and seventh week (the same week you gave the treatment), but not between any of the other weeks.

Reversal Time Series Designs   You can also extend your time series design by administering and withdrawing the treatment. That is, you can imitate the single-subject experimenter's reversal design, by pretesting, administering the treatment, posttesting, withdrawing the treatment, and testing again. You might even withdraw and introduce the treatment several times.

TABLE 10-1   How Pretest–Posttest Designs and Time Series Designs Compare in Terms of Threats to Internal Validity

	Type of Design	
Threat to Validity	**Pretest–Posttest Design**	**Time Series Design**
SELECTION	A	A
SELECTION MATURATION INTERACTION	A	A
MORTALITY	C	C
INSTRUMENTATION	C	C
MATURATION	P	E
TESTING	P	E
HISTORY	P	E
REGRESSION	P	D

KEY: A = Automatically eliminated by design.
C = Can be eliminated by using common sense, see Box 9-1.
D = The design allows you to determine whether this factor is a plausible explanation for the apparent treatment effect.
E = Design allows you to estimate and then subtract out the effects of this factor. However, estimates may be wrong if the factor exerts an inconsistent effect.
P = This factor is a real threat with this design.

To see the beauty of this reversal design, imagine that you were able to get increases each time the professor tells her class about her marital problems, then decreases when she stops talking about her problems, followed by increases when she again tells her class about her marital woes. With that pattern of results, you'd be very confident that the disclosures made a difference.

Despite the elegance of this reversal design, there are cases when you shouldn't use it. In some situations, you can't ethically withdraw the treatment after you've administered it (e.g., psychotherapy, reinforcement for wearing seatbelts).

In other situations, withdrawing and readministering the treatment may alert subjects to your hypothesis. However, you may be able to prevent subjects from guessing the hypothesis or becoming resentful when you withdraw the treatment by using placebo treatments or multiple levels of the treatment. Thus, if you were to use this design for your teacher evaluation study, you might have the professor disclose innocuous facts about her marriage (placebo treatment) or you might vary the degree of discord she discloses (several levels of the treatment variable).

Two-Group Time Series Design· A final way of extending the time series design is to collect time series data on two groups. One group, the control group, wouldn't get the treatment. The advantage of using a control group is that it allows you to rule out certain history effects. In your disclosure study, the control group might be another section of the same professor's class. If, after the treatment was administered, the ratings went down only in the treatment group, you could rule out general history effects (midterm blues, spring fever) as an explanation of the results. However, you can't rule out every history effect because the two classes may have different histories. For example, the professor may have gotten mad at one class and not the other, one class may have better midterm grades than the other. To better understand the problems and strengths of using a time series with control group design, let's look at the parent of this design: the nonequivalent control group design.

The nonequivalent control group design is the simple experiment without randomization. Because of the nonequivalent control group design's similarity to the simple experiment, it has many of the simple experiment's strengths.

Nonequivalent Control Group Design

For example, because every subject is only tested once, the nonequivalent control group design, like the simple experiment, isn't bothered by maturation, testing, or instrumentation. Furthermore, because of the control group, the nonequivalent group design, like the simple experiment, can successfully deal with the effects of history, maturation, and mortality.

But because this design doesn't use random assignment, the control and treatment groups are not equivalent. Since the control and treatment groups aren't equivalent, comparing them may be like comparing apples and oranges. Thus, with the nonequivalent control group design, the threat of selection is serious.

To address the selection threat, some investigators match subjects. Subjects may be matched on a few background variables (age, gender, IQ) that may be expected to correlate with task performance or subjects may be matched on actual task performance (pretest scores). Although matching seems effective, realize two important points about matched subjects:

1. matched subjects are only matched on a few variables;
2. matched subjects are matched on observed scores (observed scores are not the same as true scores).

Just because two groups are matched on a few variables, you shouldn't think that they're matched on all variables. They aren't. The unmatched variables may affect responses and cause the two groups to score differently on the dependent measure. For instance, suppose you decide to use a nonequivalent groups design to test your hypothesis about the effect of marital disclosure. You want two classes that are similar, so you match the classes on IQ scores, grade point average, proportion of psychology majors, proportion of females and males, and proportion of sophomores, juniors, and seniors. Unfortunately, you have not matched them in terms of when classes meet (morning versus afternoon), interest in going on to graduate school, number of times they'd taken classes from this professor before, and a few other hundred variables that might affect their ratings of the professor. These unmatched variables, not the treatment, may account for the difference between your treatment and control groups.

Since investigators realize that they can't match subjects on every single factor that may influence task performance, some investigators try to match subjects on task performance (pretest scores). Yet, even when groups are matched on pretest scores, unmatched variables can cause the groups to score differently on the posttest. That is, just because two groups of students start out with the same enthusiasm for a course, you can't be sure that they'll end the term with the same amount of enthusiasm. For example, one group may end the term with more enthusiasm because it had a clearer understanding of what the course would be like, what the tests woud be like, and how much work was involved. Consequently, although both groups might rate the professor the same at first, they may differ after the first exam is returned. That is, because of their naïveté, the naïve group may rate the professor more harshly than the experienced group after the first exam. Although this change in student attitudes toward the professor might appear to be a treatment effect, it isn't. Instead, the difference between the two groups is due to the fact that subjects changed over time in different ways because of variables they weren't matched on. Technically, there was a selection by maturation interaction. Because of interactions between selection and other variables, even matching on pretest scores doesn't free you from selection problems.

What can be done about interactions between selection and other variables? One approach is to assume that nature prefers simple, direct main effects to complex interactions. Thus, if an effect could be due to either a treatment main effect or an interaction between selection and maturation, assume that the effect is a simple treatment main effect. Be aware, of course, that your assumption may be very wrong.

Beyond assuming that selection interactions are unlikely, you can make them less likely. One way to make selection interactions less likely is to make the groups similar on as many selection variables as possible. That is, you can match the groups not only on pretest scores, but also on other variables. Since there would be fewer variables on which the groups differed, there would be fewer selection variables to interact with maturation, testing, history, etc. Hence, you'd reduce the chance of these interactions occurring.

You can prevent interactions with selection not only by minimizing selection differences but by eliminating the variables that could interact with selection. For instance, you can reduce the chances of the most common selection interaction, the selection by maturation interaction, by minimizing opportunities for maturation. After all, if neither group can mature, then you won't have a selection maturation interaction. To do this, you should present the posttest as soon after the pretest as possible so that maturation has very little time to occur.

Another problem with matching is that subjects must be matched on observed scores, rather than on true scores. Unfortunately, observed scores aren't the same as true scores. Observed scores are merely imperfect reflections of true scores because they're contaminated by measurement error. As a result of this measurement error, two groups might appear to be similar on certain variables, although actually being very different on these same variables.

To illustrate this point, suppose you were matching college students and mental patients on depression. After testing hundreds of students and patients, you obtain a group of six college students that scores the same on the depression scale as a group of six mental patients. But are the two groups equal in terms of depression?

Since the scores of both groups are likely to be heavily contaminated by random error, the answer is "probably not." You can say that both groups' scores are probably substantially affected by random error because extreme scores tend to have an extreme amount of random error, and both groups' scores are extreme. The six college student subjects' scores are extremely depressed relative to the average college student. The six mental patients' scores are extremely elated relative to the average mental patient.

When both groups are tested again, their scores will be less extreme because their scores will not be as dramatically swayed by random error. Thus, both groups' scores will regress back toward their respective group means. Therefore, on the posttest, the college student subjects will score more like average college students—less depressed, whereas the six mental patients will score more like average mental patients—more depressed. Because the groups are regressing toward different means, this regression effect could easily be mistaken for treatment effect.

How can you stop from mistaking such a regression effect for a treatment effect? The obvious approach is to reduce regression. Since regression takes advantage of random measurement error, you can reduce regression by using a measure that is relatively free of random measurement error—a reliable measure. Or, since extreme scores tend to have more random error than less extreme scores, don't select subjects who have extreme pretest scores.

A trickier approach to combat regression is to obtain results that can't be accounted for by regression. In our depression example, regression would tend to make it look as if the college students had improved in mood more than the mental patients. Thus, if you found that college students improved more than mental patients, your results might be due to regression. However, if you found the opposite result—mental patients improving in mood more than college students, regression wouldn't be an explanation for your results. So, the key is to get results exactly opposite from what regression would predict. Unfortunately, there's no way to guarantee that result. However, you could stack the odds by giving the college students no treatment and mental patients an antidepressant drug. If the antidepressant drug works, you should find that the mental patients had improved in mood much more than college students. Since these results would be opposite of what would happen if regression had occurred, you'd be confident that your results weren't due to regression.

Although regression to different means and interactions with selection are formidable problems, they aren't the only problems you can have when you match. You may also have practical problems with matching. For example, suppose you only have one person who scored an 86. You could drop this subject from your study. But if you drop every subject who doesn't have an exact match, you may end up dropping several subjects from the study. Because of all the subjects you eliminate, you may have trouble generalizing your results.

Therefore, you might try to use all your subjects. So, you might match the "86" with the next closest score, "92". This approach uses all your subjects, but, unfortunately, doesn't match them perfectly. As a result, you might not know whether your results were due to poor matching or to the treatment.

TABLE 10-2 How Two Nonequivalent Control Group Designs Compare in Terms of Threats to Internal Validity

Threat to Validity	Type of Nonequivalent Control Group	
	Unmatched	Matched
SELECTION	P!!!!	p
SELECTION MATURATION INTERACTION AND OTHER INTERACTIONS WITH SELECTION	p	p
MORTALITY	C	C
INSTRUMENTATION	C	C
MATURATION	A	A
TESTING	A	A
HISTORY	A	A
REGRESSION	p	P

KEY: A = Automatically eliminated by design.
C = Can be eliminated by using common sense, see Box 9-1.
p = This factor is a threat to this design.
P = This factor is a very serious and likely threat to this design's internal validity.

To study the effects of age, developmental psychologists have cleverly modified several quasi-experimental designs. When age researchers adapt quasi-experimental designs, they don't look for treatment effects because age is not a treatment variable. Age can't be manipulated. Instead, they look for aging effects, or what quasi-experiment researchers call maturation effects. Thus, the threat to validity in the quasi experiment (maturation) becomes the age researcher's variable of interest.

Tactics for Studying Age

Cross-sectional Designs

One of the most common modifications of a quasi-experimental design is the **cross-sectional design**: A modification of the nonequivalent control group design. As with the nonequivalent control group design, the main threat to validity is selection. That is, although you hope that the two groups will be identical except for age, they may be different on other variables, such as education level or income. As with the nonequivalent control design, the best way to avoid the threats of these non-age variables is to match on as many variables as possible. However, even with extensive matching, you can't rule out the possibility that what you call the effects of age are really the effects of growing up in a different generation, what developmental psychologists call **cohort effects.** Despite the cross-sectional design's vulnerability to selection and cohort effects, it's very popular because it's less time-consuming than other designs.

Longitudinal Designs

Another popular method of studying age-related changes is the longitudinal design. The **longitudinal design** involves taking multiple measurements of each individual over time. Sometimes this period of time can be 50 years!

In effect, the longitudinal design is a variation of the time series design. As you'll recall, the purpose of multiple measurements in the time series design was to assess the combined effects of maturation, instrumentation, mortality, and testing. Although longitudinal researchers use basically the same design, they want to assess the effects of only one of these variables: maturation. Unfortunately, longitudinal researchers can't measure maturation in isolation. Instead, they must measure the combined effects of maturation, instrumentation, mortality, and testing. Thus, the researchers' task is to rule out instrumentation, mortality, and testing effects. They may rule out the effects of instrumentation by consistently using the same measure, and rule out the effects of mortality by only including subjects who make it through the entire length of the study.

Ruling out the effects of testing is more difficult, but might be done by using unobtrusive measures or by using tests in which practice doesn't affect performance. As a last resort, researchers might use tests in which the effects of practice are well known, and then subtract out those effects. However, even if you rule out mortality, instrumentation, and testing, you still have to worry about the time series' old nemesis—history.

Sequential Strategies

In an attempt to disentangle cohort, age, and history effects, Baltes (1968) proposed two additional methods: the cross-sectional sequence and the longitudinal sequence.

These two hybrids are most appropriate when your objective is to describe, rather than explain, age and cohort changes.

Both the cross-sectional and longitudinal sequences parallel the multiple-group, time series design by combining the cross-sectional design with the longitudinal design. To get a better idea of how these hybrid designs work, imagine you have an age effect for the cross-sectional aspect of the design. If you have a group of 25-year-olds who behave differently from a group of 20-year-olds this "age" effect could be a selection effect. For example, the older group might come from a different part of the country than the younger group. However, an age effect for the longitudinal aspect of the design (25-year-olds behave differently from when they were 20), can't be explained by selection. In a sense, because the two designs that make up the **sequential design** have different weaknesses, they cover for each other. Therefore, a researcher finding an age effect for both the cross-sectional and longitudinal aspects of the design, would probably conclude that age caused the observed effect.

The Cross-sectional Sequence   With the cross-sectional sequence, you simultaneously study different age groups (as in the cross-sectional design), but retest them after a period of time (like in the longitudinal design). For example, this year you might measure attitude towards parents in a group of 15-year-olds, a group of 20-year-olds, and a group of 25-year-olds. Five years from now you'd measure their attitudes again.

The Longitudinal Sequence   In the longitudinal sequence you'd conduct the study by measuring the attitudes of a group of 15-year-olds this year. Five years later you'd retest that group (when they're 20), and test a new group of 15-year-olds. Five years later you'd retest both groups. Five years later you'd retest them again. Thus, you'd have information on two different cohorts (cross-sectional) when they were both 15, 20, and 25 years old (longitudinal).

Evaluation of Sequential Strategies   Although the sequential strategies are welcomed improvements over the cross-sectional and longitudinal designs, critics point out that the sequential strategies' abilities to disentangle cohort, age, and history effects are built on the assumption that the effects of history are minimal or nonoperative. This is a very big assumption.

For additional information on age designs see Baltes, Reese, and Nesselroade (1977).

Conclusions about Quasi-experimental Designs

Users of quasi experiments ensure temporal precedence and assess covariation. However, they don't automatically establish ceteris paribus.

They use a variety of tactics to compensate for the limitations of their designs. They may combine quasi-experimental designs to invent the perfect design for their particular research problem. They may eliminate instrumentation biases by administering the same measure, the same way, every time. Finally, they may eliminate some threats by arguing that the particular threat is not a likely explanation for the effect.

To make these arguments, researchers using quasi-experiments often rely on the law of parsimony: Nature will be most likely to choose the simplest course. For example, the time series researcher argues that the effects of maturation, instrumentation, testing, and mortality should be consistent over time. Therefore, a dramatic change after introducing the treatment shouldn't be viewed as a complex, unexpected maturation effect, but as a simple, straightforward treatment effect.

Quasi-experiment researchers don't use the law of parsimony only to suggest that simple, straight-line relationships among variables are more likely than complex, curvy, cyclical relationships. They also use it to suggest that main effects are more likely than interactions. Therefore, a matched groups researcher would argue that an effect that could be explained either as a selection maturation interaction or as a treatment main effect, should be interpreted as a treatment main effect.

Clearly, the quasi-experiment researcher's job is a difficult one, requiring much creativity and effort. But there are rewards. These researchers can often study the effects of treatments that couldn't be experimentally investigated because treatments couldn't (or wouldn't) be randomly assigned. Furthermore, because these researchers often study real-world treatments, their studies sometimes have more external validity than traditional experimental designs.

CONCLUDING REMARKS

If you want to infer causality, the methods you learned about in this chapter are extremely useful. But what if you don't want to infer causality? What if you want to describe or predict behavior? Then, you'll want to use one of the methods discussed in Chapters 11 and 12.

MAIN POINTS

1. To infer that a treatment causes an effect, you must show that changing the amount of the treatment is accompanied by changes in your dependent measure (covariation), that changes in the treatment come before changes in the effect (temporal precedence), and that no other variables are responsible for the effect (ceteris paribus).

2. By comparing treatment and no-treatment conditions, you can see whether the cause and the effect covary.

3. When you manipulate the treatment, you make sure that the cause comes before the effect, ensuring temporal precedence.

4. Randomization is an effective way of establishing a close approximation to ceteris paribus.

5. Like randomized experiments, single-subject experiments manipulate the treatment to ensure temporal precedence, and compare conditions to assess covariation.

6. Single-subject experiments approximate ceteris paribus by knowing what the relevant variables are and keeping them constant.

7. Single-subject experimenters keep relevant individual difference variables constant by using a single subject.
8. Single-subject experimenters keep relevant environmental variables constant by keeping the subject in a highly controlled environment.
9. The A–B–A or reversal design and the multiple-baseline design are used by single-subject experimenters to control for the effects maturation and testing.
10. When it comes to construct validity, the single-subject experimenter and the within-subject experimenter are very similar. Both may choose to use few levels of the independent variable, placebo treatments, or gradual changes in the levels of the independent variable to prevent subjects from becoming sensitized to the hypothesis.
11. Unlike single-subject experimenters, quasi-experimenters don't know what all the relevant variables are and can't exercise control over them.
12. Researchers using quasi experiments must explicitly rule out the eight threats to validity: history, maturation, testing, instrumentation, mortality, regression, selection, and interactions with selection.
13. Instrumentation can be ruled out simply by using the same measure, the same way, every time.
14. Mortality can be eliminated merely by keeping subjects in your study.
15. You can rule out regression if subjects were not chosen on the basis of their extreme scores or if your measuring instrument is extremely reliable.
16. The time series design is very similar to the single-subject design. The main difference is that the time series design doesn't isolate subjects from history the way the single-subject design does. As a result, the time series Achilles' heel is history.
17. The nonequivalent control group design resembles the simple experiment. However, because subjects aren't randomly assigned to groups, selection is a serious problem.
18. Although the cross-sectional and longitudinal designs are more common among age researchers, the sequential strategies are most useful because they're more effective in disentangling the effects of cohort, age, and history.
19. Although quasi-experimental designs are not as good as experimental designs for inferring causality, they are more versatile.

KEY TERMS

covariation
temporal precedence
ceteris paribus
spurious
single-subject designs
stable baseline
A–B design
A–B–A reversal design

multiple-baseline design
quasi experiments
time series design
nonequivalent control group design
cross-sectional design
cohort effects
longitudinal design
sequential designs

EXERCISES

1. Compare how single-subject experiments and randomized experiments establish precedence, and ceteris paribus.

2. Argue for the external validity of the single-subject experiment. How do single-subject time series designs differ?

3. Design a quasi experiment that looks at the effects of the stock market on presidential assass. What kind of design would you use?

4. An ad depicts a student who has improved his grade point average from 2.0 to 3.2 after a stint the military. Consider the spurious eight. Is the military the only possible explanation for the improve-ment?

5. What problems are there in determining the effects of age?

covariation, temporal

t designs and

nations.

OUTLINE

Overview

Uses for descriptive methods

Descriptive research and causality

Description for description's sake

Description for prediction's sake

Sources of data

Ex-post-facto research data you have already collected

Archival data

Observation

Testing

Describing your data

Graph it!

Correlation coefficients: When a number may be worth a thousand points

Summary of describing correlational data

Making inferences from your data

Making inferences from correlation coefficients

Analyses not involving correlation coefficients

Interpreting results

A look ahead

The case of the insignificant significant clue

Main points

Key terms

Exercises

OVERVIEW

In this chapter, you'll be introduced to methods of describing behavior. Descriptive research is fairly easy to do because all you need to do to describe behavior is measure variables.

In fact, at the most primitive level of describing behavior, you only have to measure a single variable. Your description might be the result of counting how many times something happens. For instance, the earliest research on "date rape" involved finding out how frequently women were raped by their dates.

At a more sophisticated level of description, you'd measure your original variable and several other variables to see if they're related. Thus, research on date rape evolved from counting the number of date rapes to looking at variables that might be associated with being a date rapist or victim. For example, researchers studied whether date rapists exhibited aggressive tendencies prior to raping their victims and whether certain situations were more likely to lead to a date rape (e.g., blind date).

As you can see, descriptive research quickly progresses from describing a single variable to describing relationships among variables. Almost as soon as researchers had estimated the number of date rapes, they were finding factors that related to date rape. Because descriptive research almost always involves determining how variables **co**vary, or how variables **relate** with one another, its methods are also called **correlational** methods.

USES FOR DESCRIPTIVE METHODS

When you use descriptive methods, you gain the ability to study virtually any variable in virtually any situation. You can use descriptive methods without manipulating variables. You can even use descriptive methods without limiting or accounting for the effects of extraneous variables. In short, with descriptive methods, you're free to discover whatever relationships exist between whatever variables you care to explore.

Descriptive Research and Causality

But this flexibility comes at a cost. Without being able to manipulate variables or account for the effects of extraneous variables, you can't infer causality. As a result, you can't determine the reason for the relationships you find. Thus, if you find a relationship between low self-esteem and people who've been raped, you can't say why low self-esteem and rape are related. Certainly, you can't say that low self-esteem causes one to be raped.

Why not? First, because you don't know that rape victims had low self-esteem before they were raped. It may be that prior to being raped, rape victims had high self-esteem but that being raped lead to low self-esteem. Instead of low self-esteem being the cause of rape, it may be an effect of rape.

Second, you haven't controlled for or accounted for variables that might be responsible for the relationship between self-esteem and rape. Many factors might lead one to have low self-esteem and to be raped. For example, being short may lead to low self-esteem and decrease one's ability to fight off an attacker. Or, having a low income may lead to low self-esteem and also make one more vulnerable to rape because low-income people may live in more dangerous neighborhoods, and the dangerousness of a neighborhood may be related to rape.

To repeat a very important point, correlational methods do not establish causality. When you use a correlational method to find a relationship between two variables, you don't know whether the relationship is due to:

1 changes in the first variable causing the second variable to vary;
2 changes in the second variable causing the first variable to vary; or
3 a third variable causing both variables to vary.

Stimulating Causal Hypotheses

Although correlational methods don't allow you to infer causality, they may stimulate causal hypotheses. As you can see from Box 11-1, there are two ways this may happen.

First, if you find a relationship between two variables, you may want to do an experiment to determine whether the relationship is a causal relationship. For instance, knowing there was a correlation between smoking and lung cancer led to experiments to find out whether smoking caused lung cancer.

Second, even if you find that the two related factors are not causally related, you may try to find out why they are related. You may try to find out what third factor accounts for the relationship. For example, the finding that students who study more have lower grade point averages might stimulate you to see if some studying strategies are less effective than others.

In summary, although descriptive research doesn't allow you to infer causality, it may stimulate research that will allow you to infer causality: Once you know what happens, you can try to find out why it happens.

BOX 11-1 Generating Causal Hypotheses from Correlational Data

For each correlational finding listed below, develop an experimental hypothesis.

1. The correlation between studying and good grades is $-.1$, indicating that some of the people who study the longest do below average in school.
2. People report being more persuaded by newspaper editorials than by television editorials.
3. People with high self-esteem believe that vigilantes should not be arrested.
4. People are more depressed around holidays.
5. First born children are less curious than their younger siblings.
6. The more people drink, the higher they tip.
7. Couples that laugh at the same things like each other more.

By hinting at possible causal relationships, descriptive research can indirectly help psychologists achieve two goals of psychology—explaining behavior and controlling behavior. But the main purpose of descriptive research is to achieve another important goal of psychology—describing behavior.

Description for Description's Sake

But is description really an important, scientific goal? Yes, in fact, description is a major goal of every science. What is chemistry's famed periodic table, but a description of the elements? What is biology's Linnean system of classifying plants and animals into Kingdom, Phyla, Genus, and Species, but a way of describing living organisms? What is astronomy, but a description of outerspace? What is science, but systematic observation and measurement? Thus, one reason psychologists like descriptive methods is because description is an important goal of psychology.

Description for Prediction's Sake

Psychologists also like descriptive methods because knowing what is happening helps us in predicting what will happen. In the case of suicide, for example, psychologists discovered that certain signals (giving away precious possessions, abrupt changes in personality) were associated with suicide. Since past behavior is a good predictor of future behavior, psychologists realize that people sending out those signals are more likely to attempt suicide than people not behaving this way.

Do We Need Science to Describe Behavior?

Certainly, describing behavior is an important goal of psychology. But do we need to use scientific methods to describe what's all around us? Yes! Intuition alone can't objectively measure variables, keep track of these measurements, measure the degree to which variables are related, or determine the generalizability of these results.

We Need Scientific Measurement   We need scientific methods to accurately measure the variables we want to describe. As you saw in Chapter 3, objective, reliable, valid, and sensitive measurement of psychological variables isn't automatic. If you're to observe psychological variables in a systematic and unbiased way, you must use scientific methods. Imagine using intuition to measure the number of sexist remarks, level of motivation, intelligence, or some other psychological variable!

We Need Systematic, Scientific Record Keeping   Even if your intuition gave you accurate measurements of psychological variables, you couldn't rely on your memory to keep track of your observations. Memory is, after all, "that strange deceiver." Therefore, if you're to accurately describe behavior, you need to systematically record your observations so that your conclusions aren't biased by memory's selectivity.

We Need Objective Ways to Determine Whether Variables Are Related - Obviously, if you're poor at keeping track of observations of one variable, you're going to be even worse at keeping track of two variables and the relationship between them. Therefore, you can't rely on your judgment to determine whether or not two things are related.

People seem so eager to see relationships, that they see variables as being related, even when they're not. In several experiments, (Ward & Jenkins, 1965; Chapman & Chapman, 1967), people have been exposed to random data and have "found" relationships in this random data. Out of the lab, we know that people "see" systematic patterns in the stock market, even though the stock market behaves in an essentially random fashion (Shefrin & Statman, 1986). Many people also believe that the interview is an invaluable selection device, even though research shows that interviews have virtually no validity.

Even when there is a relationship between two variables, the relationship people see between those two variables may be exactly opposite of the relationship that exists. For example, basketball players and coaches swear (both literally and figuratively) that if a player makes a shot, that player will be more likely to make the next shot. In fact, as Kahneman and Tversky (1985) have discovered, a shooter is less likely to make the next shot if he's made the previous shot. Many people are aware of the famed "*Sports Illustrated* Jinx"—the "fact" that a team or person will perform worse after being featured on the cover of *Sports Illustrated*. The belief in the "jinx" is so strong that many fans hate to see their favorite team on the magazine's cover. But fans needn't fear; the truth is that players and teams do better after appearing on the cover of *Sports Illustrated*.

Of course, sports fans aren't the only ones to totally misperceive relationships. Many Americans think that terrorism has increased since the late 1970s; in fact, terrorism has declined fairly steadily since the late 1970s. Many bosses and parents swear that rewarding people doesn't work whereas punishment does, even though research shows that rewards are more effective than punishments. And many students swear that cramming for exams is more effective than studying consistently, even though research contradicts this claim.

We Need Scientific Methods to Generalize from Our Experience   But even if you accurately describe your own experience, how can you generalize the results of your experience? After all, your experience is an extremely limited sample of behavior. Even with the best of small samples, small random samples, scientists have to worry about overlooking real relationships. Thus, it's not surprising that one man wrote to "Dear Abby" saying that it was hogwash that lung cancer and smoking were related: He knew many smokers and none had lung cancer.

With small samples, the relationship you observe may simply be due to a coincidence. For example, if we go by some people's experiences, playing the lottery is a financially profitable thing to do. How can you intuitively discount the role of coincidence?

To discount the role of coincidence, you need statistics and a random sample. Even if you were an intuitive statistician, what's to say that your experience is a random sample of behavior? Your experience may be a biased sample of behavior. Results from such biased samples are apt to be wrong. For example, some ardent Mondale supporters thought that Mondale would beat Ronald Reagan. Why? Because everyone they knew was voting for Mondale.

Conclusions about the Need for Descriptive Research   As you can see, we need descriptive research if we're to accurately describe how people behave. Fortunately, descriptive research is fairly easy to do. To describe a single variable, you need a way to accurately measure and record it from a representative sample of behavior. To describe how two variables are related, you need to get a representative sample of behavior; accurately measure both variables; and then objectively assess the association between those variables. Thus, the bottom line in doing descriptive research is getting measurements of a representative sample of behavior.

In the next few sections, we'll look at several ways to get accurate measurements of samples of behavior. We'll start by examining ways of making use of data that have already been collected, then we'll move to creating our own data.

SOURCES OF DATA

Ex-Post-Facto Research Data You've Already Collected

One possible source of data for descriptive research is the data you've already collected. For example, you might have done an experiment looking at the effects of time pressure on performance of a verbal task. At the time you did the study, you may not have cared about the age, gender, personality type, or other personal characteristics of your subjects. For testing your experimental hypothesis, these individual difference variables were just nuisance variables because they caused unwanted random error. However, like saving money for a rainy day, you collected this information anyway.

After the experiment is over, you might want to go back and look for relationships between these "nuisance variables" and task performances. This kind of research is called **ex post facto research**: research done after the fact.

External Validity

Suppose your ex-post-facto research revealed that women did better than men on the verbal task. Although this finding is interesting, you should be careful about generalizing your results. Unless the men and women in your study are a random sample drawn from the entire population of men and women, you can't say that women do better at this verbal task than men do. Your effect may simply be due to sampling men of average intelligence and women of above average intelligence. This sampling bias could easily occur, especially if your school was one that had higher admissions standards for women than for men. (Some schools did this when they switched from being an all-female college to a coeducational institution.)

You could have a bit more confidence that your results were not due to sampling error if you'd included a mathematical task and found that although the women did better than the men on the verbal task, the reverse was true on the mathematical task. If, in this case, your results are due to sampling error, they aren't due to simply having sampled women who are above average in intelligence. Instead, your sampling error would have to be due to something rather strange such as sampling women who were better than the average woman in verbal ability and who were worse than the average woman in mathematical ability. Although such a sampling bias is possible (you sampled female poets), it's not as likely as having merely sampled women who are above average in intelligence. Therefore, with this pattern of results, you'd be a little more confident that your results weren't due to sampling error.

Construct Validity

Even if you could show that your results were not due to sampling error, you couldn't automatically conclude that women had greater verbal ability than men. To make this claim, you'd have to show that your measure was a valid measure of verbal ability and that the measure was just as valid for men as it was for women.

Internal Validity

Through careful random sampling and choice of measures, you might be able to determine that women had better verbal ability than men. However, you couldn't say why women had superior verbal ability. As you'll recall, correlational methods aren't useful for inferring causality. Therefore, you couldn't say whether the difference in male and female verbal ability was due to inborn differences between men and women or to differences in how men and women are socialized.

Conclusions about Ex-Post-Facto Research

In summary, ex-post-facto research takes advantage of data you've already collected. Therefore, the quantity and quality of ex-post-facto research depends on the quantity and quality of data you collect during the original study. The more information you collect about your subjects' personal characteristics, the more ex-post-facto hypotheses you can examine. The more valid your measures, the more valid your conclusions. The more representative your sample of subjects, the more generalizable your results will be. Therefore, if you're doing a study, and there's any possibility that you'll do ex-post-facto research, you should prepare for that possibility by using a random sample of subjects and/or by collecting a lot of data about each subject's personal characteristics.

Archival Data   Rather than using data that you've collected, you can use **archival data**: data that's already been collected. Basically, there are two kinds of archival data—coded data and uncoded data.

Collected and Tabulated Data

The first kind are data that have been collected and tabulated by others. Market researchers, news organizations, behavioral scientists, and government researchers are all collecting and tabulating data. How much data? To give you some idea, over 5,000 Americans are surveyed every day—and surveys are just one way that these researchers collect data.

If you can get access to archival research, you can often look at data that you could never have collected yourself. Unfortunately, much of this data you'd never want to collect because it was collected and coded in a way that's inappropriate for your research problem.

Recorded but Uncoded Data

If you want to code data yourself, but you don't want to collect them, you can use the second kind of archival data—data that've been recorded, but are uncoded. Records of behavior range from letters to the editor, to transcripts of Congressional hearings, to videotapes of "The People's Court," to baseball statistics, to ads in the personal columns for a husband or a wife.

The primary advantage of using records of data is that they've already been collected for you. All you have to do is code them. And you can code them as best suits your needs.

The disadvantage of this kind of data is that you have to code them. As we mentioned in Chapter 3, a useful way to code behavior is content analysis. Content analysis has been used to categorize a wide range of free responses—from determining whether a threatening letter is from a terrorist or a prankster to determining whether someone's response to an ambiguous picture shows that he has a high need for achievement.

To use content analysis to categorize behavior, you must first carefully define your categories. Next, you should provide examples of each category. Finally, train yourself and your raters to use these categories.

A primary aim in content analysis is to define your categories as objectively as possible. Some researchers define their categories so objectively that all the coder has to do is count the number of times certain words come up. For example, to get an indication of America's mood, a researcher might count the number of times words like "war," "fight," and so on appear in *The New York Times*. These word-counting schemes are so easy to use that even a computer can use them. In fact, researchers have invented a computer program that can tell genuine suicide notes from fake ones (Stone et al., 1966).

Unfortunately, objective criteria aren't always so valid. To get totally objective criteria, you often have to ignore the context—and the meaning of behavior often depends on the context. For example, you might use the number of times the word "war" appears in the newspaper as a measure of how eager we are for war. This method would be objective, but what if the newspaper was merely reporting wars in other countries? Or, what if the newspaper was full of editorials urging us to "avoid war"? In that case, our measure would be objective, but invalid.

For measuring some variables, context is so important that totally objective scoring criteria are virtually impossible. Whether a remark is sarcastic, humorous, or sexist may depend more on when, where, and how the statement is made than on what is said.

To illustrate both the advantages and disadvantages of archival research, suppose you wanted to know whether people were more superstitious when they were concerned about the economy. As your measure of concern about the economy, you use government statistics on unemployment. As your measure of how superstitious people are, you have the computer count the number of key words such as "magic," "superstition," and "ouiji board" that appear in local newspapers and then divide this number by the total number of words in the newspaper. This would give you the percentage of superstitious words in local newspapers.

Internal Validity

Once you had your measures of the economy and of superstition, you'd correlate the two. Suppose you found that the more unemployment, the more superstitious words were used in the newspaper. Since you've done a correlational study, you can't say why the two variables are related. That is, you don't know whether:

1. the economy caused people to become superstitious;
2. superstitious beliefs caused the downfall of the economy;
3. or some other factor (a bad freeze or drought ruining crops) is responsible for both an increase in superstitious beliefs and a decline in the economy.

Construct Validity

In addition to the normal problems associated with correlational data, you have several problems specific to archival data. You're using measures of a construct, not because they're the best, but because they're the only measures that someone else bothered to collect. Although you're using unemployment records as an index of how insecure people felt about the economy, you'd rather have asked people about how they felt. To the degree to which the relationship between how many people were unemployed and how people felt about the economy is questionable, your measure's construct validity is questionable.

Even if there is a strong relationship between unemployment and concerns about the economy, your measure may lack construct validity because it may not even assess unemployment. It may have poor construct validity because of instrumentation bias: the criteria for who is considered unemployed changing over time. Sometimes this change in criteria is planned and is formally announced. For example, the government may change the definition from "being unemployed" to "being unemployed and showing documentation that he or she looks for three jobs every week." Other times, the change may not be announced. For instance, computerization and unemployment compensation make current unemployment statistics more complete than they were in the early 1900s. Or, since the people who'd collect unemployment statistics—social workers and other government workers—are sometimes laid off during hard economic times, unemployment statistics might be less complete during periods of high unemployment. Or, more sinisterly, politicians or administrators may distort unemployment data to make things seem better than they are.

Of course, the construct valdity of your measure of superstition is also questionable. Is the number of times superstitious terms are mentioned in newspapers a good index of superstition? Perhaps these articles sell papers and major newspapers only stoop to using these articles when sales are very low. About the only advantage of this measure over having results of some nation-wide survey that questioned people directly about their superstitious beliefs is that your measure is **nonreactive**: your collecting it doesn't change subjects' behavior.

External Validity

Because you can collect so much data so easily, your results should have good external validity. In some cases, your results may apply to millions of people because you have data from millions of people. For example, you can easily get unemployment statistics for the entire United States. Furthermore, because you can collect data for a period of years rather than for just the immediate present, you should be able to generalize your results across time.

The Limits of Aggregate Data

Being able to obtain group data (e.g., the unemployment rate for the entire United States for 1931) is convenient and may aid external validity. However, as psychologists, we're interested in individuals and what individuals do. Therefore, we want individual data. Consequently, even if we find that there is a correlation between unemployment for the nation as a whole and superstition for the nation as a whole, we're still troubled. We don't care about the nation as a whole, we care about individual behavior. Are the people who are unemployed the ones who are superstitious? Or, are the superstitious ones the people whose friends have been laid off? Or, do the rich become superstitious? With aggregate data, we can't say.

Conclusions about Archival Research

By using archival data you can get access to a great deal of data that you didn't have to collect. Having access to these data may allow you to test hypotheses you'd otherwise be unable or unwilling to test. Furthermore, because the data often summarize the behavior of thousands of people, your results may have impressive external validity.

Unfortunately, relying on others to collect data has its costs. You may find that data were not collected as carefully and as consistently as you'd have collected them. You may find that others used measures that have less construct validity than the measures you'd have used. You may find that you have data about groups, but no data about individuals. As a result of these problems with archival data, you may decide that the best way to get data is to get it yourself.

Observation

One way to collect your own data is through observation. As the name implies, observation involves simply watching behavior. As such, observation is often incorporated in many research methods. For example, observation is sometimes used to measure behavior in experiments.

Observation is also of interest for its own sake. Describing behavior is a vital concern of every field of psychology. Developmental psychologists use observation to describe child–parent interactions, social psychologists to describe cults, clinical psychologists to describe abnormal behavior, counseling psychologists to describe human sexual behavior, and comparative psychologists to describe animal behavior.

Types of Observational Research

Basically, there are two kinds of observation: naturalistic observation and participant observation. In **naturalistic observation**, you try to unobtrusively observe the subject, adopting a detached attitude. In **participant observation**, on the other hand, you actively interact with your subjects. In a sense, you become "one of them."

Which method is better? It depends on who you talk to. Advocates of participant observation claim that you get more "inside" information by using participant observation. Advocates of naturalistic observation counter that the information you get through participant observation may be tainted. As a participant, you're in a position to influence (bias) what your subjects do. Furthermore, as an active participant, you may be unable to sit back and record behavior as it occurs. Instead, you may have to rely on your (faulty) memory of what happened.

Problems with Observation

Effects of the Observer on the Observed   Whether you use participant or naturalistic observation, you want to minimize the degree to which you change behavior by observing it. One way to do this is by observing subjects unobtrusively. For example, you might want to observe subjects through a one-way mirror. If you can't be unobtrusive, you may try to become less noticeable.

There are two basic strategies for becoming less noticeable. First, you can observe subjects from a distance, hoping they'll ignore you. Second, you can let subjects become familiar with you, hoping they'll eventually habituate to you. Once subjects are used to you, they may forget you're there and revert back to normal behavior.

Objective Coding of Behavior   Of course, while you're observing behavior, you'll be recording it. As was the case with archival data, one problem with observation is that different coders may code data differently. The solution is to develop a content analysis scheme. You need to define your categories, develop a set of criteria to determine whether or not a given behavior meets that criteria, develop a checksheet to mark off each time a target behavior is exhibited, and then train your raters to use your checksheet.

Training and motivating your raters is even more important in observational research than in archival research for two reasons. First, in observational research, the rater codes *and* collects the data. Second, in observational research, there usually aren't permanent records of data so you can't check your raters' work.

Therefore, your training should involve at least three steps. First, you should spell out what each category means, giving both a definition of each category and some examples of behaviors that do and do not belong in each category. Second, you should have raters judge several videotapes, then explain why their ratings are right or wrong. Third, you should continue the training until each rater is at least 90% accurate.

Testing   If you don't want to rely on observers, you may decide to use tests. Tests are especially useful if you want to study personality variables. For instance, you might correlate scores on an intraversion–extraversion test with scores on an intelligence test.

External Validity

As was the case with ex-post-facto research, the external validity of your findings depends on the representativeness of your sample. You can't generalize your results to a population unless you have a random sample of that population. Therefore, you can't say that women are more extroverted than men unless you have a random sample of all men and women. Similarly, you can't say that extroverts are more intelligent than introverts unless you have a random sample of all introverts and extroverts.

Internal Validity

As is the case with all correlational research, if you find a relationship, it's not necessarily a causal relationship. This is important to keep in mind because many researchers try to show genetic basis for some characteristics (career preferences, schizophrenia, introversion, etc.) by showing a correlation between identical twins on that trait. However, identical twins could be similar on the trait because they share a similar environment or because they've influenced one another.

Even when researchers show that twins raised apart score similarly on tests, it doesn't necessarily mean that heredity accounts for the similarity. Identical twins raised apart tend to live in similar environments. Why? Because great care is taken to select parents that are as similar to their natural parents as possible. Since twins have the same natural parents, they tend to be raised in similar environments.

Conclusions about Testing

By using tests, you can take advantage of measures that other people have spent years developing. As a result, construct validity is usually less of a problem than if you'd devised your own measures. Furthermore, tests are often easier to use than other measures. Because of these advantages, tests are often used in experimental as well as nonexperimental research. However, when tests are used in nonexperimental research, this research has the same weaknesses as other correlational research: it doesn't allow you to establish causality, and the generalizability of your results will only be as good as the representativeness of your sample.

DESCRIBING YOUR DATA

Graph It!

After collecting your data, graph it. Start by labeling the x-axis (the horizontal axis) with one of your variables and labeling the y-axis (the vertical axis) with the other variable. Then, plot each observation.

For example, suppose we were looking at the relationship between scores on impulsivity and grade point average. Figure 11-1 shows the beginning of such a

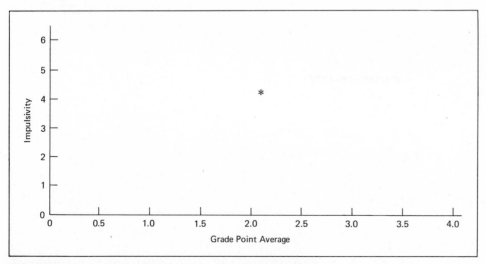

FIGURE 11-1   The Beginning of a Scatterplot

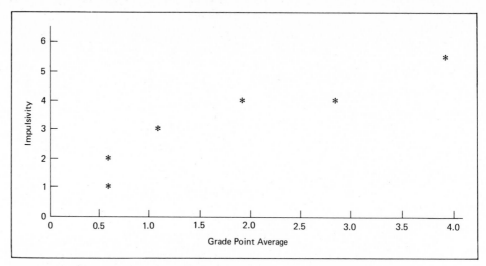

FIGURE 11-2   A Scatterplot Revealing a Positive Correlation

graph. As you can see, we've plotted the source of our first subject, a subject who has a grade point average of 2.0 and a score of 4 on the impulsivity scale. For reasons that will be obvious after we plot all our data, this graph is called a **scatterplot**.

There are four basic relationships that the scatterplot could reveal. First, it could reveal a pattern like the one shown in Figure 11-2, where the more impulsive one is, the higher one's grade point average is likely to be. Or, put another way, the less impulsive one is, the lower one's grade point average. This kind of relationship is called a **positive relationship**. One common example of a positive relationship is the relationship between height and weight; the taller you are, the more you're likely to weigh.

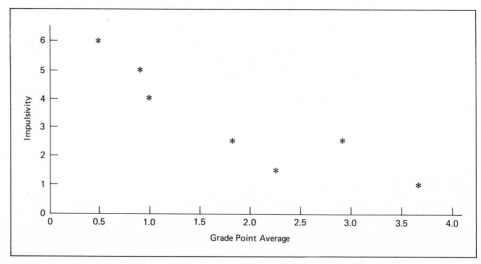

FIGURE 11-3   A Scatterplot Revealing a Negative Correlation

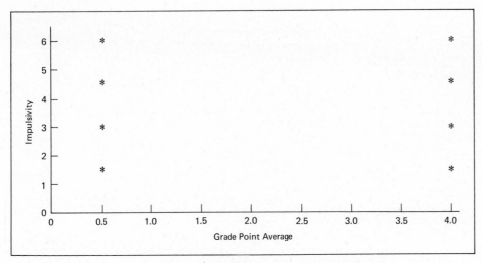

FIGURE 11-4   A Scatterplot Revealing a Zero Correlation

Second, the scatterplot could reveal a pattern like the one shown in Figure 11-3, where the more impulsive one is, the lower one's grade point average. Or, put another way, the less impulsive one is, the higher one's grade point average. This relationship is called a **negative relationship**. Many variables are inversely or negatively related. One common example of a negative relationship is that between exercise and weight: the more you exercise, the less you tend to weigh.

Third, the scatterplot might reveal that there is no relationship between impulsivity and grade point average. This pattern is depicted in Figure 11-4.

Fourth, you could have a complex relationship between impulsivity and grade point average. An example of such a relationship is depicted in Figure 11-5.

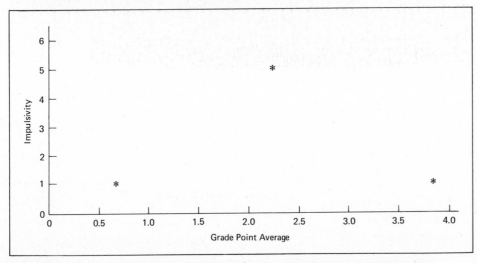

FIGURE 11-5   A Scatterplot Revealing a Nonlinear Relationship

Correlation Coefficients: When a Number May Be Worth a Thousand Points

Although a graph gives a good picture of your data, you may want to summarize your data with a single number: a correlation coefficient. The kind of correlation coefficient you use will depend on the nature of your data (see Table 11-1).

Like all correlation coefficients, the Pearson r summarizes the relationship described in your scatterplot with a single number. Like most correlation coefficients, the Pearson r ranges from -1 to $+1$.

Also like most correlation coefficients, the Pearson r should corroborate your scatterplot. If your scatterplot indicates a positive relationship between the two variables, your correlation coefficient should also be positive. If the scatterplot indicates that your variables are not related, then your correlation coefficient should be near 0. Finally, if your variables are negatively related, then the correlation coefficient should be negative.

The Logic behind the Pearson r

While Box 11-2 shows you how to compute the Pearson r, it doesn't explain the logic behind the Pearson r. Basically, the Pearson r is calculated by drawing a straight line through the points in your scatterplot. If the line slopes upward, the correlation is positive. If the line slopes upward and every single point in your scatterplot fits on that line, you have a perfect correlation of $+1.00$. Usually, however, there are points that aren't on the line. For each point that isn't on the line, the correlation coefficient is made closer to zero by subtracting a value from the coefficient. The farther the point is from the line, the larger the value that's subtracted. Once all the misfit points are accounted for, you end up with the correlation coefficient.

If the line that best fits the points slopes downward, the correlation is negative. If every single point fits on that line, you have a perfect negative relationship so your correlation coefficient equals -1.00. However, perfect negative relationships

---

TABLE 11-1   Different Kinds of Correlation Coefficients

Name of Coefficient	Uses
PEARSON r	When both variables are interval (height with weight)
POINT BISERIAL	When one variable is interval, the other nominal (weight with gender)
BISERIAL	When one variable is interval, the other is a dichotomized interval variable (weight with high versus low scorers on a test)
TETRACHORIC	Both variables are dichotomized interval variables (heavy versus light with tall versus short)
PHI COEFFICIENT	Both variables are nominal (gender with race)
SPEARMAN'S r	Data are ordinal—ranked data (high-school rank with military rank)

BOX 11-2 Calculating the Pearson *r*

If you collected data from five students at your school on impulsivity (*X*) and grade point average (*Y*) and wanted to see if the variables were related, use a Pearson *r* as shown below.

STEP 1: List each pair of scores in the following manner:

	Score for *X*	Score for *Y*	*X* times *Y*
1ST PAIR OF SCORES	1	1	1
2ND PAIR OF SCORES	2	2	4
3RD PAIR OF SCORES	3	2	6
4TH PAIR OF SCORES	4	4	16
5TH PAIR OF SCORES	5	3	15

STEP 2: Sum the scores in each column.

15   12   42

STEP 3: Calculate the means for variables *X* and *Y*.

$15/5 = 3$ $12/5 = 2.4$

STEP 4: Calculate the sum of squares for variables *X* and *Y*.

$$(X-\bar{X})$$
$(1-3)^2$ $(1-2.4)^2$
$(2-3)^2$ $(2-2.4)^2$
$(3-3)^2$ $(2-2.4)^2$
$(4-3)^2$ $(4-2.4)^2$
$(5-3)^2$ $(3-2.4)^2$
$10/4 = 2.5$ $5.2/4 = 1.3$

STEP 5: Calculate the standard deviations for variables *X* and *Y*.

$$SD = \sqrt{(X-\bar{X})^2/N\text{-}1}$$

$\sqrt{2.5} = 1.58$ $\sqrt{1.3} = 1.14$

STEP 6: Multiply the sum of *X* by the sum of *Y* and divide by the number of pairs.

$(15 \times 12)/5 = 180/5 = 36$

STEP 7: Subtract this term (36) from the sum of *X* × *Y* (42).

$42 - 36 = 6$

STEP 8: Divide this term (6) by (the number of pairs times the standard deviation of *X* times the standard deviation of *Y*).

$6/(5 \times 1.58 \times 1.14) = .58$

are rare. Therefore, many points probably aren't on that line. For each point that isn't on the line, the correlation coefficient is made closer to zero by adding a value to the coefficient. The farther the point is from the line, the larger the value that's added. After all the misfit points are accounted for, you end up with the correlation coefficient.

As you can see, the correlation coefficient describes the nature of the linear relationship between your variables. However, it ignores nonlinear relationships, such as the one depicted in Figure 11-5.

The fact that the correlation coefficient only examines the degree to which variables are linearly related is not as severe a drawback as you may think. Why? First, because totally nonlinear relationships among variables are rare. Second, even if you encounter a nonlinear relationship, you'd know you had such a relationship by looking at your scatterplot.

The Coefficient of Determination

The sign of the correlation coefficient tells you the kind of relationship you have (positive or negative). However, you may want to know not only what kind of relationship you have, but how strong this relationship is.

To find out how closely two variables are associated, square the correlation coefficient. This gives you the **coefficient of determination**. The coefficient of determination, as the name suggests, tells you the degree to which knowing one variable helps you know (determine) the other. The coefficient of determination can range from 0 (knowing a subject's score on one variable is absolutely no help in guessing what her score on the other variable will be) to $+1.00$ (if you know a subject's score on one variable, you'll know exactly what her score is on the other variable).

So, if you have a correlation of $+1.00$ ($1 \times 1 = 1$), you have a coefficient of determination of $+1.00$. This means that if you know one variable, you can predict the other one with 100% accuracy. The same would be true if you had a correlation coefficient of -1.00. (because, $-1 \times -1 = +1$).

Essentially, the coefficient of determination tells you the amount of scatter in your scatterplot. If the coefficient of determination is near 1, there is little scatter in your scatterplot. If you draw a line through your scatterplot, most of the points would be on or near that line. If, on the other hand, the coefficient of determination is near 0, there is a lot of scatter in your scatterplot. If you draw a line through the scatterplot, few of the points will be close to that line.

Summary of Describing Correlational Data

You now have two ways to summarize data from a correlational study. First, you can visually summarize your data with a scatterplot. Second, you can use two numbers that summarize the essence of your scatterplot: the correlation coefficient and the coefficient of determination.

MAKING INFERENCES FROM YOUR DATA

Often, you're only interested in describing what happened in your particular study. For example, you may find that in one of your courses, there was a relationship between impulsivity and grade point average. And that may be all you're interested in. You don't care what happens in other classes, you just wanted to describe what happened in that particular class. In that case, there's no need to go beyond describing your data by using scatterplots or correlation coefficients.

Sometimes, however, you're interested in generalizing the results you obtained in your limited sample to a larger population. To do this, you first need a random sample of that population. If you want to generalize results based on observing a few students in your class to all the students in your class, then the subjects you examine should be a random sample of class members. If you want to generalize the results based on measuring a few people to all Americans, you must have measured a random sample of Americans. If you want to generalize results based on observing two rats for an hour a day to all the times that the rats are awake, then the times you observe the rats must be a random sample from the rats' waking hours.

Of course, random samples aren't perfect samples. Even with a random sample, you're going to have sampling error. Thus, if you studied a random sample of sophomores at your school and you found a correlation of $-.30$ between grade point average and impulsivity, you can't say that if you'd studied all sophomores at your school, you'd have obtained a negative correlation coefficient. Your results may be due to random sampling error.

Making Inferences from Correlation Coefficients

Therefore, you need to use inferential statistics to infer whether or not your results may be due to random sampling error. Specifically, you should ask the statistical question: "Can I get this size of correlation coefficient in this big a random sample if there's no relationship in the population?". If the answer to your statistical question is "no," then you can be confident that the correlation coefficient in the population is not 0 (In this example, since your correlation was $-.30$, you can be confident that the correlation in the population is negative). To use proper terminology, you'd say that your correlation coefficient is significantly different from 0.

How you determine whether a correlation coefficient is statistically different from 0 depends on what kind of data you have. If you have nominal data, you should use a chi-square test (see Box 11-3). If you have interval data, you should use the statistical test described in Box 11-4. Regardless of what test you use, the test will rely on two principles. First, the further the sample's correlation coefficient is from 0, the less likely the population coefficient is 0. Thus, a correlation coefficient of .8 is more likely to be significantly different from 0 than a correlation coefficient of .2. Second, the larger the sample, the less the sample will be influenced by sampling error. Thus, a correlation coefficient of .30 is more likely to be significantly different from 0 if it comes from a sample of 100 observations than if it comes from a sample of 10 observations.

Determining whether the correlation coefficient is statistically significant from 0 is one kind of test you can perform on your correlation coefficients. If you want to perform other kinds of significance tests (Is the correlation between impulsivity and grade point average higher among women than among men?), read Cohen and Cohen's (1975) book on correlational analysis.

BOX 11-3 Computing a 2 × 2 Chi Square

If you asked men and women whether they watched "MTV" and wanted to know if there was a gender difference in their responses, you could find out by calculating a chi square using the following steps.

STEP 1: Set up a table like the one below.

"MTV" Viewers

	Female	Male	Total
YES	A 20	B 15	35
NO	C 55	D 10	65
TOTAL	75	25	100

STEP 2: Multiply B and C. Then multiply A and D.

$$B \times C = 15 \times 55 = 825$$
$$A \times D = 20 \times 10 = 200$$

STEP 3: Plug in the appropriate numbers in the following formula:

$$X^2 = \frac{n(BC - AD)^2}{(A+B)\,(C+D)\,(A+C)\,(B+D)}$$

$$X^2 = \frac{100(825 - 200)^2}{35 \times 75 \times 75 \times 25}$$

$$X^2 = \frac{100 \times 390625}{4921875}$$

$$X^2 = \frac{39062500}{4921875}$$

$$= 7.937$$

STEP 4: Turn to the chi-square table in Appendix E (Table 2) and find the row corresponding to 1 *df*. (For a 2 × 2, your *df* will always be 1. The degrees of freedom equals the number of rows minus 1, times the number of columns minus 1.)

STEP 5: Determine whether your chi square is one-tailed or two-tailed. You should be able to decide based on your hypothesis. For example, if you just predicted that there would be a difference between the genders in "MTV" watching, you have a two-tailed test. However, if you predicted that women were more likely to watch "MTV" than men, you have a one-tailed test. A one-tailed test is more powerful than a two-tailed test.

STEP 6: If you have a two-tailed test with a value of 3.84 or more, your test is significant at the .05 level. If your two-tailed test value is at least 5.41, then your test is significant at the .02 level. If you have a one-tailed test, you're in even better shape. The significance level of a one-tailed test is one-half of the probability of a two-tailed test. Thus, to be significant at a .05 level, you need only a value of 2.71. A value of 5.41 will be significant at the .01 level.

STEP 7: What is the significance level of our example for a two-tailed test? What about a one-tailed test?

BOX 11-4 How to Determine the Significance of a Correlation Coefficient

If your data on impulsivity and grade point average were collected from a random sample of students at your school, you could use those data to determine whether there is a relationship between impulsivity and grade point average for the entire school. All you need do is determine whether the observed Pearson r is significantly different from zero by following the steps listed below. In this case let's suppose that $r = +.58$.

STEP 1: Compute a t value, using the formula:

$$t = \frac{r \times \sqrt{(N-2)}}{\sqrt{(1 - (r \times r))}}$$

(r = the Pearson r; and N = number of subjects)

$$t = \frac{(.58)\sqrt{(5-2)}}{\sqrt{1-(.58 \times .58)}}$$

$$t = \frac{.58 \times 1.73}{\sqrt{1 - .34}}$$

$$t = \frac{1.00}{.81}$$

$$= 1.23$$

STEP 2: After computing the t value, look the value up in the t table under 3 $(N-2)$. Since 1.23 does not reach the t value required for significance at the .05 level (1.984), you'd conclude that the correlation failed to reach significance.

Analyses Not Involving Correlation Coefficients

You don't have to use correlations to analyze data from correlational research. Often, if researchers have interval scale data, they'll use *t* tests or analysis of variance instead. For example, if the mean score for women on a test was 53 and the mean for men was 50, they might do a *t* test.

To do a *t* test, of course, you need two groups. But what if you don't have two groups? For example, what if you have a bunch of people's test scores and their grade point averages? In that case, you could create two groups using test scores to divide your subjects into high scorers or low scorers. Then, you'd compare the average grade point average for subjects who scored high (above average) on the test with the average grade point average for subjects who scored low (below average) on the test. The procedure of dividing subjects into two groups depending on whether they scored above or below the median (the middle score) is called doing a **median split**.

With a *t* test or a simple correlation, you can only study the relationship between two variables. However, if you do an analysis of variance, you can look at the relationships among three or more variables. For instance, you could look at the relationship between impulsivity, introversion, and grade point average. In this case, you might find an interaction showing that high impulsivity is related to low grade point averages for extroverts, but is related to high grade point averages for introverts.

Interpreting Results

Interpreting Significant Results

No matter what statistical tests you use, remember what a statistically significant result means. It means that the relationship you observed is probably not due to sampling error. Instead, it probably also exists in the population from which you randomly sampled.

Keep in mind that statistical significance doesn't mean that one variable caused the other. As we've said previously, to infer causality, you must do much more than establish that your variables are related. To infer that impulsivity caused low grade point averages, you'd have to show not only that impulsivity and grade point average are related, but also that:

1. no other differences between your high and low impulsives could account for this relationship; and

2. the people were impulsive before they got low grades.

Also keep in mind that if you have a .05 significance level, you're saying that there is less than 5 chances in a 100 that the particular statistical test will be significant by chance alone. That's fine if you're only testing a single relationship. However, since correlational data are often easy to obtain, some researchers correlate hundreds of variables with hundreds of other variables. If they do hundreds of statistical tests, many results will be significant by chance alone.

Therefore, we urge you to resist temptation. Don't go crazy and compute every possible correlation coefficient. Decide what hypotheses you have and test those correlations.

If you're doing more than one statistical test, make your significance level more conservative than .05. Use a .01 or even a .001 level. Or, repeat your study with another random sample of subjects to see if the correlations that were significant the first time are significant the second time around.

Interpreting Null Results

If your results are not significant, it means that you failed to show that your results were not due to sampling error. It doesn't mean your variables aren't related, it means only that you didn't make a good case that they were related.

There are several reasons why you may get null results, even though a relationship exists between your variables. First, you may not have had enough observations. Even if you observed a fairly strong relationship in your sample, it's hard to say that your relationship isn't a fluke unless you have enough observations.

Second, your measures might be insensitive. As a result, the true relationship is obscured by measurement error.

Third, your variables may be related in a nonlinear way. This would be a problem because your statistical tests would be most sensitive to linear relationships. You could tell if this is the problem by looking at a scatterplot of your data.

Fourth, you may have failed to find a significant relationship because of **restriction of range**: you sampled from a population where everyone scores similarly on one of the variables. You see, to say that variables vary together, you need both variables to vary. If they don't, you have problems. For example, suppose you were looking at the relationship between IQ and grade point average, but everyone in your sample scored between 125 and 130 on the IQ test. In this case, the correlation between IQ and grade point average would be pretty small. Consequently, the correlation might not be significant. However, if your subjects had ranged in IQ from 85 to 185, you'd probably have a sizeable and statistically significant correlation between IQ and grade point average.

A LOOK AHEAD

In this chapter, you've been introduced to the logic of descriptive research. However, you haven't learned about the most common method of doing descriptive research: asking questions. Therefore, the next chapter is devoted to showing you how to conduct surveys, perform interviews, and write questionnaires.

THE CASE OF THE INSIGNIFICANT CLUE

INSPECTOR LESTRADE: As you can see from my research, the average Type Z personality is more likely to have been convicted of murder than the average Type Q personality. Obviously, this has important implications for our case. We have two suspects—one has Type Z personality (Mr. Zimski), and one has Type Q (Mr. Quirk). Clearly, the Type Z suspect is our murderer because being a Type Z causes people to murder.

HOLMES: Inspector, you don't know that being a Type Z causes one to commit murders. Correlational evidence is very good for describing what has happened, but as evidence of causality, it is circumstantial at best. You don't know if these people would have scored a certain way on your test—what you call a Type Z personality—**before** they committed murder. Thus, although you think that being a Type Z causes one to be a murderer, it could be that committing a murder causes one to become a Type Z. I can easily imagine how the effects of being convicted of murder—the guilt, the shame, and having received a life sentence, to name a few—could affect a person's responses to certain questions.

LESTRADE: Are you finished?

HOLMES: No, there's also the possibility that some third factor accounts for the relationship you've found. It may be that Type Zs are more likely to be men than women, that they are more likely to come from disadvantaged backgrounds, that they are more likely to be unemployed. Any of these factors might cause someone to both score a certain way on your test and to be more likely to commit murder. For example, it's quite possible that two effects of unemployment are to cause a person to answer certain questions in a particular way and to increase the chances that he would commit murder.

LESTRADE: So, you disagree with me that Zimski committed the murder because he's a Type Z. I haven't proved that being a Type Z causes murder. But, you will agree that since correlational evidence is useful for describing what happens (if not why), that the personality test results are a vital piece of the puzzle.

HOLMES: I should say that the link between personality type and murder is highly significant.

LESTRADE: So, I'll arrest Zimski as I planned. As usual, I don't really need the great Holmes, as stimulating as your conversation may be. Good day.

WATSON: Lestrade has gotten sharper, eh, Holmes. I guess you can teach an old dog new tricks. A little knowledge doesn't hurt anyone, I suppose.

HOLMES: On the contrary, Lestrade's behavior in this case is proof that a little knowledge can be dangerous.

WATSON: But you yourself congratulated him.

HOLMES: I did no such thing, Watson. I merely pointed out that the link between murder and personality type was statistically significant.

WATSON: Isn't that the same thing as agreeing that his research was important and relevant?

HOLMES: Definitely not. I said nothing about the importance or relevance of his information.

WATSON: But you did say there was a strong link between murder and personality.

HOLMES: Watson, you disappoint me. Know you nothing of statistics? A significant correlation is not necessarily a large one, it merely means that a relationship exists. To know the strength of a relationship, we need to square the correlation coefficient to get the coefficient of determination. In this case, when we calculate the coefficient of determination, we find that the relationship between personality type and murder is miniscule. In fact, as it turns out, 51% of all murderers are Type Z, whereas 49% are Type Q. This difference is small and of no practical value.

WATSON: So, if the correlation was large and significant, we would know that the Type Z suspect was the murderer. For example, if Lestrade had given the suspects your Moriarty test and one had scored higher than the other, we would know that the high scorer would be the one who is not telling the truth because the correlation between scoring high on the Moriarty test and honesty is $-.80$, so the coefficient of determination is .64 ($-.8 \times -.8$).

HOLMES: In that case, we would be much more likely to suspect the high M personality, but remember that we could not be positive. We could only be 100% positive if the coefficient of determination was 1.00.

WATSON: So, how will we know who the murderer is, Holmes?

HOLMES: Look for the motive, Watson. Find out why the murder occurred. Since nothing was taken and since the poor woman was so brutally stabbed, I think we can say that this was a crime of passion. And, when we combine this with the dog's strange behavior on the night of the murder, we can safely presume that Quirk was the murderer.

WATSON: What do you mean, the dog's strange behavior. The dog did nothing.

HOLMES: Precisely. Since the dog was on the grounds and was not drugged, the only reason it would not have barked at someone entering and leaving the grounds after midnight was if it had known the intruder. The dog didn't know Zimski, but he did know Quirk.

MAIN POINTS

1. Descriptive research allows you to accurately describe behavior. The key to descriptive research is to precisely measure and record your variables using a representative sample.
2. Although descriptive research can't tell you whether one variable causes another, it may stimulate causal hypotheses.
3. Description is an important goal of science for its own sake. It's also useful because it paves the way for prediction.
4. Ex-post-facto research uses data that you collected before you invented your hypothesis.
5. Archival research uses data collected and sometimes coded by someone else.
6. With both ex-post-facto and archival research the data may not have been measured, collected, or coded in a way appropriate for testing your hypothesis.
7. Observational research is equally applicable to correlational and experimental research.

8. In both naturalistic observation and participant observation, the researcher must be careful that the observer doesn't affect the observed and that objective coding is used.

9. Using preexisting, validated tests in your correlational research will not only increase the validity of your study but save you from having to develop your own (a time-consuming endeavor). As with most research, external validity is dependent on the representativeness of your sample.

10. Using a scatter plot to graph your correlational data will tell you the direction of the relationship (positive or negative) and give you an idea of the strength of the relationship.

11. Correlational coefficients give you one number that represents the direction of the relationship (positive or negative).

12. A positive correlation between two variables means that if a subject scores high on one of the variables, he will probably score high on the other.

13. A negative correlation between two variables means that if a subject scores high on one of the variables, she will probably score low on the other.

14. By squaring the correlation you get the coefficient of determination, which tells you the strength of the relationship.

15. If your results are based on a random sample, you may want to use inferential statistics to analyze your data.

16. Remember, statistical significance only means that your results can be generalized to the population from which you randomly sampled. Statistical significance doesn't mean that you've found a causal relationship.

17. You may obtain null results even though your variables are related. Common culprits are: insufficient number of observations, insensitive measures, nonlinear relationships, and restriction of range.

18. Beware of doing too many tests of significance. Remember, if you do 100 tests and use a .05 level of significance, 5 of those tests might be significant by chance alone.

KEY TERMS

ex-post-facto research	scatterplot
archival data	positive relationship
content analysis	negative relationship
nonreactive	coefficient of determination
naturalistic observation	median split
participant observation	restriction of range

EXERCISES

1. The more ———, the less ——— describes what kind of correlation?
2. The less ———, the less ——— describes what kind of correlation?

3. Which of the following indicates a stronger relationship between two variables? $+.70$ or $-.71$?

4. Why is it hard to infer causality from correlational research?

5. Suppose you wanted to see whether the magazine *Psychology Today* became more psychological after the American Psychological Association took it over in 1984. Your strategy might be to count the number of articles that dealt with psychology. But to determine whether an article was psychological or not, you'd want to set up a content analysis system. How would you operationalize the term "psychological"? How would you sample the articles?

6. A physician looked at 26 instances of crib death in a certain town. She found that some of these deaths were due to parents suffocating their children. As a result, she concluded that most crib deaths in this country are not due to problems in brain development, but to parental abuse and neglect. What problems do you have with the physician's conclusions?

7. List some reasons why a result from a correlational study might not reach significance. Look at Box 11-4. Why do you think those results failed to reach significance?

8. Why is describing behavior important?

12

ASKING QUESTIONS: AN INTRODUCTION TO SURVEY RESEARCH

OUTLINE

OVERVIEW

If you want to know what people are thinking, feeling, or doing, you could survey them. You might survey them orally through an interview. Or, you might give them a questionnaire survey, having them read your questions and write their answers.

Because asking questions seems easy, survey research is the most common method of tapping people's attitudes, beliefs, and behaviors. Because conducting surveys is not as easy as it seems, the survey method is also the most abused research method.

Good survey research is at least as difficult to conduct as other research. Careful planning, execution, and analysis are vital for reliable and valid information. In addition, practice and skill are necessary for writing and sequencing survey questions. In this chapter, you'll learn the methods and skills necessary to conduct sound survey research.

APPLICATIONS AND CONSIDERATIONS FOR SURVEY RESEARCH

The most obvious (but least asked) question in survey research is, "Why should I use a survey to answer my research question?" To appropriately respond to this question, you must understand the strengths and weaknesses of survey research.

Applications

With a survey, you can gather information from a large sample of people with less effort and expense than most other data gathering techniques. Surveys are used most often to assess people's beliefs, attitudes, and self-reported behaviors. You can use surveys as your main research tool, as a way of collecting preliminary data on a research area, or as a dependent measure in experimental or quasi-experimental designs.

Surveys as a Main Research Tool

As a main research tool, a survey can yield much descriptive data on your variables. It's especially useful if you want to know about people's attitudes, values, beliefs, experiences, and intentions. For example, the Gallup Poll surveys people all over the country about their attitudes toward political candidates, and market researchers question people about products they buy or might buy.

Identifying Relationships among Variables

A survey can be a helpful tool for identifying relationships among variables. Knowing that a relationship exists should lead you to a hypothesis about the reason for that relationship. Your survey could be followed up by a more controlled study that would enable you to determine causality among your variables. For example, if you conducted a survey that demonstrated a relationship between professors who watch "MTV" and their sympathy toward students, you might hypothesize that watching "MTV" causes professors to be more sympathetic toward students. This hypothesis could lead to an experiment where professors were randomly assigned to either a

"MTV" or no-"MTV" viewing condition and then later measured on sympathy toward students.

Supplementing Other Methods

A survey is also a useful supplement to other research methods. Questionnaires are often used as a dependent variable in experiments or quasi experiments. For example, you might study attitude change toward "MTV." Your manipulation might be to have people argue for or against "MTV." For your pretest and posttest, you could use a questionnaire designed to tap attitudes toward "MTV."

Considerations If you do survey research, you have to be concerned with five major questions:

1. What is my hypothesis?
2. Am I only interested in describing and predicting behavior, or do I want to infer causality?
3. Will I know what to do with the data after the survey is finished?
4. Are my respondents answering accurately?
5. Do my results apply only to those people who responded to the survey, or do the results apply to a larger group?

Know Your Hypothesis

Good research begins with a hypothesis. Knowing what your hypothesis is before you write your survey will help you focus and structure your questions in a useful and meaningful way. Many inexperienced researchers try to write surveys without clear research questions. What they haven't learned is that you can't ask pertinent questions if you don't know what you want to ask. Therefore, before you write your first survey question, make sure you have a clear hypothesis on which to base your questions.

Surveys: Not for Causality

Because surveys are a correlational method, don't use a survey if you have a causal hypothesis and don't make causal inferences from your survey data. For example, if you find that professors who watch "MTV" are most sympathetic toward students, you can't say that "MTV" causes student sympathy. Since correlational methods don't establish temporal precedence, you haven't ruled out the possibility that sympathy towards students causes professors to watch "MTV." Furthermore, since correlational methods don't establish ceteris paribus, you haven't eliminated the possibility that some other factors (e.g., similarity to students), causes both "MTV" watching and sympathy toward students.

Ask Pertinent Questions and Ask Few Questions If you aren't careful, you can produce an overwhelming amount of data—and still not find out what you wanted to know. For example, the USFL spent millions of dollars on surveys to find out whether they should be a spring or fall league. Despite the fact that it took over 20 books to summarize the survey results, the surveys didn't answer the research question. So, beware and don't be seduced by how easy it is to ask a question. Instead, ask questions with a purpose.

To make sure that we ask useful questions, we determine what analyses we plan to do before we administer the questionnaire. If we find that we don't plan on doing any analyses involving responses to that question or that no pattern of answers to that question would give us useful information, we eliminate that question.

Don't Accept Respondent's Answers as Gospel

There are numerous reasons why subjects' answers may be inaccurate. Sometimes, subjects deliberately distort the truth, giving you the answer that will impress you the most or the answer you want to hear instead. A common example of this is when a waiter asks if everything is okay.

Occasionally, subjects will lie. Subjects are most likely to lie if your questions are extremely personal (e.g., "Have you cheated on your taxes?"). Therefore, don't ask personal questions unless they're crucial to your study.

Of course, deliberate distortions aren't the only reasons why people may give you inaccurate answers. Sometimes, people don't know the right answer, but the survey doesn't allow the subjects to say they don't know. For example, an immigrant to the United States might be asked to reply Yes or No to the question "Was Jimmy Carter a good president?" Chances are this newcomer doesn't have enough information to answer. Therefore, you should allow subjects to say they don't know.

Often people don't know the right answer, but they think they know. Sometimes this is because their memories are inaccurate. For example, obese people tend to underreport what they've eaten and students tend to overreport how much they study. Both groups are surprised when they actually record their behavior (Williams and Long, 1983). Because memory is fallible, you should be very careful when interpreting responses that place heavy demands on subjects' memories.

Sometimes people don't know the correct answer because they never knew it. This is particularly true when you ask people why they behaved in a certain manner. Certainly, respondents can give reasons for their behavior, but these reasons may not be accurate. For example, Nisbett and Wilson (1977) showed that if people are shown a row of television sets they'll prefer the TV furthest to the right. Yet, people have no idea that the reason they prefer the TV is because it's on the right. The moral: Although asking people questions about why they behave the way they do is interesting, don't accept their answers at face value.

To Whom Do Your Results Apply?

Usually, you want to generalize your results beyond the people who responded to your survey. For example, you might survey a couple of classes at your university, not because you want to know what those particular classes think but because you think those classes are a representative sample of your college as a whole. But are they? Unfortunately, they probably aren't. Instead, they're probably a biased sample.

Even if you start out with an unbiased sample, your sample may be biased by the end of the study. Why? People often fail or refuse to respond to a questionnaire. In fact, if you do a mail survey, don't be surprised if only 10% of your sample returns the survey. Are these 10% typical of your sample? Probably not—it's very likely that they feel more strongly about the issue than nonrespondents.

Summary

In summary, a survey can be a relatively inexpensive way to get information about people's attitudes, beliefs, and behaviors. With a survey, you can collect a lot of information on a large sample in a short time.

Although surveys are obviously useful, they should be used with care. You must watch out for: the inaccuracy of self-report data, obtaining too much data to analyze, and biased samples. Finally, you should be aware that you can't use a survey to make causal inferences.

After weighing the advantages and disadvantages of surveys, you may decide that the survey is the best approach for your research question. In that case, you need to decide whether to use a questionnaire or an interview.

THE ADVANTAGES AND DISADVANTAGES OF MAJOR KINDS OF SURVEYS

Questionnaires   If you're considering a questionnaire survey, you have two basic options: self-administered and investigator administered. In this section, we'll discuss the advantages and disadvantages of both types of questionnaires.

Self-administered Surveys

A **self-administered survey** is a questionnaire filled out by subjects in the absence of an investigator. Self-administered surveys are used by behavioral scientists, as well as manufacturers, business people, special interest groups, and magazine publishers. You've probably seen some of these surveys in your mail, at restaurant tables, in newspapers or magazines, or attached to stereo warranties.

Self-administered surveys have several advantages. First, they're easily distributed to a large number of people. Second, they're relatively inexpensive to conduct. And third, they allow anonymity (if desired) thus encouraging frankness and honesty if highly personal or threatening information is requested.

Drawbacks   Although self-administered surveys can yield reliable data with ease and economy, there are some major drawbacks to this method. First, self-administered surveys usually have a low return rate. Since you don't know whether the few individuals who return the questionnaire are typical of the people you want to survey, you must be concerned with having a biased sample.

Second, because the researcher and the subject aren't interacting, errors or oversights in the questionnaire can't be corrected. Thus, if the survey contains an ambiguous question, the researcher can't help the subject understand it and the subject probably won't let the researcher know that the question is ambiguous. For example, Question 14 in Box 12-1, reads, "College students work hard." One respondent might think this question refers to a job a student might hold down in addition to school. Another respondent might interpret this to mean students work hard at their studies. Still another might interpret this item to mean students are serious about life. Because subject and researcher aren't interacting, the researcher will have no idea that these three respondents are answering three different questions.

Third, just as you have no way of knowing whether respondents are correctly interpreting your questions, you have no way of knowing whether they object to your question format. For example, if fixed-alternative items are used, respondents may object that their attitudes aren't represented by the alternatives—their responses are too restricted by the format. On the other hand, if you use open-ended questions, respondents may resist spending the time to write a response. In either case, if potential respondents are annoyed by the question format, they probably won't bother to respond. If they do, answers may be superficial or misleading to save time and vent annoyance.

Investigator-administered Questionnaire

The investigator-administered questionnaire is filled out in the presence of a researcher. Answers may be recorded by either the respondent or the investigator. These surveys share many of the advantages of the self-administered survey. With both methods, many subjects can be surveyed at the same time. Both methods can be administered in a wide variety of times and places.

But because the investigator must be present, the investigator-administered survey is slightly more limited in terms of where and when it can be administered. Still, investigator-administered surveys can be conducted in a variety of locations, including: the lab, the street, in class, over the phone, and at subjects' homes.

A major advantage of having an investigator present is that the investigator can clarify questions for the respondent. In addition, the investigator's presence encourages subjects to respond. As a result, investigator-administered surveys have a higher response rate than self-administered.

Unfortunately, the investigator's presence may do more than just increase response rates. This type of questionnaire may reduce perceived anonymity, and because respondents feel their answers are less anonymous, they may be less candid.

Interviews

In an interview, the investigator asks respondents a series of questions and records responses. Interviews are more expensive than questionnaires for two reasons. First, they are more time-consuming than questionnaires because you can only interview one person at a time. If you interview several people at once, some people may go along with the group rather than giving their true opinions. Second, it takes more energy and personal involvement to administer an interview.

What does the added expense of the interview buy you? Basically, it buys you more interaction with the subject. Because of this interaction, you can clarify questions the subjects don't understand. You can follow-up on ambiguous or interesting responses—a tremendous asset in exploratory studies where you haven't yet identified all the important variables. Finally, this personal touch may increase your response rate.

Unfortunately, the personal nature of the interview creates two major problems. First, there's the problem of **interviewer bias:** the interviewer may influence subjects' responses by verbally or nonverbally encouraging or rewarding "correct" answers. Second, because subjects are interviewed by the investigator, they may be more apt to give socially desirable responses than if they were merely writing their answers on an anonymous questionnaire.

Telephone Interviews

Psychologists have found that a certain kind of interview is less affected by demand characteristics and interviewer bias than the personal interview. Furthermore, this method generates such a high response rate, that it's less vulnerable to sampling bias than any other method: the telephone interview.

Since the telephone interviewer can't see the subjects, the interviewer can't bias their responses via subtle visual cues. Furthermore, by monitoring and tape-recording all the interviews, you can discourage interviewers from saying anything that might bias subjects' responses (changing wording of questions, giving more favorable verbal feedback for expected answers).

The telephone survey also appears to reduce the effects of demand characteristics by giving subjects a greater feeling of anonymity (Groves & Kahn, 1979). This feeling of anonymity is also partly responsible for the fact telephone surveys have a higher response rate than personal interviews. Thanks to anonymity, the telephone survey is less vulnerable to both response bias and sampling bias than other survey methods.

How to Conduct a Telephone Interview   In a few pages, we'll discuss the general things you should consider when planning a survey—whether it's a telephone survey, a mail survey, or whatever. But, at this point, we'd like to give you a few words of advice that apply only to the unique situation of conducting a telephone survey.

Your first step is to determine what population you wish to sample and determine a way of getting all of their phone numbers. Often your population is conveniently represented in a telephone book, membership directory, or campus directory. Once you obtain the telephone numbers you're ready to draw a random sample from your population by following the instructions given later in this chapter.

When you draw your sample, pull more names than you actually plan to survey. You won't be able to reach everyone that you attempt to phone so you'll need some alternate names. Usually we draw 25% more names than we actually plan on interviewing.

Before you start calling people, practice your survey. You might practice by interviewing a friend on the phone, or having someone read the interview to you. Often you'll need to improve your questions to make them sound more understandable. Remember there are differences between the spoken word and the written word. Make your questions short and concise, and keep your voice clear and slow. Be careful not to bias your interview through inflection. Tape yourself reading the questions and play it back. Is your voice hinting at what answer you want subjects to give? If not (and you've followed the advice we gave in our "Planning a Survey" section), you're ready to begin calling subjects.

If you get a busy signal or a phone isn't answered, try again later. A good rule of thumb is to phone a person 3 to 4 times at different times of the day before giving up and replacing them with an alternate name. If the number has been disconnected, use an alternate number.

When you do reach a person, identify yourself and ask for the person on the list. As with any study, informed consent is a necessary ingredient. So, after you identify yourself, give a brief description of what the interview is about and ask the person if she or he is willing to participate.

Again ask the questions slowly and clearly. Be prepared to repeat questions or clarify them.

Once the survey is completed, thank your subject and follow standard debriefing policy.

Conclusions about Telephone Interviews   You've seen that the telephone survey is superior to the personal interview for reducing response, interviewer, and sampling biases. However, the main reason for the popularity of the telephone interview is practicality: the telephone survey is more convenient, less time-consuming, and cheaper than the personal interview.

While there are many advantages to using the telephone interview, you should be aware of its limitations. First, as with any survey method, there is the possibility of a biased sample. Even if you followed proper random sampling techniques, telephone interviews are limited to those households with phones. Although this may not seem serious, you should be aware that not everyone has a telephone. Furthermore, some people won't be available to answer their phones. Still others may refuse to answer your questions. In fact, some people get very angry when they receive a phone call regarding a telephone survey. The authors have been yelled at on more than one occasion by people who believe that telephone interviews are a violation of their privacy.

With telephone surveys, you're limited to asking very simple and short questions. Often, subjects' attention spans are very short because your phone call interrupted a family fight, or the baby is crying in the background, etc.

Finally, by using the telephone survey, you limit yourself to only learning what subjects tell you. You can't see anything for yourself. Thus, if you want to know what race the subject is, you must ask. You don't see the subject or the subject's environment, and the subjects know you don't. Therefore, a 70-year-old bachelor living in a shack could tell you he's a 35-year-old millionaire with a wife and five kids. He knows you have no way of verifying his story.

PLANNING A SURVEY

What is Your Hypothesis?

As with all psychological research, the first step in designing a survey is to have a clear research question. You need a hypothesis as a guide in the development of a cohesive and useful set of survey questions. Writing a survey without a hypothesis to unify it is like writing a story without a plot—in the end all you have is a set of disjointed facts that tell you nothing.

You not only want a clear research question, you want an important one. Therefore, before you write your first survey item, write down in your research proposal why your study is important. As you'll learn in Chapter 13, in order to establish the importance of any study, you need to conduct a thorough literature review. You must demonstrate how your research question builds on existing work and the contribution your survey will make to the field of psychology. For example, are there any practical applications for your survey results? What useful information about human behavior will your survey provide?

Format of Questions

You've decided that your research question is appropriate. In addition, you've decided what kind of survey will give you the best information. Now, you're ready to decide what kind(s) of questions to use.

Fixed Alternative

A **fixed alternative question** resembles an item on a multiple-choice test. With this type of question, respondents are given several choices. Fixed alternatives usually yield two basic kinds of data: nominal (qualitative) data (e.g., male/female) and interval-scale data (e.g., strongly agree, agree, disagree, strongly disagree).

Nominal Dichotomous Data   Dichotomous questions—questions that allow only two responses (usually yes or no)—give you qualitative data. That is, they ask whether or not a person has a given quality. Often, respondents are asked whether they're a member or nonmember of a category (e.g., "are you employed?").

Sometimes, several dichotomous questions are asked at once. For example, "are you Black, Hispanic, Asian, or Caucasion (non-Hispanic)"? Note however, that this question can be rephrased as several dichotomous questions: "Are you Black?" (yes or no), "Are you Hispanic" (yes or no), etc. Thus, the information is still dichotomous—either subjects claim to belong to a category or they don't. Consequently, the numbers you get from these kinds of questions are on a nominal scale: if you get numbers from these questions, they're just stand-ins for words (e.g., 1 = yes, 2 = no). In other words, different numbers stand for different types (different qualities) rather than for different amounts (quantities).

There are several advantages to **nominal dichotomous items.** Well-constructed nominal items can be easier to answer and score than other types of questions. Specifically, it's a lot easier for respondents to decide between two alternatives (e.g., "Are you for or against animal research?") than five (e.g., "Rate how favorably you feel toward animal research on a 5-point scale"), or a potentially infinite number of alternatives (open-ended questions). Furthermore, because there are only two (usually very different) options, there is a greater chance respondents and investigators will have similar interpretations of the items. Therefore, a well-constructed dichotomous item can be a highly reliable and valid measure.

Although there are many advantages to nominal dichotomous items, there are some disadvantages. One problem is that some respondents will resist the fixed alternative nature of the question. To illustrate, consider the following question:

"Do you approve or disapprove of abortion?" (Disapprove/Approve)

Many respondents may want to say, "It depends. Is the mother's life in danger? Was rape or incest involved? Will the baby be born with severe birth defects?" Yet, the fixed alternatives don't allow for any of these conditions.

Another problem is that some respondents may not think their viewpoint is represented by the two alternatives given. For example, how would people who are neutral toward abortion respond? What about those who are adamantly opposed or ardently in favor?

If you've artificially limited your respondents to two alternatives, your respondents may not be the only ones irritated by the fact that your alternatives prevent them from accurately expressing their opinions. You too should be annoyed—because by depriving yourself of information about subtle differences among respondents, you deprive yourself of power: the ability to find relationships among variables.

Likert-type and Interval Items   On a Likert-type scale, subjects usually respond to a statement by checking either "strongly agree" (scored as 5), "agree" (scored as 4), "undecided" (3), "disagree" (2), or "strongly disagree" (1). Traditionally, most psychologists have assumed that a subject who "strongly agrees" (a "5") and a subject who merely "agrees" (a "4") differ by as much $(5 - 4 = 1)$ as a subject who is "undecided" (a "3") differs from someone who "disagrees" (a "2"). In other words, Likert-type scales are assumed to yield **interval data:** there is an equal psychological interval between each consecutive number. Questions 9 through 14 in Box 12-1 are examples of Likert-type, interval scale items.

Likert-type items are extremely useful in questionnaire construction. Whereas dichotomous items only allow subjects to agree or disagree, Likert-type items give subjects the freedom to: strongly agree, agree, be neutral, disagree, or strongly disagree. Thus, Likert-type items yield more information than nominal dichotomous items. Furthermore, because Likert-type items yield interval data, responses to them can be analyzed by more powerful statistical tests than nominal dichotomous items.

The major disadvantage of Likert-type items is that respondents may resist the fixed-alternative nature of the question. In an interview you can get around this by reading the question as if it were an open-ended question. Then, you'd record the answer under the appropriate alternative. In fact, all the questions in Box 12-1 can be read like open-ended items. Another tip, for either an interview or questionnaire, is to have a "Don't Know", "Undecided", or "Neutral" option. This way, respondents won't feel forced into an answer that doesn't reflect their true position.

Summating Scores   If you have several Likert-type items that are designed to measure the same variable (e.g., student sympathy), you can sum each respondent's answers to these questions. For example, the possible answers for questions 9 through 14 in Box 12-1 are based on the same 5-point interval scale, where strongly agree could be a 1, agree a 2, undecided a neutral 3, disagree a 4, and strongly disagree a 5. Once each response has been transformed into a number that ranges from 1 to 5, the answers for questions 9 through 14 can be added (summed) to produce a **summated score.** Thus, if Question 9 were given a "1", Question 10 a "2", Question 11 a "1", Question 12 a "3", Question 13 a "1", and Question 14 a "2", the summated score (total score for liking students) would be "10".

There are two statistical advantages to using summated scores. First, just as a 50-question multiple-choice test is more reliable than a 1-question test, a score based on several questions is more reliable than a single question. Second, analyses are often simpler for summated scores. If we summed the responses for the six Likert-type items in Box 12-1, we could compare "MTV" watchers and nonwatchers on "student sympathy" by doing one *t* test. Without a summated score, you'd have to perform six separate *t* tests and then correct the *t* test for the effects of having done multiple analyses.

Open-ended Questions

Open-ended items, like essay questions, pose a question without predetermined response options. This format gives respondents more freedom about how they answer questions than fixed alternative and scaled items. This flexibility makes open-ended questions a useful exploratory device because it allows unexpected, but important, responses.

Open-ended questions also enable you to assess your respondents' degree of sophistication and knowledge on your survey topic. This will give you insight into whether your respondents really have the information you're seeking and why they give the answers they do. For example, one professor may respond to Question 9 in Box 12-1 ("I like college students") with an undecided because he is new to the college and doesn't know. Still another professor may give the same rating because she has mixed feelings about students. Asking open-ended questions would allow you to see that these two respondents have different reasons for giving the same response.

Although there are numerous advantages to open-ended questions, these are tempered by some potentially serious disadvantages. First, open-ended questions take more time to ask and record than other question formats. This not only places greater demands on you, it also requires more from your respondents. Subjects will often skip open-ended questions because of the difficulty of generating their own responses.

You should also be aware that it takes some skill to ask open-ended questions. For example, you have to be very careful not to bias subjects responses through inflection, and nonverbal behavior. Often subjects will be looking at you for signs of whether they're answering the question correctly. Your nonverbal behavior may guide them, whether you're aware of it or not.

It will also take some skill to accurately and sufficiently record responses to open-ended interview questions. If you don't take shorthand, you might consider video-recording or tape-recording the interview.

But perhaps the biggest disadvantage of open-ended questions, whether in an interview or questionnaire, is that they're difficult to score. Answers may be so varied that you won't see an obvious way to code them. Often the coding strategy you finally adopt will be arbitrary. To help you devise a logical and systematic method of coding open-ended questions, use a content analysis scheme (see Chapter 11) before you start collecting data.

Once you've done a content analysis, you may convert the information from your open-ended questions into nominal or interval data where appropriate. For example, if you ask people how old they are, you'd analyze this quantitative data as interval data. If you ask subjects what gender they are, you'd analyze this qualitative, categorical data as nominal data.

Survey Format

Structured

The **structured survey** is the kind most often used in psychological research. In a structured survey, all respondents are asked a standard list of questions in a standard order.

The structured format will ensure that each subject is asked the same ques-

---

BOX 12-1 Sample Telephone Survey

Hello my name is _____ . I'm conducting a survey for my Research Design Class at Bromo Tech. Your name was drawn as a part of a random sample of university faculty. I'd greatly appreciate if you'd answer a few questions about your job and your TV viewing habits. The survey should take only five minutes. Will you help me?

		#	%
Demographics			
1. **Gender** (Don't ask)		—	—
__ Male	1	—	—
__ Female		—	—
2. **What is your position at Bromo Tech?**			
__ Instructor	2	—	—
__ Assistant professor		—	—
__ Associate professor		—	—
__ Professor		—	—
__ Other (If other terminate interview)			
3. **How long have you been teaching college?**			
__ 0–4 years	3	—	—
__ 5–9 years		—	—
__ 10–14 years		—	—
__ 15–19 years		—	—
__ 20 or more years		—	—
4. **What department do you teach in?**			
__ Anthropology	4	—	—
__ Art		—	—
__ Biology		—	—
__ Business		—	—
__ Chemistry		—	—
__ English		—	—
__ History		—	—
__ Math		—	—
__ Physical Education		—	—
__ Physics		—	—
__ Political Science		—	—
__ Psychology		—	—
__ Sociology		—	—
5. **What is the highest academic degree you've earned?**			
__ B.A.	5	—	—
__ M.A./M.D.		—	—
__ Ph.D./Ed.D		—	—

(continued)

BOX 12-1 (continued)

6. How old are you?
   — ≤25   6 __   __
   — 26–34   __   __
   — 35–44   __   __
   — 45–54   __   __
   — 55–64   __   __
   — ≥65   __   __

End of Demographics

7. **Do you watch "MTV" (Music Television)?**
   — Yes   7 __   __
   — No   __   __

8. **How many hours a week do you estimate
   you watch "MTV"?**
   — ≤1 hour   8 __   __
   — 2–4 hours   __   __
   — 5–9 hours   __   __
   — 10–14 hours   __   __
   — 15–19 hours   __   __
   — ≥20 hours   __   __

Please indicate how much you agree or disagree with the following
statements. State whether you strongly agree, agree, disagree, strongly
disagree, or are undecided.

9. I like college students.   SA A U D SD
10. College is stressful for students.   SA A U D SD
11. Colleges need to spend more time on students' SA A U D SD
    emotional development.
12. Colleges need to spend more time on students' SA A U D SD
    physical development.
13. College students should be allowed to postpone SA A U D SD
    tests when they're sick.
14. College students work hard.   SA A U D SD

Thank you for your help.

Note: Questions 2 through 8 can be read as open-ended questions.

tions and has the same response options (e.g., yes or no). Furthermore, by using a standard list of questions, the risk of interviewer bias is reduced. Thus, by controlling the questions and limiting the response range, you can obtain accurate and easily interpretable responses.

Of course, once you've developed your structured questions, you need to pretest them. Again, questions may look fine on paper but have weaknesses that only emerge when given to your actual study population. Thus, when you pretest your questions, ask respondents how they interpreted each question, and why they responded the way they did.

Semistructured

A **semistructured survey** is constructed around a core of standard questions. However, unlike the structured survey, the interviewer may expand on any question in order to explore a given response in greater depth. Like the structured questionnaire, the semistructured survey can yield accurate and comprehensive data. In addition, it has the advantage of being able to probe for underlying factors or relationships that may be too elusive for the structured survey.

Unfortunately, these advantages may be outweighed by two major disadvantages. First, data from an unstructured survey may be hard to interpret. It's difficult to compare subjects' responses when different subjects are asked different follow-up questions. Second, in giving the interviewer more freedom to follow up answers, you may be giving the interviewer more freedom to bias the results. Which answers are probed and how they're probed may affect subsequent answers to fixed items.

The semistructured questionnaire is best when you're surveying a topic on which there's little data—an exploratory survey. It provides you with enough standard information to make meaningful interpretations and gives you new information that may be useful for future surveys or studies.

As with structured questions, you should pretest any unstructured questions. How will potential subjects interpret the question? What kinds of follow-up questions are likely? What are common responses to these follow-up questions?

Unstructured

Unstructured surveys are very popular in the news media, in the analyst's office, and by the inexperienced researcher. In the unstructured survey, interviewers have objectives that they believe can be best met without an imposed structure. Therefore, there isn't a set of standard questions. The interviewer is free to ask what she wants, in the way she wants, and the respondent is free to answer how he pleases. Without standardization, the information is extremely vulnerable to interviewer bias and is usually too disorganized for analysis.

Because of these problems, the unstructured interview is best used as an exploratory device. As a research tool for reaping meaningful and accurate information, the unstructured survey is limited.

The Art of Asking Good Questions

Although it's important to decide how subjects should respond to questions (open-ended, Likert-type, dichotomous), it's more important to ask good questions. Although asking questions is a part of everyday life, asking good survey questions is not. In this section, you'll learn the criteria for good questionnaire construction. By adhering to these criteria, you'll get the most out of your surveys.

Framing Questions

Accurate communication is the major goal in questionnaire construction. To accurately communicate, your questionnaire must adhere to several criteria.

1. USE WORDS A THIRD-GRADER WOULD UNDERSTAND. Your task is not to impress respondents with your command of vocabulary and technical jargon: Your task is to make sure subjects understand you. Therefore, use very basic vocabulary and avoid jargon.

2. USE WORDS AND TERMS THAT WON'T BE MISINTERPRETED. There are several steps you can take to make sure that subjects know exactly what you're talking about. First, avoid slang terms. Slang terms often have different meanings to different groups. Thus, if you want to know people's attitudes toward marijuana, use the word "marijuana" rather than a slang term like "dope". "Dope" may be interpreted as meaning marijuana, heroine, or all drugs. Second, be specific. If you want to know how people feel about college students, don't ask "How do you feel about students?" Finally, you can avoid misinterpretations through extensive pretesting. Only through experience will you find that a question or term may be misinterpreted. Through extensive pretesting, you may find that a seemingly straighforward question such as "Should Pittsburgh increase coke production?" may be interpreted in at least five different ways:

1. Should Pittsburgh increase cocaine production?
2. Should Pittsburgh increase coal production?
3. Should Pittsburgh increase steel production?
4. Should Pittsburgh increase soft-drink production?
5. Should Pittsburgh increase Coca-Cola production?

3. AVOID PERSONAL QUESTIONS UNLESS YOU REALLY NEED THE INFORMATION. Personal questions tend to arouse suspicion and resistance.

4. MAKE SURE THAT YOUR SAMPLE HAS THE INFORMATION YOU SEEK. Obviously, subjects can't give you accurate answers if they don't know the answer. You should therefore avoid asking questions such as, "How much marijuana do your children smoke a month?" If you suspect that some subjects won't know the answer to a question you've decided to ask, allow them to say that they don't know the answer. Such a question might read, "I spent _____ hours advising students on personal matters last year: less than 20, between 20 and 40, between 40 and 60, between 60 and 80, more than 80, don't know."

5. AVOID LEADING QUESTIONS. Remember your aim is to get accurate information, not conformity. Therefore don't ask, "Don't you disapprove of the horrible way MTV presents graphic violence?" Instead ask, "Do you approve or disapprove of MTV's presentation of violence?"

6. AVOID QUESTIONS THAT ARE LOADED WITH SOCIAL DESIRABILITY. Don't ask questions that have a socially correct answer, e.g., "Do you donate money to student causes?" Generally, subjects will respond with the desirable answer and will be "on guard" during the rest of the survey.

7. AVOID DOUBLE-BARRELED QUESTIONS. Obviously, you wouldn't think of asking a subject more than one question at the same time. But that's exactly what happens when you ask a **double-barreled question:** several questions packed into a single question, e.g., "How much do you agree with the following statement, 'Colleges need to spend more time on students' emotional and physical development'?" The data from this question are uninterpretable because you don't know whether subjects were responding to the first statement "Colleges need to spend more time on students' emotional development," the second statement "Colleges need to spend more time on students' physical development," or both statements.

As you can see, the conjunction "and" allowed this question to be double-barreled. Almost all double-barreled questions are joined by "and" or some other conjunction. So when looking over your questions, look suspiciously at all "and's," "or's," and "but's."

8. KEEP QUESTIONS SHORT AND CONCISE. This will help you avoid ambiguity, confusion, and double-barreled questions. Remember, short questions are easier to understand. A useful rule of thumb is to keep most of your questions under 10 words (one line) and all your questions under 20 words.

9. AVOID NEGATIONS. The appearance of a negation in a questionnaire item increases the possibility of misinterpretation. Furthermore, it takes more time to process and interpret a negation than a positively stated item. To illustrate, compare the next two statements: "Don't you not like it when students don't study?"; versus "Do you like it when students study?"

10. AVOID IRRELEVANT QUESTIONS. Be sensitive to the relevancy of a questionnaire item for your population and your research question. For example, "Do you eat quiche?" is irrelevant to the research question, "Are professors who watch MTV more sympathetic to students?"

Although there are many obvious reasons for not including irrelevant questions, the most important reason is that irrelevant questions irk respondents. If you ask an irrelevant question, many respondents will conclude that you're either incompetent or disrespectful. Since they've lost respect for you, they'll be less likely to give accurate answers to questions. In fact, they may even refuse to continue with the survey.

11. Finally, **PRETEST THE QUESTIONNAIRE** in a pilot study to eliminate weaknesses.

Sequencing Questions

Once you've developed a good set of questionnaire items, you need to decide in what order to ask them. Ordering questions is important because the sequence of questions can influence results. To appropriately order questions, follow these four general rules.

1. PUT INNOCUOUS QUESTIONS FIRST, PERSONAL QUESTIONS LAST. Subjects are often tense or anxious at the beginning of a survey. They don't know what to expect. They don't know whether they should continue the survey. The questions you ask at the beginning set the tone for the rest of the survey. Thus, if the first question is extremely personal, subjects may decide to withdraw from the survey. Even if they don't withdraw, they'll be very defensive throughout the survey. If, on the other hand, your initial questions are innocuous, subjects may relax and feel comfortable enough to respond frankly to personal questions later on.

Putting the most sensitive questions at the end of your survey won't only increase the number of candid responses, it will also yield more data. To illustrate, suppose that you have a 20-item survey in which all but one of the questions are relatively innocuous. If you put the sensitive item first, respondents may quit the survey immediately. Since this item was the first question you asked, you've gathered no information whatsoever. If, on the other hand, you put the sensitive item last, respondents may still quit. Nevertheless, you still have their responses to 19 of the 20 questions.

2.   QUALIFY EARLY. If people must meet certain qualifications to be included in your sample or to be asked certain questions in your battery, find out if they qualify before you ask them the questions. In other words, don't ask people questions that don't apply to them. There's no need to waste their time, and yours, by collecting useless information. Subjects don't like saying "no, doesn't apply" 10 times. Box 12-1 has two qualifying questions. The first is Question 2, "What is your position at Bromo Tech?" This question establishes the presence of two qualifications for the survey: 1) that the person is a professor; and 2) the person teaches at Bromo Tech. If people don't meet these qualifications, the survey is terminated at the start of the interview, not at the end. This saves time and energy. Can you identify the second qualifying question?

3.   BE AWARE OF RESPONSE SETS. If all your questions have the same response options, people sometimes get locked into one answer. For example, if each question has the alternatives "Strongly Agree, Agree, Undecided, Disagree, Strongly Disagree," respondents may answer each question with the same alternative, e.g., "Undecided." The undecided response allows them to get the questionnaire over with as soon as possible. To avoid the undecided **response set,** you may want to eliminate the undecided option. Of course, the undecided response set isn't the only response bias. You'll also encounter the "Yea Sayers" and the "Nay Sayers" that you read about in Chapter 3.

One of the most common ways of dealing with response styles is to alternate the way you phrase the questions. That is, you might ask subjects to strongly agree, agree, disagree, or strongly disagree to the statement, "Students are hard working." Then, later in the questionnaire ask them to strongly agree, agree, disagree or strongly disagree to the statement, "Students are lazy."

4.   KEEP SIMILAR QUESTIONS TOGETHER. There are several reasons why you get more accurate responses when you keep related questions together. First, your subjects perceive the survey to be organized and professional, and, therefore, take it seriously. Second, subjects don't get confused about what your questions apply to as they do when surveys constantly skip between topics. Third, by asking all the related questions together, subjects are already thinking about the topic before you ask the question. And since they are, they can respond quickly and accurately. If subjects aren't thinking about the topic before you ask the question, it may take some of them a while to think of the answer. At best, this makes for some long pauses. At worst, subjects will avoid long pauses by saying they don't know.

Add Demographic Questions

In addition to writing items that directly address your research question, you should ask some questions that will reveal your sample's **demographics:** characteristics, such as age, gender, and education level. Thus, in our survey of college professors (see Box 12-1), we asked six demographic questions. By comparing our sample's responses to these demographic questions with the population's demographics, we can see how representative our sample is. That is, we can look in the catalog or go to the personnel office to find out what percentage are women. Then, we can compare our sample demographics to these population demographics. If we found that 75% of the faculty was male, but that only 25% of our sample was male, we'd know that our sample wasn't representative of faculty.

Note that we put the demographic questions first (Questions 1–6). Why? We put our demographic questions first because they were relatively innocuous. Thus, these questions would put our respondents at ease before we asked more personal questions.

Add the Finishing Touches

You've written your questions, carefully sequenced them, and pretested them. Now, you should carefully proof and pretest your questionnaire to make sure that it's accurate, easy to read, and easy to score.

Obviously, subjects are more likely to take your research seriously if your questionnaire looks professional. Therefore, your final copy of the questionnaire should be free of smudges and spelling errors. The spaces between questions should be uniform.

Even though the questionnaire is neatly typed, certain key words may have been scrambled or omitted. At best, these words could cause embarrassment. At worst, they would cause you to lose data. Bear in mind, that although you should proof the questionnaire to ensure that it looks professional in form, you should also pretest it to ensure that the content is professional.

Once you've verified both the form and the content of the questionnaire, you should code your pretest subjects responses. After doing this, you should consider ways of making coding easier. Basically there are four strategies you can use to facilitate coding:

1. Line up responses in either the far right or far left margin. This will allow you to score each page quickly because you can go straight down the page without shifting your gaze from left to right or filtering out extraneous information. If you put information in the far left margin, you're less likely to miscode items because the number of the item is right next to the relevant answer.
2. Have subjects put their answers on an answer sheet. With an answer sheet, you don't have to look through and around questions to find the answers. The answer sheet is an especially good idea when your questionnaire is more than one page long because it saves you the trouble of turning pages.
3. Have subjects put their responses on a coding sheet that can be scored by computer. Computer scoring is more accurate than hand scoring. Besides, since computers like dull, time-consuming tasks, why not let them code responses?
4. If you really want to employ computers, you could have the computer administer the questionnaire, print out the responses, and even score the questionnaire. (See Appendix C for more information on computer applications.)

SAMPLING

Once you've decided what questions you'll ask and how you'll ask them, you need to decide who you'll ask. To decide that, you first have to decide exactly what population you want to study. If your population is extremely small (all art history teachers at your school), you may decide to survey all members of your population. Usually, however, your population is so large that you can't survey everyone, so you survey a sample of those people. Whether you acquire your sample by random sampling, stratified random sampling, convenience sampling, or quota sampling, your goal is to get a sample that's representative of your population.

Random Sampling

In **random sampling,** each member of the population has an equal probability of being selected. Furthermore, the selection of subjects is independent. In other words, the selection of a given person has no influence on the selection or exclusion of other members of the population from the sample.

As you can imagine, random assignment can be very time-consuming. First, you have to identify every member of the population. That can be a chore, depending on your population. If you're interested in a student sample, then a trip to the Registrar's Office should yield a list of all currently enrolled students. In fact, some schools can generate a computerized random sample of students for you. If you're interested in sampling a community, the local telephone company is a good place to start. Or, if you're willing to spend the money, you can buy census tapes from the government or from marketing research firms.

After you've identified the population, you have to assign random numbers to your subjects. Just this step—assigning random numbers to all members of a population—can be cumbersome and time-consuming. Imagine assigning one million random numbers to names! But after that's done, you have to use the random number table to determine who you'll sample. Fortunately, many of the headaches of random sampling can be computerized if you have a computerized list of your population.

Despite the hassles involved with random sampling, researchers are willing to tolerate it because it allows one to generalize the results of a study to a larger population. As you'll recall, you can use inferential statistics to infer the characteristics of a population from a random sample of that population.

Determining Sample Size

As you know, your random sample may differ from the population by chance. That is, although your population may be 51% women, your random sample may be 49% women. You also know that you can reduce random sampling error by increasing your sample size. In other words, a sample of 10 thousand will tend to more accurately reflect the population than a sample of 10. However, surveying 10 thousand people may cost more time and energy than the added accuracy it buys. To determine how many people you'll need to survey if you use random sampling, consult Table 12-1.

TABLE 12-1 Required Sample Size as a Function of Population Size, Desired Accuracy (within 5, 3 or 1%), and Level of Confidence

Confidence Level: Sampling Error: Size of Universe	95% 5%	90% 5%	85% 5%	80% 5%	95% 3%	90% 3%	85% 3%	80% 3%	95% 1%	90% 1%	85% 1%	80% 1%
50	44	42	40	39	48	47	46	45	50	50	50	49
100	79	73	167	63	92	88	85	82	99	99	98	98
200	132	116	102	92	169	159	148	140	196	194	193	191
500	217	178	147	126	343	302	268	242	476	466	456	447
1,000	278	216	172	145	521	434	365	319	907	873	838	809
2,000	322	242	188	156	705	554	447	380	1661	1550	1443	1357
5,000	357	261	199	163	894	664	516	429	3311	2897	2545	2290
10,000	370	268	203	166	982	711	545	448	4950	4079	3414	2970
20,000	377	272	205	168	1033	737	560	459	6578	5124	4117	3488
50,000	381	274	207	168	1066	754	569	465	8195	6055	4697	3896
100,000	383	275	207	169	1077	760	573	467	8926	6445	4929	4054
1,000,000	384	275	207	169	1088	765	576	469	9706	6842	5157	4207
100,000,000	384	275	207	169	1089	765	576	469	9800	6889	5184	4225

Example of use of table: If you are sampling from a universe of 50 people and you want to be 90% confident that your results will be within 5% of the true percentage in the population, you need to randomly sample 42 people.

Note: Table provided by David Van Amburg of Market Source, Inc.

With pure random sampling, you leave everything to chance. You count on using a large sample size so that the effects of chance will be small. This isn't the case with **stratified random sampling.** Instead of leaving everything to chance, you make sure that the sample is similar to the population in certain respects. For example, if you know that the population is 75% male and 25% female, you make sure your sample is 75% male and 25% female. You accomplish this goal by dividing your population (stratum) into two subpopulations, or substrata. One substratum would consist of male members of the population, the other of female members. Next, you'd decide on how many subjects to sample from each substratum (e.g., 75 from the male stratum, 25 from the female stratum). Finally, you'd draw random samples from each substratum, following the same basic procedures you used in random sampling. The only difference is that you're collecting two samples from two substrata, rather than one sample from the main population.

By using stratified random sampling, you have all the advantages of random sampling, but you don't need to sample nearly as many people. As a result, the Gallup Poll can predict the outcome of presidential elections based on samples of only 300 people. Furthermore, a stratified random sample ensures that your sample matches the population exactly on certain key variables.

Stratified Random Sampling

Convenience Sampling

In **convenience sampling,** you simply sample people who are easy to survey. Convenience surveys are very common. Newspapers ask people to mail in their responses to a survey question, and radio stations ask people to call in their reactions to a question. Even television stations have gotten into the act, asking people to call one number if they're in favor of an issue, another number if they're opposed to it.

To see how you'd get a convenience sample, suppose that you were given one week to get 1,000 responses to a questionnaire. What would you do? You might go to areas where you'd expect to find large numbers of people, such as a shopping mall. Or, you might ask your professors if you could survey their classes. Or, you might put an ad in the newspaper, offering people money if they'd respond to a questionnaire.

As you can see, the convenience sample can provide you with a lot of data. Unfortunately, you don't know whether the sample represents your population. It's more likely that it doesn't. In fact, if your subjects are actively volunteering to be in your survey, you can bet that your sample is extremely biased. The average person doesn't call in to radio shows, write letters in response to questions in the newspaper, or respond to ads asking for people to be in a survey.

Quota Sampling

Quota sampling is designed to make your convenience sample more representative of the population. Like stratified random sampling, quota sampling is designed to guarantee that your sample matched the population on certain characteristics. For instance, you might make sure that 25% of your sample was female, or that 20% of your sample was Black American.

Unlike stratified random sampling, however, quota sampling doesn't involve random sampling. Consequently, even though you met your quotas, your sample may not reflect the population at all. For example, you may meet your 20% quota of Blacks by hanging around a hotel hosting a convention of Black cowboys. Obviously the Blacks in your survey are not representative of the Black Americans in your community.

Conclusions about Sampling Techniques

To get samples that represent your population, we recommend that you use either random sampling or stratified random sampling. However, no sampling technique is totally free of sampling bias because, ultimately, subjects choose the sample. That is, you can sample them, but they may not answer you. As a result, your sample won't represent members of the population who choose not to respond.

There are two things you can do about the bias caused by nonresponse. First, you can try to have a very low nonresponse rate. Some investigators have 97% response rates by using fairly brief telephone surveys. Second, keep detailed records on the people who refused. If possible, unobtrusively record their gender, race, and estimated age.

ADMINISTERING THE SURVEY

You have your survey questions. You've carefully sequenced your questions and you've determined your sampling technique. Now it's time for you to actually administer your survey. Basically, you're going to follow the same advice you received for administering experiments, quasi experiments, and other correlational studies. In essence, you must conduct yourself professionally in every step of your survey.

For example, subjects should always be greeted, whether in person or in print. Thus, a mail questionnaire should always be accompanied by a cover letter—a written greeting. Just as with a personal greeting, your cover letter should introduce you, explain the nature of your study, and request your subjects' help.

Subjects should always be given clear instructions, either orally (in an interview) or in writing (in a questionnaire). Of course, if an investigator is administering the questionnaire, any written instructions can be backed up with oral ones.

After subjects complete a survey, they should be debriefed and thanked. Thus, at the end of a mail questionnaire, you should write a debriefing, thank your subjects, and give them any additional instructions. For example, "Please mail your questionnaire in the stamped and addressed envelope provided. To find out more about the survey, put a check mark in the upper left-hand corner of the questionnaire and we'll send you a summary of the results once the survey is completed."

ANALYZING SURVEY DATA

Summarizing Data

The first step in analyzing survey data is to determine what data are relevant to your hypotheses. Once you know what data you want, you need to summarize those data. How you summarize them will depend on what kind of data you have—and the type of data will depend on the type of questions you ask. When you ask rating scale questions or when you ask people to quantify their behavior ("How many hours do you watch 'MTV'?"), then you can probably assume that your data are interval scale data. If you ask questions the answers to which are yes or no ("Do you watch 'MTV'? Do you like students?"), or questions where people have to classify themselves ("Are you male or female? Are you a sophomore, junior, or a senior?"), then you have nominal data.

Summarizing Interval Data

If you simply want to know the typical response to an interval scale question, ("How many hours do people in the sample watch 'MTV'?"), then you need only to calculate the mean for that question. More often, however, you'll be interested in the relationship between one or more variables. In that case, you'll probably want to construct tables of means that reflect these relationships. In our example, we expected that there would be a relationship between "MTV" watching and sympathy for students. Therefore, we compared "MTV" watchers average sympathy for students (see Table 12-2). In addition, we were interested in seeing whether male or female professors were more sympathetic to students (see Table 12-2). To supplement your tables of means, you may want to compute a correlation coefficient to get an idea of the strength of the relationship between your two variables.

TABLE 12-2   Table of Means and Interactions

**Table of Means for "MTV" on Question 9:
"I Like College Students"**

No-"MTV"	"MTV"
4.0	3.0

Average score on a 1- (strongly disagree) to-5 (strongly agree) scale.

**Table of Means for Gender on Question 9:
"I Like College Students"**

Male	Female
3.25	3.75

Average score on a 1 (strongly disagree) to 5 (strongly agree) scale.

**Interaction for Gender by "MTV" on Question 9:
"I Like College Students"**

	No-"MTV"	"MTV"
MALE	3.5	3.0
FEMALE	4.5	3.0

Average score on a 1 (strongly disagree) to 5 (strongly agree) scale.

Looking at Complex Relationships

Thus far, you've seen how to compare the relationship between pairs of variables (e.g., "MTV" and sympathy, gender and sympathy, gender and "MTV"). Sometimes, however, you may want to see how three or more variables are related. The easiest way to compare three or more variables is to construct a table of means, as we've done in Table 12-2. As you can see, this 2 × 2 table of means allows us to look at how both "MTV" watching and gender are related to sympathy (Table 12-2).

Summarizing Ordinal or Nominal Data

If your data aren't interval scale data, don't summarize your data by computing means. Instead, use percentages (Table 12-3).

To look at relationships among variables use tables of percentages to compare different groups' responses. These tables are called **crosstabs** because they allow you to compare across groups. As you can see in Table 12-3, crosstabs are a powerful way to graphically display similarities and differences between groups.

TABLE 12-3 Contingency Table: "MTV" by Gender

Do You Watch "MTV"?	Male		Female	
YES	20	(A)	15	(B)
NO	55	(C)	10	(D)

If you want to compute a measure to quantify how closely two variables are related, you can calculate a correlational coefficient. But don't compute the Pearson *r* as you would for nominal data, instead compute the **phi coefficient** (see Box 12-2). Like most correlation coefficients, phi ranges from −1 (strong negative correlation) to +1 (strong positive correlation).

Looking at Complex Relationships

If you want to look at how three or more variables are related, don't use the phi coefficient. Instead, construct a table of percentages, as we've done in Table 12-3. This 2 × 2 table of percentages does for our nominal data what the 2 × 2 table of means did for our interval data—allows us to look at three variables at once.

BOX 12-2 Computing the phi Coefficient

Once you've drawn your crosstabs, the **phi coefficient** is extremely easy to calculate. The formula is:

$$\phi = \frac{BC - AD}{\sqrt{(A + B) \times (C + D) \times (A + C) \times (B + D)}}$$

Thus, for our crosstabs between "MTV" and gender (see Table 12-3), the computations would be:

$$\phi = \frac{(15 \times 55) - (20 \times 10)}{\sqrt{(20 + 15) \times (55 + 10) \times (20 + 55) \times (15 + 10)}}$$

$$= \frac{825 - 200}{\sqrt{35 \times 65 \times 75 \times 25}}$$

$$= \frac{625}{\sqrt{4265625}}$$

$$= \frac{625}{2065.34}$$

$$= .30$$

Using Inferential Statistics

In addition to using descriptive statistics to define the characteristics of your sample, you may wish to use inferential statistics. Inferential statistics may allow you to generalize the results of your sample to the population it represents.

There are two reasons why you might want to use inferential statistics. First, you might want to estimate certain **parameters:** characteristics of the population, such as the population mean. Thus, if you wanted to estimate the average amount of time students spend watching "MTV," use inferential statistics. This is called **parameter estimation.**

Second, you might want to determine whether the relationship you found between two or more variables would hold in the population or if it's merely due to sampling error. For example, you might want to determine whether watching "MTV" and grade point average are related in the population. Since you're deciding whether or not to reject the null hypothesis that the variables are not related in the population, this use of inferential statistics is called **hypothesis testing.**

Despite the obvious value of parameter estimation and hypothesis testing, you should carefully consider whether or not to use these techniques. Remember, you can only use inferential statistics if you can assume that you've randomly sampled from a given population. If, however, you can't assume that your sample represents a random sample from a given population, *don't* use inferential statistics.

Even if you can assume that your sample is a random sample, be wary of doing too many analyses. Remember, if you use the .05 level of significance but do 100 separate analyses, 5 of them are likely to be significant by chance alone.

Parameter Estimation with Interval Data

One reason for using statistics is to estimate population parameters. For example, from our survey of "MTV" watching and student sympathy, we might want to estimate the amount of sympathy the average professor has.

You can establish 95% confidence intervals for any population mean from the sample mean, if you know the standard error of the mean. (If you don't have a computer or calculator that will compute the standard error of the mean for you, see Chapter 5). You establish the lower limit of your confidence interval by subtracting two standard errors from the sample mean. Then, you establish the upper limit of your confidence interval by adding two standard errors to the sample mean. Thus, if the average sympathy rating for all the professors in our sample was 4.0 and the standard error was .5, we could be 95% confident that the true population mean is somewhere between 3.0 and 5.0.

Hypothesis Testing with Interval Data

You can also use statistics to see if there are significant differences between groups. For example, we might want to know if the differences we observe in our sample also apply to the population at large. Through a *t* test we could see whether the differences in sympathy we observed between "MTV" watchers and non-"MTV" watchers was a true difference (not due to sampling error).

The *t* test between means is not the only way to determine whether there is a relationship between "MTV" watching and student sympathy. Determining whether the correlation coefficient between those two variables was significant is another way. To determine whether a correlation coefficient is significant, refer to Box 11-4.

If you're comparing more than one pair of variables, you can do several *t* tests or test the significance of several correlations. In either case, you should correct for doing more than a single statistical test by using a more stringent significance level than the conventional .05 level. For example, if you looked at 5 comparisons, you might use the .01 level; if you looked at 50 comparisons, you might use the .001 level.

Relationships among More than Two Variables   If you want to look at more than two variables at once ("MTV" and gender on sympathy, Table 12-2), you might use analysis of variance (ANOVA). If you perform multiple ANOVAs, you should correct your alpha level for the number of ANOVAs you computed, just as you would if you use multiple *t* tests.

More Complicated Procedures   You should be aware that we've just scratched the surface of how interval data from a survey can be analyzed. Factor analysis, multivariate analysis of variance, and multiple regression are all techniques that could be used to analyze survey research data. However, these statistical techniques are beyond the scope of this book.

Estimating Overall Percentages in Population

If you select your sample size according to Table 12-1, you're 95% confident that your sample percentages are within 5% of the population's percentages. Thus, if you found that 35% of your subjects were female, you'd be 95% confident that between 30% and 40% of your population was female.

Relationships between Variables

With nominal data, you can use significance tests to determine whether differences between sample frequencies reflect differences in population frequencies. But instead of using *t* tests, as you would with interval data, you'd use the chi-square test (see Box 11-3).

If you're performing more than one **chi-square** test, you should correct for the number of analyses performed. Just as with the *t* test, you should raise your significance level to compensate for doing multiple analyses. Thus, if you're comparing five chi squares, you should use a .01 significance level rather than a .05.

Using Inferential Statistics with Nominal Data

CHAPTER SUMMARY

In this chapter you learned the essence of good survey research. Early in the chapter you were introduced to the applications and limitations of survey research. You saw the advantages and disadvantages of different survey formats, as well as the strengths and weaknesses of different kinds of questions. First, you learned how to write a survey, and then you learned how to administer, score, and analyze survey data.

Now that you know the basics of survey research, you're ready to apply your knowledge. Experience will make you even more aware of the need for careful planning, execution, and analyses. Through direct application of the principles you learned in this chapter, you'll become a skillful survey researcher.

MAIN POINTS

1. Surveys can help you describe what people are thinking, feeling, or doing.
2. Surveys allow you to gather information from a large sample with less effort and expense than most other data-gathering techniques.
3. In a survey it's important to ask only pertinent questions. Otherwise, your research question could be lost in a lot of irrelevant information.
4. Don't accept respondents' answers as gospel. People don't always tell the truth.
5. Know who you want to generalize your results to before you start your study.
6. Remember, surveys only yield correlational data. You cannot determine causality.
7. There are several drawbacks to self-administered questionnaires: they have a low return rate, respondents may misinterpret questions, and subjects may object to question format.
8. Investigator-administered questionnaires have a higher response rate than self-administered questionnaires.
9. Interviews are especially useful for exploratory studies.
10. Telephone surveys have higher response rates, are easier to administer, and offer greater anonymity than personal interviews.
11. Your first step in survey research is to have a hypothesis.
12. There are three basic question formats: nominal dichotomous, Likert-type, and open-ended.
13. Structured surveys are generally more useful than unstructured ones.
14. Asking good questions is the key to good survey research.
15. Be sure to edit your questions according to our 10 major points.
16. Careful attention should be placed on sequencing questions. Keep similar questions together, qualify early, and put personal questions last.
17. Be aware of response sets.
18. Some time spent deciding how to code your questionnaire can save time in the end.
19. Random and stratified random sampling allow you to make statistical inferences from your data.
20. Subjects in survey research should be treated with the same respect as subjects in any other kind of study.

KEY TERMS

self-administered survey
interviewer bias
fixed alternative question
nominal dichotomous items
Likert-type items
summated score
open-ended items
structured survey
semistructured survey
leading question
double-barreled question
response set

demographics
random sampling
stratified random sampling
convenience sampling
quota sampling
crosstabs
phi coefficient
parameters
parameter estimation
hypothesis testing
chi square

EXERCISES

1. Develop a hypothesis that can be tested by administering a survey.

2. Is a survey the best way to test your hypothesis? Why?

3. Is an interview or a questionnaire the best way to test your hypothesis? Why?

4. For the three basic question formats list their advantages and disadvantages.

5. Based on your hypothesis, write three nominal dichotomous questions.

6. Based on your hypothesis, write three Likert-type items.

7. Based on your hypothesis, write three open-ended questions.

8. Edit your questions using the 10 points presented in this chapter.

9. Why can you make statistical inferences from data based on random sampling and stratified random sampling?

13

PUTTING IT ALL TOGETHER

"What it boils down to is that you've got to know the bottom line"

—BODY HEAT

"An ounce of prevention is worth a pound of cure"

OVERVIEW

Your research should be carefully planned before you test your first subject. Finding out after the fact that your study has already been done, that you didn't have a clear hypothesis, or that your measures were invalid are heartaches easily avoided through a little forethought. In short, poor planning leads to poor execution.

Poor execution is unethical. At best, it wastes subjects time; at worst, it may harm them. Therefore, the purpose of this chapter is to help you avoid unethical research by showing you how to carefully plan, implement, and report the results of your study. If you follow our advice, your research should be humane, valid, and meaningful.

AIDS TO DEVELOPING YOUR IDEA

In this section you'll learn about two major research tools—the research journal and the research proposal. Many scientists regard these two tools as essential to the development and implementation of sound, ethical research.

The Research Journal

We recommend that you keep a research journal: a diary of your research idea and experiences. Keeping a journal will help you in at least three ways. First, you won't have to rely on memory to explain later why and how you did what you did. Second, writing to yourself helps you think through design decisions. Third, the research journal can help you in preparing a research proposal.

Since the journal is for your eyes only, it doesn't have to be neatly typed or free of spelling and grammatical errors. What's in the journal is much more important than how it's written.

What should you put in your journal? Every idea you have about your research project. So, at the beginning of the research process, when you're trying to develop a research hypothesis, use your research journal for brainstorming by writing down any research ideas you think of and indicating what stimulated each idea. As you narrow down your choices, explain why you eliminated certain ideas and chose to focus on others. When you decide on a given idea, explain why you decided on that particular research idea. When reading related research, summarize and critique it in your journal. Remember to write down the authors, year, title, publication, and publisher for each source. This information will come in very handy when you write your research proposal.

In short, whenever you have an insight, find a relevant piece of information, or make a design decision, record it in your journal.

The Proposal Like the research journal, the purpose of the research proposal is to help you think through each step of your research project. In addition, it lets others (e.g., friends, professors) think through your study so that they can give you advice on how to improve your study. Thus, by writing the proposal you'll have the opportunity to try out ideas and explore alternatives without damaging a single subject. The process of writing the proposal will help you make intelligent and ethical research decisions.

Although the research proposal builds on the research journal, it is much more formal than the journal. The proposal should conform in content, style, and organization to the guidelines given in the American Psychological Association's Publication Manual (1983). In your research proposal, you'll state your hypothesis, how you arrived at it, how you define and operationalize your variables, who your subjects will be, and how your study fits in with existing research. In essence, your research proposal will become the introduction and method sections for your final report and the first draft of your abstract, results, and discussion sections.

WRITING THE INTRODUCTION TO YOUR RESEARCH PROPOSAL

Now that you know what a research proposal is, it's time for you to begin writing one. We'll first show you how to write your introduction.

The Elements of an Introduction The purpose of the introduction is to demonstrate to your readers that you've read relevant research and thoroughly understand your research question. Once you've articulated the reasoning behind your hypothesis, you explain what you plan to do and why you plan to do it. After reading the introduction, your reader should know what your hypothesis is, why it's interesting, and why your study is the best way to test the hypothesis.

Establishing the Importance of Your Study

To convince people that your study is important and interesting, you must first let them know exactly what you're studying. You must define your concepts. Once you've explained what your concepts are, then you can explain why the concepts are important.

Historical Precedence To establish the importance of your study, you might show that there is a historical precedence for your study. You could emphasize the great minds that have pondered the concept you'll study, the number of people through the ages who have tried to understand the behavior, or merely the length of time that the concept has existed.

Statistical Evidence   Alternatively, you might document the importance of the concept by presenting statistical evidence. Thus, if you're studying widowhood, you might present statistics on the percentage of people who are widowed. In the absence of statistics, you could use quotes from influential people or organizations (e.g., American Psychological Association) to stress the importance of your concept.

Case Studies   Finally, you might present a case study—a real-life situation where your concept is in action. Giving an example of the concept is a very good way to simultaneously define the concept and provide a vivid picture of its importance. If you use an example that's analogous to your study, so much the better.

The Research Summary   Another way of establishing that your concepts are important is to cite research pertaining to them. Citing a quantity of research not only informs your reader about the concept, but stresses its importance. After all, if other people have studied a concept, it must be important.

When citing research, review several older, classic works as well as recent research. Critiquing, rather than merely summarizing, these articles will show that you've thought about what you've read.

Obviously, you aren't doing a research summary merely to establish yourself as a scholar. Your aim is to show how your study follows from existing research. In other words, your evaluations of other work should set up your own work so well that a very astute reader could guess what your manipulations will be just from reading the research summary.

Of course, you won't require your readers to guess the rationale for your hypothesis and for your study. After carefully summarizing the relevant research, spell out, step-by-step, the reasoning that led to your hypothesis. Be very explicit.

State Your Hypothesis

Even though your readers may have guessed your hypothesis, leave nothing to chance: State your hypothesis. To emphasize a point that can't be overemphasized enough, state your hypothesis boldly and clearly so that readers can't miss it. Let them know what your study is about by writing, "The hypothesis is. . . ."

When you state your hypothesis, be sensitive to whether you'll be testing it with an experiment or a correlational study. If you'll be directly manipulating the predictor (independent) variable, you'll be conducting an experiment. Only with an experiment may you use the word "cause" ("A sedentary life-style causes depression"). If you don't plan on directly manipulating your predictor variable then you have a correlational study—you can only test whether two or more variables "relate" ("A sedentary life-style is related to depression").

Once you've stated your hypothesis, you need to convince people that your study is the best way to test your hypothesis. Thus, you must describe what you're going to do and why you're going to do it.

Justify Your Manipulations and Measures

You should justify your method of testing your hypothesis with the same care you took in justifying the hypothesis itself. Early in the introduction, foreshadow your choice of procedures. Near the end of the introduction, carefully build on what you've already said, explicating your reasons for choosing your methods or procedures.

For example, suppose your justification for using a set of procedures, manipulations, or measures is that these procedures are commonly used and accepted. Then, when you summarize the relevant research, let your readers know about the procedures and how well accepted they are.

But what if you're using novel procedures or measures? In this case, when you review the relevant research, let your readers know that you're dissatisfied. Later in the proposal, when you justify your procedures, you'll draw on your earlier criticisms to show why your methods are best. For instance, if you're using a new measure, you'll refer to your definition of the concept, and point out how your measure captures the essence of this definition. Then, you'll remind your readers of the weaknesses you spotted in other measures and point out that your measure avoids these weaknesses.

Overview of the Introduction

We've given you some general advice on how to write an introduction. You've seen the importance of clearly defining your concepts, critically summarizing research, explicating your hypothesis, and justifying your way of testing the hypothesis.

Justifying Specific Types of Studies

Thus far, you've only been given general advice because the specific way in which you'll justify your study will depend on the kind of study you're doing. In the next section, you'll learn how to justify five kinds of studies.

The Exploratory Study

In introducing an **exploratory study:** a study investigating a new area of research, you must take special care to justify your study, your hypothesis, and your procedures. You must compensate for your readers' lack of knowledge about your research area.

New Is Not Enough   Unlike most introductions, you can't state that your research area is important merely by showing that the area has inspired a lot of research. In this case it hasn't—that's why your study is an exploratory study. To justify an exploratory study, don't merely state that your research question has been ignored. Many dull research areas have been ignored. Convince your readers that your research question deserves top priority to help psychology advance as a science.

One approach you can use to justify your exploratory study is to discuss real-life examples, case studies of your research area. Once your readers feel the area is important, you can further excite them by emphasizing that you're exploring new frontiers, boldly going where no investigators have gone before.

Explain Your Reasoning   In an exploratory study, as in all studies, you must explain the rationale for your hypothesis in detail. Since you're studying an unexplored dimension, you must give your readers the background to understand your predictions.

Therefore, be extremely thorough in detailing the logic behind your predictions—even if you think your predictions are just common sense. Not everyone will share your common sense.

How do you detail the logic behind "common sense" predictions? Even common sense predictions can often be justified by theory or research on related variables. For example, suppose you're interested in seeing how low-sensation seekers and high-sensation seekers differ in their reactions to stress. You might argue that differences would be expected based on the arousal optimization theory—the theory that we all have an ideal level of arousal. Thus, you might argue that high-sensation seekers like stress because it increases their arousal levels, whereas low-sensation seekers hate stress. In addition, you could argue that introversion–extroversion and sensation seeking are related concepts. Since they're related and stress has different effects on introverts and extroverts, stress should also have different effects on low-sensation seekers versus high-sensation seekers.

Defend Your Procedures   Finally, in an exploratory study you may be studying variables that have never been studied before. In that case, you can't use other people's measures and manipulations of your concepts. Explain why your manipulations and measures are valid.

Direct Replication

Demonstrate the Importance of the Original Study   To justify a direct replication, you should first show that the original study was important. To establish the study's importance, discuss its influence on psychology. To get some objective statistics to support your opinion, note the number of times the study has been cited using the *Citation Index* described in Appendix B.

Explain Why the Results Might Not Replicate   After establishing the study's importance, convince your readers that the study's results might not replicate. That is, argue that the original study was flawed, that the findings wouldn't occur today, that the findings contradict other published work, or that Type I or Type II errors occurred.

For instance, if the results from the original study were barely significant, you can justify a direct replication by arguing that a Type I error may have been committed. On the other hand, if the original study reported null results, you might argue that a Type II error occurred by claiming that random error or poor execution of the study may have hidden real differences. If the original study's finding seems to conflict with several other published papers, you have a compelling rationale for replicating the study.

Finally, you can justify a replication if you think the study wouldn't come out the same today. For example, you might want to replicate a conformity study because you feel that people are no longer as conforming as they were when the original study was conducted. Regardless of what approach you take, you must present a compelling rationale for any study that's merely a rerun of another study.

Systematic Replication

The systematic replication accomplishes everything the direct replication does and more. Therefore, every reason for doing a direct replication is also a reason for doing a systematic replication. In addition, you can justify a systematic replication by showing that modifying the procedures would improve the original study's power, construct validity, or external validity.

Improved Power   If you thought the original study's null results were due to Type II error, you might make a minor change in procedure to improve power. For example, you might use more subjects, more extreme levels of the predictor variable, or a better way of collecting the dependent measure (e.g., a more accurate stopwatch) than the original study.

Improved Construct Validity   You might also want to alter slightly the original study if you were concerned that the original study's results could be biased by demand characteristics. Thus, you might repeat the study using a double-blind procedure or you might use multiple levels of the treatment factor to help reduce or evaluate the effects of subject bias.

Improved External Validity   If you're systematically replicating a study to improve external validity, you should explain why you suspect the results may not generalize to different stimulus materials, levels of the treatment variable, or subjects. Even if it seems obvious to you why a study done on rats might not apply to humans; why a study done on college students may not apply to factory workers; why a study done on men may not apply to women; or why the results wouldn't hold if different levels of the treatment were used—spell out your reasons for suspecting that the results won't generalize.

Conceptual Replication

Most of the reasons for conducting a systematic or direct replication are also relevant for introducing and justifying a conceptual replication. In addition, the conceptual replication has several other unique selling points, depending on how you changed the original study.

Measurement Changes   Your conceptual replication might differ because you used a different way of measuring the criterion variable than the original authors. In that case, you should support your choice by showing how your measure is more reliable, sensitive, or valid than the original measure. To make the case for your measure, you may want to cite other studies that used it. As in the legal arena, precedent carries weight in psychology. If someone else published a study using a given measure, then the measure automatically gains some credibility.

Changes in the Manipulation of the Predictor Variable   If you manipulate the predictor variable differently from the original authors, you should start by defining the predictor variable. Next, you should discuss possible weaknesses with previous manipulations and then show why the one you're using avoids these weaknesses. Conclude by showing that your manipulation is consistent with conceptual definitions of the variable.

Changing the Design If you're changing the original study's design, explain why. If you're replicating a between-subjects design using a within-subjects design to improve power, tell your readers. If you're converting a within-subjects design to a between-subjects design because you feel subjects will be less likely to guess the hypothesis, tell your readers. Your readers will not instantaneously realize the advantages of using a different design.

Replication and Extension

Your study may go beyond a conceptual replication to looking at additional factors or measures. In that event, your introduction would contain everything a conceptual replication would and a rationale for the additional factors or measures as well.

Rationale for Additional Factors or Measures For example, suppose the original author found that people loaf in groups. You might think of a situation (e.g., a group where all members were good friends) where social loafing wouldn't occur. Thus, you might include friendship as a factor in your design. Be sure to justify your reasoning for including the factor, defend your manipulation of it, and state your predictions regarding it.

Rationale for Additional Criterion Variables Instead of adding a predictor variable to a study, you might add a criterion variable. Your purpose would be to discover the process behind the effect. Thus, in social loafing, you might collect measures of subjects' perceptions of others to find out the cognitive processes responsible for social loafing (e.g., perceptions that their efforts aren't being noticed). Or, you might record their interactions with others to find out the behavioral processes responsible for social loafing (e.g., working being punished, socializing being rewarded). Or, you might monitor arousal levels in an attempt to discover the physiological reasons for social loafing (e.g., lower physiological arousal in a group setting).

The tricky part about writing an introduction to a "process" study is convincing your readers that you really are measuring the underlying causes of a phenomenon. You must do more than merely show that these "processes" occur before the phenomenon. These processes could be incidental side effects of the treatment. For instance, a fever comes before you get ill and intensifies as you get sicker, but it doesn't cause you to be ill. It's just a symptom or side-effect of your illness. In the same way, a criterion variable may correlate with a phenomenon but not cause that phenomenon.

Theory Testing

If you're testing a prediction from a theory, there's good news and bad news. The good news is that you won't have to spend much effort justifying your study's importance. Almost everyone assumes that testing a theory is important.

The bad news is that not everyone will agree that your predictions follow from the theory. To protect yourself, you must clearly detail how your predictions follow from theory. By being clear, everyone will follow your logic, and some may even agree with it.

PLANNING YOUR PROCEDURES

You've reviewed the literature, developed a hypothesis, operationalized your variables, and stated your reasons for testing your hypothesis. But, your preliminary work is still not done. You must now plan the nitty gritty of your study. In other words, although you've probably decided on the general design (e.g., a 2 × 2) your plan is not complete until each minute detail has been thought through and written down. In your journal determine exactly, what procedure each subject will go through. For example, what instructions will they be given? Who will administer the treatment? Where? Will subjects be tested in groups or individually? How should the researcher interact with subjects? Although your answers must be accountable to issues of validity and reliability, your paramount concern must always be ethics. You don't have the right to harm another person.

Ethical Con-siderations: Human Research

Ethics should be the foundation of your research plan. You must be careful not to damage your subjects. Ideally, they should feel as well when they leave the study as when they began. Unfortunately, even in the most innocuous studies, protecting your subjects from discomfort is much easier said than done.

Weighing the Risks

Know the Risks Realize that any experience may be traumatic to some subjects. Trauma can occur from things you'd never think of as being traumatic. Because any study has risks and because you can't know all of them, don't test a single subject without your professor's permission.

To begin to sensitize yourself to the risks involved in your proposed study, list the 10 worst things that could possibly happen to subjects. If you're testing human subjects, be aware that not all subjects will react in the same way. Some may experience trauma because the study triggers some painful memory. Some may feel bad because they did poorly. Others may feel bad because they felt their behavior ruined your study. Realize that some of your subjects may be mentally imbalanced and any attack on their self-esteem might lead to disastrous consequences. Since subjects are so fragile, you should list some serious consequences in your worst case scenario.

Reducing Risks

Since any study has the potential for harm, the possibility of severe consequences doesn't mean that your professor won't allow you to do the study. However, you and your professor should think about ways to minimize the risks.

Screening Subjects   One method of minimizing risks is to screen out "vulnerable subjects." For instance, if there's any reason to believe that your study may increase heart rate or blood pressure, you may want to make sure that only people in good health participate in your study. If your study might harm people with very low self-esteem, you may want to only use subjects who are well adjusted and have high levels of self-esteem. Therefore, you might give a measure of self-esteem to potential subjects to eliminate those with low self-esteem.

Informed Consent   Not only should you screen subjects, but you should let subjects screen themselves. That is, subjects should be volunteers who give their **informed consent:** know what the study is about before volunteering for it.

But, how informed is informed consent? Very informed, when it comes to telling subjects about any unpleasant aspect of the study. If subjects are going to get shocked, exposed to loud noises, or extreme cold, they should be informed of this before volunteering to be in the study. Consequently, if your study does involve unpleasantness, you may have difficulty getting subjects to volunteer.

Informed consent is considerably less informed when it comes to more innocuous aspects of the study. After all, the study would be ruined if subjects knew everything that would happen (and why it happened) beforehand. So, although subjects are usually told the truth, they aren't always told the whole truth. For example, a memory experiment's description would mention that subjects have to memorize words, but might omit the fact that the researcher is looking at the order in which facts are recalled or that there's a surprise recall of all the lists at the end of the study.

Since subjects are not fully informed about your study, there may be some things about it that they dislike (e.g., the task may be too hard for them). Had they known about these features, they wouldn't have participated. What can you do about the problem of subjects being traumatized by something you didn't warn them about because you didn't think it would be traumatic? For example, suppose a subject finds it upsetting to try the surprise recall tasks?

One protection against these unexpected problems is to make sure subjects understand that they can quit the study at any time. So, before the subjects begin your study, tell them that if they find any aspect of the study uncomfortable, they can and should escape this discomfort by quitting the study. Assure them that it's their duty to quit if they experience discomfort and that they'll still get full credit.

Modifying the Study

You've seen that you can minimize ethical problems by letting subjects know what they're getting in for and by letting them gracefully withdraw from the study. You should also minimize harm by making your study as humane as possible. You can make your study more ethical by reducing the strength of your treatment manipulation, carefully selecting stimulus materials, and by being a conscientious researcher.

Reducing the Treatment Strength   Although using extreme levels of your predictor variable may help you get a significant change in the criterion variable, extreme levels may harm your subjects. For example, 24 hours of food deprivation is more likely to cause hunger than 12 hours. However, 24 hours of deprivation is more stressful to the subject. If you plan an unpleasant manipulation, remember your subjects' welfare and minimize the unpleasant consequences as much as possible. Consider using levels of the predictor variable that are less severe than you originally intended.

Modifying Stimulus Materials   By modifying your stimulus materials, you may be able to prevent them from triggering unpleasant memories. For instance, if you're interested in the effects of caffeine on memory for prose, you wouldn't want the prose passage to cover some topic like death, divorce, alcoholic parents, or rape. Instead, you'd want to use a passage covering a less emotional topic, such as sports. If the sports article referred to someone's death or car accident, you might want to delete that section.

The Conscientious Researcher

Often, it's not the study that's unethical, it's the researcher's arrogance. Although we know of a few subjects who were hurt as a direct result of a research manipulation, we know of many more who were hurt because the researcher treated them discourteously.

To ensure that you're sensitive, courteous, and respectful to all of your human subjects, you should do two things. First, when scheduling your research sessions, make sure you leave a 10-min gap between the end of one session and the beginning of the next session. Some investigators feel that, like a physician, they should efficiently schedule people one after another. Their "efficiency" results in subjects having to wait for the investigator, the investigator having to rush through the formalities of greeting subjects, or—even worse—investigators rushing through debriefing. Thus, the "efficient" investigator, like the efficient physician, is seen as unconcerned. Although this conduct doesn't become physicians, it's intolerable for psychological researchers! After a subject has given an hour of his or her time, you should be more than willing to answer any questions he has. Furthermore, if you rush through greeting the subject or debriefing, the subject will see you as uncaring, and as a result, you'll be less likely to be able to detect or remedy any harm your study may have caused. Therefore, we advise that you walk, not run, subjects.

Second, empower your subjects. That is, allow them to rate your study on a scale such as the one in Box 13-1. Give each subject's rating sheet to your instructor. Following this simple procedure helps you to appreciate each subject's individuality and makes them aware that you value their opinions.

Debriefing

Although you should try to anticipate and prevent every possible bad reaction to a subject, you won't be successful. Inevitably, your procedures will still cause some unpleasantness. After the study is over, you should try to remove this unpleasantness by debriefing your subjects, i.e., informing them about the study, reassuring them that their reactions were normal, and expressing your appreciation for their participation.

You should also listen to subjects and be sensitive to any unexpected, un-

---

BOX 13-1 Sample Debriefing Rating Scale

Serving as a subject in psychology studies should provide people with a first-hand look at research. On the scale below, please indicate how valuable or worthless you found today's study by circling a number from +3 to −3.

WORTHLESS: −3 −2 −1   +1 +2 +3 :VALUABLE

If you wish to explain your rating or to make comments on this study, either positive or negative, please do so below.

---

happy reactions to your study. By being a good listener, you should be able to undo any damage you may have unwittingly done.

In summary, you should be very concerned about ethics. Since ethics involve weighing the costs of the study against its potential benefits, you should do everything you can to minimize the risks to your subjects. If, despite your efforts, a subject experiences discomfort, you should try to reduce that discomfort during debriefing.

Ethical Considerations: Animal Research

With animals you incur the same responsibilities that you did with human subjects—you must protect them from undue stress and discomfort. In many ways you have even more responsibility to animal subjects because they're completely dependent on you for their mere existence. To fulfill your responsibility to animal subjects, you must follow the A.P.A.'s guidelines for proper housing, food and water, and handling (see Appendix A).

Furthermore, because your animal subjects don't have the power to give their informed consent (they aren't volunteers) nor to quit the study, you must carefully question the value of your study. Ask yourself and your professor this question: "Is the potential knowledge gained from the study worth the cost to the animals?". Finally, if you must euthanize your animal subjects at the end of your study, follow A.P.A.s guidelines to ensure that this is done in the most humane way.

Maximize the Benefits

For your study to be ethical, the potential benefits must be greater than the potential harm. Thus, an extremely harmless study can be unethical if the study has no potential benefits. So, just as you owe it to your subjects to reduce potential harm, you owe it to them to maximize the potential benefits of your study. You do this by making sure your study provides accurate information. That requires power, internal validity, and construct validity.

Power Is Knowledge

One of the most serious obstacles to obtaining accurate information is lack of power. Remember, null results don't prove the null hypothesis. They only make people wonder about the study's power. There's no point in doing a study that's so powerless that it will lead to inconclusive, null results.

To have power, you should have a strong predictor variable manipulation, a reliable, sensitive criterion variable, well-standardized procedures, homogeneous subjects, a sensitive design, and enough subjects.

Sample Size   Perhaps your most important obstacle to finding a significant effect is a lack of subjects. As a rule, you should have at least 16 subjects in each group. Of course, this number will be affected by the sensitivity of your design, the heterogeneity of your subjects, the number of observations you can get from a subject, the size of the difference you expect to find between conditions, and the reliability and sensitivity of your criterion variable.

If you have a within-subjects design, a reliable and sensitive criterion variable, and expect a rather large difference between your conditions, you may be able to use fewer than 16 subjects per group.

If, on the other hand, you're using a simple, between-subjects design, heterogenous subjects, a manipulation that may have little effect, and a relatively insensitive and unreliable criterion variable, you may want at least 60 subjects per group.

Hunting for Subjects
How are you going to get all the volunteer subjects you need to conduct a powerful study?

The Draft   Some researchers rely on "captive" samples. For example, many colleges "volunteer" students in introductory psychology courses for the research draft. In fact, most of the research strength of modern psychology has been built using this research draft. If your school has such a draft, count yourself among the blessed. All you have to do is ask your research design professor how to become a recruiter.

Enlisting Volunteers   If your school doesn't have a draft, an effective way of getting subjects is to ask professors to request volunteers from their classes. Many professors will gladly do this. Some will even give volunteers extra credit as an incentive for participating in your study.

Noncollege Samples   But what if you don't want to use college students in your study? For example, suppose you want to study children or retirees? Or suppose you agree with skeptics who claim that results from studies done on college students can't be applied to "normal people." Then, look beyond college classrooms for subjects. A note of caution: You may find that getting "real-world" subjects takes as much work and creativity as planning your study.

Children   If you're interested in studying children, you may still be able to take advantage of the "captive" audience approach. After all, most children can be found in classrooms. However, obtaining access to those children may turn into a bureaucratic nightmare. You'll have to obtain permission from all or many of the following: the school board, the superintendent, principal, teacher, parent, child, your professor, and your university. If you're going to get these permissions in time for your study, you'll need to plan ahead—and be very lucky.

Adults   Finding adult subjects can be even more challenging than finding children. For example, one of your text's authors wanted an adult population for her doctoral dissertation. Her first thought was to contact a major company and gain access to its employees. This tactic failed. Next, she tried to run a newspaper ad asking for volunteers. One newspaper refused to print it. Another would only run it in the "Personal" section with the ads for dates, astrology, and massages. Although a few "volunteers" called, most wanted a date or obscene conversation. We don't recommend newspaper ads.

Older Adults   The authors have had greater success recruiting elderly subjects. Nutrition centers, retirement communities, friendship networks, and nursing homes have been fruitful sources of subjects. In addition, we recommend the "grandmother connection": have an older relative or friend introduce you to other prospective subjects.

Obviously, finding human subjects will take planning, perseverance, and luck. Once you contact prospective subjects, you should explain your study to them and have them sign a permission form. The permission form will protect both you and your subjects. Basically, it states that you've explained the study to the volunteers and that they agree to participate. A sample permission form appears in Box 13-2. If minors are participating in your study, you need to have separate forms for both the subjects and their parents.

Animal Subjects   In many ways, animals are better subjects than humans. You don't have to worry about permission slips, extra credit, or obscene phone calls. Consult with your instructor about obtaining animals for your research. Often schools have rat colonies or purchase animals for student research.

Reducing Threats to Construct Validity

After ensuring that your study has adequate power, we'd like to be able to tell you that you can take it easy and relax. Unfortunately, you can't. Power is not your only concern when conducting psychological research. You must also be wary that the construct validity of your results may be destroyed by researchers failing to conduct your study in an objective, standardized way or subjects reacting in the way they think you want them to react to the treatment, rather than simply reacting.

Researcher Effects   If you use more than one investigator, you may be able to detect researcher effects by simply including the researcher as a factor in your design. In other words, randomly assign subjects to condition and to researcher. If you have two researchers and two treatment conditions (A and B), you'd have four conditions: A1, B1 (conditions run by Researcher 1), and A2, B2 (conditions run by Researcher 2). Then, do an analysis of variance (ANOVA) using the researcher as a factor to see whether different researchers got different results.

However, using ANOVA to detect researcher effect is not the solution to reducing researcher effects for two reasons. First, this statistical approach will only tell you if one researcher is getting different results from the other researchers. If all your researchers are biased, you may not obtain a significant researcher effect. Of course, if you're the only researcher, you can't use researcher as a factor in an ANOVA.

BOX 13-2   Consent Form

Students taking PSY 455, Research Design, are conducting research assessing the effects of noise and sleep deprivation on anxiety.

If you participate in this study, you will be deprived of sleep for two nights and exposed to common city noise for one hour. During that hour, you will be asked to fill out two questionnaires, and your pulse and blood pressure will be measured several times.

You will be asked to spend two nights in a special dorm room so that your sleep can be monitored. In addition, it will take 90 minutes for the noise treatment and measures to be completed.

You will receive $20 for participating in the study.

Physical injury, psychological injury, or deception are not part of this study. In addition, all your responses and answers will be held confidential. No one other than the investigators will see this information.

Any questions you have regarding this project should be addressed to the investigators or to Dr. _____, faculty supervisor.

If you agree to participate in this study, please sign the following statement.

_____

I have read the above consent form and understand the proposed project. I consent to participate in this study. I understand that I can quit the study at any time.

I will be paid $20 whether or not I complete the study.

_____   _____
Signature   Date

Second, and more importantly, detecting researcher effects is not the same as preventing them.

To prevent researcher effects, you must address the three major causes of researchers failing to conduct studies in an objective and standardized manner. First, researchers may not know how to behave because the procedures may not have been spelled out. Second, researchers may not be motivated or may not be able to follow the instructions. Third, the researchers may strongly expect or hope for subjects to behave in certain ways.

Loose Protocol Effect: The Importance of Developing a Protocol   Often, the researchers aren't behaving in an objective and standardized way because of the **loose protocol effect:** the instructions aren't detailed enough. Fortunately, the loose protocol effect can be avoided.

Before you start your study, carefully plan everything. As a first step, you should write out a set of instructions that chronicles the exact procedure for each subject. These procedures should be so specific that another person could test your subjects the same way you do.

To make your instructions specific, you might want to write a computer program based on them. Since computers don't assume anything, writing such a program forces you to spell everything out to the last detail. If you can't program, just write the script as if a robot were to administer the study. Write out each step, including the actual words that are spoken to subjects. The use of such a script will help standardize treatment, thus reducing threats to validity.

Once you have a detailed draft of your protocol, give it a test run. For example, to ensure that you're as specific as you think you are, pretend to be a subject and have several different people run the study using only your instructions. See how the different individuals behave. This may give you clues for tightening up your procedures. In addition, you should test several practice subjects. Notice if you change procedures in some subtle way across subjects. If so, adjust your instructions to eliminate this variability.

At the end of your practice runs, you should have a detailed set of instructions that you and any co-investigator can follow to the letter. To double-check your protocol consult Box 13-3.

Inspiring the Troops to Avoid Researcher Effects   Of course, even if you write your protocol (procedures) in detail, you or your co-investigators may still fail to follow that protocol. To avoid the researcher failure to follow protocol effect, you need to make sure that all investigators know the procedures and that everyone is motivated to follow them.

To make sure investigators learn the procedures, you should hold training sessions. Supervise investigators while they practice the procedures on each other and on practice subjects.

Once researchers know the right way to run the study, the key is to make sure that they're motivated to do so the same way every time. To increase researchers' motivation to be consistent, you might have them work in pairs. One researcher tests the subjects, the other takes notes while listening in through an intercom or watching through a one-way mirror. You may even wish to record research sessions.

If your researchers still have trouble following procedures, you may need to partially automate your study. For instance, you might use a computer to present instructions, administer the treatment, or collect the criterion measure. Computers have the reputation for following instructions exactly, therefore helping standardize your procedures. Of course, computers aren't the only machines that might help you. Some others include automated slide-projectors, tape recorders, and videotape recorders. Countless other devices can be used to record your data accurately, from electronic timers and counters to noise-level meters.

Researcher Expectancy Effect   The final source of researcher bias is the **researcher expectancy effect** or investigator bias: researcher's expectations are affecting the results. You can take three steps to prevent the researcher expectancy effect:

1. Be very specific about how investigators are to conduct themselves. Remember, researcher expectancies probably affect the results by changing the investigator's

---

BOX 13-3   Protocol Checklist

What is your hypothesis?

How will you manipulate your treatment variables?

How will you measure your dependent (criterion) variables?

How many subjects will you need?

Do you have your professor's permission?

Do you have a suitable place to test your subjects?

How will you get your subjects?

If you're using animals, how will they be cared for?

What will you do with your animals after the study?

If you're using human subjects, how will you make your sign-up sheets available to potential subjects?

Have you included a description of the study on the sign-up sheet?

Will subjects be rewarded for participating in your study (e.g., money or extra credit)?

If you're conducting an experiment, how will you assign subjects to condition?

Have you written a detailed research protocol?

If you're using human subjects, have you developed a consent form?

If you use volunteers from college classes, how will you notify professors about which students participated?

Will you inform participants about the outcome of your study? How?

---

behavior rather than by causing the investigator to send a telepathic message to the subjects.

2.   Don't let the investigators know the hypothesis.

3.   Don't let investigators know what condition the subject is in—making the investigator blind. Although making investigators blind is easiest in drug experiments where subjects take either a placebo or the real drug, it can be done in other experiments. For example, if you present stimuli in booklets, you can design your booklets for different conditions to look very similar. In that way, an investigator testing a group of subjects might not know what condition each subject is in. For some studies, you may be able to use a second investigator who does nothing except collect the criterion variable. This second investigator could easily be kept in the dark as to subject condition.

Whether you're the only investigator or one of a team, researcher effects may bias your results. Therefore, you should always try to prevent the loose protocol effect, the failure to follow protocol effect, and the researcher expectancy effect.

Subject Effects   Unfortunately, in psychological research, you must beware not only of researcher effects, but also of **subject effects** or biases: subjects may see through the study and try to play along with what the investigator wants. Fortunately, there are various ways of preventing subject bias.

1.   PREVENTING SUBJECT BIAS. For starters, you might make your researcher blind to reduce the chance that the subject will get any ideas from her. In experimental investigations, you might use a between-subjects design rather than a within-subjects design because subjects who are only exposed to one treatment condition are less likely to guess the hypothesis than subjects who are exposed to all treatment conditions.

2.   PLACEBO TREATMENTS. A related tactic is to prevent subjects from knowing whether they're in the comparison or treatment condition. Therefore, if you have comparison conditions, use placebo treatments rather than empty comparison conditions. To further confuse subjects who may behave differently simply because they think they're in the treatment group, you might use several treatment conditions rather than a single one.

3.   UNOBTRUSIVE RECORDING. Subjects are less likely to know the hypothesis if they don't know what you're measuring. Obviously, if they don't even know they're being observed—as in some field studies—they won't know what you're measuring. Thus, if your hypothesis is an obvious one, you may try to do a field study. (But make sure that you aren't invading subjects' privacy!)

Although field studies lend themselves more easily to unobtrusive recording, unobtrusive recording can even occur in a laboratory study. For example, subjects may not know they're being observed if you can observe their behavior while you're out of the room by using an intercom or a one-way mirror.

4.   UNOBTRUSIVE MEASURES. Even if the subject knows you're watching, she doesn't have to know what you're watching. That is, you can use unobtrusive measures. For example, you might ask the subject to type an essay, using a computer keyboard. Although she thinks you're measuring the quality of the essay, you may have the computer programmed to monitor speed of typing, time in between paragraphs, number of errors made, or times a section was rewritten. In addition, you might also have tape-recorded and videotaped the subject, monitoring her facial expressions, number of vocalizations, and loudness of vocalizations.

Research Realism

Rather than trying to obscure or confuse subjects about the purpose of the study, you may try to prevent them from even thinking about it. How? By designing a study that has a high degree of **research** or experimental **realism:** a study that involves subjects in the task. Research realism means that subjects aren't playing a role or merely going through the motions, saying, "What does she really want me to do?" or "If I were a typical person, how would I behave in this situation?" Note that research

---

BOX 13-4 Ethics Checklist

Is a physically unpleasant stimulus going to be used in your study? If so, this fact should be clearly stated on the sign-up sheet and consent form.

What precautions are you taking to reduce potential harm to your subjects caused by a physically unpleasant stimulus?

Are you going to use stress of some sort (e.g., sense of insecurity or failure, assault upon values, fatigue, or sleep deprivation) in your study? If so, this fact should be clearly stated on the sign-up sheet and consent form.

What precautions are you going to take to reduce potential harm to your subjects caused by stress?

What will you do if subjects exhibit signs of harm (e.g., crying, disoriented behavior)?

Are you prepared to describe the purpose and nature of your study to your subjects during debriefing?

Will you use deception in your study? If so, what will you tell them during debriefing?

Are you aware that subjects can quit your study at any time? If a subject does drop out, will you give her/him credit for participating?

What educational gain do you think subjects will obtain from participating in your study?

How will you ensure the confidentiality of each subject's data?

---

realism doesn't mean the study is like real life; it means that subjects are engrossed in the task. In this age of videogames, even a fairly artificial task can be very high in research realism.

Ethics Summary

You should now understand how vital ethics are to the plan of your study. You must not only ensure the safety of your subjects but demonstrate the validity of your methods. To help you evaluate the ethics of your proposed study, consult Box 13-4, Appendix A, and your professor.

WRITING THE METHOD SECTION

Now that you've thoroughly thought out each step of your study, you're ready to write the method section of your proposal. This is the how section—here you'll explain exactly how you plan to conduct your study.

There are several subsections to the method section: subjects, design, apparatus, and procedure. To help you write each subsection, we recommend you review several journal articles to get a feeling for the amount of detail you should include.

Subjects

In the subjects section, you'll describe the general characteristics of your subjects. State how many subjects you plan to have, how many will be male, how many will be female, their ages, how you plan to obtain them, and any other relevant information (e.g., what strain of rat). You should also indicate when and where they'll be tested and whether they'll be tested individually or in groups. If they'll be tested in groups, you should state the size of the groups. If you plan to exclude data from some subjects (e.g., extreme scores), state your reasons and criteria for exclusion.

The subjects section is written in a straightforward and somewhat mechanical fashion. In fact, it's so mechanical that you can use the fill-in-the-blank example in Box 13-5 to write most subjects sections.

Design

The design is also easy to write. Merely describe the design of your study. For an experiment, state the number of levels for each independent variable, whether the variable is a between- or within-subjects variable, and the dependent variable. Again, if you consult Box 13-5 you can write a design section by filling in the blanks.

Apparatus

In the apparatus section, describe the equipment you plan to use. This includes laboratory equipment, tests, computers, etc.

If you plan to use equipment made by a company, list the brand name and the make of the product. If you designed your equipment, briefly describe it. You need to give enough detail so that readers will have a general idea of how it looks. If it's a test or questionnaire, reference the source of the test, and give at least one example of a typical item. This gives readers a feel for what the subjects will see. In the appendix of your proposal, include a copy or diagram of your apparatus.

Procedure

The procedure section tells your readers what happened to subjects in your study. In essence, it's a summary of your protocol. How much detail should you include? Here are two tips to help you answer this question. First, include any methodological wrinkles that you feel are critical to the study's internal, external, and construct validity. Second, read the procedure sections of several related studies and mimic their style. Don't worry if it seems too brief. You'll be including your complete protocol in the appendix of your proposal.

Putting the Method Section Together

Place your method section directly after the introduction. Identify the start of the method section with a centered heading labeled **Method** one double-spaced line below the last line of the introduction. On the next double-spaced line, label your subjects section. The word **Subjects** should be at the left margin and underlined. The text for the subjects section should start on the next line. The apparatus and procedures sections should be presented in the same fashion as the subjects section. That is, they should be at the left margin, underlined, and the text for each should start on the line below the heading.

STUDENT SUBJECTS

Subjects were _____ (#) (__ (#) male, __ (#) female) undergraduates who participated in the study/experiment:

1. to receive extra credit for introductory psychology
2. to fulfill a course requirement
3. for money
4. other

During the (fall, winter, spring, summer) of 19 __ subjects were tested (individually, in groups of _____) .

IF APPROPRIATE ADD

Subjects were randomly assigned to (#) __ conditions.

Data from (#) __ subjects were not analyzed because:

1. they didn't follow instructions
2. they quit the study
3. their data were lost
4. other

_____ Subjects were in the _____ condition, and (#) _____ subjects were in the _____ condition.

ANIMAL SUBJECTS

Subjects were (#) _____ (__ (#) male, (#) __ female):

1. rats
2. pigeons
3. other

They were (#) __ days old at the start of the experiment and were maintained at (%) __ of their free-feeding weight. They were randomly assigned to condition.

Fill-in-the-Blank Design Section

The design was an (name of the treatment variable or brief description of levels × name of the treatment variable or brief description of levels within/ between subjects, factorial/functional design. The dependent/criterion variable(s) were _____ .

WRITING THE RESULTS SECTION

In the results section of your proposal you should state how you plan to analyze your data. Remember that the primary goal of selecting particular statistical tests is to accurately and fairly test your hypotheses. Therefore, this is a good place to restate each of your hypotheses and explain how each will be tested. What statistical tests will you use? Will your data conform to the assumptions of those tests? For example, if you plan to use analysis of variance, will your study yield at least interval data? If not, you better choose another statistic.

If you're conducting a manipulation check, explain how you plan to analyze it at the start of the proposal's results section. Then present the analyses for each hypothesis.

Your results section should immediately follow the methods section. Center the title **Results** one double-spaced line below the last line of the method section.

WRITING THE DISCUSSION SECTION

Once you've decided how you'll analyze your data, you're ready to discuss how you'll interpret them. If your hypotheses are supported, how will this information relate to the literature and arguments you covered in the introduction? How will you interpret results that don't confirm your hypotheses?

In addition, the discussion is the place to present the limitations of your study and to speculate about future research needs stemming from your study.

Your discussion section will come directly after the results section. Once again, the title **Discussion,** should be centered one double-spaced line below the last line of the Results section.

PUTTING ON THE FRONT AND BACK

You've written the introduction, method, results, and discussion sections. Now it's time to return to the beginning of your proposal and write the title and abstract.

The Front

Title
The title is the first thing readers will see. It should be simple, direct, honest, and informative. Ideally, it should be a brief statement about your predictor and criterion variables.

Avoid being too cute or obscure. If there's some catchy saying or title that you must include, use a colon to add this extra title to the simpler title. Such a title might be, "The effect of eating sugar on anxiety: A bittersweet effect."

The title should appear centered on a separate piece of paper. Two lines below the title, center your name. Two lines below your name, center the name of the course (e.g., PSY 250: Research Methods).

The title should also appear, centered, at the top of the first page of your introduction.

Abstract

The abstract comes after your title. The abstract is a short, one-page summary of your research proposal.

Jolley, Murray, & Keller (1984) give six basic sentences that can be used to write most abstracts. The first sentence describes the general research topic (e.g., Love is a common topic in popular music). The order of the next five sentences often varies. However, there should be a sentence that gives the number of subjects and their treatment (e.g., sixteen subjects will listen to love ballads for one hour, while 16 control subjects will sit in a quiet room for one hour). In a third sentence, you should explain how you plan to measure the criterion variable (e.g., Subjects will fill out the Reuben Love-Like Scale 10 minutes after treatment). You should describe the hypothesis in a fourth sentence (e.g., It is hypothesized that listening to love ballads will raise scores on the Love-Like Scale). The final sentence will be reserved for your research report. In this sentence, you'll describe the main results—the results that relate to your hypothesis.

The abstract should appear on a separate sheet of paper following the title page. The heading **Abstract** should appear centered at the top of the page. The text of your abstract should begin one double-spaced line below the heading.

The Back Now that you've written the title and abstract, it's time to write your reference list. To help you organize your references, we suggest you write each reference on an index card and alphabetize the cards. If you have more than one reference for an author, put the cards for that author in chronological order. By writing them on cards before you type them up, you reduce the chances of omitting a reference or typing them out of order.

You should use the reference style given in the American Psychological Association's *Publication Manual* (1983) pp. 118–33. This style is also consistent with the Modern Language Association's style manual (MLA). For a few examples of proper referencing see Box 13-6.

References should be typed on a separate sheet of paper and appear at the end of your proposal.

THE VALUE OF PRACTICE

Even after you've carefully designed your study, modified it based on comments from your instructor, and been given your professor's "go ahead" to run it, you may still want to conduct a pilot study: test several subjects (friends, family members, other members of the class), just for practice. By testing practice subjects, you'll get some of the "bugs" out of your study. You'll discover:

1. whether subjects perceive your manipulation the way you intend
2. whether you can perform the study the same way every time
3. whether you're providing the right amount of time for each of the research tasks and whether you're allowing enough time in between tasks
4. whether your instructions are clear

BOX 13-6   Sample References

BOOK

Lifton, R.J. (1968). <u>Death in life</u>. New York: Random House.

EDITED BOOK (REFERENCE FOR ENTIRE WORK)

Etzold, T.H., & Gaddis, J.L. (Eds.). (1978). <u>Containment: Documents on American policy and strategy, 1945–1950</u>. New York: Columbia University Press.

ARTICLE OR CHAPTER IN AN EDITED VOLUME

Gaddis, J.L. (1978). The strategy of containment. In T.H. Etzold & J.L. Gaddis (Eds.), <u>Containment: Documents on American policy and strategy, 1945–1950</u> (pp. 25–41). New York: Columbia University Press.

JOURNAL ARTICLE

Hatch, O.G. (1982). Psychology, society, and politics. <u>American Psychologist</u>, 42, 29–33.

UNPUBLISHED MANUSCRIPT

Hilgard, E. (1945). <u>Psychological problems of the coming peace</u>. Unpublished manuscript, SPSSI Archives, University of Akron, Akron, OH.

---

5. whether your cover story is believable
6. how subjects like the study
7. how long it takes you to run and debrief a subject

   In short, testing practice subjects helps you to fine-tune your study and hone your investigative skills.

CONDUCTING THE STUDY

The dress rehearsal is over. Final changes in your proposal have been made. Now you're ready for the real thing—to run your study! This section will show you how.

Establishing Rapport
As you might imagine, your prospective subjects may be apprehensive about the study. Subjects often aren't sure whether they're in the right place, whether they know what's going to happen to them, or whether the researcher is a Dr. Frankenstein.

To put them at ease, let your subjects know they're in the right place. And be courteous. You should be both friendly and business-like. Greet the subject warmly, pays close attention to her and seem concerned that she knows what will happen in the study. Be obviously concerned that each subject is treated humanely and that the study is done professionally.

Being professional enhances your image with your subjects. Why? Most subjects like knowing that they're involved in something important. And some will view your efficiency as a way of showing that you value their time—which you should.

So, how can you exude a professional manner? Some novice investigators think that being professional means acting casually. Nothing could be further from the truth. Subjects are very put off by a disinterested attitude. They feel that you are unconcerned with the study and with them.

To appear professional, you should be neatly dressed, enthusiastic, well organized, and prompt. Not only should you have written out a detailed script, but you should be ready and waiting for your subjects at least 10 minutes before the study is scheduled to begin. Once your subjects arrive, concentrate exclusively on the job at hand until the study is over. Never ask a subject to wait a few minutes while you socialize with friends.

What do you lose by being a "professional" investigator? Problem subjects. If you seem enthusiastic and professional, your subjects will also become involved in doing your study—even if the tasks are relatively boring. Thus, if you're professional in your manner and attitude, you'll probably not even have to ask the subjects to refrain from chatting throughout the study. Similarly, if you're professional, subjects will stop asking questions when you say, "I'll explain the purpose at the end of the study."

After you've established rapport with your subjects, you need to give them instructions. To get them to follow instructions exactly, you might:

1. be repetitive
2. have subjects read the instructions, and then you should orally paraphrase those instructions
3. run subjects individually
4. ask subjects to ask questions
5. have subjects demonstrate they understand the instructions by quizzing them or by giving them a practice trial before beginning the study

Once the study has begun, try to follow the procedure to the letter. Don't let subjects change your behavior by reinforcing you or punishing you. For instance, suppose subjects are asked to count backwards by threes for 20 seconds. Some subjects will thank you for telling them they can stop; others will plead nonverbally for you to stop. Don't let any of these strategies affect how long you have them count.

Once the study is over, you should debrief your subjects. Generally, in debriefing you should first try to find out whether the subjects suspected the hypothesis. Simply ask what they thought the study was about. Then, you should explain the purpose of your study. **Debriefing**

If you deceived your subjects, you need to make sure they aren't upset about the deception and that they understand why deception was necessary. Subjects should leave the study appreciating the fact that deception was the only way to get good information about an important issue.

Making sure subjects accept your rationale for deception is crucial for three reasons. First, you don't want them to feel humiliated or angry at you. Second, if they get mad, they may not only be mad at you but at psychologists in general. Perhaps the anger or humiliation might stop them from visiting a psychologist when they need help. Third, the unhappy subject may spread the word about your deception, ruining your chances of deceiving other subjects.

After explaining the purpose of the study, you should answer any questions the subjects have. Although answering questions may sometimes seem like a waste of time, you owe it to your subjects. They gave you their time, now it's your turn.

After subjects' questions and doubts have been dealt with, give them an opportunity to rate how valuable they felt the study was. These ratings: 1) encourage you to be courteous to your subjects, 2) let you know if your study is more traumatic than you originally thought, and 3) make subjects feel that you value their opinions.

After the rating, you should assure subjects that their responses during the study will be kept confidential. Tell them that no one but you will know their responses. Then, ask the subjects not to talk about the study because it's still in progress. For example, you might ask them not to talk about the study until next week. Finally, you should thank your subjects, escort them back to the waiting area, and say good-bye.

PROTECTING DATA: CONFIDENTIALITY

You might think that once a subject leaves the study, your responsibilities to him end. Wrong! You're still responsible for guaranteeing that subject's privacy. Knowledge about a given subject is between you (the investigator) and the subject—no one else. Never violate this confidentiality. To ensure confidentiality the following precautions should be taken:

1. Assign each subject a number. When you refer to a given subject, always use the assigned number, never that subject's name.
2. Never store a subject's name and data in a computer—this could be a hacker's delight.

3. If you have subjects write their names on booklets, tear off and destroy the cover of the booklet after you've analyzed your data.

4. Store a list of subjects and their numbers in one place and the data with the subjects' numbers on it in another place.

5. Watch your mouth. There is rarely a reason to talk casually about a subject's behavior. Even if you don't mention any names, other people may guess or think they've guessed the identity of your subject.

ANALYZING DATA

After you've finished testing your subjects and made plans to protect the data, you're ready to start analyzing and interpreting it. The statistical tests you perform depend on the nature of your hypothesis, the kind of data you have, and the particular design you selected. To perform that analysis, consult the chapter in this book that corresponds to the design you selected.

WRITING THE FINAL REPORT

Much of the work on your research report has already been done. Essentially, your research proposal was the first draft of your research report. To complete your final report follow the advice in this section.

What Stays the Same or Changes Very Little

The title page, introduction, and references from your proposal can be transferred to your research report without any changes. The method section needs to be rewritten adding changes in procedures that resulted from the pilot study. Remember to rewrite the method section in the past tense: in the proposal you told people what you were going to do, in the report you need to tell them what you did.

The abstract should also be rewritten to reflect what you found. Remember to add that sixth sentence, i.e., describe the main results.

Writing the Results Section

Depending on the study, you'll report anywhere from one to three kinds of results: results of the manipulation check, results relating to your hypothesis, and other significant results.

Results of the Manipulation Check

If you used a manipulation check, you should put these findings at the beginning of the results section. Although these results will usually be statistically significant and unsurprising, it's important to demonstrate that you manipulated what you said you were going to manipulate. Thus, reporting the outcome of your manipulation check is a good lead into discussing results relating to your hypothesis.

Results Relating to Your Hypothesis

Once you've reported the results of your manipulation check, present the results relating to your hypothesis. As you introduce these results, clearly connect them to your hypotheses so that your readers can easily tell how the hypotheses fared. For example, if you hypothesized that people who own cats are less likely to hit their children, report what the data said about this hypothesis: "The hypothesis that people who own cats are less likely to hit their children was supported. Cat owners hit their children on the average 2.3 times a month per child, whereas people who did not own cats hit their children on the average 4.6 times, $F(1,64) = 18.2$, $p<.05$."

Other Significant Results

After reporting results relating to your hypotheses (whether or not the results were significant), you should report any other statistically significant results. Even if the results are unwanted and make no sense to you, significant results must be reported. Therefore you might report: "There was an unanticipated interaction between gender of the child and cat ownership. Parents of females were more likely to own cats, $F(1,64) = 20.1$, $p <.05$."

Tips on Writing the Results Section

Report the Statistic in the Text   When you report a result, always give the statistic, value, and level of significance. For examples of how to report specific statistical tests in text see Table 13-1.

Table It   Create a table listing all the analyses relating to your hypotheses. Make sure to indicate in the table: the statistical test used, the criterion and predictor variables, the statistical values, and the level of significance. Tables 13-2 and 13-3 are two examples.

When you type your report, make sure to refer to the tables in the text of your paper (e.g., "As Table 1 indicates . . ."). Tables should be numbered sequentially

TABLE 13-1   How to Report Statistical Tests in Text

Statistic	df	Numerical Value	Probability
F	(2,46)	= 3.85,	$p <.05$
t	(24)	= 3.0	$p <.001$
r		= .71,	$p <.01$
χ^2	(6,$N^* = 80$)	= 11.48,	$p <.05$

*Note: With χ^2 report *df* and sample size (*N*).

TABLE 13-2 Pearson Product Moment Correlation for Self-Esteem

Group	Body Concept attractiveness	fitness
Female	.65***	.50**
Male	.35*	.70***

*$p<.05$, **$p<.01$, ***$p<.001$

as they appear in the text of your paper. Although you'll actually place all tables and graphs at the end of your report, your professor will probably want you to indicate where each table would be inserted if you were to place it in the results section. Generally, you'll sandwich this information between the first paragraph that mentions the table and the next paragraph. Centered between these two paragraphs type "Insert Table *table number* about here."

You may be asking yourself, why not put the actual table there, rather than indicate an intention to do so? Most journals require research reports to be submitted this way because it's easier to typeset tables separately and insert them as close as possible to the reference later. Regard this research report as preparation for your first journal article.

Graph It As the saying goes, "A picture is worth a thousand words." Therefore, graphing the means for all predicted effects (effects relating to your hypotheses) and all other significant findings is an effective way of showing your results. Remember to label the axes and give an informative heading for each graph. In your research report, you'll refer to all graphs as figures. As with tables, you should refer to all figures in text, number them sequentially, and indicate where they should be inserted. Place all graphs at the end of your report.

TABLE 13-3 Analysis of Variance: for Self-Esteem Data

Source	SS	df	MS	F
Between (exercise)	499.41	2	249.71	9.75
Within (error)	145.76	57	2.56	

WRITING THE DISCUSSION SECTION

In the discussion section of your report you should summarize the main findings of your study. Relate these findings to the literature and the arguments you presented in your introduction. Speculate about the reasons for any surprising results. Finally, discuss the limitations of your study, and reemphasize the importance of the research problem.

SUMMARY

Well, you've done it! If you followed the instructions in this book, and carefully followed all the advice in this chapter, you should have just completed a carefully planned, meaningful, and ethical research project. Congratulations and best wishes for your continued success as a psychological researcher!

MAIN POINTS

1. The research journal is a way to document and think through your research decisions.
2. The research proposal will also aid you in planning your research. However, it's more formal than the journal and should conform to the *Publication Manual* of the American Psychological Association.
3. In the introduction of your proposal you need to demonstrate the importance of your study. Critique and summarize relevant research. This critique should be the springboard for you to articulate the reasoning behind your hypothesis. Next explain what you plan to do in your study and why.
4. Before you write the rest of your proposal you should carefully plan out each step of your study in your journal.
5. Ethics should be your primary concern when planning your research.
6. You must carefully weigh the potential harm your manipulations may cause subjects against the potential benefits your study might yield. Every effort should be made to reduce risks by: screening subjects, using informed consent, modifying your design or stimulus materials, and debriefing subjects.
7. When using animal subjects you must plan for 24-hour care of the animal. An ethical researcher is a humane researcher.
8. Ethics don't just apply to the treatment and care of subjects. An ethical study is a well-planned study that maximizes the probability of finding existing differences between your groups. Thus, your study should have power and construct validity.
9. Once you've planned out every detail of your study you should formalize your plan in the method, results, and discussion sections of your proposal.
10. The method section is the "how" section, where you explain how you plan to conduct your study.

11. In the results section you'll plan your statistical analyses. What kind of data will you have? What kind of statistical tests are appropriate to test your hypotheses?

12. In the discussion section you'll explore the implications of possible research findings for your hypotheses and the future of psychology.

13. Once the body of the paper is finished, write your abstract (a brief summary of your proposal) and the title and reference sections of your proposal.

14. The pilot study is recommended as a way to get the "bugs" out of your proposal and get your proposal in shape for the actual study.

15. In addition to a well-developed plan, the key to conducting good research is to be a courteous and professionally mannered investigator. This includes establishing rapport with your subjects and properly debriefing them.

16. Remember all data is confidential.

17. When you analyze your data make sure that it conforms to the assumptions of the statistical test you plan to use.

18. Much of your final research report will be based on your proposal.

19. The title page, introduction, methods, and reference sections of your proposal can be transferred directly to your research report.

20. In the results section of your report, present the results of your manipulations check and your hypotheses and other significant findings.

21. In the discussion section of your report, summarize the main findings of your study and relate these to the literature and arguments you presented in your introduction.

Appendix A

ETHICAL GUIDELINES FOR RESEARCH

AMERICAN PSYCHOLOGICAL ASSOCIATION'S PRINCIPLES GOVERNING THE TREATMENT OF HUMAN PARTICIPANTS

A. In planning a study, the investigator has the responsibility to make a careful evaluation of its ethical acceptability. To the extent that the weighing of scientific and human values suggests a compromise of any principle, the investigator incurs correspondingly serious obligation to seek ethical advice and to observe stringent safeguards to protect the rights of human participants.

B. Considering whether a participant in a planned study will be a "subject at risk" or a "subject at minimal risk," according to recognized standards, is of primary ethical concern to the investigator.

C. The investigator always retains the responsibility for ensuring ethical practice in research. The investigator is also responsible for the ethical treatment of research participants by collaborators, assistants, students, and employees, all of whom, however, incur similar obligations.

D. Except in minimal-risk research, the investigator establishes a clear and fair agreement with research participants, prior to their participation, that clarifies the obligations and responsibilities of each. The investigator has the obligation to honor all promises and commitments included in that agreement. The investigator informs the participants of all aspects of the research that might reasonably be expected to influence willingness to participate and explains all other aspects of the research about which the participants inquire. Failure to make full disclosure prior to obtaining informed consent requires additional safeguards to protect the welfare and dignity of the research participants. Research with children or with participants who have impairments that would limit understanding and/or communication requires special safeguarding procedures.

E. Methodological requirements of a study may make the use of concealment or deception necessary. Before conducting such a study, the investigator has a special responsibility to: i) determine whether the use of such techniques is justified by the study's prospective scientific, educational, or applied value; ii) determine whether alternative procedures are available that do not use concealment or deception; and

iii) ensure that the participants are provided with sufficient explanation as soon as possible.

F. The investigator respects the individual's freedom to decline to participate in or to withdraw from the research at any time. The obligation to protect this freedom requires careful thought and consideration when the investigator is in a position of authority or influence over the participant. Such positions of authority include, but are not limited to, situations in which research participation is required as part of employment or in which the participant is a student, client, or employee of the investigator.

G. The investigator protects the participant from physical and mental discomfort, harm, and anger that may arise from research procedures. If risks of such consequences exist, the investigator informs the participant of that fact. Research procedures likely to cause serious or lasting harm to a participant are not used unless the failure to use these procedures might expose the participant to risk of greater harm, or unless the research has great potential benefit and fully informed and voluntary consent is obtained from each participant. The participant should be informed of procedures for contacting the investigator within a reasonable time period following participation should stress, potential harm, or related questions or concerns arise.

H. After the data are collected the investigator provides the participant with information about the nature of the study and attempts to remove any misconceptions that may have arisen. Where scientific or humane values justify delaying or withholding this information, the investigator incurs a special responsibility to monitor the research and to ensure that there are no damaging consequences for the participant.

I. Where research procedures result in undesirable consequences for the individual participant, the investigator has the responsibility to detect and remove or correct these consequences, including long-term effects.

J. Information obtained about a research participant during the course of an investigation is confidential unless otherwise agreed upon in advance. When the possibility exists that others may obtain access to such information, this possibility, together with the plans for protecting confidentiality, is explained to the participant as part of the procedure for obtaining informed consent.

Note. From *American Psychologist*, 1981, *36*, pp. 633–638. Copyright 1981 by the American Psychological Association. Reprinted by permission.

AMERICAN PSYCHOLOGICAL ASSOCIATION'S PRINCIPLES GOVERNING THE CARE AND USE OF ANIMALS

I. General

A. The acquisition, care, and use of all animals must be in compliance with relevant federal, state, and local laws and regulations and with international conventions to which the U.S. is a party.

B. Psychologists working with animals must be familiar with Principle 10 (Care and Use of Animals) of the "Ethical Principles of Psychologists" of the APA (*American Psychologist*, 1981, *36*, 633–638) and research must be conducted in a manner consistent with that principle.*

C. The guidelines shall be conspicuously posted in every laboratory, teaching facility, or other setting in which animals are maintained and used by psychologists and their students.

D. Considerations limited to the time, convenience, or expense of a procedure do not justify violations of any of the principles included in this document.

E. Violations of these guidelines should be reported to the facility supervisor. . . . If not resolved on the local level, allegations of violations of these guidelines or Principle 10 of the Ethical Principles of Psychologists should be referred to the APA Ethics Committee, which is empowered to impose sanctions.

F. Psychologists may consult with the Committee on Animal Research and Experimentation at any stage preparatory to, or during, a research project for advice about the appropriateness of research procedures or ethical issues related to experiments with animals. Individuals with any questions concerning these guidelines should consult with the Committee on Animal Research and Experimentation.

G. Psychologists are strongly encouraged to become familiar with the ethical principles of animal research. To facilitate this, the Committee on Animal Research and Experimentation will maintain a list of appropriate references.

II. Personnel

A. A supervisor, experienced in the care and use of laboratory animals, shall closely monitor and be responsible for the health, comfort, and humane treatment of all animals within the particular facility.

B. A veterinarian shall be available for consultation regarding housing, nutrition, animal care procedures, health, and medical attention. The veterinarian should conduct periodic inspections of the facility at least twice a year.

C. Psychologists shall ensure that all individuals using animals under their supervision have received explicit instruction in experimental methods and in the care, maintenance, and handling of the species being studied. Responsibilities and activities of all individuals dealing with animals shall be consistent with their respective competencies, training, and experience.

D. It is the responsibility of the psychologist to be cognizant of and to comply with all federal, state, city, or local laws pertaining to the acquisition, care, use, and disposal of animals. Investigators should also be fully familiar with the "NIH Guide for the Care and Use of Laboratory Animals."

---

*An investigator of animal behavior strives to advance understanding of basic behavioral principles and/or to contribute to the improvement of human health and welfare. In seeking these ends, the investigator ensures the welfare of animals and treats them humanely. Laws and regulations notwithstanding, an animal's immediate protection depends upon the scientist's own conscience.

Note. Reprinted from New animal guidelines. (1985, April). *APA Monitor*, p. 6. Used with the kind permission of the American Psychological Association.

E. It is the responsibility of the supervisor of the facility to ensure that adequate records of the utilization and disposition of animals are maintained.

F. It is the responsibility of the supervisor of the facility to ensure that all personnel involved in the care, maintenance, and handling of animals be familiar with these guidelines.

III. Facilities

A. The facilities housing animals shall be designed to conform with specifications in the "NIH Guide for the Care and Use of Laboratory Animals" and in relevant legislation.

B. Investigators are encouraged to seek accreditation of their facilities from such organizations as the American Association for Accreditation of Laboratory Animal Care (AAALAC).

C. Research may not be conducted until it has been reviewed by a local institutional committee to ensure that procedures are appropriate and humane. The committee should have representation from within the institution and, when possible, from the local community.

IV. Acquisition of Animals

A. When appropriate, animals intended for use in the laboratory should be bred for that purpose.

B. Animals not bred in the researcher's facility must be acquired lawfully from reliable sources. The U.S. Department of Agriculture (USDA) may be consulted for information regarding suppliers.

C. Animals taken from the wild should be trapped in a humane manner and in accordance with local, state, and federal laws.

D. Investigators should ensure that those responsible for transporting animals to the research facility provide adequate food, water, ventilation, and space, and impose no unnecessary stress on the animals.

E. Endangered species or taxa should be utilized only with full attention to required permits and ethical concerns not covered by legislation. Information can be obtained from the Office of Endangered Species, U.S. Department of the Interior, Fish and Wildlife Service, Washington, D.C. 20240. Similar caution should be used in work with threatened species.

V. Care and Housing Animals

Responsibility for the conditions under which animals are kept, both within and outside of the context of active experimentation or teaching, rests jointly upon the investigator or instructor and those individuals appointed by the institution to administer animal care. Housing must be consistent with all relevant laws and standards and, when feasible, should enable the animals to express their natural behavior. Animals should be provided with humane care and healthful conditions during their entire stay in the facility.

VI. Justification of the Research

A.   Research should be undertaken with a clear scientific purpose. There should be a reasonable expectation that the research will:

> **1.**   Increase our knowledge of the processes underlying the evolution, development, control, or biological significance of behavior;
> **2.**   Increase understanding of the species under study in the research; or
> **3.**   Provide results that benefit the health or welfare of humans or other animals.

B.   The contributions to knowledge or to health expected to result from the research should be sufficient to benefit as to outweigh any distress to the animals used.
C.   The psychologist should monitor the animals' welfare throughout the course of an investigation in order to ensure continued justification for the research.

VII. Experimental Design

A.   The investigator should consider the possibility of using alternatives to animals in research and teaching whenever appropriate.
B.   Humane considerations should constitute one of the major sets of factors that enter into the design of research. In particular, several relevant considerations should be noted:

> **1.**   The species chosen for study should be well suited to answer the question(s) posed. When the research involves procedures that are likely to cause pain or discomfort to the animal and when any of several species are equally appropriate to answer the scientific questions asked, the researcher should employ the species that appears likely to experience least distress.
> **2.**   The number of animals utilized in a study should be sufficient to provide a clear answer to the question posed. Care should be exercised to use the minimum number of animals consistent with sound experimental design, especially where the procedures might cause pain or discomfort to the animals.

VIII. Experimental Procedures: Humane considerations for the well-being of the animal should be incorporated into the design and conduct of all procedures involving animals.

A.   Procedures which involve no pain or distress to the animal, or in which the animal is anesthetized and is euthanized before regaining consciousness, are acceptable if the investigator abides by the principles enunciated in these guidelines.
B.   Experiments involving pain that is not relieved by medication or other acceptable methods should be undertaken only with justification as noted above (Section VI).

C. An animal observed to be in a state of severe distress or pain which cannot be alleviated should be euthanized immediately, using a humane, approved method.

D. The use of aversive stimuli should be undertaken only with justification as noted above (Section VI). Care should be taken to adjust the parameters of aversive stimulation to levels that appear minimal, though compatible with the aims of the research. Investigators are encouraged and should be able to control the effects of acute experimental pain (e.g., by escape or avoidance behavior).

E. Procedures involving food or water deprivation should be used only when less stressful procedures are inappropriate to the design and purpose of the experiment. Minimal levels of deprivation consistent with the goals of the research should be used.

F. Prolonged physical restraint should be used only after less stressful procedures are inappropriate to the design and purpose of the experiment. Minimal levels of deprivation consistent with the goals of the research should be used.

G. Procedures that entail extreme environment conditions, such as high or low temperatures, high humidity, modified atmospheric pressure, etc. should be undertaken only with justification as noted above (Section VI).

H. Studies entailing prey killing or intensive aggressive interactions among animals should be fully justified and conducted in a manner that minimizes extent and duration of pain.

I. Procedures entailing the deliberate infliction of trauma should be restricted and used only with very strong justification. Animals used in such experiments should be anesthetized.

J. Procedures involving the use of paralytic agents without reduction in pain sensation require particular prudence and humane concern. Utilization of muscle relaxants or paralytics alone during surgery or other invasive procedures, without general anesthesia, is unacceptable, and should not be used for surgical restraint.

K. Surgical procedures, because of their intrusive nature, require close supervision and attention to humane considerations by the investigator.

1. All surgical procedures and anesthetization should be conducted under the direct supervision of a qualified scientist who is competent in the use of the procedure.

2. If the surgical procedure is likely to cause greater discomfort than that attending anesthetization, the animals should be rendered incapable of perceiving pain and maintained in that condition until the experiment or procedure is ended.

3. Sound postoperative care and monitoring must be provided to minimize discomfort, prevent infection and other untoward consequences of the procedure.

4. As a general rule, animals should not be subjected to successive surgical procedures unless this is required by the nature of the research. However, there may be occasions when it is preferable to carry out more than one procedure on a few animals than to carry out a single procedure on several animals. The alternatives must be carefully weighed, and the guiding principle is to cause the least possible distress on the fewest possible animals.

IX. Field Research

A. Field workers should disturb their populations as little as possible. Investigators should make every effort to minimize potential harmful effects of the study on the population and on other plant and animal species in the area.

B. Research conducted in populated areas should be done in a manner that is in accordance with all laws and with respect for the property and privacy of the inhabitants of the area.

C. Particular justification is required for the study of endangered species. Such research should not be conducted unless all requisite permits are obtained.

X. Educational Use of Animals

A. When animals are used solely for educational rather than research purposes, the consideration of possible benefits accruing from their use versus the cost in terms of animal distress must take into account the fact that no new knowledge is likely to be acquired and some of the procedures which can be justified for educational purposes.

B. Classroom demonstrations involving animals should be used only when instructional objectives cannot effectively be achieved through the use of videotapes, films or other alternatives. Careful consideration should be given to the question of whether the type of demonstration is warranted by the anticipated instructional gain.

C. Student projects involving pain or distress to animals should be undertaken judiciously and only when the training objectives cannot be achieved in any other way. Greater justification is required if there is no anticipated new scientific knowledge but only learning or practice of established procedures by students.

D. Demonstrations of scientific knowledge in such contexts as exhibits, conferences, or seminars do not justify the use of painful procedures or multiple surgical interventions. Audio-visual alternatives should be considered.

XI. Disposition of Animals

A. When an animal is no longer needed, alternatives to euthanasia should be considered.

    1. Animals may be distributed to colleagues who can utilize them. Care should be taken that such a procedure does not expose the animal to excessive surgical or other invasive or painful procedures. The investigator donating animals should be assured that the proposed use by the recipient colleague has the approval of or will be evaluated by the appropriate institutional animal care committee and that humane treatment will be continued. It may sometimes be feasible to return wild-trapped animals to the field. This should be done only when there is reasonable assurance that such release will not detrimentally affect the fauna and environment of the area and when the ability of the animal to survive in nature has not been seriously impaired. Unless conservation efforts dictate otherwise, release should normally occur within the same area from which animals were originally trapped. Animals reared in the laboratory generally should not be released; either they cannot survive or they may survive and disrupt the natural ecology.

B. When euthanasia constitutes the most humane form of disposition of an animal at the conclusion of an experiment:

    1. Euthanasia must be carried out in compliance with all federal, state, city, and local laws.

    2. Euthanasia must be accomplished in such a humane manner, appropriate for the species under anesthesia or in such a way as to ensure immediate death in accordance with procedures approved by the institutional care committee.

    3. No animal is to be discarded until its death is verified.

    4. Disposal of euthanized animals should be accomplished in a manner that is in accord with all relevant legislation, consistent with health, environmental, and aesthetic concerns, and approved by the institutional animal care committee.

Appendix B

LIBRARY RESOURCES

This appendix is your introduction to library references for psychology and other behavioral sciences. By reading this appendix you'll learn what references to look for and how to use them.

Library research is a necessary and useful component of any research project. It can help you devise your basic research question and refine it, and inform you about research and theories that relate to your question. Furthermore, a thorough search through your library's resources can save you from wasting time and effort by directing your attention to designs and manipulations that other researchers have found fruitless or promising.

PSYCHOLOGICAL ABSTRACTS

The *Psychological Abstracts* give brief summaries of work published in psychology and related fields. Although *Psychological Abstracts* are a very useful resource, finding your references can be very tedious and time consuming. A good first step is to look in the *Psychological Thesaurus* that's usually located with the abstracts. The thesaurus will tell you other subject titles under which your criterion variable might be listed. For example, "self" is also called identity, personality, and ego. Once you've found your criterion variable in the thesaurus you're ready to tackle the abstracts.

Several issues of *Psychological Abstracts* are published each year. All of the issues published in a given year are identified by the same volume number. For example, all of the issues published in 1985 are classified as Volume 72. Most libraries bind together the abstract issues that bear the same volume number. However, the abstracts for this year have not yet been bound together and can be found in several soft-bound issues that share the same volume number.

In the back of each issue are author and subject indexes for that issue. And for each of the hardbound volumes there is a corresponding hardbound index. This index will bear the same volume number as the abstracts it indexes. In these hardbound indexes, both author and subject listings are given. For all indexes, abstracts are identified by an abstract number, e.g., 129 in volume 58's index. This tells you that the abstract is the 129th abstract in volume 58. Although this sounds rather complicated, this method gives you many alternative ways of finding references.

Looking up Abstracts by Subject

If you're trying to find recent references, locate the abstract issues for this year. In the back of each issue find your criterion variable in the subject index. For easy referral, write the numbers of the abstracts indexed under your criterion variable and look them up in that issue.

If you want to locate references for previous years, find the hardbound indexes that correspond to those years. Look up your criterion variable in the subject index. Write down the volume number of the index and the abstract numbers.

Looking up References by Author

If you know the names of researchers who've investigated your criterion variable, simply look up their names in either an issue or volume index.

Browsing through the Abstracts

The *Psychological Abstracts* are organized by both year and subject. That is, in a given volume, all abstracts on the same topic are located together. Thus, once you find an abstract that addresses your criterion variable examine the abstracts located near it.

Finding the Original Resource

From reading an abstract you'll have a good idea whether you want to read the original source. If so, you'll find a reference for the original publication with the abstract. Go to your library's catalogue files to locate the original source. If your library doesn't own it, try interlibrary loan.

SOCIAL SCIENCES INDEX

This is a comprehensive source for journal references in all the social sciences. In addition to psychology, such fields as anthropology, sociology, social work, and geography are included. Since psychologists aren't the only people that conduct behavioral research, *Social Science Index* can help you locate useful references published in nonpsychological journals.

Like *Psychological Abstracts*, several issues are published each year. The issues for a particular year are identified by the same volume number and bound together in hardback. However, the issues for this year won't be bound together. Therefore, to find the most recent indexes, look for several softbound issues that bear the same volume number.

In the front of each index, you'll find a list of abbreviations for the journals indexed, a list of addresses for those journals, an explanation of other abbreviations used in the index, and a sample entry. These lists and this example will help you interpret the references given under your criterion variable.

To use this index, look up your criterion variable under the appropriate subject heading. You may wish to take a look at the *Psychological Thesaurus* located with the *Psychological Abstracts* to find other subject headings related to your criterion variable. Each index entry (reference) is organized in the following order:

Title, author, brief description, journal, volume number, pages, month, and year.

Most of this information is presented in abbreviated form. Remember to look at the guides presented at the beginning of each index to interpret these abbreviations. An index entry might read:

Reactivity of adults in timed tests. M. Davis, bibl. J. Gent.P. *19:*907–14, D, '85.

In this example, the "bibl." means it is a bibliography—you've hit a goldmine! In other words, this is a list of references on your criterion variable. The article was published in the *Journal of Genetic Psychology*, Volume *19*, pages 907–914, in December of 1985.

As you've noted, indexes don't provide summaries of the articles referenced.

SOCIAL SCIENCE CITATION INDEX

This is a superior index to the *Social Sciences Index* because it offers you several different ways to locate references. Each year, the *Social Science Citation Index* indexes over 70 thousand articles that appear in more than two thousand journals. This resource actually consists of three separate, but related indexes. Included are a subject index, author index, and citation index. Each index covers the same journal articles but indexes them in different ways. Depending on the kind of information you're seeking, and the information already available on the topic, any one of these indexes can be an effective starting point. Once you locate relevant articles, the information they provide (title words, reference citations, authors, etc.) can be used to enter the other indexes to continue the search.

The Subject Index

In the PERMUTERM SUBJECT INDEX (PSI) every major word from the title of an article is paired with every major word in that title. For example, if an article was titled "Sex differences in the effect of television viewing on aggression" the article would be indexed under Sex Differences and Aggression; Sex Differences and Television Viewing; and Television Viewing and Aggression. These permuted (arranged in all possible ways) pairs are alphabetically listed as two-level indexing entries and linked to the names of the authors who used them in the titles of their articles. For example,

Aggression
    SEX DIFFERENCES   ERON M
    TELEVISION VIEWING   BUNKER A

Sex Differences
    AGGRESSION   ERON M
    TELEVISION VIEWING   MUTIN SS

Television Viewing
    AGGRESSION   BUNKER A
    SEX DIFFERENCES   MUTIN SS

Thus, the PSI tells you that during the period indexed, the authors Bunker and Mutin used the words shown opposite their name ("Aggression" and "Sex Differences" respectively).

To use PSI, simply think of words and word pairs that are likely to appear in the titles of articles related to your criterion variable. By looking up these words you'll discover the names of authors who've used the words in the titles of their articles. Once you've found those names, look them up in the Source Index.

The Source Index

The SOURCE INDEX is a straightforward author index to the articles covered each year. For each article indexed, you're given the language in which it's written (if it isn't English), its title, authors, journal, volume number, page numbers, year, the number of references cited in the article, and the journal issue number. In addition, beginning with the May-August 1974 issue, references contained in each indexed article are listed. To facilitate reprint requests and other correspondence, a mailing address is often provided for each first author. Below is a sample entry of the SOURCE INDEX:

> BUNKER, A
>   (SP) THE RELATIONSHIP OF AGGRESSION AND TV VIEWING
>   *J APPL PSY*   25   09   87   20R N3
>   CTR FOR REHABILITATIVE CHANGE, CENTER AVENUE
>   NEW MEXICO, MEXICO
>   ADAMS 2   *INTERN. J OF PSY*   45   60   12
>   ALISTAR F   *J OF BEH MED*   20   21   09

One of the sections of the SOURCE INDEX lists current authors according to the organization with which they're affiliated. Another section lists anonymously authored articles according to the name of the publication in which it appeared.

The Citation Index

The final index is the CITATION INDEX. This index is based on the concept that authors' references (citations) to previously published material indicate that the current article is related to the same topic as the older (cited) reference. In addition, articles that refer to (cite) the same publications, usually address the same topic.

Applying these relationships, the CITATION INDEX shows for the time period covered which previously published items are being cited in the current literature, who is doing the citing, and in what journals they're being cited. It is organized alphabetically by the names of the authors of the items receiving the citations. Following each cited item is a list of the current articles that're giving the citations. These are also arranged alphabetically by the names of their authors. Special sections of the CITATION INDEX cover journal articles that cite anonymously authored items, and articles that cite items that are authored by an organization rather than an individual. Cited items can be books, articles, letters, theses, or any other type of published material and can be from any time period.

To start a search in the CITATION INDEX, look up the name of an author or organization known to have published material relevant to your criterion variable. If any of the previously published works of that author or organization have been cited during the indexing period specified, the item will appear and those doing the citing will be listed. The names of the citing authors are then used to enter the Source Index for a complete description of the citing articles.

In summary, there are four basic types of searches you can do with the *Social Sciences Citation Index*. You can do a Citation search when an earlier key paper relevant to your variable is known. You can use a Permuterm search when you don't know of an earlier, relevant paper. An Author search is best used when you have the name of an author who's published work on your criterion variable. Finally, you can do an Organization search when you know the name of an organization that's involved with your criterion variable.

CURRENT CONTENTS

This volume lists the table of contents for several journals. This can be very useful since the criterion variable is usually mentioned in the title of the article. Thus, by looking at titles you can determine which articles you want to find and read. Although you might initially prefer that the articles were organized by topic rather than by journal, you'll soon find that most journals only cover certain topics. That is, if you're looking for a measure of aggression, you wouldn't look at the contents for *The Journal of Memory and Cognition*.

COMPUTER SEARCHES

Your most thorough and efficient method of locating references is an "on-line" computer search. This service gives you rapid access to indexes and abstracts that are stored in the computer. If you plan ahead, a computer search can save you hours of looking through abstracts and indexes. It will look through all of the resources we've discussed in this section, plus many more. Why not let the computer do the searching so you can have more time to plan and execute your study?

A major advantage of a computer search is that you can cross-reference two or more variables. To cross-reference variables on a computer search you must first come up with the variables. Once you have your research idea this shouldn't be very difficult. For example, if your topic is aggression in food-deprived monkeys, the computer will find only those references that concern "aggression" in "food-deprived" "monkeys". If you were using just an abstract or index, you could only look up one (two at the most) of these variables at a time. Thus, if you looked up aggression you'd have to read through all the references concerning aggression in humans, rats, birds, and lions to find ones that dealt with monkeys. You'd then have to sort through all the scattered monkey listings to find "food-deprived" monkeys. Obviously an on-line computer search can save you a lot of time in the library.

The actual search is usually conducted by a specialist in the library. Your task is to give this person a list of key words that will locate the references you need. Once you provide these key words, it may take a week or two to get your list of references. This is why you must plan ahead. Find out from your library how much time it will take.

An additional word of caution regarding on-line searches is that they may cost you money. Although many schools provide this service free to students, it's not uncommon for students to be charged $5.00 or more. Generally, the more variables you use in the search, the more the search will cost.

ADDITIONAL INFORMATION

For more information about these and other resources consult your reference librarian or professor. By doing library research, you'll learn how people have measured your criterion variable. You'll learn about measures that seem to work well and others that don't. Finding a measure that doesn't work can be valuable because it will save you from repeating someone else's mistake. Finding a measure that does work is obviously valuable because you could use or copy that measure.

Appendix C

USING THE COMPUTER TO ASSIST IN RUNNING SUBJECTS

There are numerous advantages to using a computer to run subjects. Most of these advantages stem from the fact that the computer will do exactly what it's told.

Since you must tell the computer exactly what to do, you're forced to think through every detail of your procedure before you run a single subject. Then, you must write out (program) each step. By comparing the programs for the different conditions, you can readily observe every single difference between your various treatment conditions. Thus, you can easily see whether all differences between conditions are relevant to the treatment variable. If there are any nontreatment differences between conditions, you can try to eliminate them. Consequently, programming can help you make your treatment manipulation as pure as possible.

Another consequence of having to program every step of the procedure is that you become aware of the decisions you're making at each step. By focussing your concentration in these ways, programming may improve your procedures. In addition, this keen awareness of what the procedure is and why should make writing the method section easier.

Although you get some benefits from writing a program, the major benefits come from having the computer use your program. Because the computer follows instructions exactly, a computerized study is the ultimate in standardization: Everyone receives the same instructions and stimuli—procedures are not inadvertently changed as the study goes on. This high degree of standardization reduces error variance, thereby increasing your study's power.

This high degree of standardization also ensures that subjects aren't reinforced for responding in a way that supports the hypothesis. Whereas a human experimenter might nod and smile for "correct" answers and frown for "incorrect" answers, the computer responds the same way, regardless of how the subject responds. Therefore, a computerized study reduces experimenter bias. Finally, because the computer follows the program to the letter, anyone who has your program can exactly replicate your study.

In addition to standardizing the presentation of instructions and stimuli, programming can also help you collect data. Computers have three advantages over humans when it comes to collecting data. First, they can sometimes collect data more unobtrusively than humans. The computer can stealthily monitor how fast the subject is typing, how fast she's answering questions, etc. Second, computers don't get tired or bored and can thus tirelessly record hours of bar-pressing or physiological responses. Third, computers record without bias. Since computers are blind to the hypothesis, they never deliberately change a response or interpret an answer to make the data more consistent with the hypothesis.

Beyond being consistent about presenting stimuli and collecting data, computers can also motivate subjects to attend to the task. Some subjects are more impressed with a study if it's on computer. After all, if it's computerized, it must be scientific. Others are motivated by a computer study because the computer interacts with them; it reacts immediately to their responses. To capitalize on the motivating aspect of the computer's responsiveness, some investigators program the computer to call the subject by name. Other investigators go even farther by making their study resemble a video game.

Of course, all this programming takes time and effort. But in the final analysis, it may save time and effort. For example, you may save time by running several subjects at once if you have more than one computer. You may also save time by running fewer subjects because your high degree of standardization has reduced error variance. Finally, running subjects on a computer should be less draining. The computer, by presenting and recording data, is doing your job for you!

Fortunately, you can also take advantage of the computer's ability to run subjects even if you know nothing about programming. How? You can take advantage of "user-friendly" programs especially designed to run subjects—if you're lucky enough to have access to one of these programs. If you aren't that fortunate, you can quickly learn the rudiments of programming. In two hours, you can learn enough to program a computer to help you test subjects for certain kinds of studies. Although you may have heard that learning programming is like learning another language, most of the commands you'll need don't sound very foreign. That is, the commands "print," "end," "goto," "if," "clear screen" should all have a familiar ring.

We don't mean to say that in two hours you'll know enough to make the computer randomly assign subjects to condition, present instructions, present stimulus materials, record and store data, debrief subjects, and analyze your data. You won't.

But having the computer do everything isn't necessary. In fact, for both ethical and practical reasons, we don't believe that researchers should have computers do everything.

For ethical reasons, we feel that you shouldn't have the computer debrief subjects. Instead, you should personally debrief subjects. Why? Beyond the obvious arguments that subjects may have questions that they wouldn't ask a computer or questions that a computer couldn't answer, we feel that to debrief subjects by computer is dehumanizing.

For practical reasons, we feel that you shouldn't have the computer do anything that could be done just as well by other means. In other words, we urge you to fight the urge to "overprogram." The most common overprogramming error is to have the computer store the data for all the subjects in the study. We know of many researchers who wrote—or paid professional programmers to write—programs that ended up incorrectly storing data. Only after the study was over, did these researchers realize that they didn't have any data they could analyze. Therefore, we urge that you have the computer print out each subject's data right after the subject has been debriefed.

Of course, what constitutes an overprogramming error depends both on your ability as a programmer and on the advantages of having that particular task computerized. For example, suppose you can easily write a program to do everything in a study except randomly assign subjects to condition. Some people would spend hours trying to program the computer to randomly assign subjects. However, we suggest that you consider randomly assigning the subjects yourself. In other words, don't program just for sake of programming, program to improve your study.

You can dramatically improve your study by programming only a small aspect of it. For example, you might write a program that only gives instructions. Such a program might improve your study by standardizing some of the procedures and reducing experimenter bias.

If you had a program that only presented stimuli, you'd also standardize your procedures and reduce experimenter bias. In addition, such a program might eliminate the time and expense of other ways of presenting stimuli. For example, if you were going to present your stimuli in a booklet, computer presentation would save you the trouble of duplicating, collating, and stapling them together. Finally, and most importantly, such a program would force you to think through your procedures very carefully before you ran the study. As a result, writing the method section should be easier.

If you had a program that only recorded responses, you'd again reduce the possibility of experimenter bias. In addition, you could have the program record behavior unobtrusively. For example, the program could record how long it took subjects to respond without them knowing they were being timed. Finally, since the computer is not easily bored, you could have it record responses for hours. For example, if you were measuring physiological responses or bar-pressing behavior over a period of hours, the computer could record the data continuously.

What can go wrong? If you're having the computer run any part of your study, you have to be concerned about two things:

1. will subjects do what you want and
2. will the computer do what you want

There are several things you can do to maximize the chances that subjects will do what you want. First, you should greet them and find out if they have computerphobia. If they do, you should do your best to allay this fear. By all means, tell them that you're available if they don't understand something. Beyond that, your efforts to get subjects to warm up to the computer could range from showing them how to press the keys to having them play a game on it.

Once you've done your best to assure subjects that the computer won't bite, the rest is up to your program. You should have made sure that your instructions are extremely detailed, clear, and repetitious. Try to get some people who know nothing about computers to be pilot subjects in your study to ensure that your instructions are clear enough. Once your instructions are clear, see what happens when a subject presses the wrong button. For example, if a subject is supposed to answer "a, b, c, or d," see what happens when "4" or "e" is pressed. Ideally, the program should tell the subject that the wrong button was pressed and to please try again.

Once you have the study set up so that the subject will follow instructions, make sure that the computer is doing what you want. Unfortunately, just because the computer is doing what it's supposed to in one condition, doesn't mean that's the case for all conditions. Therefore, check each condition. Generally, we find that **numerous** test runs are necessary because fixing one error may cause other errors or cause you to have to make other changes. Consequently, we recommend that you spend at least one day more than you think necessary to test a program. The first day, we check to make sure it's working. Then, we print out a listing of the program. The listing makes it easier for us to catch spelling errors and to compare programs side by side. On the second day, we fix any small errors we catch and recheck the program. On the third day, we recheck the program again. If we don't change anything, then we're finished. However, if we change anything at all, we come back for a fourth day of testing.

Once the program is working to your satisfaction, you should make at least one back-up copy (An unwritten rule of research with computers is that diskettes will go bad). Then, as an extra precaution, you should print out a listing of your program.

Appendix D

MARKETING YOUR RESEARCH SKILLS

In this course, you've learned how to conduct and evaluate research. In the process, you've refined your ability to think critically, logically, and creatively. Furthermore, you've demonstrated the ability to plan and complete projects. In short, you now possess some highly marketable skills.

ABILITY TO ASK QUESTIONS

One of the skills you've refined is the ability to ask questions. Not only have you formulated your own research questions, but you've learned how to question research findings and practices.

Your mastery of the art of question asking—often called critical thinking—will be respected by researchers and nonresearchers alike. On a superficial level, this skill will help you because people will frequently judge you based on the kinds of questions you ask. From your questions, others can decide how educated, informed, or intelligent you are. The key to impressing people is often not what you know, nor who you know, but what you ask.

On a deeper level (and the reason people value intelligent questioners), the ability to question is vital to success. When people make disastrous decisions, it's usually because they failed to ask the right questions. Because critical thinking is so vital to success, entrance exams to medical, law, business, and graduate schools incorporate tests of critical thinking.

Ability to Ask Questions of Data

Although most intelligent people can ask intelligent questions, not all can ask intelligent questions of data. To most people, data are data. But you know that not all data are created equal. That is, you know that how data are collected affects how they can be interpreted. Before accepting data at face value, you try to determine what kind of design was used and whether that design was used properly. Thus, in looking at data from an "experiment," you ask how subjects were assigned, how independence was achieved, how subject and experimenter bias were reduced, etc. In looking at an observational design, you question whether temporal precedence could be inferred, what threats to ceteris paribus were present, how observer bias was reduced, etc.

In addition to questioning how data were collected, you also question how they were analyzed. Your eyes no longer glaze over when you hear terms like "interaction," "statistically significant," etc. In fact, you're so familiar with data that you may be able to suggest alternative ways of presenting, interpreting, or analyzing existing information. In short, you're aware of what the analyses say—and what they don't.

ABILITY TO GET ANSWERS

Although your finesse at scrutinizing, interpreting, and using existing data is very marketable, your most marketable asset may be your ability to create new data. That is, not only do you know how to ask questions, you know how to get answers because you know how to make the abstract concrete.

By operationalizing variables, you can turn unanswerable questions into answerable ones. Thus, the question: "Will a diet plan be a financial success?" becomes the question: "Will a diet plan with these features, marketed in this way, get X number of sales at Z price?"

You might be surprised at how rare and valuable this skill is. Even very intelligent people are mystified by individuals who can create the desired information. For example, in a recent trial, a lawyer was defending a cartoonist in a libel suit. The prosecutor claimed that everyone knew that the devious cartoon character was supposed to be his client. The cartoonist was so apprehensive about the case that he hired a psychologist to help him in selecting the jury. Even with the right jury, the lawyer was concerned. How could he defend his client against such a subjective charge? The psychologist mentioned that one way to answer such a question would be to survey people in the community and ask them who, if anybody, they thought the cartoon resembled. The lawyer's response: "You mean you could do that?" This true story shows that although you may tend to undervalue your ability to get answers, others won't.

MAKING LOGICAL ARGUMENTS

In this course, you've also refined your ability to think logically. You've had to be explicit about your logic and the assumptions you're making. In writing introductions and discussion sections, you've practiced spelling out the rationale and assumptions behind your thinking.

MAKING LOGICAL ARGUMENTS SUPPORTED BY DATA

In writing introduction, results, and discussion sections not only have you argued logically, but you've also used data to support your arguments. You've used data to support the assumptions behind your arguments as well as to support your conclusions. In addition to supporting your conclusions, you can refute arguments supported by data. For example, because you're aware of the limits of correlational data, you know that the statement, "Profits have increased since Jim took over. Therefore, Jim is a good manager," is not necessarily true. In short, you're well aware of the uses and abuses of data.

COMMUNICATING COMPLEX OR TECHNICAL INFORMATION

In this course, you've learned not only to think creatively, critically, and logically, but to articulate your reasoning. You've spelled out the rationale behind your study, the procedures you used, the results, and your conclusions. In addition, you've summarized the results of other studies, some of which contained complex and technical information. Your ability to coherently present complex information should be an asset, no matter what profession you enter.

PLANNING AND COMPLETING PROJECTS

Your skills in manipulating data, thinking logically, and articulating both your logic and your assumptions, and asking questions, analyzing, and interpreting data are only some of the skills you used in carrying out your research project. Planning the research project required those skills, in addition to the skills required in designing and implementing any kind of project. You had to take initiative, map out all your steps, anticipate potential flaws and problems, challenge your basic assumptions, choose from among several alternative courses of action, prepare a timeline, overcome inevitable obstacles to your progress, aggregate all the information, come to a conclusion, and compile the final report. We can't imagine a more strenuous test of your planning and problem-solving abilities.

SELLING YOURSELF

Clearly, you have much to offer a prospective employer. To get a good job, however, you must convince your employer that you have these skills. Your initial efforts to convince anyone of your value will involve sending a résumé and cover letter. To help you, we've prepared a sample (see Box D-1).

Prospective employers will want you to be able to back up your claims about your abilities. To convince them that you have the skills you claim, use your skills at constructing operational definitions to describe yourself in objective and quantifiable terms (e.g., don't say, I'm a good student; say I have a 3.7 G.P.A.). To help convince employers of your abilities, you may want to send them copies of your final research project.

Once you've convinced your prospective employers of your skills, you'll have to convince them that these skills will generalize to the job. That is, your prospective

```
                          RESUME

                     Ms. Ima Sharpe
                    100 Resource Drive
                  City of Industry, CA  76278
                     (426) 754-5533
```

OBJECTIVE: To be an asset to your company through the
application of my skills in writing, logical thinking,
organizing, research, communication, and leadership.

EDUCATION: B.A. The Wright University
               Major: Psychology
               Senior Thesis: Reducing errors on a motor task

WRITING SKILLS: The rigors of conducting good research have
honed my competencies in research proposal and report
writing.
     - I received an "A" for my research proposal.
     - My research report was handed out in class as an
       example of how a research report should be written.

LOGICAL THINKING SKILLS: Training in research methodology
has finely tuned my inductive and deductive reasoning.
These powers of critical thinking are vital for optimal
problem solving in any business situation.
     - independent thinking
     - ability to recognize problems
     - ability to ask the right questions
     - ability to make the abstract concrete
     - ability to generate possible solutions
     - ability to recognize the flaws of each solution
     - ability to determine the best solution through
       research and analysis of relevant variables

ORGANIZATIONAL SKILLS: In order to plan, execute, interpret,
and apply research I have developed organizational skills.
     - arranged for experimental facilities and equipment
     - recruited participants (subjects)
     - supervised and conducted an experiment
     - organized The Wright University's Annual Rat Olympics

RESEARCH SKILLS: As a consequence of my course in research
design I know many research techniques.
     - how to set up timetables for studies
     - survey research
     - experimental research
     - library research
     - how to use computer packages to analyze data
     - how to interpret statistics

ORAL PRESENTATION SKILLS: To effectively speak about
research I had to make the complex sound simple, the
technical sound basic. To speak convincingly about research
I had to be a good salesperson.
     - I presented an experimental report at a regional
       psychology conference.
     - I received an A^+ for a verbal critique of technical
       research in class.

LEADERSHIP:
     - President of PSI CHI
     - Vice-president of The Student Experimental Psychology
       Club

Reference: My research methods professor.

employer might say, "Sure, you're a good student and had a rigorous class, but how do I know you'll do well at this firm?" Respond to that question by asking another, "Would you hire a typist who had an excellent record as a typist at another company?" This implies that your skills were so basic that they, like typing, would generalize to any company. To successfully show the value of your skills, you should give specific examples of how they would apply to this particular job. Although Table D-1 should give you a general idea of how research skills might apply to business, you'll want your examples to be so specific and relevant that the interviewer could visualize you succeeding on the job. Of course, to generate these specific examples, you must learn as much about the job as possible before the interview. (As we've implied all along, everything boils down to having done your research.)

Despite your best efforts, some interviewers may not feel that your skills will generalize to their business. Some may say, "If you were a business major, I'd hire you without reservation. But you're not." At this point, it may be tempting to give up. After all, the interviewer is judging you on the basis of a superficial criterion—face validity. Although you may be sorely tempted to quit, don't.

Instead, try to see whether you can make a case for yourself on the basis of face validity. Mention any courses or internships you've had in business.

Because face validity has a big influence in the real world, you may want to acquire experiences that will improve the face validity of your candidacy. Fortunately, since face validity is superficial, it's often easy to acquire. For example, you can improve the face validity of your candidacy by

1. picking up the jargon of that field
2. subscribing to newspapers or journals in that field (*Wall Street Journal*)
3. doing a survey for a company (even free of charge), so you can put it on your résumé.

TABLE D-1 Similarities between the Executive and the Researcher

Executive	Researcher
Identifies problem	Identifies problem
Collects background data on problem	Collects background data on problem
Makes proposals to collect other needed information	Makes proposals to collect other needed information
Establishes timeline	Establishes timeline
Attends to detail	Attends to detail
Analyzes data	Analyzes data
Reports findings	Reports findings

4. doing research in the area in which you want a job. For example, one of our students wanted a job in personnel, so she did a research project on productivity and sent it to a prospective employer. She got the job.

In addition to marketing the general skills that you possess, you may want to market your specific research skills. These skills might be especially attractive to a small firm. Small companies may find that your ability to do research will save them from paying large fees to outside research consulting firms.

There are many ways in which a small firm might be able to use your skills. For example, you might conduct research relating to the company's workers. In this capacity, you might design surveys to assess worker's attitudes and opinions toward the company. Alternatively, you could assess the impact of training programs or policy changes on productivity.

You might also do some research to get feedback from customers. This could be as simple as designing questionnaires to find out who your customers are and what they like about your company, or it could be more complex. For instance, you might do research that would pretest the effectiveness of the ads your company is designing. Or, you might evaluate the effectiveness of a new advertising campaign. You may end up saving the company a lot of money by telling them where not to spend their advertising dollar.

Another avenue would be to use consumer input to develop a new product or service. For example, you might question them regarding features they desire in a product, cost they're willing to tolerate, where they would buy such a product, etc. You might also do a content analysis of the features of successful products of the same general nature—"What objective features do they all have in common?" Such advance planning could save your company from creating another Edsel.

If you want a job where you're constantly involved in research, there are several careers you should consider. If you enjoy the hands-on, interpersonal part of research, but don't like the writing, planning, and statistical analyses parts, you could become a field interviewer or a telephone interviewer. In addition, you might be able to get a job at a mental hospital as a psychological test administrator.

If you desire a job that would fully immerse you in research, you should consider market research jobs and research assistant jobs. Market research is one of the fastest growing fields in the country. Primarily, you'd conduct and analyze consumer surveys, but you might be able to do some laboratory research. Market researchers are hired by market research companies (of course), large advertising agencies, and most large companies.

Research assistant jobs are not as common, but they can be found. Many of these jobs focus on evaluation research. The purpose of evaluation research is to determine the effects of a program (job training program) or decide if a treatment (wellness center) is working. Thus, large hospitals and the federal government do a substantial amount of evaluation research.

Other jobs involve analyzing data the government has collected. The federal government collects data about almost anything you can imagine—from people's attitudes toward life to how much meat they buy. The government needs research assistants to help analyze the data collected from the census and from numerous other surveys.

There are also jobs working for institutions who do research for the federal government. That is, universities and large research companies, (Rand Company, Battelle) which receive government money to do ground-breaking research, often have research assistant jobs. In addition, some universities also have jobs for laboratory assistants—people who will maintain their animal laboratory.

CONCLUSION

As you know, research design requires the ability to clearly define problems, propose solutions to those problems, and implement those solutions **on time.** In performing your projects, you demonstrated initiative in problem solving, attention to detail, logical thinking, and lucid writing. In short, you're able to ask questions and get answers. Virtually all employers need people with your skills.

Certain employers (research firms) will immediately recognize that they need your skills. Other employers, equally desperate for your skills, may not recognize that they need you. You'll need to convince them by using your persuasive ability and the strategies we suggested earlier. In addition, you may want to improve the appearance of your application by taking courses that will improve its face validity (see Table D-2). Good Luck!

TABLE D-2   Specific Jobs Available to a Good Research Design Student and Courses that Would Help in Obtaining that Job

Job Title	Supplementary Course
Business person	Accounting
Interviewer	Public Speaking
Laboratory Assistant	Neuropsychology with lab
Marketing Researcher	Marketing
Newspaper Reporter	English/Journalism
Personnel Administrator	Personnel Psychology
Public Health Statistician	Biology
Public Opinion Researcher	Computer Science
Research Assistant—Company	Computer Science
Research Assistant—Government	Computer Science
Research Assistant—Hospital	Biology with lab
Research Assistant—Mental Health	Testing
Technical Writer	English/Journalism

Appendix E

STATISTICS AND RANDOM NUMBERS TABLES

TABLE A-1 Critical Values of *t*

Level of Significance for Two-tailed *t*-Test

df	0.2	0.1	0.05	0.02	0.01
1	3.078	6.314	12.706	31.821	63.657
2	1.886	2.920	4.303	6.965	9.925
3	1.638	2.353	3.182	4.541	5.841
4	1.533	2.132	2.776	3.747	4.604
5	1.476	2.015	2.571	3.365	4.032
6	1.440	1.943	2.447	3.143	3.707
7	1.415	1.895	2.365	2.998	3.499
8	1.397	1.860	2.306	2.896	3.355
9	1.383	1.833	2.262	2.821	3.250
10	1.372	1.812	2.228	2.764	3.169
11	1.363	1.796	2.201	2.718	3.106
12	1.356	1.782	2.179	2.681	3.055
13	1.350	1.771	2.160	2.650	3.012
14	1.345	1.761	2.145	2.624	2.977
15	1.341	1.753	2.131	2.602	2.947
16	1.337	1.746	2.120	2.583	2.921
17	1.333	1.740	2.110	2.567	2.898
18	1.330	1.734	2.101	2.552	2.878
19	1.328	1.729	2.093	2.539	2.861
20	1.325	1.725	2.086	2.528	2.845
21	1.323	1.721	2.080	2.518	2.831
22	1.321	1.717	2.074	2.508	2.819
23	1.319	1.714	2.069	2.500	2.807
24	1.318	1.711	2.064	2.492	2.797
25	1.316	1.708	2.060	2.485	2.787
26	1.315	1.706	2.056	2.479	2.779
27	1.314	1.703	2.052	2.473	2.771
28	1.313	1.701	2.048	2.467	2.763
29	1.311	1.699	2.045	2.462	2.756
30	1.310	1.697	2.042	2.457	2.750
40	1.303	1.684	2.021	2.423	2.704
60	1.296	1.671	2.000	2.390	2.660
120	1.289	1.658	1.980	2.358	2.617
∞	1.282	1.645	1.960	2.326	2.576

This table is abridged from Table 12 of the *Biometrika Tables for Statisticians*, (Vol. 1, 3rd ed.) by E. S. Pearson and H. O. Hartley, (Eds.), 1970, New York: Cambridge University Press. Used with the kind permission of the Biometrika trustees.

TABLE A-2 Upper Percentage Points of the Chi Square Distribution

df \ Q	0.250	0.100	0.050	0.025	0.010	0.005	0.001
1	1.32330	2.70554	3.84146	5.02389	6.63490	7.87944	10.828
2	2.77259	4.60517	5.99147	7.37776	9.21034	10.5966	13.816
3	4.10835	6.25139	7.81473	9.34840	11.3449	12.8381	16.266
4	5.38527	7.77944	9.48773	11.1433	13.2767	14.8602	18.467
5	6.62568	9.23635	11.0705	12.8325	15.0863	16.7496	20.515
6	7.84080	10.6446	12.5916	14.4494	16.8119	18.5476	22.458
7	9.03715	12.0170	14.0671	16.0128	18.4753	20.2777	24.322
8	10.2188	13.3616	15.5073	17.5346	20.0902	21.9550	26.125
9	11.3887	14.6837	16.9190	19.0228	21.6660	23.5893	27.877
10	12.5489	15.9871	18.3070	20.4831	23.2093	25.1882	29.588
11	13.7007	17.2750	19.6751	21.9200	24.7250	26.7569	31.264
12	14.8454	18.5494	21.0261	23.3367	26.2170	28.2995	32.909
13	15.9839	19.8119	22.3621	24.7356	27.6883	29.8194	34.528
14	17.1170	21.0642	23.6848	26.1190	29.1413	31.3193	36.123
15	18.2451	22.3072	24.9958	27.4884	30.5779	32.8013	37.697
16	19.3688	23.5418	26.2962	28.8454	31.9999	34.2672	39.252
17	20.4887	24.7690	27.5871	30.1910	33.4087	35.7185	40.790
18	21.6049	25.9894	28.8693	31.5264	34.8053	37.1564	42.312
19	22.7178	27.2036	30.1435	32.8523	36.1908	38.5822	43.820
20	23.8277	28.4120	31.4104	34.1696	37.5662	39.9968	45.315
21	24.9348	29.6151	32.6705	35.4789	38.9321	41.4010	46.797
22	26.0393	30.8133	33.9244	36.7807	40.2894	42.7956	48.268
23	27.1413	32.0069	35.1725	38.0757	41.6384	44.1813	49.728
24	28.2412	33.1963	36.4151	39.3641	42.9798	45.5585	51.179
25	29.3389	34.3816	37.6525	40.6465	44.3141	46.9278	52.620
26	30.4345	35.5631	38.8852	41.9232	45.6417	48.2899	54.052
27	31.5284	36.7412	40.1133	43.1944	46.9630	49.6449	55.476
28	32.6205	37.9159	41.3372	44.4607	48.2782	50.9933	56.892
29	33.7109	39.0875	42.5569	45.7222	49.5879	52.3356	58.302
30	34.7998	40.2560	43.7729	46.9792	50.8922	53.6720	59.703
40	45.6160	51.8050	55.7585	59.3417	63.6907	66.7659	73.402
50	56.3336	63.1671	67.5048	71.4202	76.1539	79.4900	86.661
60	66.9814	74.3970	79.0819	83.2976	88.3794	91.9517	99.607
70	77.5766	85.5271	90.5312	95.0231	100.425	104.215	112.317
80	88.1303	96.5782	101.879	106.629	112.329	116.321	124.839
90	98.6499	107.565	113.145	118.136	124.116	128.299	137.208
100	109.141	118.498	124.342	129.561	135.807	140.169	149.449
z_Q	+0.6745	+1.2816	+1.6449	+1.9600	+2.3263	+2.5758	+3.0902

This table is taken from Table 8 of the *Biometrika Tables for Statisticians*, (Vol. 1, 3rd ed.) by E.S. Pearson and H.O. Hartley, (Eds.), 1970, New York: Cambridge University Press. Used with the kind permission of the Biometrika trustees.

370

TABLE A-3 Critical Values of F for p < .10

2nd df \ 1st df	1	2	3	4	5	6	7	8	9	10	12	15	20	24	30	40	60	120	∞
1	39·86	49·50	53·59	55·83	57·24	58·20	58·91	59·44	59·86	60·19	60·71	61·22	61·74	62·00	62·26	62·53	62·79	63·06	63·33
2	8·53	9·00	9·16	9·24	9·29	9·33	9·35	9·37	9·38	9·39	9·41	9·42	9·44	9·45	9·46	9·47	9·47	9·48	9·49
3	5·54	5·46	5·39	5·34	5·31	5·28	5·27	5·25	5·24	5·23	5·22	5·20	5·18	5·18	5·17	5·16	5·15	5·14	5·13
4	4·54	4·32	4·19	4·11	4·05	4·01	3·98	3·95	3·94	3·92	3·90	3·87	3·84	3·83	3·82	3·80	3·79	3·78	3·76
5	4·06	3·78	3·62	3·52	3·45	3·40	3·37	3·34	3·32	3·30	3·27	3·24	3·21	3·19	3·17	3·16	3·14	3·12	3·10
6	3·78	3·46	3·29	3·18	3·11	3·05	3·01	2·98	2·96	2·94	2·90	2·87	2·84	2·82	2·80	2·78	2·76	2·74	2·72
7	3·59	3·26	3·07	2·96	2·88	2·83	2·78	2·75	2·72	2·70	2·67	2·63	2·59	2·58	2·56	2·54	2·51	2·49	2·47
8	3·46	3·11	2·92	2·81	2·73	2·67	2·62	2·59	2·56	2·54	2·50	2·46	2·42	2·40	2·38	2·36	2·34	2·32	2·29
9	3·36	3·01	2·81	2·69	2·61	2·55	2·51	2·47	2·44	2·42	2·38	2·34	2·30	2·28	2·25	2·23	2·21	2·18	2·16
10	3·29	2·92	2·73	2·61	2·52	2·46	2·41	2·38	2·35	2·32	2·28	2·24	2·20	2·18	2·16	2·13	2·11	2·08	2·06
11	3·23	2·86	2·66	2·54	2·45	2·39	2·34	2·30	2·27	2·25	2·21	2·17	2·12	2·10	2·08	2·05	2·03	2·00	1·97
12	3·18	2·81	2·61	2·48	2·39	2·33	2·28	2·24	2·21	2·19	2·15	2·10	2·06	2·04	2·01	1·99	1·96	1·93	1·90
13	3·14	2·76	2·56	2·43	2·35	2·28	2·23	2·20	2·16	2·14	2·10	2·05	2·01	1·98	1·96	1·93	1·90	1·88	1·85
14	3·10	2·73	2·52	2·39	2·31	2·24	2·19	2·15	2·12	2·10	2·05	2·01	1·96	1·94	1·91	1·89	1·86	1·83	1·80
15	3·07	2·70	2·49	2·36	2·27	2·21	2·16	2·12	2·09	2·06	2·02	1·97	1·92	1·90	1·87	1·85	1·82	1·79	1·76
16	3·05	2·67	2·46	2·33	2·24	2·18	2·13	2·09	2·06	2·03	1·99	1·94	1·89	1·87	1·84	1·81	1·78	1·75	1·72
17	3·03	2·64	2·44	2·31	2·22	2·15	2·10	2·06	2·03	2·00	1·96	1·91	1·86	1·84	1·81	1·78	1·75	1·72	1·69
18	3·01	2·62	2·42	2·29	2·20	2·13	2·08	2·04	2·00	1·98	1·93	1·89	1·84	1·81	1·78	1·75	1·72	1·69	1·66
19	2·99	2·61	2·40	2·27	2·18	2·11	2·06	2·02	1·98	1·96	1·91	1·86	1·81	1·79	1·76	1·73	1·70	1·67	1·63
20	2·97	2·59	2·38	2·25	2·16	2·09	2·04	2·00	1·96	1·94	1·89	1·84	1·79	1·77	1·74	1·71	1·68	1·64	1·61
21	2·96	2·57	2·36	2·23	2·14	2·08	2·02	1·98	1·95	1·92	1·87	1·83	1·78	1·75	1·72	1·69	1·66	1·62	1·59
22	2·95	2·56	2·35	2·22	2·13	2·06	2·01	1·97	1·93	1·90	1·86	1·81	1·76	1·73	1·70	1·67	1·64	1·60	1·57
23	2·94	2·55	2·34	2·21	2·11	2·05	1·99	1·95	1·92	1·89	1·84	1·80	1·74	1·72	1·69	1·66	1·62	1·59	1·55
24	2·93	2·54	2·33	2·19	2·10	2·04	1·98	1·94	1·91	1·88	1·83	1·78	1·73	1·70	1·67	1·64	1·61	1·57	1·53
25	2·92	2·53	2·32	2·18	2·09	2·02	1·97	1·93	1·89	1·87	1·82	1·77	1·72	1·69	1·66	1·63	1·59	1·56	1·52
26	2·91	2·52	2·31	2·17	2·08	2·01	1·96	1·92	1·88	1·86	1·81	1·76	1·71	1·68	1·65	1·61	1·58	1·54	1·50
27	2·90	2·51	2·30	2·17	2·07	2·00	1·95	1·91	1·87	1·85	1·80	1·74	1·70	1·67	1·64	1·60	1·57	1·53	1·49
28	2·89	2·50	2·29	2·16	2·06	2·00	1·94	1·90	1·87	1·84	1·79	1·74	1·69	1·66	1·63	1·59	1·56	1·52	1·48
29	2·89	2·50	2·28	2·15	2·06	1·99	1·93	1·89	1·86	1·83	1·78	1·73	1·68	1·65	1·62	1·58	1·55	1·51	1·47
30	2·88	2·49	2·28	2·14	2·05	1·98	1·93	1·88	1·85	1·82	1·77	1·72	1·67	1·64	1·61	1·57	1·54	1·50	1·46
40	2·84	2·44	2·23	2·09	2·00	1·93	1·87	1·83	1·79	1·76	1·71	1·66	1·61	1·57	1·54	1·51	1·47	1·42	1·38
60	2·79	2·39	2·18	2·04	1·95	1·87	1·82	1·77	1·74	1·71	1·66	1·60	1·54	1·51	1·48	1·44	1·40	1·35	1·29
120	2·75	2·35	2·13	1·99	1·90	1·82	1·77	1·72	1·68	1·65	1·60	1·55	1·48	1·45	1·41	1·37	1·32	1·26	1·19
∞	2·71	2·30	2·08	1·94	1·85	1·77	1·72	1·67	1·63	1·60	1·55	1·49	1·42	1·38	1·34	1·30	1·24	1·17	1·00

TABLE A-3 (continued)

1st df / 2nd df	1	2	3	4	5	6	7	8	9	10	12	15	20	24	30	40	60	120	∞
1	161.4	199.5	215.7	224.6	230.2	234.0	236.8	238.9	240.5	241.9	243.9	245.9	248.0	249.1	250.1	251.1	252.2	253.3	254.3
2	18.51	19.00	19.16	19.25	19.30	19.33	19.35	19.37	19.38	19.40	19.41	19.43	19.45	19.45	19.46	19.47	19.48	19.49	19.50
3	10.13	9.55	9.28	9.12	9.01	8.94	8.89	8.85	8.81	8.79	8.74	8.70	8.66	8.64	8.62	8.59	8.57	8.55	8.53
4	7.71	6.94	6.59	6.39	6.26	6.16	6.09	6.04	6.00	5.96	5.91	5.86	5.80	5.77	5.75	5.72	5.69	5.66	5.63
5	6.61	5.79	5.41	5.19	5.05	4.95	4.88	4.82	4.77	4.74	4.68	4.62	4.56	4.53	4.50	4.46	4.43	4.40	4.36
6	5.99	5.14	4.76	4.53	4.39	4.28	4.21	4.15	4.10	4.06	4.00	3.94	3.87	3.84	3.81	3.77	3.74	3.70	3.67
7	5.59	4.74	4.35	4.12	3.97	3.87	3.79	3.73	3.68	3.64	3.57	3.51	3.44	3.41	3.38	3.34	3.30	3.27	3.23
8	5.32	4.46	4.07	3.84	3.69	3.58	3.50	3.44	3.39	3.35	3.28	3.22	3.15	3.12	3.08	3.04	3.01	2.97	2.93
9	5.12	4.26	3.86	3.63	3.48	3.37	3.29	3.23	3.18	3.14	3.07	3.01	2.94	2.90	2.86	2.83	2.79	2.75	2.71
10	4.96	4.10	3.71	3.48	3.33	3.22	3.14	3.07	3.02	2.98	2.91	2.85	2.77	2.74	2.70	2.66	2.62	2.58	2.54
11	4.84	3.98	3.59	3.36	3.20	3.09	3.01	2.95	2.90	2.85	2.79	2.72	2.65	2.61	2.57	2.53	2.49	2.45	2.40
12	4.75	3.89	3.49	3.26	3.11	3.00	2.91	2.85	2.80	2.75	2.69	2.62	2.54	2.51	2.47	2.43	2.38	2.34	2.30
13	4.67	3.81	3.41	3.18	3.03	2.92	2.83	2.77	2.71	2.67	2.60	2.53	2.46	2.42	2.38	2.34	2.30	2.25	2.21
14	4.60	3.74	3.34	3.11	2.96	2.85	2.76	2.70	2.65	2.60	2.53	2.46	2.39	2.35	2.31	2.27	2.22	2.18	2.13
15	4.54	3.68	3.29	3.06	2.90	2.79	2.71	2.64	2.59	2.54	2.48	2.40	2.33	2.29	2.25	2.20	2.16	2.11	2.07
16	4.49	3.63	3.24	3.01	2.85	2.74	2.66	2.59	2.54	2.49	2.42	2.35	2.28	2.24	2.19	2.15	2.11	2.06	2.01
17	4.45	3.59	3.20	2.96	2.81	2.70	2.61	2.55	2.49	2.45	2.38	2.31	2.23	2.19	2.15	2.10	2.06	2.01	1.96
18	4.41	3.55	3.16	2.93	2.77	2.66	2.58	2.51	2.46	2.41	2.34	2.27	2.19	2.15	2.11	2.06	2.02	1.97	1.92
19	4.38	3.52	3.13	2.90	2.74	2.63	2.54	2.48	2.42	2.38	2.31	2.23	2.16	2.11	2.07	2.03	1.98	1.93	1.88
20	4.35	3.49	3.10	2.87	2.71	2.60	2.51	2.45	2.39	2.35	2.28	2.20	2.12	2.08	2.04	1.99	1.95	1.90	1.84
21	4.32	3.47	3.07	2.84	2.68	2.57	2.49	2.42	2.37	2.32	2.25	2.18	2.10	2.05	2.01	1.96	1.92	1.87	1.81
22	4.30	3.44	3.05	2.82	2.66	2.55	2.46	2.40	2.34	2.30	2.23	2.15	2.07	2.03	1.98	1.94	1.89	1.84	1.78
23	4.28	3.42	3.03	2.80	2.64	2.53	2.44	2.37	2.32	2.27	2.20	2.13	2.05	2.01	1.96	1.91	1.86	1.81	1.76
24	4.26	3.40	3.01	2.78	2.62	2.51	2.42	2.36	2.30	2.25	2.18	2.11	2.03	1.98	1.94	1.89	1.84	1.79	1.73
25	4.24	3.39	2.99	2.76	2.60	2.49	2.40	2.34	2.28	2.24	2.16	2.09	2.01	1.96	1.92	1.87	1.82	1.77	1.71
26	4.23	3.37	2.98	2.74	2.59	2.47	2.39	2.32	2.27	2.22	2.15	2.07	1.99	1.95	1.90	1.85	1.80	1.75	1.69
27	4.21	3.35	2.96	2.73	2.57	2.46	2.37	2.31	2.25	2.20	2.13	2.06	1.97	1.93	1.88	1.84	1.79	1.73	1.67
28	4.20	3.34	2.95	2.71	2.56	2.45	2.36	2.29	2.24	2.19	2.12	2.04	1.96	1.91	1.87	1.82	1.77	1.71	1.65
29	4.18	3.33	2.93	2.70	2.55	2.43	2.35	2.28	2.22	2.18	2.10	2.03	1.94	1.90	1.85	1.81	1.75	1.70	1.64
30	4.17	3.32	2.92	2.69	2.53	2.42	2.33	2.27	2.21	2.16	2.09	2.01	1.93	1.89	1.84	1.79	1.74	1.68	1.62
40	4.08	3.23	2.84	2.61	2.45	2.34	2.25	2.18	2.12	2.08	2.00	1.92	1.84	1.79	1.74	1.69	1.64	1.58	1.51
60	4.00	3.15	2.76	2.53	2.37	2.25	2.17	2.10	2.04	1.99	1.92	1.84	1.75	1.70	1.65	1.59	1.53	1.47	1.39
120	3.92	3.07	2.68	2.45	2.29	2.17	2.09	2.02	1.96	1.91	1.83	1.75	1.66	1.61	1.55	1.50	1.43	1.35	1.25
∞	3.84	3.00	2.60	2.37	2.21	2.10	2.01	1.94	1.88	1.83	1.75	1.67	1.57	1.52	1.46	1.39	1.32	1.22	1.00

TABLE A-3 (continued)

2nd df \ 1st df	1	2	3	4	5	6	7	8	9	10	12	15	20	24	30	40	60	120	∞
1	647.8	799.5	864.2	899.6	921.8	937.1	948.2	956.7	963.3	968.6	976.7	984.9	993.1	997.2	1001	1006	1010	1014	1018
2	38.51	39.00	39.17	39.25	39.30	39.33	39.36	39.37	39.39	39.40	39.41	39.43	39.45	39.46	39.46	39.47	39.48	39.49	39.50
3	17.44	16.04	15.44	15.10	14.88	14.73	14.62	14.54	14.47	14.42	14.34	14.25	14.17	14.12	14.08	14.04	13.99	13.95	13.90
4	12.22	10.65	9.98	9.60	9.36	9.20	9.07	8.98	8.90	8.84	8.75	8.66	8.56	8.51	8.46	8.41	8.36	8.31	8.26
5	10.01	8.43	7.76	7.39	7.15	6.98	6.85	6.76	6.68	6.62	6.52	6.43	6.33	6.28	6.23	6.18	6.12	6.07	6.02
6	8.81	7.26	6.60	6.23	5.99	5.82	5.70	5.60	5.52	5.46	5.37	5.27	5.17	5.12	5.07	5.01	4.96	4.90	4.85
7	8.07	6.54	5.89	5.52	5.29	5.12	4.99	4.90	4.82	4.76	4.67	4.57	4.47	4.42	4.36	4.31	4.25	4.20	4.14
8	7.57	6.06	5.42	5.05	4.82	4.65	4.53	4.43	4.36	4.30	4.20	4.10	4.00	3.95	3.89	3.84	3.78	3.73	3.67
9	7.21	5.71	5.08	4.72	4.48	4.32	4.20	4.10	4.03	3.96	3.87	3.77	3.67	3.61	3.56	3.51	3.45	3.39	3.33
10	6.94	5.46	4.83	4.47	4.24	4.07	3.95	3.85	3.78	3.72	3.62	3.52	3.42	3.37	3.31	3.26	3.20	3.14	3.08
11	6.72	5.26	4.63	4.28	4.04	3.88	3.76	3.66	3.59	3.53	3.43	3.33	3.23	3.17	3.12	3.06	3.00	2.94	2.88
12	6.55	5.10	4.47	4.12	3.89	3.73	3.61	3.51	3.44	3.37	3.28	3.18	3.07	3.02	2.96	2.91	2.85	2.79	2.72
13	6.41	4.97	4.35	4.00	3.77	3.60	3.48	3.39	3.31	3.25	3.15	3.05	2.95	2.89	2.84	2.78	2.72	2.66	2.60
14	6.30	4.86	4.24	3.89	3.66	3.50	3.38	3.29	3.21	3.15	3.05	2.95	2.84	2.79	2.73	2.67	2.61	2.55	2.49
15	6.20	4.77	4.15	3.80	3.58	3.41	3.29	3.20	3.12	3.06	2.96	2.86	2.76	2.70	2.64	2.59	2.52	2.46	2.40
16	6.12	4.69	4.08	3.73	3.50	3.34	3.22	3.12	3.05	2.99	2.89	2.79	2.68	2.63	2.57	2.51	2.45	2.38	2.32
17	6.04	4.62	4.01	3.66	3.44	3.28	3.16	3.06	2.98	2.92	2.82	2.72	2.62	2.56	2.50	2.44	2.38	2.32	2.25
18	5.98	4.56	3.95	3.61	3.38	3.22	3.10	3.01	2.93	2.87	2.77	2.67	2.56	2.50	2.44	2.38	2.32	2.26	2.19
19	5.92	4.51	3.90	3.56	3.33	3.17	3.05	2.96	2.88	2.82	2.72	2.62	2.51	2.45	2.39	2.33	2.27	2.20	2.13
20	5.87	4.46	3.86	3.51	3.29	3.13	3.01	2.91	2.84	2.77	2.68	2.57	2.46	2.41	2.35	2.29	2.22	2.16	2.09
21	5.83	4.42	3.82	3.48	3.25	3.09	2.97	2.87	2.80	2.73	2.64	2.53	2.42	2.37	2.31	2.25	2.18	2.11	2.04
22	5.79	4.38	3.78	3.44	3.22	3.05	2.93	2.84	2.76	2.70	2.60	2.50	2.39	2.33	2.27	2.21	2.14	2.08	2.00
23	5.75	4.35	3.75	3.41	3.18	3.02	2.90	2.81	2.73	2.67	2.57	2.47	2.36	2.30	2.24	2.18	2.11	2.04	1.97
24	5.72	4.32	3.72	3.38	3.15	2.99	2.87	2.78	2.70	2.64	2.54	2.44	2.33	2.27	2.21	2.15	2.08	2.01	1.94
25	5.69	4.29	3.69	3.35	3.13	2.97	2.85	2.75	2.68	2.61	2.51	2.41	2.30	2.24	2.18	2.12	2.05	1.98	1.91
26	5.66	4.27	3.67	3.33	3.10	2.94	2.82	2.73	2.65	2.59	2.49	2.39	2.28	2.22	2.16	2.09	2.03	1.95	1.88
27	5.63	4.24	3.65	3.31	3.08	2.92	2.80	2.71	2.63	2.57	2.47	2.36	2.25	2.19	2.13	2.07	2.00	1.93	1.85
28	5.61	4.22	3.63	3.29	3.06	2.90	2.78	2.69	2.61	2.55	2.45	2.34	2.23	2.17	2.11	2.05	1.98	1.91	1.83
29	5.59	4.20	3.61	3.27	3.04	2.88	2.76	2.67	2.59	2.53	2.43	2.32	2.21	2.15	2.09	2.03	1.96	1.89	1.81
30	5.57	4.18	3.59	3.25	3.03	2.87	2.75	2.65	2.57	2.51	2.41	2.31	2.20	2.14	2.07	2.01	1.94	1.87	1.79
40	5.42	4.05	3.46	3.13	2.90	2.74	2.62	2.53	2.45	2.39	2.29	2.18	2.07	2.01	1.94	1.88	1.80	1.72	1.64
60	5.29	3.93	3.34	3.01	2.79	2.63	2.51	2.41	2.33	2.27	2.17	2.06	1.94	1.88	1.82	1.74	1.67	1.58	1.48
120	5.15	3.80	3.23	2.89	2.67	2.52	2.39	2.30	2.22	2.16	2.05	1.94	1.82	1.76	1.69	1.61	1.53	1.43	1.31
∞	5.02	3.69	3.12	2.79	2.57	2.41	2.29	2.19	2.11	2.05	1.94	1.83	1.71	1.64	1.57	1.48	1.39	1.27	1.00

TABLE A-3 (continued)

2nd df \ 1st df	1	2	3	4	5	6	7	8	9	10	12	15	20	24	30	40	60	120	∞
1	4052	4999.5	5403	5625	5764	5859	5928	5982	6022	6056	6106	6157	6209	6235	6261	6287	6313	6339	6366
2	98.50	99.00	99.17	99.25	99.30	99.33	99.36	99.37	99.39	99.40	99.42	99.43	99.45	99.46	99.47	99.47	99.48	99.49	99.50
3	34.12	30.82	29.46	28.71	28.24	27.91	27.67	27.49	27.35	27.23	27.05	26.87	26.69	26.60	26.50	26.41	26.32	26.22	26.13
4	21.20	18.00	16.69	15.98	15.52	15.21	14.98	14.80	14.66	14.55	14.37	14.20	14.02	13.93	13.84	13.75	13.65	13.56	13.46
5	16.26	13.27	12.06	11.39	10.97	10.67	10.46	10.29	10.16	10.05	9.89	9.72	9.55	9.47	9.38	9.29	9.20	9.11	9.02
6	13.75	10.92	9.78	9.15	8.75	8.47	8.26	8.10	7.98	7.87	7.72	7.56	7.40	7.31	7.23	7.14	7.06	6.97	6.88
7	12.25	9.55	8.45	7.85	7.46	7.19	6.99	6.84	6.72	6.62	6.47	6.31	6.16	6.07	5.99	5.91	5.82	5.74	5.65
8	11.26	8.65	7.59	7.01	6.63	6.37	6.18	6.03	5.91	5.81	5.67	5.52	5.36	5.28	5.20	5.12	5.03	4.95	4.86
9	10.56	8.02	6.99	6.42	6.06	5.80	5.61	5.47	5.35	5.26	5.11	4.96	4.81	4.73	4.65	4.57	4.48	4.40	4.31
10	10.04	7.56	6.55	5.99	5.64	5.39	5.20	5.06	4.94	4.85	4.71	4.56	4.41	4.33	4.25	4.17	4.08	4.00	3.91
11	9.65	7.21	6.22	5.67	5.32	5.07	4.89	4.74	4.63	4.54	4.40	4.25	4.10	4.02	3.94	3.86	3.78	3.69	3.60
12	9.33	6.93	5.95	5.41	5.06	4.82	4.64	4.50	4.39	4.30	4.16	4.01	3.86	3.78	3.70	3.62	3.54	3.45	3.36
13	9.07	6.70	5.74	5.21	4.86	4.62	4.44	4.30	4.19	4.10	3.96	3.82	3.66	3.59	3.51	3.43	3.34	3.25	3.17
14	8.86	6.51	5.56	5.04	4.69	4.46	4.28	4.14	4.03	3.94	3.80	3.66	3.51	3.43	3.35	3.27	3.18	3.09	3.00
15	8.68	6.36	5.42	4.89	4.56	4.32	4.14	4.00	3.89	3.80	3.67	3.52	3.37	3.29	3.21	3.13	3.05	2.96	2.87
16	8.53	6.23	5.29	4.77	4.44	4.20	4.03	3.89	3.78	3.69	3.55	3.41	3.26	3.18	3.10	3.02	2.93	2.84	2.75
17	8.40	6.11	5.18	4.67	4.34	4.10	3.93	3.79	3.68	3.59	3.46	3.31	3.16	3.08	3.00	2.92	2.83	2.75	2.65
18	8.29	6.01	5.09	4.58	4.25	4.01	3.84	3.71	3.60	3.51	3.37	3.23	3.08	3.00	2.92	2.84	2.75	2.66	2.57
19	8.18	5.93	5.01	4.50	4.17	3.94	3.77	3.63	3.52	3.43	3.30	3.15	3.00	2.92	2.84	2.76	2.67	2.58	2.49
20	8.10	5.85	4.94	4.43	4.10	3.87	3.70	3.56	3.46	3.37	3.23	3.09	2.94	2.86	2.78	2.69	2.61	2.52	2.42
21	8.02	5.78	4.87	4.37	4.04	3.81	3.64	3.51	3.40	3.31	3.17	3.03	2.88	2.80	2.72	2.64	2.55	2.46	2.36
22	7.95	5.72	4.82	4.31	3.99	3.76	3.59	3.45	3.35	3.26	3.12	2.98	2.83	2.75	2.67	2.58	2.50	2.40	2.31
23	7.88	5.66	4.76	4.26	3.94	3.71	3.54	3.41	3.30	3.21	3.07	2.93	2.78	2.70	2.62	2.54	2.45	2.35	2.26
24	7.82	5.61	4.72	4.22	3.90	3.67	3.50	3.36	3.26	3.17	3.03	2.89	2.74	2.66	2.58	2.49	2.40	2.31	2.21
25	7.77	5.57	4.68	4.18	3.85	3.63	3.46	3.32	3.22	3.13	2.99	2.85	2.70	2.62	2.54	2.45	2.36	2.27	2.17
26	7.72	5.53	4.64	4.14	3.82	3.59	3.42	3.29	3.18	3.09	2.96	2.81	2.66	2.58	2.50	2.42	2.33	2.23	2.13
27	7.68	5.49	4.60	4.11	3.78	3.56	3.39	3.26	3.15	3.06	2.93	2.78	2.63	2.55	2.47	2.38	2.29	2.20	2.10
28	7.64	5.45	4.57	4.07	3.75	3.53	3.36	3.23	3.12	3.03	2.90	2.75	2.60	2.52	2.44	2.35	2.26	2.17	2.06
29	7.60	5.42	4.54	4.04	3.73	3.50	3.33	3.20	3.09	3.00	2.87	2.73	2.57	2.49	2.41	2.33	2.23	2.14	2.03
30	7.56	5.39	4.51	4.02	3.70	3.47	3.30	3.17	3.07	2.98	2.84	2.70	2.55	2.47	2.39	2.30	2.21	2.11	2.01
40	7.31	5.18	4.31	3.83	3.51	3.29	3.12	2.99	2.89	2.80	2.66	2.52	2.37	2.29	2.20	2.11	2.02	1.92	1.80
60	7.08	4.98	4.13	3.65	3.34	3.12	2.95	2.82	2.72	2.63	2.50	2.35	2.20	2.12	2.03	1.94	1.84	1.73	1.60
120	6.85	4.79	3.95	3.48	3.17	2.96	2.79	2.66	2.56	2.47	2.34	2.19	2.03	1.95	1.86	1.76	1.66	1.53	1.38
∞	6.63	4.61	3.78	3.32	3.02	2.80	2.64	2.51	2.41	2.32	2.18	2.04	1.88	1.79	1.70	1.59	1.47	1.32	1.00

This table is abridged from Table 18 of the *Biometrika Tables for Statisticians*, (Vol. 1, 3rd ed.) by E.S. Pearson and H.O. Hartley, (Eds.), 1970, New York: Cambridge University Press. Used with the kind permission of the Biometrika trustees.

TABLE A-4 Coefficients of Orthogonal Polynomials

	3-Condition Case Trend		4-Condition Case Trend			5-Condition Case Trend			
	1 (Linear)	2 (Quad)	1 (Lin)	2 (Quad)	3 (Cubic)	1 (Lin)	2 (Quad)	3 (Cubic)	4
CONDITION 1	−1	1	−3	1	−1	−2	2	−1	1
CONDITION 2	0	−2	−1	−1	3	−1	−1	2	−4
CONDITION 3	1	1	1	−1	−3	0	−2	0	6
CONDITION 4			3	1	1	1	−1	−2	−4
CONDITION 5						2	2	1	1
WEIGHTING FACTOR	2	6	20	4	20	10	14	10	70

	6-Condition Case Trend					7-Condition Case Trend					
	1 (Lin)	2 (Quad)	3 (Cubic)	4	5	1 (Lin)	2 (Quad)	3 (Cub)	4	5	6
CONDITION 1	−5	5	−5	1	−1	−3	5	−1	3	−1	1
CONDITION 2	−3	−1	7	−3	5	−2	0	1	−7	4	−6
CONDITION 3	−1	−4	4	2	−10	−1	−3	1	1	−5	15
CONDITION 4	1	−4	−4	2	10	0	−4	0	6	0	−20
CONDITION 5	3	−1	−7	−3	−5	1	−3	−1	1	5	15
CONDITION 6	5	5	5	1	1	2	0	−1	−7	−4	−6
CONDITION 7						3	5	1	3	1	1
WEIGHTING FACTOR	70	84	180	28	252	28	84	6	154	84	924

	8-Condition Case Trend						9-Condition Case Trend					
Condition	1 (Lin)	2 (Quad)	3 (Cub)	4	5	6	1 (Lin)	2 (Quad)	3 (Cub)	4	5	6
1	−7	7	−7	7	−7	1	−4	28	−14	14	−4	4
2	−5	1	5	−13	23	−5	−3	7	7	−21	11	−17
3	−3	−3	7	−3	−17	9	−2	−8	13	−11	−4	22
4	−1	−5	3	9	−15	−5	−1	−17	9	9	−9	1
5	1	−5	−3	9	15	−5	0	−20	0	18	0	−20
6	3	−3	−7	−3	17	9	1	−17	−9	9	9	1
7	5	1	−5	−13	−23	−5	2	−8	−13	−11	4	22
8	7	7	7	7	7	1	3	7	−7	−21	−11	−17
9							4	28	14	14	4	4
WEIGHTING FACTOR	168	168	264	616	2184	264	60	2772	990	2002	468	1980

TABLE A-4 *(continued)*

	10-Condition Case Trend						11-Condition Case Trend					
Condition	**1** (Lin)	**2** (Quad)	**3** (Cub)	**4**	**5**	**6**	**1** (Lin)	**2** (Quad)	**3** (Cub)	**4**	**5**	**6**
1	−9	6	−42	18	−6	3	−5	15	−30	6	−3	15
2	−7	2	14	−22	14	−11	−4	6	6	−6	6	−48
3	−5	−1	35	−17	−1	10	−3	−1	22	−6	1	29
4	−3	−3	31	3	−11	6	−2	−6	23	−1	−4	36
5	−1	−4	12	18	−6	−8	−1	−9	14	4	−4	−12
6	1	−4	−12	18	6	−8	0	−10	0	6	0	−40
7	3	−3	−31	3	11	6	1	−9	−14	4	4	−12
8	5	−1	−35	−17	1	10	2	−6	−23	−1	4	36
9	7	2	−14	−22	−14	−11	3	−1	−22	−6	−1	29
10	9	6	42	18	6	3	4	6	−6	−6	−6	−48
11							5	15	30	6	3	15
WEIGHTING FACTOR	330	132	8580	2860	780	660	110	858	4290	286	156	11220

	12-Condition Case Trend						13-Condition Case Trend					
Condition	**1** (Lin)	**2** (Quad)	**3** (Cub)	**4**	**5**	**6**	**1** (Lin)	**2** (Quad)	**3** (Cub)	**4**	**5**	**6**
1	−11	55	−33	33	−33	11	−6	22	−11	99	−22	22
2	−9	25	3	−27	57	−31	−5	11	0	−66	33	−55
3	−7	1	21	−33	21	11	−4	2	6	−96	18	8
4	−5	−17	25	−13	−29	25	−3	−5	8	−54	−11	43
5	−3	−29	19	12	−44	4	−2	−10	7	11	−26	22
6	−1	−35	7	28	−20	−20	−1	−13	4	64	−20	−20
7	1	−35	−7	28	20	−20	0	−14	0	84	0	−40
8	3	−29	−19	12	44	4	1	−13	−4	64	20	−20
9	5	−17	−25	−13	29	25	2	−10	−7	11	26	22
10	7	1	−21	−33	−21	11	3	−5	−8	−54	11	43
11	9	25	−3	−27	−57	−31	4	2	−6	−96	−18	8
12	11	55	33	33	33	11	5	11	0	−66	−33	−55
13							6	22	11	99	22	22
WEIGHTING FACTOR	572	12012	5148	8008	15912	4488	182	2002	572	68068	6188	14212

TABLE A-4 *(continued)*

| Condition | 14-Condition Case Trend | | | | | | 15-Condition Case Trend | | | | | |
	1 (Lin)	2 (Quad)	3 (Cub)	4	5	6	1 (Lin)	2 (Quad)	3 (Cub)	4	5	6
1	−13	13	−143	143	−143	143	−7	91	−91	1001	−1001	143
2	−11	7	−11	−77	187	−319	−6	52	−13	−429	1144	−286
3	−9	2	66	−132	132	−11	−5	19	35	−869	979	−55
4	−7	−2	98	−92	−28	227	−4	−8	58	−704	44	176
5	−5	−5	95	−13	−139	185	−3	−29	61	−249	−751	197
6	−3	−7	67	63	−145	−25	−2	−44	49	251	−1000	50
7	−1	−8	24	108	−60	−200	−1	−53	27	621	−675	−125
8	1	−8	−24	108	60	−200	0	−56	0	756	0	−200
9	3	−7	−67	63	145	−25	1	−53	−27	621	675	−125
10	5	−5	−95	−13	139	185	2	−44	−49	251	1000	50
11	7	−2	−98	−92	28	227	3	−29	−61	−249	751	197
12	9	2	−66	−132	−132	−11	4	−8	−58	−704	−44	176
13	11	7	11	−77	−187	−319	5	19	−35	−869	−979	−55
14	13	13	143	143	143	143	6	52	13	−429	−1144	−286
15							7	91	91	1001	1001	143
WEIGHTING FACTOR	910	728	97240	136136	235144	497420	280	37128	39780	6446460	10581480	426360

This table is adapted from Table VII of *Statistics* (pp. 662-664) by W. L. Hays, 1981, New York: Holt, Rinehart & Winston. Copyright © 1982 by Holt, Rinehart & Winston, Inc. Adapted by permission.

USING TABLE A-4 TO COMPUTE TREND ANALYSES

Suppose you had the following significant effect for sugar on aggression.

	df	SS	MS	F
Sugar Main Effect	2	126.95	63.47	6.35
Error Term	21	210.00	10.00	

How would you compute a trend analysis for this data? In other words, how would you calculate an F ratio for the linear and quadratic effects so that you could complete the ANOVA table below?

	df	SS	MS	F
Sugar Main Effect	2	126.95	63.47	6.35
Linear Component	1			
Quadratic Component	1			
Error Term	21	210.00	10.00	

Before you generate an F ratio, you must have a sum of squares. To compute the sum of squares for a trend, you must first get the sum of the scores for each condition. Simply add up all the scores for each condition or, if you prefer, multiply each condition's average by the number of scores making up each average. Thus, if one condition's mean was 10 and there were 5 scores making up that mean, the sum for that condition would be 5 × 10 or 50.

Next, arrange these totals, starting with the total for the lowest level of independent variable and ending with the total for the highest level of the independent variable. That is, place the sum for the condition with the lowest level of the independent variable first, the sum for the condition with the next highest level of the independent variable next, and so on. In our example, you would order your sums like so:

Total Number of Violent Instances per Condition

Amount of Sugar	Total Number of Violent Instances
0 mg	10.0
50 mg	50.0
100 mg	12.0

Now, you are ready to consult the tables of orthogonal polynomials in Table A-4. Because this example involves three conditions, you would look for the three-condition table. The table reads:

Three-Condition Case

	1st—Trend—2nd	
	(Linear)	(Quadratic)
CONDITION 1	−1	1
CONDITION 2	0	−2
CONDITION 3	1	1
WEIGHTING FACTOR	2	6

To get the numerator for the sum of squares for the linear trend, multiply the sum for the lowest level of the independent variable by the first value in the Linear column of the table (-1), the second sum by the second value in the Linear column of the table (0), and the third sum by the third value in the Linear column of the table $(+1)$. Next, get a sum by adding these three products together. Then, square that sum. So, for the sugar example we just described, you would do the following calculations:

$$(-1 \times 10) + (0 \times 50) + (1 \times 12)^2$$

or

$$(-10 + 0 + 12)^2$$

or

$$(2)^2$$

or

$$4$$

To get the denominator for the sum of squares, multiply the weighting factor for the linear trend (2) by the number of observations in each condition. Since there were eight observations in each condition, the denominator would be 16 (2×8). The sum of squares linear would be the numerator (4) divided by the denominator (16) or .25.

Once you've computed the sum of squares for the linear trend, the rest is easy. All you have to do is compute an F ratio by dividing the mean square linear by the mean square error and then see if that result is significant.

Calculating the mean square linear involves dividing the sum of squares linear by the degrees of freedom linear. Since the degrees of freedom for any trend is always 1.00, you could divide your sum of squares .25 by 1.00 and get .25. Or, you could simply remember that a trend's mean square is always the same as its sum of squares.

Getting the mean square error is also easy: just find the mean square error in the print-out that was used to test the overall main effect. In this example, that would be 10.0.

So, to get the F value for this linear comparison, you would divide the mean square for the comparison (.25) by the mean square error used on the overall main effect (10.0). Thus, the F would be .25/10, or .025. Since the F is below 1, this result is obviously not significant.

But how large would the F have had to be to be significant? That depends on how many trends you were analyzing. If you had decided to look only at the linear trend, the significant F at the .05 level would have to exceed the value in the F table for 1 degree of fredom (the df for any trend) and 21 degrees of freedom, the df for the error term. The value is 4.32.

However, if you are going to analyze more than one trend, you must correct for the number of Fs you are going to compute. The correction is simple: you divide the significance level you want (say .05), by the number of trends you will test. In this example, you are computing two Fs. Therefore, you should use the F for .05/2 or .025. So, in this example, you would only declare a trend significant if the F for that trend exceeds the tabled value for $F_{(1,21)}$ at the .025 level: 5.83.

Obviously, the F for the linear component $F(1,21) = .025$, falls far short of the critical value of 5.83. But what about the quadratic component? To determine whether the quadratic component is significant, you would follow the same steps as before. The only difference is that you would look at the quadratic column of the table instead of the linear column.

Thus, you would first multiply the treatment sums by the constants listed in the column labelled "quadratic", add them together, and square that sum. In other words,

$$((1 \times 10) + (-2 \times 50) + (1 \times 12))^2$$

or

$$(10) + (-100) + 12)^2$$

or

$$2(-78)$$

or

$$6084.$$

Then, you would divide 6084 by 8 (the number of observations in each condition) $\times$ 6 (the weighting factor for the quadratic effect). So, SS quadratic is $6084/(8 \times 6) = 6084/48 = 126.7$, as is the MS quadratic (SS (126.7)/ DF (1) = MS (126.7)).

To get the F, you would divide the MS quadratic by MS error. Therefore, the F would be $126.7/10 = 12.67$. As before, the critical value for the comparison is the F value for the .025 significance level with 1 and 21 degrees of freedom: 5.83. Since our F of 12.67 exceeds the critical value of 5.83, we have a statistically significant quadratic trend.

So, our complete ANOVA table, including the linear and quadratic components would be as follows:

	df	SS	MS	F
Sugar Main Effect	2	126.95	63.47	6.35*
Linear	1	0.25	0.25	0.02
Quadratic	1	126.70	126.70	12.67*
Error Term	21	210.00	10.00	

*Significant at .05 level.

From looking at the table, you see that if you add up the degrees of freedom for all the trends involved in the main effect (1 + 1), you get the total *df* for that main effect (2). More importantly, note that if you add up the sum of squares for the components (126.70 + .25), you get the sum of squares for the overall effect (126.95). This fact gives you a way to check your work. Specifically, if the total of the sums of squares for all the components doesn't add up to the sum of squares for the overall effect, you have made a mistake.

TABLE A-5 Critical Values for the Tukey Test

Number of Means

df_{error}	αFW	2	3	4	5	6	7	8	9	10	11	12	13	14	15	16	17	18	19	20	αFW	df_{error}
5	.05	3.64	4.60	5.22	5.67	6.03	6.33	6.58	6.80	6.99	7.17	7.32	7.47	7.60	7.72	7.83	7.93	8.03	8.12	8.21	.05	5
	.01	5.70	6.98	7.80	8.42	8.91	9.32	9.67	9.97	10.24	10.48	10.70	10.89	11.08	11.24	11.40	11.55	11.68	11.81	11.93	.01	
6	.05	3.46	4.34	4.90	5.30	5.63	5.90	6.12	6.32	6.49	6.65	6.79	6.92	7.03	7.14	7.24	7.34	7.43	7.51	7.59	.05	6
	.01	5.24	6.33	7.03	7.56	7.97	8.32	8.61	8.87	9.10	9.30	9.48	9.65	9.81	9.95	10.08	10.21	10.32	10.43	10.54	.01	
7	.05	3.34	4.16	4.68	5.06	5.36	5.61	5.82	6.00	6.16	6.30	6.43	6.55	6.66	6.76	6.85	6.94	7.02	7.10	7.17	.05	7
	.01	4.95	5.92	6.54	7.01	7.37	7.68	7.94	8.17	8.37	8.55	8.71	8.86	9.00	9.12	9.24	9.35	9.46	9.55	9.65	.01	
8	.05	3.26	4.04	4.53	4.89	5.17	5.40	5.60	5.77	5.92	6.05	6.18	6.29	6.39	6.48	6.57	6.65	6.73	6.80	6.87	.05	8
	.01	4.75	5.64	6.20	6.62	6.96	7.24	7.47	7.68	7.86	8.03	8.18	8.31	8.44	8.55	8.66	8.76	8.85	8.94	9.03	.01	
9	.05	3.20	3.95	4.41	4.76	5.02	5.24	5.43	5.59	5.74	5.87	5.98	6.09	6.19	6.28	6.36	6.44	6.51	6.58	6.64	.05	9
	.01	4.60	5.43	5.96	6.35	6.66	6.91	7.13	7.33	7.49	7.65	7.78	7.91	8.03	8.13	8.23	8.33	8.41	8.49	8.57	.01	
10	.05	3.15	3.88	4.33	4.65	4.91	5.12	5.30	5.46	5.60	5.72	5.83	5.93	6.03	6.11	6.19	6.27	6.34	6.40	6.47	.05	10
	.01	4.48	5.27	5.77	6.14	6.43	6.67	6.87	7.05	7.21	7.36	7.49	7.60	7.71	7.81	7.91	7.99	8.08	8.15	8.23	.01	
11	.05	3.11	3.82	4.26	4.57	4.82	5.03	5.20	5.35	5.49	5.61	5.71	5.81	5.90	5.98	6.06	6.13	6.20	6.27	6.33	.05	11
	.01	4.39	5.15	5.62	5.97	6.25	6.48	6.67	6.84	6.99	7.13	7.25	7.36	7.46	7.56	7.65	7.73	7.81	7.88	7.95	.01	
12	.05	3.08	3.77	4.20	4.51	4.75	4.95	5.12	5.27	5.39	5.51	5.61	5.71	5.80	5.88	5.95	6.02	6.09	6.15	6.21	.05	12
	.01	4.32	5.05	5.50	5.84	6.10	6.32	6.51	6.67	6.81	6.94	7.06	7.17	7.26	7.36	7.44	7.52	7.59	7.66	7.73	.01	
13	.05	3.06	3.73	4.15	4.45	4.69	4.88	5.05	5.19	5.32	5.43	5.53	5.63	5.71	5.79	5.86	5.93	5.99	6.05	6.11	.05	13
	.01	4.26	4.96	5.40	5.73	5.98	6.19	6.37	6.53	6.67	6.79	6.90	7.01	7.10	7.19	7.27	7.35	7.42	7.48	7.55	.01	
14	.05	3.03	3.70	4.11	4.41	4.64	4.83	4.99	5.13	5.25	5.36	5.46	5.55	5.64	5.71	5.79	5.85	5.91	5.97	6.03	.05	14
	.01	4.21	4.89	5.32	5.63	5.88	6.08	6.26	6.41	6.54	6.66	6.77	6.87	6.96	7.05	7.13	7.20	7.27	7.33	7.39	.01	
15	.05	3.01	3.67	4.08	4.37	4.59	4.78	4.94	5.08	5.20	5.31	5.40	5.49	5.57	5.65	5.72	5.78	5.85	5.90	5.96	.05	15
	.01	4.17	4.84	5.25	5.56	5.80	5.99	6.16	6.31	6.44	6.55	6.66	6.76	6.84	6.93	7.00	7.07	7.14	7.20	7.26	.01	
16	.05	3.00	3.65	4.05	4.33	4.56	4.74	4.90	5.03	5.15	5.26	5.35	5.44	5.52	5.59	5.66	5.73	5.79	5.84	5.90	.05	16
	.01	4.13	4.79	5.19	5.49	5.72	5.92	6.08	6.22	6.35	6.46	6.56	6.66	6.74	8.82	6.90	6.97	7.03	7.09	7.15	.01	
17	.05	2.98	3.63	4.02	4.30	4.52	4.70	4.86	4.99	5.11	5.21	5.31	5.39	5.47	5.54	5.61	5.67	5.73	5.79	5.84	.05	17
	.01	4.10	4.74	5.14	5.43	5.66	5.85	6.01	6.15	6.27	6.38	6.48	6.57	6.66	6.73	6.81	6.87	6.94	7.00	7.05	.01	
18	.05	2.97	3.61	4.00	4.28	4.49	4.67	4.82	4.96	5.07	5.17	5.27	5.35	5.43	5.50	5.57	5.63	5.69	5.74	5.79	.05	18
	.01	4.07	4.70	5.09	5.38	5.60	5.79	5.94	6.08	6.20	6.31	6.41	6.50	6.58	6.65	6.73	6.79	6.85	6.91	6.97	.01	
19	.05	2.96	3.59	3.98	4.25	4.47	4.65	4.79	4.92	5.04	5.14	5.23	5.31	5.39	5.46	5.53	5.59	5.65	5.70	5.75	.05	19
	.01	4.05	4.67	5.05	5.33	5.55	5.73	5.89	6.02	6.14	6.25	6.34	6.43	6.51	6.58	6.65	6.72	6.78	6.84	6.89	.01	
20	.05	2.95	3.58	3.96	4.23	4.45	4.62	4.77	4.90	5.01	5.11	5.20	5.28	5.36	5.43	5.49	5.55	5.61	5.66	5.71	.05	20
	.01	4.02	4.64	5.02	5.29	5.51	5.69	5.84	5.97	6.09	6.19	6.28	6.37	6.45	6.52	6.59	6.65	6.71	6.77	6.82	.01	
24	.05	2.92	3.53	3.90	4.17	4.37	4.54	4.68	4.81	4.92	5.01	5.10	5.18	5.25	5.32	5.38	5.44	5.49	5.55	5.59	.05	24
	.01	3.96	4.55	4.91	5.17	5.37	5.54	5.69	5.81	5.92	6.02	6.11	6.19	6.26	6.33	6.39	6.45	6.51	6.56	6.61	.01	
30	.05	2.89	3.49	3.85	4.10	4.30	4.46	4.60	4.72	4.82	4.92	5.00	5.08	5.15	5.21	5.27	5.33	5.38	5.43	5.47	.05	30
	.01	3.89	4.45	4.80	5.05	5.24	5.40	5.54	5.65	5.76	5.85	5.93	6.01	6.08	6.14	6.20	6.26	6.31	6.36	6.41	.01	
40	.05	2.86	3.44	3.79	4.04	4.23	4.39	4.52	4.63	4.73	4.82	4.90	4.98	5.04	5.11	5.16	5.22	5.27	5.31	5.36	.05	40
	.01	3.82	4.37	4.70	4.93	5.11	5.26	5.39	5.50	5.60	5.69	5.76	5.83	5.90	5.96	6.02	6.07	6.12	6.16	6.21	.01	
60	.05	2.83	3.40	3.74	3.98	4.16	4.31	4.44	4.55	4.65	4.73	4.81	4.88	4.94	5.00	5.06	5.11	5.15	5.20	5.24	.05	60
	.01	3.76	4.28	4.59	4.82	4.99	5.13	5.25	5.36	5.45	5.53	5.60	5.67	5.73	5.78	5.84	5.89	5.93	5.97	6.01	.01	
120	.05	2.80	3.36	3.68	3.92	4.10	4.24	4.36	4.47	4.56	4.64	4.71	4.78	4.84	4.90	4.95	5.00	5.04	5.09	5.13	.05	120
	.01	3.70	4.20	4.50	4.71	4.87	5.01	5.12	5.21	5.30	5.37	5.44	5.50	5.56	5.61	5.66	5.71	5.75	5.79	5.83	.01	
∞	.05	2.77	3.31	3.63	3.86	4.03	4.17	4.29	4.39	4.47	4.55	4.62	4.68	4.74	4.80	4.85	4.89	4.93	4.97	5.01	.05	∞
	.01	3.64	4.12	4.40	4.60	4.76	4.88	4.99	5.08	5.16	5.23	5.29	5.35	5.40	5.45	5.49	5.54	5.57	5.61	5.65	.01	

This table is abridged from Table 29 in Pearson, F. S. and Hartley, H. O., (Eds.), (1970), *Biometrika tables for statisticians* (3rd ed., Vol. 1). New York: Cambridge University Press. Used with the kind permission of the *Biometrika* Trustees.

USING TABLE A-5 TO COMPUTE POST-HOC TESTS

Post-hoc tests, such as the Tukey test, can be used after finding a significant main effect for a multilevel factor. These tests help determine which conditions are significantly different from one another.

To see how you could use Table A-5 to compute post-hoc tests, suppose that an investigator uses 24 subjects (eight in each group) to examine the effect of color (blue, green, or yellow) on mood. As you can see from the table below, the investigator's ANOVA table reveals a significant effect of color.

Source	Sum of Squares	Degrees of Freedom	Mean Square	F
Color	64	2	32.0	4.0*
Error	168	**21**	**8.0**	

*Significant at .05 level.

The means for the three color conditions are

Blue	Green	Yellow
10.0	5.0	8.0

Now, the question is: which conditions differ from one another. Does yellow cause a different mood than green? Does blue cause a different mood than yellow? To find out, we need to do a post-hoc test. For this example, we will do the Tukey test. The formula for the Tukey test is

$$\frac{\text{Mean 1} - \text{Mean 2}}{\text{SQR RT (MSE} * \text{1/number of observations per condition)}}$$

Since the mean square error is 8 (see original ANOVA table) and there are 8 subjects in each group, the denominator in this example will always be:

$$\text{SQR RT (8} * \tfrac{1}{8})$$

or

$$\text{SQR RT } (\tfrac{8}{8})$$

or

$$SQR \ RT \ 1$$

or

$$1$$

The numerator will change, depending on what means you are comparing. Thus, if you are comparing blue and green, the numerator would be $10 - 5$ or 5. So, to see whether the blue and green conditions differ significantly, you would do the following calculations:

$$\frac{\underset{(Blue \ mean)}{10.0} - \underset{(green \ mean)}{5.0}}{SQR \ RT \ (8 * \frac{1}{8})} = \frac{5.0}{SQR \ RT \ 1} = \frac{5.0}{1.0} = 5.0$$

To find out whether 5.0 is significant, go to the Table 5 and look for the column 3 because you have three means you are comparing. Then, go down and look at the row numbered 21 because you have 21 degrees of freedom in your error term (as you can see by looking at the original ANOVA table). The value in that table is 3.58. This is the critical value that you will use in all your comparisons. If your Tukey statistic for a pair of means is larger than this critical value, there is a significant difference between conditions. Since 5.0 is greater than 3.58, your result is significant at the .05 level.

But, do blue and yellow differ? To find out, compute the Tukey statistic

$$\frac{10.0 - 8.0}{SQR \ RT \ (8 * \frac{1}{8})} = \frac{2.0}{SQR \ RT \ 1} = \frac{2.0}{1.0} = 2.0$$

Since 2.0 is less than our critical value of 3.58, the difference between blue and yellow is not statistically significant at the .05 level.

Do yellow and green differ?

$$\frac{8.0 - 5.0}{SQR \ RT \ (8 * \frac{1}{8})} = \frac{3.0}{SQR \ RT \ 1} = \frac{3.0}{1.0} = 3.0$$

Since 3.0 is less than our critical value of 3.58, the difference between yellow and green conditions is not statistically significant at the .05 level.

12	13	98	21	39	36	74	39	83	77	79	37	89	4	20	21	91	98	90	37	49	
39	31	69	14	22	50	40	54	12	71	98	25	26	20	61	52	93	90	76	46	19	
53	10	28	46	41	29	74	46	64	39	4	47	55	98	22	69	9	15	34	94	16	
29	95	79	80	35	0	9	65	42	99	69	90	22	16	34	81	44	3	24	96	70	
20	59	12	35	63	52	35	2	56	40	85	2	85	2	58	26	94	48	0	85	70	
2	19	26	78	95	1	4	72	81	80	60	49	67	32	10	28	90	72	25	28	53	
37	40	96	68	6	95	55	82	16	36	58	68	68	69	7	11	31	17	39	82	85	
1	0	13	31	19	63	90	75	17	33	49	13	54	32	26	66	38	1	7	35	16	
63	88	20	20	75	16	70	26	75	22	48	6	1	89	99	21	48	6	9	67	85	
64	93	100	50	95	76	94	84	25	67	98	94	23	75	40	33	86	87	76	24	98	
95	13	66	49	11	48	20	54	51	65	63	33	98	80	13	84	70	85	93	74	22	
18	35	10	64	79	70	5	55	92	41	92	14	63	52	94	56	5	40	55	50	17	
40	62	28	72	82	81	51	7	45	9	26	47	34	47	47	95	45	38	82	85	20	
33	7	97	68	76	44	73	73	0	80	55	84	77	74	27	5	17	57	75	63	2	
15	60	83	28	56	78	9	27	52	79	68	90	48	12	51	55	77	48	10	55	21	
58	1	28	1	64	50	28	8	69	70	96	26	100	6	31	89	0	31	91	5	23	
71	94	59	17	43	50	34	12	14	45	30	79	63	76	72	18	67	87	47	90	93	
73	24	19	13	98	0	64	44	90	20	13	66	81	97	81	11	38	7	37	93	64	
97	82	87	98	29	97	69	24	62	100	12	28	84	86	10	69	25	66	93	21	57	
2	23	76	42	76	87	64	99	5	7	13	33	19	18	37	96	73	95	91	24	24	
17	85	42	29	80	53	92	6	44	100	18	24	31	5	6	37	63	93	42	5	97	
83	42	53	54	93	63	19	59	30	80	75	8	91	48	79	2	40	6	56	57	60	
30	3	41	73	63	76	18	82	8	13	30	78	45	43	77	77	99	98	40	14	82	
64	7	19	80	64	4	34	30	65	63	11	72	20	15	22	30	82	77	51	87	61	
90	24	25	98	38	79	45	84	30	49	64	98	48	25	14	0	12	63	67	12	77	
20	40	25	87	45	88	52	19	33	17	63	60	62	46	12	59	99	5	88	74	89	
87	62	78	25	71	57	6	98	59	79	34	20	77	87	83	12	74	29	12	16	99	
54	10	53	29	37	82	5	77	54	4	69	7	40	18	32	85	37	73	42	49	49	
45	35	11	73	30	16	3	75	56	58	98	46	93	58	96	29	73	6	71	8	46	
69	17	54	7	86	29	18	86	98	5	56	78	0	78	24	34	73	95	11	44	36	
72	60	78	88	27	45	80	66	25	37	73	7	67	29	27	12	90	60	97	15	94	
93	9	58	84	88	90	73	47	49	53	95	62	28	11	61	0	91	49	32	82	28	
74	75	27	81	28	48	4	65	87	69	32	14	46	52	52	36	21	13	70	24	76	
36	42	53	92	96	19	52	38	2	22	47	26	94	34	57	81	28	49	74	68	50	
93	76	77	19	31	74	40	5	0	23	61	15	11	82	35	77	9	28	11	32	30	
54	75	23	75	34	69	93	93	20	29	78	24	71	92	75	70	60	80	88	21	11	
72	99	15	97	27	48	50	88	2	89	57	18	25	7	100	80	84	97	84	18	53	
99	6	34	98	33	77	44	86	95	0	30	34	91	25	98	77	14	95	100	84	19	
94	13	95	44	22	63	18	88	37	89	95	98	80	72	72	71	66	13	33	24	12	
48	56	64	63	75	27	69	63	29	51	59	22	83	2	33	32	91	78	53	45	63	
7	66	52	91	70	34	54	25	71	91	12	41	39	35	37	66	52	80	1	33	94	
77	83	71	83	68	55	85	11	69	32	10	30	54	73	21	43	68	65	83	26	90	
95	28	92	53	63	46	36	45	62	24	39	65	100	85	12	69	3	72	55	43	5	
54	59	91	34	52	75	87	95	30	97	33	57	69	37	7	62	65	36	9	57	73	
76	13	93	41	42	27	80	85	61	11	42	44	51	38	59	85	91	51	79	14	26	
59	84	46	41	29	7	44	63	27	29	41	39	76	88	46	46	65	72	62	92	67	
15	91	53	78	85	78	77	80	36	89	88	84	60	42	55	48	99	44	66	77	27	

54	69	27	97	71	52	38	45	35	14	74	40	96	40	88	38	67	44	81	5
55	2	76	36	72	7	28	55	13	31	78	67	98	50	25	94	39	71	28	0
56	3	4	20	8	63	33	69	31	69	32	35	18	23	84	69	64	13	43	86
57	79	55	89	1	25	68	100	58	44	92	73	29	70	47	3	51	37	24	24
58	99	6	65	35	66	98	66	47	47	22	1	54	94	13	0	31	40	55	69
59	46	98	1	46	43	86	42	91	63	1	93	84	51	8	79	47	54	85	90
60	6	14	71	51	7	10	79	41	58	3	27	33	74	67	18	94	4	57	99
61	92	31	31	40	12	19	74	73	20	94	33	41	40	74	79	42	23	41	29
62	87	8	68	74	61	66	94	27	71	81	37	82	83	7	8	46	65	63	37
63	50	48	52	100	68	75	38	65	59	57	78	24	29	52	24	98	78	48	77
64	67	96	52	88	76	79	16	12	42	33	35	50	54	69	21	57	62	21	84
65	54	42	22	99	28	90	74	46	26	13	48	45	99	3	38	94	86	53	41
66	99	51	72	2	75	81	92	71	85	26	77	73	23	14	2	46	7	13	2
67	35	63	58	46	91	44	56	26	59	56	21	91	19	83	6	61	47	53	10
68	81	98	63	17	77	45	47	96	25	38	23	26	80	20	47	40	39	14	71
69	90	47	44	40	40	9	60	62	13	79	39	0	99	57	37	39	2	8	42
70	29	30	16	54	83	76	50	0	61	100	51	74	78	15	9	16	17	22	44
71	47	94	70	80	51	26	11	78	34	29	10	55	90	42	4	6	83	72	95
72	69	14	17	73	79	25	71	14	52	98	77	82	15	25	8	34	38	80	82
73	54	58	47	9	0	6	36	94	27	3	18	5	36	98	74	36	30	8	87
74	24	63	57	91	8	58	38	29	72	5	56	71	81	50	67	59	41	9	17
75	14	24	69	85	97	51	68	80	16	92	59	72	97	23	89	44	16	71	19
76	86	21	31	59	72	17	77	45	43	29	34	97	67	45	23	88	91	68	12
77	5	28	80	31	99	77	39	23	69	0	15	49	100	2	22	64	73	92	53
78	29	71	48	4	87	32	17	90	89	9	99	34	58	8	61	73	98	48	89
79	90	94	19	80	70	36	2	17	48	63	82	39	85	26	65	27	81	69	83
80	62	66	48	74	86	6	66	41	15	65	6	41	85	57	84	64	70	39	64
81	67	54	3	54	23	40	25	95	93	55	59	46	77	55	49	82	26	8	87
82	75	27	62	15	81	36	22	26	69	42	44	91	55	0	84	48	68	65	5
83	70	19	7	100	94	53	81	76	73	40	22	58	49	42	96	18	66	89	8
84	75	7	9	20	58	92	41	42	79	26	91	44	63	87	45	21	23	15	6
85	55	70	10	23	25	73	91	72	29	47	93	58	21	75	80	52	9	12	36
86	83	42	62	53	55	12	11	54	19	2	45	43	67	13	5	74	30	93	11
87	94	20	76	23	65	72	55	27	44	19	10	72	50	67	83	18	67	22	49
88	51	10	72	9	59	47	66	32	17	6	75	8	54	22	37	3	46	83	95
89	99	50	22	2	92	9	98	9	40	23	34	8	63	58	49	31	70	39	83
90	9	12	3	23	2	0	82	75	36	63	71	19	78	26	66	63	16	75	7
91	20	40	50	29	51	82	81	47	73	69	74	100	80	37	14	67	1	90	92
92	90	92	54	52	74	0	88	71	45	49	38	54	80	2	85	42	75	47	20
93	25	6	92	30	19	31	22	41	0	22	79	87	84	61	6	19	67	97	60
94	13	12	94	76	29	61	50	67	29	76	27	70	97	16	83	88	100	22	48
95	91	77	51	3	92	85	46	22	0	58	84	64	87	93	94	94	13	98	41
96	29	12	39	35	32	47	30	81	40	32	37	8	48	81	50	77	18	39	7
97	43	96	86	14	91	24	22	85	16	51	42	37	41	100	94	76	45	50	67
98	57	44	72	45	87	21	7	29	26	82	69	99	10	39	76	29	11	17	85
99	63	10	10	76	7	75	19	91	2	31	45	94	54	72	10	48	52	7	12
100	34	28	11	95	4	82	51	7	69	53	93	36	81	66	93	88	15	73	54

This table is taken from the Random numbers table in Appendix D of *Foundations of Behavioral Research*, 3rd ed. (p. 642-643) by F. N. Kerlinger, 1986, New York: Holt, Rinehart & Winston. Copyright © 1986 by Holt, Rinehart & Winston. Reprinted by permission.

Appendix F

SAMPLE RESEARCH PAPER

Self-Monitoring

1

Self-Monitoring and Attitude Similarity in

Established Couples

Mark L. Mitchell

Janina M. Jolley

Clarion University of Pennsylvania

Running Head: SELF-MONITORING AND ATTITUDE SIMILARITY

Abstract

To determine whether existing research on self-monitoring could be extrapolated to long-term interactions, we studied existing couples. As would be expected from previous research, high self-monitoring men were less similar in attitudes to their partners than were low self-monitoring men. However, contrary to what might be expected from previous research, high self-monitoring men loved more and were more loved than low self-monitoring men; high self-monitoring men were not perceived to be more similar to their partner than low self-monitoring men; and high self-monitors did not link up with other high self-monitors.

Self-Monitoring

3

Self-Monitoring and Attitude Similarity in

Established Couples

Self-monitoring is the degree to which people

adjust their behavior to the social situation. Most research on

self-monitoring has focused on short interactions. Because of

the risks of extrapolating existing research on self-monitoring

to established couples, we decided to study existing couples

directly. Specifically, we wanted to answer these questions:

1) Would high self-monitoring men choose

partners who were less similar to themselves in attitudes than

would low self-monitoring men? Although high self-monitors

might place less importance on the prospective partner's

interior personal attributes than low self-monitors (Snyder,

Berscheid, & Glick, 1985), high self-monitors might still choose

mates who are very similar to themselves in terms of attitudes.

After all, Snyder, et al. (1985) report that when the date was

not to take place in a public place, low self-monitors and high

self-monitors did not differ in their dating choices.

Furthermore, since high self-monitors are more out-going,

more likely to initiate a conversation, more socially skilled

(Ickes & Barnes, 1977), and have more dating partners than

low self-monitors, they may be able to select a partner who has desirable exterior and interior qualities. That is, high self-monitoring men may have their cake and eat it too.

2) If high self-monitoring men choose partners who are less similar to themselves in terms of values, do they love their partners less? After all, attitude similarity is an important determinant of attraction (Byrne, 1971). Furthermore, much of Snyder's work has suggested that high self-monitors have qualities that are not conducive to forming strong attachments such as being "image conscious" (Snyder & DeBono, 1985), superficial (Snyder, Gangestaad, & Simpson, 1983; Snyder, Berscheid, & Glick, 1985), and willing to date someone other than their current partner (Snyder, Berscheid, & Glick, 1985). Finally, because high self-monitoring men have more partners than low self-monitors, Helson's adaptation level theory (Helson, 1964) would suggest that they might be less pleased with their partners than low self-monitoring men.

3) Do high self-monitors tend to pair off with other high self-monitors, as Ickes's and Barnes's (1977) research would indicate?

Method

Subjects

From four undergraduate psychology classes, we recruited every student who claimed to be currently engaged in a heterosexual relationship. These 35 students received extra credit for both their own and their partner's participation.

Procedure

Subjects were assured that their partner would not see their responses. Then, each subject responded to the Contemporary Topics Questionnaire (Lerner, Karson, Meisels, & Knapp, 1975) twice—once responding for themselves, a second time as they believed their partner would fill it out. They then completed the Rubin Love-Like Scale (Rubin, 1970), the Self-monitoring Scale (Snyder, 1974), and a short questionnaire about the length and intensity of the present relationship.

Results

Characteristics of the Sample

As we had hoped, our sample was made up of well-established couples. On the average, the couples had dated for

1.64 years. On a 1 (relationship definitely won't lead to marriage) to 9 (relationship definitely will lead to marriage) scale, the average response was 7.41. On the Rubin Love Scale, the average Love score was 104.65 for the women, 103.85 for the men.

<u>Primary Measures</u>

To obtain an index of attitude similarity, we compared each couple's responses to the Contemporary Topics Questionnaire. Specifically, for each of the 36 items of the questionnaire, we subtracted the men's self-rating from the women's self-rating. We took the absolute value of these differences and summed them to get a score than could range from 0 (no difference in attitudes) to 216 (extremely dissimilar in attitudes).

Table 1 shows that the correlation between attitude dissimilarity and male self-monitoring was positive and significant ($\underline{r}$ = .35, $\underline{p}$ < .05), indicating that the higher a man's self-monitoring score, the less similar he was to his partner. These results support Snyder, Berscheid, and Glick's (1985) findings that high self-monitors are less concerned than low self-monitors about interior characteristics.

Self-Monitoring

7

Insert Table 1 about here

However, despite their tendency to be less similar to their partners than low self-monitoring men, high self-monitoring men were more loved than low self-monitoring men: The correlation between a man's self-monitoring score and the woman's love for her partner was positive and significant, $r(35) = .43$, $p < .01$. Furthermore, this love was not one-sided: Male high self-monitors tended to love their partner more than low self-monitoring men, $r(35) = .39$, $p < .05$.

The relationship between women's levels of self-monitoring and dissimilarity of attitudes was smaller and not significant, $r(35) = .13$, n.s. Surprisingly, however, there was a tendency for high self-monitoring women to love their partners less, $r(35) = -.40$, $p < .05$, and be loved less, $r(35) = -.23$, n.s., than low self-monitoring women (see Table 1).

Finally, contrary to what Ickes's and Barnes's (1977) study would suggest, there was not a strong relationship between male self-monitoring and female self-monitoring within these couples. In fact, the relationship was close to zero, $r(35) = .04$, n.s.

Discussion

The results of this study of existing couples indicate that high self-monitoring men are less concerned with attitude similarity than low self-monitoring men. Even though high self-monitoring men select partners who are less similar to themselves, and even though they and their partner are aware of their dissimilarities, they love more and are loved more than low self-monitoring men. For the high self-monitoring man, love is more than attitude deep. However, the pattern is practically reversed for women. Thus, although our results confirm some of the findings of Snyder and his colleagues, they point to the need to study the female self-monitor.

Self-Monitoring

6

References

Byrne, D. (1971). The attraction paradigm. New York: Academic Press.

Helson, H. (1964). Adaptation-level theory. New York: Harper and Row.

Ickes, W. & Barnes, R. D. (1977). The role of sex and self-monitoring in unstructured dyadic interactions. Journal of Personality and Social Psychology, 35, 315–330.

Lerner, R. M., Karson, M., Meisels, M. & Knapp, J. R. (1975). Actual and perceived attitudes of late adolescents and their parents: The phenomenon of the generation gaps. The Journal of Genetic Psychology, 126, 195–207.

Rubin, Z. (1970). Measurement of romantic love. Journal of Personality and Social Psychology, 16, 265–273.

Snyder, M. (1974). The self-monitoring of expressive behavior. Journal of Personality and Social Psychology, 30, 526–537.

Snyder, M., Berscheid, E., & Glick, P. (1985). Focusing on the exterior and the interior: Two investigations of the initiation of personal relationships. Journal of Personality and Social Psychology, 48, 1427–1439.

Snyder, M. & DeBono, K. G. (1985). Appeals to image and
    claims about quality: Understanding the psychology of
    advertising. Journal of Personality and Social Psychology,
    49, 586–597.

Snyder, M., Gangestad, & Simpson, J. A. (1983). Choosing
    friends as activity partners: The role of self-monitoring.
    Journal of Personality and Social Psychology, 45,
    1061–1072.

Self-Monitoring

9

Table 1

Correlations for Self-Monitoring, Love, and Attitude
Dissimilarity by Gender

	Gender	
Relationship	Female	Male
Self-monitoring and attitude dissimilarity	.13	.35*
Self-monitoring and love for partner	−.40*	.39*
Self-monitoring and being loved by partner	.43**	−.23

*$p < .05$.   **$p < .01$.

GLOSSARY

A–B–A reversal design A single subject or small *n* design in which baseline measurements are made of the target behavior (A), then an experimental treatment is given (B), and the target behavior is measured again (A).

Abstract A short, one-page summary of a research proposal or article.

Analysis of variance (ANOVA) A statistical test for analyzing data from experiments. Especially useful if the experiment has more than one independent variable or more than two levels of an independent variable.

Archival data Data from existing records and public archives.

Baseline A measure of the dependent variable as it occurs without the experimental manipulation. Used as a standard of comparison in single-*n* and small-*n* designs.

Between-groups variance (mean square treatment, mean square between) A measure of the combined effects of random error and treatment. This quantity is compared to the within-groups variance in ANOVA. It's the top half of the *F* ratio. If the treatment has no effect, the between-groups variance should be roughly the same as the within-groups variance. If the treatment has an effect, the between-groups variance should be larger than the within-groups variance.

Blind A strategy of making the subject or researcher unaware of what condition the subject is in.

Blocked design Dividing experimental subjects into groups (blocks) on a subject variable (e.g., low-IQ block and high-IQ block). Then, randomly assigning members from each block to experimental condition. Ideally, a blocked design will give you more power than a simple, between-subjects design.

Carry-over The effects of a treatment condition persist into later conditions. Often a problem with single-*n* and within-subjects designs because you don't know whether the subject's behavior is due to the treatment just administered or to a lingering effect of a treatment administered some time ago.

Ceiling effect The effect of treatment(s) is underestimated because the dependent measure is not sensitive to psychological states above a certain level. The measure puts an artificially low ceiling on how high a subject may score.

Central limit theorem If numerous large samples from the same population are taken, and you were to plot the mean for each of these samples, your plot would resemble a normal curve—even if the population from which you took those samples was not normally distributed.

Ceteris paribus   Holding all variables, except the ones you're interested in constant: "everything else being equal."

Chi square (χ^2)   A statistical test you can use to determine whether two or more variables are related. Best used when you have nominal data.

Coefficient of determination   The square of the correlation coefficient; tells the degree to which knowing one variable helps to know another. Can range from 0 (knowing a subject's score on one variable tells you absolutely nothing about the subject's score on the second variable) to 1.00 (knowing a subject's score on one variable tells you exactly what the subject's score on the second variable was).

Cohort effects   The effect of belonging to a given generation (e.g., the '60s generation). Sometimes, people mistakenly assume that differences between people of different age groups is the result of biological aging when the difference is really due to the two groups having different backgrounds because they grew up in different eras.

Compensation   When subjects in the control group try to make up for being deprived of a desired treatment. May be a problem in field research when the treatment is a training program or some other desired treatment.

Conceptual replication   An attempt to demonstrate an experimental phenomenon with an entirely new paradigm or set of measures or manipulations.

Concurrent validity   Validating a measure by giving your subject the new measure and some established measures of the construct at the same time (concurrently). You then correlate performance on the established measures with performance on the new measure. Concurrent validity is to be distinguished from predictive validity; predictive validity being seeing how well your measure predicts scores on measures that you'll administer to the subject at some future time.

Confounding variables   Variables that are unintentionally manipulated. If confounding variables are present in a study, it's hard to say what caused the effect.

Construct validity   The degree to which a study measures and/or manipulates what the researcher claims it does.

Content analysis   A method used to categorize a wide range of open-ended (unrestricted) responses.

Content validity   With many measures and tests, subjects are asked a few questions from a large body of knowledge. A test has content validity if its content is a fair sample of the larger body of knowledge. Students hope that their psychology tests have content validity.

Control group   Subjects who don't receive the experimental treatment. These subjects are compared to the treatment group to determine whether the treatment had an effect.

Convenience sampling   Choosing to include people in your sample simply because they are easy (convenient) to survey.

Converging operations   A set of related studies that differ only in that they use different measures and/or manipulations of the construct.

Correlation coefficient   A number that can vary from -1.00 to $+1.00$ and indicates the kind of relationship that exists between two variables (positive or negative as indicated by the sign of the correlation coefficient) and the strength of the relationship (indicated by the extent to which the coefficient differs from 0).

Counterbalancing   Any technique used to control order effects by distributing order effects across treatment conditions.

Criterion validity   The degree to which the measure relates to other measures of the construct. Concurrent validity and predictive validity are types of criterion validity.

Cross-over (disordinal) interaction   When an independent variable has one kind of effect in the presence of one level of a second independent variable, but the opposite kind of effect in the presence of a different level of the second independent variable. Example: Getting closer to someone may increase their attraction to you if you've complimented them, but may decrease their attraction to you if you've just insulted them. Called a cross-over interaction because the lines in a graph of the interaction will cross. Called disordinal interaction because it can't be explained by having ordinal rather than interval data.

Cross-sectional design   Trying to study the effects of age by comparing different age groups at the same point in time. E.g., Today, you might compare a group of 5-year-olds with a group of 10-year-olds. To be distinguished from longitudinal designs where you study the same people at different times (e.g., study a group of 5-year-olds today, then return 5 years later and study them again when they're 10).

Crosstabs   Tables of percentages used to compare different groups' responses; allows for an examination of the relationships among variables.

Crucial studies   Studies that put two theories into competition.

Curvilinear   A relationship between an independent and dependent variable that is graphically represented by a curved line.

Debriefing   Giving subjects the details of a study at the end of their participation. Proper debriefing is one of the researcher's most serious obligations.

Deduction   Applying a general rule to a specific situation.

Demand characteristics   Characteristics of the study that suggest to the subject how the researcher wants the subject to behave.

Demographics   Characteristics of a group, such as: sex, age, social class.

Demoralization   An effect of subjects knowing that they're being denied the preferred treatment. Subjects may then feel victimized and give up. A problem in field research if some subjects get training that may improve their promotability but others get no treatment at all.

Dependent groups *t* test   A statistical test used with interval or ratio data to test differences between two conditions on a single dependent variable. Differs from the between-groups *t* test or independent groups *t* test in that it is only to be used when you're getting two scores from each subject (within-groups design) or when you're using a matched pairs design.

Dependent variable   The factor that the experimenter predicts is affected by the independent variable. The subject's response that the experimenter is measuring.

Diffusion of treatment   When the treatment given to the treatment group is spread to the no-treatment group by treatment group subjects. E.g., A professor hands out sample tests to one section of a class, but not to the other. Students who get the sample test, make copies and give them to their friends in the no-treatment class. May result in a failure to observe any difference between groups and thus falsely conclude that the treatment has no effect.

Direct replication   Repeating a study as exactly as possible, usually to determine whether or not the same results will be obtained.

Discriminant validity   When a measure doesn't correlate significantly with variables from which it should differ. E.g., A violence measure might have a degree of discriminant validity if it doesn't correlate with measures of love, and desire for world peace.

Double-barreled question   Several questions embedded into a single question. E.g., Are you happy and mad?

Double-blind   When neither the subject nor the person running the subject is aware of what treatment the subject has received.

Empty control group   A group that doesn't get any kind of treatment. The group gets nothing, not even a placebo. Usually, because of subject and experimenter biases that may result from such a group, you'll want to avoid using an empty control group.

Experimental group   Subjects who are randomly assigned to receive the treatment.

Experimental hypothesis   A prediction that the treatment will cause an effect.

Experimental realism   When a study engages the subject so much that the subject is not merely playing a role (helpful subject, good person). The subject is not treating the experimental situation as a trivial, make-believe or pretend world.

Exploratory study   A study investigating (exploring) a new area of research.

Ex-post-facto research   When a researcher goes back, after the research has been completed, looking to test hypotheses that were not formulated prior to the beginning of the study. The researcher is trying to take advantage of hindsight. Often, an attempt to salvage something out of a study that didn't turn out as planned.

External validity   The degree to which the results of a study can be generalized to other subjects, settings, and times.

Extraneous factors   Nontreatment factors.

Factorial experiment   An experiment that examines two or more independent variables (factors) at a time.

Failure to follow protocol effect   Contamination caused when investigators deviate from the protocol.

Fatigue effects   Decreased performance on a task due to being tired or less enthusiastic as a study continues.

Field experiment   An experiment performed in a nonlaboratory setting.

Fixed alternative items   Items on a test or questionnaire, in which a person must choose an answer from among a few specified alternatives.

Floor effect   The effects of treatment(s) is underestimated because the dependent measure artificially restricts how low scores can be.

Functional relationship   The shape of a relationship.

Grand mean   The mean of all the scores in a study. Often used when doing the calculations for an ANOVA.

History effect   A subject's scores change between pretest and posttest because his environment has changed between pretest and posttest.

Hypothesis   A testable prediction.

Hypothesis guessing   When subjects alter their behavior to conform to their guess as to what the research hypothesis is. Can be a serious threat to construct validity, especially if subjects guess right.

Hypothesis testing   The use of inferential statistics to determine whether the relationship found between two or more variables in a particular sample holds true in the population or whether the observed relationship is due to sampling error.

Hypothetical construct   An entity that can't be observed directly, with our present technology. E.g., Love, motivation, short-term memory, etc.

Independence   Factors are independent when they're not causally or correlationally linked.

Independent random assignment   Randomly determining for each individual subject which condition they will be in.

Independent variable   The variable being manipulated by the experimenter. Subjects are assigned to level of independent variable by independent random assignment.

Induction   Creating a general rule by seeing similarities among several specific situations.

Inferential statistics Procedures for determining the reliability and generality of a particular research finding.

Informed consent If subjects agree to take part in a study after they've been told what's going to happen to them, you have their informed consent.

Instrumentation effect Apparent treatment effects being due to changes in the measuring instrument.

Interaction When you need to know how much of another variable subjects have received to say what the effect of a given variable is, you have an interaction between those two variables. If you graph the results from an experiment that has two or more independent variables, and the lines you draw between your points are not parallel, you have an interaction.

Internal consistency The degree to which each question in a scale taps the same construct.

Internal validity The degree to which a study establishes that a factor causes a difference in behavior.

Interobserver reliability An index of the degree to which different raters give the same behavior similar ratings.

Interval data Data that gives you numbers that can be meaningfully ordered along a scale (from lowest to highest) and in which equal intervals (distances) between numbers represent equal psychological distances (e.g., the difference between a rating of 3 and a rating of 2 is the same psychological distance as the difference between a rating of 5 and a rating of 4).

Interviewer bias When the interviewer influences subjects' responses by verbally or nonverbally rewarding "correct" responses.

Known groups technique Determining the validity of a measure by seeing whether groups known to differ on a characteristic differ on a measure of that characteristic. E.g., Ministers should differ from atheists on a measure of religiosity.

Latency A type of dependent measure in which we measure not what the subject responds to, but how long it takes before she responds. Often, latency is used as a measure in reaction-time tasks.

Leading question Questions structured to lead respondents to the answer the researcher wants. E.g., "You like this book, don't you?"

Likert-type items Items that typically ask subjects whether they strongly agree, agree, are neutral, disagree, or strongly disagree with a certain statement. These items are assumed to yield interval data.

Linear A relationship between an independent and dependent variable that's graphically represented by a straight line.

Longitudinal design Trying to estimate the effects of age by testing one group of people repeatedly over time (e.g., testing them when they were 5, again when they were 10, etc.).

Loose protocol effect   Variations in procedure because the written procedures (the protocol) isn't detailed enough. These variations in procedure may result in reseacher bias.

Main effect (overall main effect)   The overall or average effect of an independent variable.

Matched pairs design   An experimental design in which the subjects are paired off by matching them on some variable assumed to be correlated with the dependent variable. Then, for each matched pair, one member is randomly assigned to one treatment condition, the other gets the other treatment condition. This design usually has more power than a simple, between-groups experiment.

Matching   Choosing your groups so that they're identical (they match) on certain characteristics.

Maturation   Changes in subjects due to natural development.

Mean   A measure of central tendency computed by dividing the sum of a set of scores by the number of scores in the set.

Median split   The procedure of dividing subjects into two groups based on whether they're above or below the median (middle score).

Mixed designs   An experimental design that contains both between-subjects and within-subjects manipulations of the independent variables.

Mortality (Attrition)   Subjects dropping out of a study before the study is completed.

Multiple baseline design   A single-n or small-n design in which different behaviors receive baseline periods of varying lengths prior to the introduction of the treatment variable. E.g., A manager might collect baseline data on employee absenteeism, tardiness, and cleanliness. Then, the manager would reward (treatment) cleanliness while continuing to collect data on all three variables. Then, the manager would reward punctuality, etc.

Multiple operations   When several different measures of the same construct are included in the same study.

Mundane realism   Extent to which the research setting or task resembles real life.

Naturalistic observation   A technique of observing events as they occur in their natural setting.

Negative correlation   An inverse relationship between two variables. E.g., Number of suicide attempts and happiness.

Nominal scale data   Qualitative data; different scores don't represent different amounts of a characteristic (quantity). Instead, they represent different kinds of characteristics (qualities).

Nonequivalent control group design   In quasi experiments, a comparison group that isn't determined by random assignment. Researcher hopes that this group is equivalent to the treatment group (before the treatment group received the treatment, of course), but it probably isn't.

Nonreactive measures   Measurements that are taken without changing the subjects behavior; also referred to as unobtrusive measures.

Null hypothesis   The hypothesis that there's no relationship between two or more variables.

Null results   Results that fail to dispute the null hypothesis. They fail to provide convincing evidence that the factors are related. Could mean that no relationship exists or it could mean that your design lacks the power to find the relationship.

Observer bias   Bias created by the observer seeing what the observer wants or expects to see.

Open-ended items   Questions that don't provide fixed response alternatives.

Operational definition   A publicly observable way to measure or manipulate a variable: a "recipe" for how you're going to measure or manipulate your factors.

Ordinal data   Numbers that can be meaningfully ordered from lowest to highest. With ordinal data, you know that a subject with a high score has more of a characteristic than a subject with a low score. But you don't know how much more. E.g., ranked data, you know the top-ranked student has a higher score than the second ranked student, but how much higher? You don't know if you only have ranked data. Furthermore, someone with a rank of 1 might be way ahead of the number 2 ranked scorer, but the number 2 scorer may be only slightly ahead of the number 3 scorer.

Ordinal interaction   Reflects the fact that an independent variable seems to have more of an effect under one level of a second independent variable than under another level. If you graph an ordinal interaction, the lines will not be parallel, but they will not cross. Called an ordinal interaction because the interaction, the failure of the lines to be parallel, may be an illusion. The independent variable may have the same effect under all levels of the second independent variable, but because equal psychological distances aren't reflected by equal distances on your measuring scale (the difference between a 1 and a 4 is the same, in terms of amount of a construct, as is the difference between a 6 and a 7). In short, the interaction may result from having ordinal rather than interval data.

Parameter estimation   The use of inferential statistics to estimate certain characteristics of the population (parameters) from a sample of that population.

Parameters   Measurements describing populatons; often inferred from statistics, which are measurements describing a sample.

Parsimonious   Explaining a broad range of phenomena with only a few principles.

Participant observation   An observation procedure in which the observer participates with those being observed.

Phi (φ) coefficient   A correlation coefficient to be used when both variables are measured on the nominal scale.

Placebo   A chemically inert material; allows experimenters to test the effects of the expectations of subjects who believe they took actual material.

Positive correlation   A relationship between two variables where the two variables tend to vary together—when one increases, the other tends to increase. E.g., height and weight: the taller one is, the more one tends to weigh; the shorter one is, the less one tends to weigh.

Post-hoc test   Usually refers to a statistical test that's been performed after an ANOVA has obtained a significant effect for a factor. Since the ANOVA only says that at least two of the levels of the independent variable differ from one another, post-hoc tests are performed to find out which levels differ from one another.

Posttest   Testing subjects on the dependent measure after they've received the treatment.

Power   The probability of rejecting the null hypothesis in a statistical test when it's in fact false. The ability to find significant differences when differences truly exist.

Practice effects   The change in a score on a test (usually a gain) resulting from previous practice with the test.

Pretest   When subjects are tested on the dependent measure before they get the treatment. After getting the treatment, subjects will probably be given the dependent measure task again (the posttest).

Pretest–posttest design   Each subject is given the pretest, administered the treatment, then given the posttest.

Quasi experiments   A study that resembles an experiment except that random assignment played no role in determining which subjects got which level of treatment. Usually have less internal validity than experiments.

Quota sampling   Making sure you get the desired numbers of (meet your quotas for) certain types of people (certain age groups, minorities, etc.). This method doesn't involve random sampling and usually gives you a less representative sample than random sampling would. It may, however, be an improvement over convenience sampling.

Random error   Variation in scores due to unsystematic, chance factors.

Random sampling   A sample that has been randomly selected from a population.

Ratio scale   The highest form of measurement. With ratio scale numbers, the difference between any two consecutive numbers is the same (see interval scale). But in addition to having interval scale properties, in ratio scale measurement, a zero score means the total absence of a quality. (Thus, Fahrenheit is not a ratio scale measure of temperature because 0° Fahrenheit doesn't mean there is no temperature. 0° Kelvin, absolute zero, on the other hand, does mean the complete absence of temperature). If you have ratio scale numbers, you can meaningfully form ratios between scores. If IQ scores were ratio (they aren't, very few measurements in psychology are), you could say that someone with a 60 IQ was twice as smart as someone with a 30 IQ (a ratio of 2 to 1). Furthermore, you could say that someone with a 0 IQ had absolutely no intelligence whatsoever.

Regression to the mean   The tendency for scores that are extremely unusual to revert back to more normal levels on the retest.

Reliability   A general term, often referring to the degree to which a subject would get the same score if retested (test–retest reliability). More generally, reliability refers to the degree to which scores are free from random error.

Replication factor   A factor sometimes included in a factorial design to see whether an effect replicates (occurs again) if different stimulus materials are used. E.g., An investigator wants to see if a new memory strategy is superior to a conventional one. Instead of having all the subjects memorize the same story, the researcher assigns different subjects to get different stories. The different stories are the replication factor in the study. The researcher hopes that the memory strategy manipulation will have the same effect, regardless of what story is used. But, if story type matters (there's an interaction between memory strategy and story type), the researcher might do further research to understand why the effect wasn't as general as had been expected.

Researcher effect   Ideally, you hope that the results from a study would be the same no matter who was running the subjects. However, it's possible that the results may be affected by the researcher. If more than one researcher is running subjects for a given study, reseacher may be included as a factor in the design to determine if different researchers get different results.

Researcher expectancy effect   When a researcher's expectations affect the results. This is a type of researcher bias.

Research realism   A study that involves the subject so that the subject is less likely to play a role during the study.

Response set   Habitual way of responding on a test that is independent of a particular test item. E.g., a subject might always check "agree" no matter what the statement is.

Restriction of range   To observe a sizeable correlation between two variables, both must be allowed to vary widely (if one variable doesn't vary, the variables can't vary together). Occasionally, investigators fail to find a relationship between variables because they only study one or both variables over a highly restricted range. E.g., comparing NFL offensive linemen and saying that weight has nothing to do with playing offensive line in the NFL on the basis of your finding that great offensive tackles don't weigh much more than poor offensive tackles. Problem: You only compared people who ranged in weight from 285–300.

Sampling statistics   The science of inferring the characteristics of a population from a sample.

Scatterplot   A graph made by plotting the scores of individuals on two variables (e.g., plotting each subject's height and weight). By looking at this graph, you should get an idea of what kind of relationship (positive, negative, zero) exists between the two variables.

Selection bias   Apparent treatment effects being due to comparing groups that differed even before the treatment was administered (comparing apples with oranges).

Selection by maturation interaction   The groups started out the same on the pre-test, but afterwards developed at different rates or in different directions.

Self-administered questionnaire   A questionnaire filled out in the absence of an investigator.

Semistructured questionnaire   A survey constructed around a core of standard questions; however the interviewer may expand on any question in order to explore a given response in greater depth.

Sensitivity   The degree to which a measure is capable of distinguishing between subjects having different amounts of a construct.

Sensitization   After getting several different treatments and performing the dependent variable task several times, subjects may realize (become sensitive to) what the hypothesis is.

Sequential designs   Designs that attempt to disentangle cohort, age, and history effects.

Simple main effect   Imagine a factorial experiment where you have two levels of attractiveness (ugly, pretty) and two levels of communication style (praising, insulting). If you were just to look at the difference between liking for the pretty person and liking for the ugly person in the praising condition, (totally ignoring the insult condition) you'd be looking at the simple main effect of attractiveness in the praising condition. To find the overall main effect for attractiveness, you'd have to average this with the simple main effect of attractiveness in the insult condition.

Single blind   To reduce either subject biases or researcher biases, you might use a single blind experiment in which either the subject (if you're most concerned about subject bias) or the person running subjects (if you're most concerned about researcher bias) is unaware of who's receiving what level of the treatment.

Single-subject designs   Designs that require only a single subject. These designs are common in operant conditioning and psychophysics research.

Social desirability   A bias resulting from subjects giving responses that make them look good rather than giving honest responses.

Spurious   A relationship between two variables is said to be spurious if the two variables don't affect one another but are instead related because of some other variable. E.g., the relationship between ice cream sales and rapes in New York is spurious, not because it doesn't exist (it does!), but because ice cream doesn't cause rape and rape doesn't cause ice cream sales. Beware of spuriousness whenever you look at correlational research.

Standard deviation   A measure of the extent to which individual scores deviate from the population mean.

Standard error of the difference   An index of the degree to which random sampling error may cause two sample means representing the same populations to differ.

Standard error of the mean   An index of the degree to which random sampling error may cause the sample mean to be an inaccurate estimate of the population mean.

Statistical regression   The tendency for extreme scores on some variable to be closer to the group mean when remeasured, due to unreliability of measurement.

Statistical significance   When, thanks to statistics, we can be confident, beyond a reasonable doubt (usually 95% sure), that the relationship observed was not due to fluke random error, but represents a real relationship.

Stratified random sampling   Making sure that the sample is similar to the population in certain respects (e.g., certain percentage of women, etc.) and then randomly sampling from these groups (strata). Has all the advantages of random sampling with even greater accuracy.

Straw theory   An oversimplified version of an existing theory. Opponents of a theory may present and attack a straw version of that theory, but claim they've attacked the theory itself.

Structured questionnaire   A survey in which all respondents are asked a standard list of questions in a standard order.

Subject biases (Subject effects)   Ways the subject can bias the results (guessing the hypothesis and playing along, giving the socially correct response, etc.).

Summated scores   When you have several Likert-type questions that all tap the same dimension (e.g., attitude toward democracy), you could add up each subject's responses from the different questions to get an overall or summated score.

Systematic replication   A study that varies from the original study only in some minor aspect.

Temporal precedence   Causes come before effects. Therefore, in trying to establish causality, you must establish temporal precedence: that the causal factor was introduced before the effect occurred.

Testing effect   Apparent treatment effects being due to subjects being changed by the pretest.

Theory   A set of propositions from which a large number of new observations can be deduced.

Time series design   A quasi-experimental design in which a series of observations are taken from a group of subjects over time before and after they receive the treatment.

Trend analysis   A post-hoc analysis to determine the shape of a relationship between the independent and dependent variable.

Type I error   Rejecting the null hypothesis when it is in fact true.

Type II error   Failure to reject the null hypothesis when it is in fact false.

Within-groups variance (mean square within, mean square error, error variance)   An estimate of the amount of random error in your data. The bottom half of the F ratio.

Within-subjects designs   Experimental designs in which each subject is tested under more than one level of the independent variable. The order in which the subjects receive the treatments is usually determined by random assignment.

REFERENCES

Adams, J. (1974). *Conceptual blockbusting.* San Francisco: Freeman.

American Psychological Association. (1981a). Ethical principles of psychologists. *American Psychologist, 36,* 633–638.

American Psychological Association. (1981b). Guidelines for the use of animals in school-science behavior projects. *American Psychologist, 36,* 686.

Anastasi, A. (1982). *Psychological Testing.* (5th ed.). New York: Macmillan.

Anderson, J. R. & Bower, G. H. (1973). *Human associative memory.* Washington, D. C.: V. H. Winston.

Aronson, E. & Carlsmith, J. M. (1968). Experimentation in social psychology. In G. Lindzey & E. Aronson (Eds.), *Handbook of social psychology* (2nd ed.), *2,* (pp. 1–79), Reading, Mass.: Addison-Wesley.

Aronson, E. & Linder, D. (1965). Gain and loss of esteem as determinants of interpersonal attractiveness. *Journal of Experimental Social Psychology, 1,* 156–171.

Ayllon, T. & Azrin, N. (1965). The measurement and reinforcement of behavior of psychotics. *Journal of the Experimental Analysis of Behavior, 8,* 171–180.

Ayllon, T. & Azrin, N. (1968). *The token economy: A motivational system for therapy and rehabilitation.* New York: Appleton-Century-Crofts.

Baltes, P. B. (1968). Longitudinal and cross-sectional sequences in the study of age and generation effects. *Human Development, 11,* 145–171.

Baltes, P. B., Reese, H. W., & Nesselroade, J. R. (1977). *Life-span developmental psychology: Introduction to research methods.* Monterey, Cal.: Brooks and Cole.

Bandura, A. (1977). *Social learning theory.* Englewood Cliffs, N.J.: Prentice-Hall.

Barber, T. X. (1976). *Pitfalls in human research: Ten pivotal points.* New York: Pergamon.

Barber, T. X. & Silver, M. J. (1968). Fact, fiction, and experimenter bias effect. *Psychological Bulletin, 70,* 1–29.

Baron, R. A., Russell, G. W., & Arms, R. L. (1985). Negative ions and behavior: Impact on mood, memory, and aggression among Type A and Type B persons. *Journal of Personality and Social Psychology, 48,* 746–754.

Blough, D. S. (1957). Effect of lysergic acid diethylamide on absolute visual threshold in the pigeon. *Science, 126,* 304–305.

Blough, D. S. (1961). Animal psychophysics. *Scientific American, 205,* 113–122.

Bousfield, W. A. (1953). The occurrence of clustering in the recall of randomly arranged associates. *Journal of General Psychology, 49,* 229–240.

Brady, J. V. (1958). Ulcers in "executive" monkeys. *Scientific American, 199,* 95–100.

Broad, W. J. & Wade N. (1982). Science's faulty fraud detectors. *Psychology Today, 16,* p. 50–57.

Buros, O. K. (Ed.). (1978). *The eighth mental measurements yearbook* (Vol. 1). Highland Park, N.J.: Gryphon Press.

Campbell, D. T. & Stanley, J. C. (1966). *Experimental and quasi-experimental designs for research.* Chicago: Rand McNally.

Campbell, J. P., Daft, R. L., & Hulin, C. L. (1982). *What to study: Generating and developing research questions.* Beverly Hills, Cal.: Sage Publications.

Chapman, L. J., & Chapman, P. J. (1967). Genesis of popular but erroneous psychodiagnostic observations. *Journal of Abnormal Psychology, 72,* 193–204.

Chlopan, B. E., McCain, M. L., Carbonell, J. L., & Hagen, R. L. (1985). Empathy: Review of available measures. *Journal of Personality and Social Psychology, 48,* 635–653.

Cohen, A. S., Rosen, R. C., & Goldstein, L. (1985). EEG hemispheric asymmetry during sexual arousal: Psychophysiological patterns in responsive, unresponsive, and dysfunctional men. *Journal of Abnormal Psychology, 94,* 580–590.

Cohen, J. & Cohen, P. (1975). *Applied multiple regression/correlation analysis for the behavioral sciences.* Hilldale, N.J.: Erlbaum.

Coile, D. C. & Miller, N. E. (1984). How radical animal activists try to mislead humane people. *American Psychologist, 39,* 700–701.

Cook, T. D. & Campbell, D. T. (1979). *Quasiexperimentation: Design and analysis for field settings.* Chicago: Rand McNally.

Dipboye, R. L. & Flanagan, M. F. (1979). Research settings in industrial and organizational psychology. *American Psychologist, 34,* 141–150.

Dutton, P. G. & Aron, A. P. (1974). Some evidence for heightened sexual attraction under conditions of high anxiety, *Journal of Personality and Social Psychology, 30,* 510–517.

Eron, L. D. (1982). Parent–child interaction, television violence, and aggression in children. *American Psychologist, 37,* 197–211.

Eysenck, H. J., & Eysenck, M. (1983). *Mindwatching.* Garden City, NY: Anchor Press/Doubleday.

Fechner, G. (1966). *Elements of psychophysics.* (H. Adler, Trans.). New York: Holt. (Originally published 1860)

Festinger L. (1954). Theory of social comparison processes. *Human Relations, 7,* 117–140.

Frank, R. (1984 August). A *half-life theory of love.* Paper presented at the 92nd Annual Convention of the American Psychological Association, Toronto, Canada.

Garner, W. R., Hake, H. & Eriksen, C. W. (1956). Operationism and the concept of perception. *Psychological Review, 63,* 149–159.

Geller, E. S. (1983). Rewarding safety belt usage at an industrial setting: Tests of treatment generality and response maintenance. *Journal of Applied Behavior Analysis, 16,* 189–202.

Graziano, W. G., Rahe, D. F., & Feldesman, A. B. (1985). Extraversion, social cognition, and the salience of aversiveness in social encounters. *Journal of Personality and Social Psychology, 49,* 971–980.

Greenwald, A. G. (1975). Significance, nonsignificance, and interpretation of an ESP experiment. *Journal of Experimental Social Psychology, 11,* 180–191.

Greenwald, A. G. (1976). Within-subjects designs: To use or not to use? *Psychological Bulletin, 83,* 314–320.

Groves, R. M., & Kahn, R. L. (1979). *Surveys by telephone: A national comparison with personal interviews.* New York: Academic Press.

Guthrie, E. R. (1952). *The psychology of learning.* New York: Harper.

Hall, C. S. (1954). *A primer of Freudian psychology.* Cleveland: World Publishing Co.

Hammond, K. R. (1948). Measuring attitudes by error-choice: An indirect method. *Journal of Abnormal and Social Psychology, 43,* 38–48.

Hays, W. L. (1981). *Statistics* (3rd ed.). New York: Holt, Rinehart & Winston.

Hernstein, R. J. (1962). Placebo effect in rat. *Science, 138,* 677–678.

Hess, E. H. & Polt, J. M. (1960). Pupil size as related to interest value of visual stimuli. *Science, 132,* 349–350.

High-handed professor's comments called hot air. (1985, August 30). *USA Today,* p. 2c.

Holmes, D. S., & Will, M. J. (1985). Expression of interpersonal aggression by angered and nonangered persons with Type A and Type B behavior patterns. *Journal of Personality and Social Psychology, 48*, 723–727.

Huck, S. W., & Sandler, H. M. (1979). *Rival Hypotheses: Alternative interpretations of data based conclusions*. New York: Harper and Row.

Hull, C. L. (1952). *A behavior system*. New Haven, CT.: Yale University Press.

Jackson, J. M., & Williams, K. D. (1985). Social loafing on difficult tasks: Working collectively can improve performance. *Journal of Personality and Social Psychology, 49*, 937–942.

James, W. (1950). *Principles of psychology*. New York: Dover. (Originally published 1890)

Johnson, V. S. (1985). *Electrophysiological changes induced by adrostenol: A potential human pherome.* Unpublished manuscript, New Mexico State University, Las Croces, New Mexico.

Jolley, J. M., Murray, J. D., & Keller, P. A. (1984). *How to write psychology papers: A student's survival guide for psychology and related fields.* Sarasota, Fla.: Professional Resource Exchange.

Kahneman, D., Slovic, P., & Tversky, A. (Eds.). (1982). *Judgment under uncertainty: Heuristics and biases.* New York: Cambridge University Press.

Kelley, H. H. (1971). *Attribution in social interaction.* Morristown, N. J.: General Learning Press.

Kenny, D. A. (1979). *Correlation and causality.* New York: John Wiley & Sons.

Kerlinger, F. N. (1973). *Foundations of behavioral research* (2nd ed.). New York: Holt, Rinehart & Winston.

Kohlberg, L. (1981). *The meaning and measurement of moral development.* Worcester, Mass.: Clark University Press.

Kohler, W. (1925). *The mentality of apes.* New York: Harcourt.

Kuhn, T. S. (1970). *The structure of scientific revolutions.* (2nd ed.). Chicago: University of Chicago Press.

Laird, J. D. (1984). The real role of facial response in the experience of emotion: A reply to Tourangeau and Ellsworth and others. *Journal of Personality and Social Psychology, 47*, 909–917.

Latane, B. (1981). The psychology of social impact. *American Psychologist, 36*, 343–356.

Latane, B. & Darley, J. M. (1968). Group inhibition of bystander intervention in emergencies. *Journal of Personality and Social Psychology, 10*, 215–221.

Latane, B. & Darley, J. M. (1970). *The unresponsive bystander: Why doesn't he help?.* New York: Appleton-Century-Crofts.

Latane, B., Nida, S. A. (1981). Ten years of research on group size and helping. *Psychological Bulletin, 89*, 307–324.

Latane, B., Williams, K., & Harkins, S. (1979). Many hands make light the work: The causes and consequences of social loafing. *Journal of Personality and Social Psychology, 37*, 822–832.

Lemon, N. (1973). *Attitudes and their measurement.* New York: Wiley.

Lewin, K. (1951). *Field theory in social science.* New York: Harper.

Light, R. J., & Pillemer, D. P. (1984). *Summing up: The science of reviewing research.* Cambridge, Mass.: Harvard University Press.

Lykken, D. T. (1979). The detection of deception. *Psychological Bulletin, 86*, 47–53.

Lykken, D. T. (1981). *A tremor in the blood: Uses and abuses of the lie detector.* New York: McGraw–Hill.

Maslow, A. H. (1970). Cited in S. Cunningham, Humanists celebrate gains, goals. APA *Monitor, 16*, p. 16.

Mayzner, M. S. & Dolan, T. R. (Eds.). (1978). *Minicomputers in sensory and information-processing research.* Hillsdale, N. J.: Erlbaum.

McCann, I. L. & Holmes, D. S. (1984). Influence of aerobic exercise on depression. *Journal of Personality and Social Psychology, 46*, 1142–1147.

McDougall, W. (1908). *An introduction to social psychology.* London: Methuen.

Milgram, S. (1966, August). Four studies using the lost letter technique. Address given at American Psychological Association, New York.

Milgram, S. (1974). *Obedience to authority: An experimental view.* New York: Harper and Row.

Milgram, S., Bickman, L., & Berkowitz, L. (1969). Note on the drawing power of crowds of different sizes. *Journal of Personality and Social Psychology, 13*, 79–82.

Mook, D. G. (1983). In defense of external invalidity. *American Psychologist, 38*, 379–387.

Morris, J. D. (1986) "MTV" in the classroom. *Chronicle of Higher Education, 32*, 25–26.

Myers, J. L. (1979). *Fundamentals of experimental design* (3rd ed.). Boston: Allyn and Bacon.

Neisser, U. (1984, August). *Ecological movement in cognitive psychology.* Invited address at the 92nd Annual Convention of the American Psychological Association in Toronto, Canada.

Nisbett, R. E. & Wilson, T. D. (1977). Telling more than we can know: Verbal reports on mental processes. *Psychological Review, 84*, 231–259.

Orne, M. (1962). On the social psychology of the psychological experiment: With particular reference to demand characteristics and their implications. *American Psychologist, 17*, 776–783.

Parsons, H. M. (1974). What happened at Hawthorne? *Science, 183*, 922–932.

Pennebaker, J. W., Dyer, M. A., Caulkins, R. S., Litowitz, D. L., Ackerman, P. L., Anderson, D. B., & McGraw, K. M. (1979). Don't the girls get prettier at closing time: A country and western application to psychology. *Personality and Social Psychology Bulletin, 5*, 122–125.

Pfungst, O. (1911). *Clever Hans.* New York: Henry Holt.

Phillips, D. P. (1985). Natural experiments on the effects of mass media violence on fatal aggression: Strengths and weaknesses of a new approach. In L. Berkowitz (Ed.), *Advances in experimental social psychology* (Vol. 19). Orlando, Fla: Academic Press.

Pronko, N. H. (1969). Are geniuses born or made? In *Panorama of Psychology.* pp. 215–219. Belmont, Col: Brooks/Cole.

Publication manual of the American Psychological Association (1983). (3rd ed.). Washington, D. C.: American Psychological Association.

Ranieri, D. J. & Zeiss, A. M. (1984). Induction of a depressed mood: A test of opponent-process theory. *Journal of Personality and Social Psychology, 47*, 1413–1422.

Rinn, W. E. (1984). The neuropsychology of facial expression: A review of the neurological and psychological mechanisms for producing facial expressions. *Psychological Bulletin, 95*, 52–77.

Roediger, H. L. (1980). The effectiveness of four mnemonics in ordering recall. *Journal of Experimental Psychology, 6*, 558–567.

Roethlisberger, F. J. & Dickson, W. J. (1939). *Management and the worker.* Cambridge, Mass.: Harvard University Press.

Rogers, C. R. (1985). Cited in S. Cunningham. Humanists celebrate gains, goals. APA *Monitor, 16*, p. 16.

Rosenthal, R. & Rosnow, R. (1969). *Artifact in behavioral research.* New York: Academic Press.

Rubin, Z. (1970). Measurement of romantic love. *Journal of Personality and Social Psychology, 16*, 265–273.

Schachter, S. (1959). *The psychology of affiliation.* Stanford, Cal.: Stanford University Press.

Schachter, S. (1971). Some extraordinary facts about obese humans and rats. *American Psychologist, 26*, 129–144.

Schaie, K. W. (1977). Quasi-experimental designs in the psychology of aging. In J. E. Birren & K. W. Schaie (Eds.), *Handbook of the psychology of aging* (pp. 39–115) New York: Van Nostrand.

Seligman, M. E. P. (1975). *Helplessness: On depression, development, and death.* San Francisco: Freeman.

Shaffer, D. R., Rogel, M., & Hendrik, C. (1975). Intervention in the library: The effect of increased responsibility on bystanders' willingness to prevent theft. *Journal of Personality and Social Psychology, 5*, 303–319.

Shefrin, H. M. & Statman, M. (1986). How not to make money in the stock market. *Psychology Today, 20*, 52–57.

Sherman, L. W. & Berk, R. A. (1984). The specific deterrent effects of arrest for domestic assault. *American Sociological Review, 49*, 261–272.

Skinner, B. F. (1938). *The behavior of organisms: An experimental analysis.* New York: Appleton-Century-Crofts.

Solomon, R. L. (1980). The opponent-process theory of acquired motivation: The costs of pleasure and the benefits of pain. *American Psychologist, 35,* 691–712.

Steele, C. M. & Southwick, L. (1985). Alcohol and Social Behavior I: The Psychology of Drunken Excess. *Journal of Personality and Social Psychology, 48,* 18–34.

Sternberg, R. J. & Grajek, S. (1984). The nature of love. *Journal of Personality and Social Psychology, 47,* 312–329.

Stevens, S. S. (1957). On the psychophysical law. *Psychological Review, 64,* 153–181.

Stone, P. J., Dunphy, D. C., Smith, M. S., & Ogilvie, D. M. (1966). *The general inquirer: A computer approach to content analysis.* Cambridge, Mass.: The M. I. T. Press.

Sudman, S. & Bradburn, N. M. (1982). *Asking Questions: A practical guide to questionnaire design.* San Francisco: Jossey-Bass.

Tversky, A. (1985). Quoted by K. McKean, Decisions, decisions. *Discover,* pp. 22–31.

Tversky, B. (1973). Encoding processes in recognition and recall. *Cognitive Psychology, 5,* 275–287.

Ward, W. C. & Jenkins, H. M. (1965). The display of information and the judgment of contingency. *Canadian Journal of Psychology, 19,* 231–241.

Webb, E. J. (1981). *Nonreactive measures in the social sciences.* (2nd ed.). Boston: Houghton-Mifflin.

Webb, E. J., Campbell, D. T., Schwartz, R. D., & Seechrist, L. (1981). *Unobtrusive measures: Nonreactive research in the social sciences.* Chicago: Rand McNally.

Williams, K. B., & Williams, K. D. (1983). Social inhibition and asking for help: The effects of number, strength, and immediacy. *Journal of Personality and Social Psychology, 44,* 67–77.

Williams, R. L., & Long, J. D. (1983). *Toward a self-managed lifestyle* (3rd ed.). Boston: Houghton-Mifflin.

Winer, B. J. (1971). *Statistical principles in experimental design.* (2nd ed.). New York: McGraw-Hill.

Wohlwill, J. F. (1970). Methodology and research strategy in the study of developmental change. In L. R. Goulet & P. B. Baltes (Eds.), *Life-span developmental psychology: Research and theory* (pp. 150–191) New York: Academic Press.

Yerkes, R. M., & Dodson, J. D. (1908). The relation of strength of stimulus to rapidity of habit-formation. *Journal of Comparative Neurology and Psychology, 18,* 459–482.

Zimbardo, P. C. (1974). On the ethics of intervention in human psychological research: with special reference to the Stanford prison experiment. *Cognition, 2,* 243–256.

Zuckerman, M., Klorman, R., Larrance, D. T., & Spiegel, N. H. (1981). Facial, autonomic, and subjective components of emotion: The facial feedback hypothesis versus the externalizer-internalizer distinction. *Journal of Personality and Social Psychology, 41,* 929–944.

INDEX

417